U.S. SPECIAL FORCES

AIRBORNE RANGERS

Alan M. and Frieda W. Landau

Lowe & B. Hould
Publishers

This edition published in 2002 by Lowe and B. Hould, an imprint of Borders, Inc., 515 East Liberty, Ann Arbor, MI 48104. Lowe & B. Hould Publishers is a trademark of Borders Properties, Inc.

Previously published in 1992 and 1993 by MBI Publishing Company, Galtier Plaza, Suite 200, 380 Jackson Street, St. Paul, MN 55101-3885 USA

Library of Congress Cataloging-in-Publication Data Available

ISBN 0-681-89056-8

On the front cover: Uniform emblems of the SEALs and the Rangers are represented with the gold Trident and namesake patch, respectively. The oval patch with an arrowhead type symbol is the icon for U.S. Special Operations, and DELTA Force. *David Bohrer*

On the back cover: Rangers receive instructions from their squad leader as they wait in a treelined area to ambush a simulated enemy force. In their role as one of the elite light infantry units in the U.S. military, Rangers are often called upon to conduct such direct action missions, which usually strike hard but are limited in duration.

Printed in China

CONTENTS

Airborne Rangers

CONTENTS

DELTA: America's Elite Counterterrorist Force

CONTENTS

U.S. Navy SEALs

Acknowledgments

We would like to thank the following, without whose cooperation and goodwill this book would not have been possible.

Col. David Grange, commander, 75th Ranger Regiment, and his staff; Sgt. First Class Ronald Hilston, Regimental S-5; Capt. Joe Stanjones and S. Sgt. Robert Gallagher, 3rd Ranger Battalion S-5; and the Rangers of the 75th.

Col. John J. Maher, commander, Ranger Training Brigade; Lt. Col. Brian M. Pentecost, deputy commander; Maj. Bernie Champoux, executive officer; Command Sgt. Maj. Frederick E. Weekley; and the staff of brigade headquarters.

Lt. Col. Clyde M. Newman, commander, 4th Ranger Training Battalion; Command Sgt. Maj. Donald E. Purdy; and the officers and men of the 4th Ranger Training Battalion.

Lt. Col. Jack Donovan, commander, 5th Ranger Training Battalion; Command Sgt. Maj. Luis C. Palacios; and the officers and men of the 5th Ranger Training Battalion.

Lt. Col. Paul J. Burton, commander, 6th Ranger Training Battalion; Command Sgt. Maj. Velda E. Welch; and the officers and men of the 6th Ranger Training Battalion.

Lt. Col. Barry E. Willey, commander, 7th Ranger Training Battalion; Command Sgt. Maj. Francisco G. Magana; and the officers and men of the 7th Ranger Training Battalion.

Lt. Col. Alexander Angelle, public affairs officer, and Griff Godwin, public affairs specialist, Fort Benning, Georgia.

Capt. Douglas Kinneard, public affairs, Hurlburt Field, Florida.

Z. Frank Hanner, curator, National Infantry Museum, Fort Benning, and his staff.

The staff of the Donovan Technical Library, Infantry Hall, Fort Benning; in particular Mrs. Geneva Brown and Mrs. Betty Van Sickle.

Minolta Corporation for the loan of camera equipment to supplement our own.

Col. Robert I. Channon, US Army (retired).

Mr. Philip B. Piazza, president, Merrill's Marauders Association.

Mr. Tom Walsh and Mr. Les Enekes of the London International Air Show, London, Ontario, for allowing us to interview pilots at their show about special operations support.

Lt. Comdr. Dave Parsons, US Navy.

And finally we wish to thank Marshall LeFavor, who patiently read the rough drafts.

Any errors are ours.

Except where noted, all photographs are by the authors.

Introduction

When Gen. Norman D. Cota urged the small group of Rangers from the 5th Ranger Battalion to "lead the way" off Omaha Beach, Pfc. Ellis E. Reed was chosen to take a bangalore torpedo to blow the concertina wire beyond the seawall. All he had to do was get over the seawall under fire, run up to the wire, and blow it up. It would be just like a training exercise, he was told. And, just as in a training exercise, Private Reed gave the safety warning of "fire in the hole" before he blew a path through the wire large enough for the thirty-five Rangers with him to reach the road above the beach.

Today's Rangers would say that Private Reed was "hooah"—he had the Ranger spirit, a combination of confidence, competence, and enthusiasm. The first question asked of a new member of a Ranger unit, whether in the Training Brigade or the Regiment, is if he is hooah. Will the new member fit into the Ranger community, which is so dependent on teamwork? Will he understand that being a Ranger is an attitude, a state of mind, as well as a matter of skills and training? For that is the most important part.

Rangers know they have received the most arduous and exacting training in the infantry. Their skills have been honed under conditions that come as close to combat as possible. This gives them the confidence to eagerly undertake any task with the conviction that they will succeed. They also know that the other members of their unit will back them up at all times. They are all Rangers, they are hooah!

The term "ranger" or "raunger" is found in England as early as 1455, according to the *Oxford English Dictionary* describing one who is "a forest officer, a gameskeeper." In the North American colonies, it was defined as "a body of mounted troops, or other armed men, employed in ranging over a tract of country." Colonies had a defensive screen of forts and block houses that could never be totally effective against infiltrating Indians. The solution was the employment of small mobile forces that ranged or patrolled the frontier.

In chapter 1 of this book, we have attempted to present a brief history of those units which performed Ranger missions, even if they were not called Rangers. Ranger missions are special light infantry military operations such as strike operations, usually deep penetration, including raids, interdictions, and recovery. Rangers may also do reconnaissance and security missions such as taking and holding an enemy airfield for use by US forces. Thus, Col. Benjamin Grierson's command is included, but some Confederate Ranger units are not. Due to the limited nature of this book, not all Ranger units operating in colonial and early national period America are mentioned.

Chapters 2 and 3 cover the Ranger Training Brigade and the 75th Ranger Regiment, respectively. We have tried to convey an idea of present-day Ranger life and training in these sections.

Anyone wishing to learn more about the history of the Rangers in the United States should consult the works listed in the bibliography.

RANGERS LEAD THE WAY!

Chapter 1

History of the Rangers

Colonial Rangers

"I cannot conceive how war can be made in such a country," wrote a British soldier from America (Beattie 1986). The territories controlled by the British colonists, larger than the mother country, were a trackless and almost uninhabited wilderness. Many of the areas' Indian inhabitants were hostile. Armies operating in America had to operate over large distances, and commanders had to control and coordinate units over these distances. Reinforcements, some supplies, and orders had to come from England, 3,000 miles away.

The British Army recognized these problems before Gen. Edward Braddock's Army met disaster in 1755. George Washington's unsuccessful campaign in 1754 necessitated building a road through what was described as "an immense uninhabited Wilderness overgrown everywhere with trees," so that "no where can anyone see twenty yards" (Gipson 1946-1947). Where roads existed they were "either Rocky or full of Boggs, we are obliged to blow the Rocks and lay Bridges every Day" (Gipson 1946-1947).

When Braddock brought his army to the colonies, they were not unfamiliar with wilderness operations. In Europe and Scotland in the 1740s, commanders experienced wilderness combat, and occasionally conducted operations against guerrillas. Braddock formed nine companies of Virginia troops, of which six were known as Rangers, and a company of light horse Rangers. Similar companies from Maryland and North Carolina were formed, but few of these men were woodsmen, most coming from the tidewater settlements. The general still hoped to employ them "to cover the Main Body of the Army, and shelter it from all Manner of Surprise" (Nichols 1947).

Braddock realized his army might be attacked by irregulars. He trained his troops in march security, created a second grenadier company in each battalion, and lightened the equipment each soldier carried. He bent his efforts toward securing provincial backwoodsmen and Indians for the expedition, but too few Indians enlisted. Even so, "these troops remain so constantly on guard, always marching in battle formation, that all the efforts that our detachments put forth against them are useless," according to French descriptions of Braddock's careful movements before his defeat, just short of his objective, Fort Duquesne (near Pittsburgh, Pennsylvania), in a battle that remains controversial (Gipson 1946-1947).

The British turned immediately to the colonists, who used Rangers all along the frontier, reinforced by defensive screens of forts and block houses, between which mobile units "ranged" or patrolled the frontier. Along the southern frontier during King George's War, defections among England's Indian allies led to the building of forts and Ranger patrols in 1746. Gorham's Rangers, active in Nova Scotia since 1750, were an example of what Rangers could do. Gorham, whose unit served the crown until 1765, was the only American Ranger to be offered a regular commission. Gorham's father had also led a Ranger company in Nova Scotia from 1744 to 1750. The British, in 1755, started recruiting frontiersmen from New York and New Hampshire.

One of those recruited was Robert Rogers, a backwoodsman from New Hampshire. Most of the Rangers from western New Hampshire and Massachusetts were to engage in scouting. As auxiliaries of the regular army, they took the Oath to Fidelity, and were subject to the Rules and Articles of War. In 1756 Rogers took command of four companies. Rogers' area of operations was the Champlain Hudson River Valley chain of rivers and lakes, whose strategic value was that they led into either French Canada or New York. These waterways were crucial to the movement of the army, its supplies, and raiders. Since these routes froze in winter, major military operations ceased as armies went into winter quarters. While their most important mission was reconnaissance, during the winter the Rangers could patrol and harass their enemies as well.

Tensions always existed between the Rangers and the regular army. In 1756 Lord Loudoun, commanding the British Army in America wrote, "It is impossible for an Army to Act in this Country, without *Rangers*; and there ought to be a considerable body of them" (Beattie 1986). Later he was less enthusiastic. Rangers proved to be more expensive than regular infantry, and it was often said they were difficult to handle; and in the case of Rogers' Rangers, that only he could control them. Others went further, claiming they were overly fond of rum, going out on patrol only when they felt like it. Regular army officers claimed Rangers would riot when exposed to military discipline. Despite these complaints more Rangers were recruited for the campaign of 1758. By 1757, Loudoun feared that even Ranger intelligence was inaccurate, and began to search for an alternative.

The army could not do without these irregulars, and they remained with the army throughout the Seven Years' War. A process began at this time to train regular officers and trusted men "to beat the woods, & act as *Irregulars*" (Beattie 1986), and to initiate a long-term commitment to develop light infantry capable of wilderness fighting. None of this, though, could be accomplished without the help of the Rangers. While Loudoun determined to convert two companies into Rangers, with the

Standing Orders, Rogers' Rangers

1. Don't forget nothing.
2. Have your musket clean as a whistle, hatchet scoured, sixty rounds powder and ball, and be ready to march at a minute's warning.
3. When you're on the march, act the way you would if you was sneaking up on a deer. See the enemy first.
4. Tell the truth about what you see and what you do. There is an army depending on us for correct information. You can lie all you please when you tell other folks about the Rangers, but don't never lie to a Ranger or officer.
5. Don't never take a chance you don't have to.
6. When we're on the march we march single file, far enough apart so one shot can't go through two men.
7. If we strike swamps, or soft ground, we spread out abreast, so it's hard to track us.
8. When we march, we keep moving till dark, so as to give the enemy the least possible chance at us.
9. When we camp, half the party stays awake while the other half sleeps.
10. If we take prisoners, we keep 'em separate till we have had time to examine them, so they can't cook up a story between 'em.
11. Don't ever march home the same way. Take a different route so you won't be ambushed.
12. No matter whether we travel in big parties or little ones, each party has to keep a scout 20 yards ahead, 20 yards on each flank, and 20 yards in the rear so the main body can't be surprised and wiped out.
13. Every night you'll be told where to meet if surrounded by a superior force.
14. Don't sit down to eat without posting sentries.
15. Don't sleep beyond dawn. Dawn's when the French and Indians attack.
16. Don't cross a river by a regular ford.
17. If somebody's trailing you, make a circle, come back onto your own tracks, and ambush the folks that aim to ambush you.
18. Don't stand up when the enemy's coming against you. Kneel down, lie down, hide behind a tree.
19. Let the enemy come till he's almost close enough to touch. Then let him have it and jump out and finish him up with your hatchet.
MAJ Robert Rogers

Col. William O. Darby, first commander of modern US Rangers. US Army

bushing, fighting, etc., that they might be better qualified for any future service against the enemy we had to contend with" (Russell 1978). Between 1757 and 1758 volunteers went on patrols with Rogers and his men. The light infantry battalion raised in England during this period had many commissioned and noncommissioned officers who had trained with the Rangers.

Lord Howe was instructed by Rogers. Observers noted that Howe made the 55th Foot in the image of the Rangers, but with traditional red uniforms. Howe ordered tails cut off coats and queues off hats, added leggings for protection in the underbrush, and ordered barrels of muskets browned to reduce reflections. By February 1759 one tenth of each battalion of regular troops was formed into a light infantry corps. Gen. Sir Jeffrey Amherst ordered light infantry armed with carbines in place of muskets, and wanted them to "swing pack"—move out—at a moment's notice, so they could move swiftly through the wilderness. In addition, they displayed discipline and staying power.

The Rangers were helping to change the tactics of the British Army in the wilderness. Every regiment was trained to skirmish, patrol, and move quickly through the forests. Regular troops were soon carrying thirty pounds of meal which they cooked. Some discarded knapsacks and, in Ranger fashion, carried a blanket roll. In 1756 some British units instructed their men in the art of firing and loading while prone or kneeling. In June 1758 ten rifles were issued in each battalion to arm the best marksmen. Movement was facilitated by discarding some equipment and training each man to move in order "slow and fast in all sorts of Ground" (Beattie 1986).

Despite these changes the regulars still needed Rangers. In 1757, Loudoun determined the army needed increased winter scouting, so he sent home many provincials raised in the northern colonies and asked these same colonies to furnish a contingent of 1,100 experienced Rangers. Rogers saw that his Rangers were specially equipped for winter scouting. Each man had a haversack for dried food and spare flints and a canteen made of wood, or tin, that carried about two quarts of a mixture of rum and water. A blanket roll was

possibility of forming a separate corps, it was necessary that these "Gentlemen Volunteers" accompany the Rangers on various missions to learn the art of "ranging." Two months later the men were ordered back to their regular units.

Lt. Col. Thomas Gage offered to raise a corps of 500 light armed foot soldiers, recruited from the colonists, with the mobility of Rangers but subject to all regulations. The first of these units was activated on the New York frontier in 1758. Rogers recorded that regulars arrived "to be trained in the ranging or wood-service." Instruction was to include "our methods of marching, retreating, and draped over one shoulder with its ends tied together at the opposite waist. Weapons consisted of a tomahawk, a scalping knife, and a musket, usually sawed down for better handling in the field, with sixty rounds of ball and powder, often supplemented by buckshot. Some carried bayonets.

During cold weather, mittens were attached to sleeves or carried around the neck on strings. Snowshoes were carried on the back when not in use. The blanket could also serve as a hood, and those who could afford them wore army capotes or watch coats. Extra supplies could be carried on hand sleighs or toboggans. Travel across frozen lakes and rivers was aided by barbed ice creepers attached to the soles of moccasins and shoes.

On the march, an advance guard was deployed. During the winter they were equipped with ice skates. Use of flankers and reconnaissance parties was standard at all times, though mistakes were made. Rest stops and camping at night meant that pickets were set out in all directions. Beds of spruce boughs were placed around a fire pit dug to a depth of three feet. The pits minimized the chances of detection by the enemy. At dawn, the usual hour for an attack, the men were drawn into ranks. If the enemy failed to attack, breakfast was taken and the march continued.

Throughout the period from 1758 to 1760, Rogers' Rangers carried out a series of long-range reconnaissance patrols against French positions in the area of Fort Ticonderoga, New York. In March of 1759, Rogers led a force of fifty-two Indians, 169 light infantry, and ninety Rangers to scout Fort Carillon at Ticonderoga. They returned with valuable intelligence, several scalps, prisoners, and a sketch of the fort.

In 1760 Amherst ordered Rogers to move against the Abenaki Indians at St. Frances. He was to take 200 Rangers and to "remember the Barbarities that have been committed by the enemy's Indian scoundrels" (Beattie 1986). The Rangers crossed 200 miles of wild terrain while losing one quarter of their strength to sickness, lameness, and injuries. The Indians were surprised: between 100 and 200 Indians were killed, and the town was burned. Only two of Rogers' men were lost in the attack. While returning, proper discipline was not

Battle flags and colors of the 2nd Ranger Battalion, World War II. US Army

Order activating Darby's Rangers.

Shoulder patch of 1st Ranger Battalion, World War II. The current patch of the 75th Ranger Regiment is modeled on this style.

enforced. One third of the men, already hungry and tired, fell prey to "enraged" pursuers or starvation.

By Gen. James Wolfe's Canadian campaign of 1759, the British Army had learned to fight in the harsh terrain of the Americas. As Wolfe's Army moved it was protected by screens of light infantry and Rangers. The general ordered detachments never to halt, encamp, or cross dangerous areas without scouting. All camps and outposts were to be fortified against sudden attacks. If they occurred the retreating force was to use light infantry to screen the withdrawal to draw the enemy into battle with the main army.

Rangers in the Revolution and the Early Republic

Throughout the American Revolution, both sides used light infantry and irregular forces,

Commando knife specially made for Darby's Rangers. The handle of the knife doubles as brass knuckles.

which often took part in the increasingly bitter intercommunal strife between Loyalist Tories and Whig Rebels.

In 1776, George Washington gave Col. Thomas Knowlton permission to form a unit of Rangers that would perform "delicate" and hazardous duty. Formed from about 120 men from New England regiments, the unit was positioned near the East River above Harlem. It reconnoitered in front of American lines and, while operating with Gen. Nathanael Greene's troops, attempted to reach the rear of the British lines to cut off the enemy.

Though the Rangers were adept at moving through difficult terrain, the operation was a failure, and Knowlton was killed. The unit surrendered with the garrison at Fort Washington 16 November 1776.

British Ranger units operated from Canada, infiltrating New York State and Pennsylvania, joining Indian allies in destroying houses, barns, grain, and grist and saw mills. They aimed at interdicting supplies from the Mohawk Valley to the Continental Army.

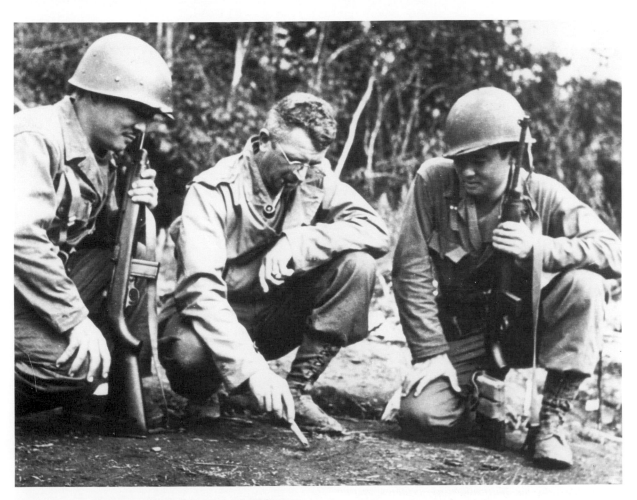

Gen. Frank D. Merrill (middle). US Army via Phil Piazza

Intercommunal warfare was particularly fierce in the south. From 1780 until war's end, Col. Francis Marion played a substantial role in combating England's southern strategy. British Army planners believed they could drive the Whigs from areas of power by using Loyalist partisans. Slowly, but inevitably, they would pacify each colony, finally restoring colonial government.

Marion's career as a partisan Ranger began in 1780. Without an independent command, and intrigued by the partisan activities of American Gen. Thomas Sumpter, he agreed to direct militia activities near Williamsburg, an area of Whig influence. American Gen. Horatio Gates consented, ordering

Marion, in August 1780, to disrupt supplies from Camden to British Gen. Charles Lord Cornwallis.

Marion and his men knew the woods and swamps well and, armed with a variety of weapons, carried out lightning raids against British and Tory forces. They often loaded their muskets with buckshot or musket ball and three or four buckshot. It was not uncommon for partisans to score the musket ball so it would break into fragments, inflicting more damage than ordinary shot.

In the fall of 1780, General Cornwallis wrote that "Col. Marion has so wrought on the minds of the people . . . that there was scarce an Inhabitant between the Santee and the Peedee who was not in

Merrill's Marauders at the start of their mission. Note the contrast to the Marauders as supplies became scarce. US Army via Phil Piazza

arms against us." British Col. Banastre Tarleton, sent to run Marion down, reported that his foe could bring his men together rapidly, and "after making incursions into the friendly districts, or threatening the communications, to avoid persuit, he disbanded his followers" (Scheer 1958). Marion frequently held up supplies sent to the British Army.

Having failed to bring his foe to bay, Tarleton is supposed to have declaimed: "Come on, my boys, let's go back. As for this damned old fox, the devil himself could not catch him" (Scheer 1958). Having eluded Tarleton, Marion continued to raid until his supplies ran low. Moving to a place in the swamps in the Lynch Creek and Great Pee Dee, both in South Carolina, he set up a supply and rest camp. From this base he continued to harass the British and their Tory allies, keeping the "whole country in continual alarm," so that regular troops were "everywhere necessary" (Scheer 1958).

In 1781 Marion joined with Gen. "Light Horse" Harry Lee and invested Fort Watson, South Carolina. They soon joined Gen. Nathanael Greene's troops at Eutaw Springs, South Carolina on 8 September, forming the right wing of Gen. Greene's line. Placed to absorb the first shock of battle, they were to fall back after firing as many rounds as possible. Greene hoped to use Daniel Morgan's successful Cowpens' strategy—having the militia and regulars retreat after firing their initial rounds. After four hours of fierce fighting, each side lost about 500 men, either killed or wounded. Though outnumbered, the British troops broke the first two Continental lines. Not wishing to risk his last unbroken regiments, Greene withdrew. Cornwallis also suffered heavily and moved to Wilmington, but later retreated into Virginia. Greene said Marion's men had a "degree of Spirit and firmness," that "would have graced the soldiers of the King of Prussia [Frederick the Great]" (Ferling 1984).

Greene, who followed Cornwallis north, was soon back in South Carolina where he was joined by Marion and others. Greene was defeated near Camden, South Carolina, but Marion cut the British line of communications at Fort Watson, forcing a British retreat. Marion spent the remainder of the war hunting Tories and trying to keep supplies from reaching British troops in Charleston. In 1782 his brigade was officially disbanded.

East Florida, along the Georgia border, was the scene of constant guerrilla activity. By 1777 the Loyalists in east Florida and nearby Georgia formed the East Florida Rangers. Supplemented by a small body of Creek Indians, their leader, Thomas Brown, carried out a series of raids into Georgia. While some raids were of little military value, they succeeded in bringing cattle and other

Merrill's Marauders crossing a primitive mountain bridge in Burma. The lack of food can be seen clearly in the skeletal appearance of the men. US Army via Phil Piazza

forage into food-poor east Florida. Brown attached his Rangers to Indian war parties to prevent "indiscriminate butchering of women and children" (Olson 1970).

Throughout the war, Brown, the governor of Florida, and the local military authorities argued over the status and rank of the Rangers. The army won, and many of the old Rangers (men of property) did not wish to accept the terms of the new provisional establishment and left the service. At the end of 1779, Brown formed a new corps, the Kings (Carolina) Rangers. They were issued new uniforms consisting of a short green coat with crimson collar and cuffs and plain green lapels. While stationed on the Georgia border, they drove cattle from rebel areas and worked among Loyalists in the back country. At war's end, many moved to Barbados.

The early national period saw continued unrest along the frontier. Consequently the states, and later the federal government, continued to use Rangers units. In the 1800s, Congress was interested in the immediate protection of the frontier from Indian raids. On 2 January 1812, six companies of Rangers, recruited from the area, were raised for the protection of settlers. Men enlisted for twelve months. They equipped and provided for themselves and their horses at an allowance of one dollar per day. While they brought security to the frontier settlements, the Rangers were not strong enough to assert American rights, as European nations still held territory on the frontier.

In 1814 there were 1,070 Rangers, and ten independent companies, patrolling the frontier from Michigan to Louisiana. In 1818, Gen. Andrew Jackson commanded Ranger units in the Florida panhandle. A mounted Ranger battalion was formed between 1832 and 1833. It was employed to show force against the Indians, especially when bargaining, and for protection of commercial routes. Essentially, it was part of Andrew Jackson's Indian policy. In 1832, the secretary of war, Lewis Cass, reported that the Rangers were merely "superior militia" who were unruly and had difficulty working with regular infantry. Costing $150,000 more than a regular dragoon regiment, they did not receive special training.

Nevertheless, the government decided mounted units were useful, and despite earlier fears that cavalry was an aristocratic threat to democracy, the secretary of the army moved to enact legislation discharging the Rangers, and enlisting dragoons.

Throughout the 1830s, Ranger units were used in Texas. In 1832 they were employed along the

Merrill's Marauders receiving a very rare resupply by parachute. Such drops were usually impossible because of climate or terrain. US Army via Phil Piazza

frontier and were separate from Texas' regular army and militia. Texas Rangers had no regular uniforms and furnished their own arms. Rangers were used in the Mexican War, despite Zachary Taylor's poor opinion of them; he found them indispensable as scouts. Twenty or more Ranger companies served Texas between the war with Mexico and the Civil War.

The Civil War

It is estimated that some 428 units were officially and unofficially known as Rangers during the Civil War. Their effectiveness has been questioned, and many were Rangers in name only. On 21 April 1862, Confederate President Jefferson Davis approved an act to form partisan Rangers to be organized as infantry or cavalry. Captured military equipment would be considered "booty," as the act declared: "The Rangers shall be paid their full value in such manner as the Secretary of War may prescribe" (Grant 1958).

From the beginning, the units were controversial. Problems arose because they siphoned troops away from regular units and were allowed to profit from confiscated goods. Brig. Gen. Henry Heth, of West Virginia, announced that they were "a terror to the loyal and true everywhere," being no better than robbers and plunderers. He found that they were "more ready to plunder friends than foes . . . they do as they please—go where they please," which meant "roaming over the country, taking what they want, and doing nothing" (Grant 1958).

While some units, such as Mosby's Rangers, had good reputations, disillusionment with their operations was rising. Confederate Secretary of War James A. Seddon believed that the advantages of such units had been only "partially realized," and that their "independent organization and the facilities and temptations thereby afforded to license and depredations grave mischiefs have resulted" (Grant 1958). He concluded that they should be disbanded and the men merged with troops of the line.

In 1864, Gen. Robert E. Lee was informed that "[Rangers] are a terror to the citizens and an infamy to the cause. They never fight; can't be made to fight." Many, he was told, "have engaged in this business for the sake of gain." Lee was

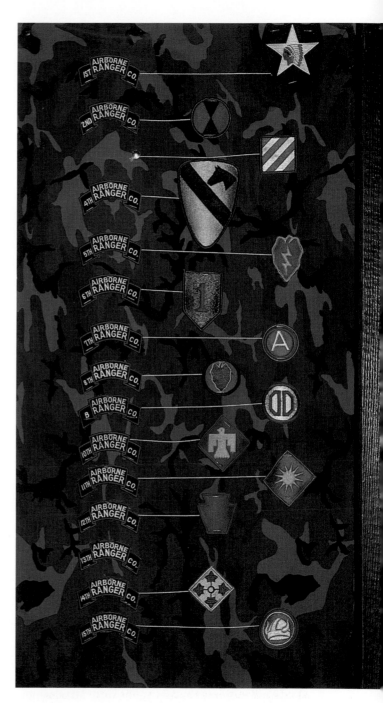

Patches and badges of the Ranger companies in Korea.

17

Shoulder patches and badges of the Ranger companies in Vietnam. The insignia in the center is the badge of the Vietnam Ranger Association. The shield in the center is the badge of Merrill's Marauders. The motto continues to be the motto of the 75th Ranger Regiment. Sfc. R. Hilston, US Army

convinced and soon recommended that "the law authorizing these partisan corps be abolished" (Grant 1958). This was done, with some exceptions, in February 1864.

Rangers were organized for the Union and were used to counter Confederate Rangers. Their contribution to the war is equally obscure. Col. Benjamin Grierson's two raids into Mississippi, though, are similar to Ranger operations. As Gen. Ulysses S. Grant prepared to move against

Vicksburg, he instructed Grierson to move south into Mississippi where he was to destroy as much as possible. Grant hoped Grierson's activities would pull Confederate troops out of Grant's operational area.

From 17 April to 2 May 1863, Grierson's mounted troops rode through parts of Mississippi. Having eluded pursuers, he wrecked more than fifty miles of railroad and destroyed several supply bases. Though Confederate leaders were aware this was a diversion, some troops were pulled away from opposing Grant's operations at Vicksburg. This raid was made famous in the movie *The Horse Soldiers*.

Less well known was Grierson's later, winter raid. In some ways this raid was more successful than the first. Gen. Henry Halleck wanted to cut supply lines to the Army of Tennessee. Once Confederate Gen. John B. Hood had been defeated by Union Gen. George H. Thomas before Nashville, a cavalry attack directed at railroads would destroy the major lines of communication to the defeated Confederates.

Very much like Merrill's Marauders of a later war, Grierson's men marched long distances. They accounted for 600 prisoners and 800 head of captured livestock. Some 1,000 slaves deserted their owners, thus denying their services to the manpower-poor Confederacy. Grierson's men destroyed as much track and rolling stock as possible. Already short of supplies, the Confederacy could ill afford the loss of the warehouses with commissary, quartermaster, and ordnance stores. A total of 5,000 stand of arms and 500 bales of cotton had now been destroyed by Grierson.

World War II

The United States did not deploy Ranger units again until World War II. Early in the war, Gen. George C. Marshall decided to train US troops in commando methods. They would gain experience accompanying the British on raids. Brig. Gen. Lucian Truscott, Jr., and Gen. Dwight D. Eisenhower discussed the planning, organization, and conduct of combined operations, eventually deciding to form a commando-type organization.

Eisenhower did not want to use the term commando, as this was already intimately associated with the British. Truscott chose Rangers because the name had been used by American units that had displayed "high standards of individual courage, determination, ruggedness, fighting ability, and achievement" (King 1981). Officially, they would be identified as the 1st Ranger Battalion. Training began at Carrickfergus, Northern Ireland, in June 1942.

Guidelines for Ranger volunteers were determined, the goal being fully trained soldiers of the highest standard. Officers and noncommissioned officers had to show leadership skills, with particular emphasis on initiative, judgment, and common sense. Selectees needed skills in self-defense, weaponry, scouting, mountaineering, seamanship, and small boat handling. Those with skills in demolition and knowledge of railway engines and public utilities, such as power plants and radio stations, were needed.

Volunteers were trained in speed marches, cliff climbing, obstacle courses, and tactical problems. During training, British commandos simulated enemy resistance by throwing grenades and firing small arms over and near the Rangers. Throughout training, the men worked in pairs—a buddy system. Having chosen partners from their platoons, both men trained and lived together. Teams negotiated the bullet and bayonet course, as well as the obstacle course, together. During movement, one team would cover another, and the street fighting course soon became known as "Me and My Pal."

During the war there were six Ranger battalions. The 1st, 3rd, and 4th fought in the Mediterranean theater. The 2nd and 5th went ashore on D-day, 6 June 1944. The 6th and Merrills Marauders fought against the Japanese. These units were originally designated Ranger battalions, but were redesignated Ranger infantry battalions in August 1943.

The 1st Ranger Infantry Battalion was formed in June of 1942 at Carrickfergus, Northern Ireland, and trained there and elsewhere in England before participating in the landings in North Africa in November 1942. The battalion took part in the invasion of Sicily in July 1943. Following Sicily, the unit landed in Italy at Salerno in September 1943,

First Lieutenant and Staff Sergeant of 2nd Platoon, L Company Rangers, 101st Airborne Division, in Vietnam, 1971. The yellow Ranger tab is on the beret. The airborne insignia is on the left shoulder. US Army via Col. David Grange

and was destroyed at Cisterna during the Anzio campaign of January 1944.

The 4th Ranger Infantry Battalion was formed in North Africa in May 1943. The 4th, along with the 1st and 3rd battalions, formed Ranger Force for the landings in Sicily and Italy. The unit suffered fifty percent casualties at Anzio. They continued to fight on into February, and were then used to conduct patrolling school for the Fifth Army.

The 2nd Ranger Infantry Battalion was formed in April 1943 at Camp Forrest, Tennessee. They arrived in England on 29 November 1943, and took part in the D-day landings, assaulting Pointe Du Hoe. They saw action in Brest, and later in the Ardennes-Alsace areas, ending the war in Czechoslovakia.

The 5th Ranger Infantry Battalion also formed at Camp Forrest. They arrived in England on 17 January 1944. The battalion landed in Normandy on D-day. After Normandy, the unit saw action in northern France, the Ardennes-Alsace area, the Rhineland, and central Europe. In April 1945 the unit was tasked by Gen. George Patton to escort 1,000 Germans through the Buchenwald death camp.

The 6th Ranger Infantry Battalion was formed at Hollandia, New Guinea, from the 98th Field Artillery Battalion and saw action in the Philippines. Three days before the first landings in the Philippines, they landed on Dinagat, securing the island. During the landings on Luzon, they landed on White Beach and participated in the drive on Manila. During this time they liberated a prisoner of war camp.

Operation Torch

The 1st Rangers, now under the command of Col. William O. Darby, were scheduled to land at Arzew east of Oran, Algeria, as part of Operation Torch (the invasion of North Africa), in November 1942. They were to reduce the main defenses nearby and capture the port of Arzew. Once this was accomplished, they were to capture and secure the beachhead for further landings. The destruction of the coastal defenses was necessary before the rest of the force could land, for if the Rangers failed, naval gunfire would be necessary, alerting the defenders. The Rangers were successful.

During operations in Tunisia and North Africa, the Rangers were employed in a variety of missions, not always in line with their training. Early in February 1943, Darby led the Rangers on a night raid against Italian front-line positions,

killing or wounding about seventy-five Italians, destroying one antitank gun and five machine guns, and capturing eleven prisoners. Ranger casualties included one killed and twenty wounded. Unfortunately, when the Rangers were used as regular infantry, as happened, especially during and after the disaster at Kasserine Pass, Tunisia, their casualties increased.

On 13 March, Gen. George S. Patton ordered Darby to assist in the attack on Gafsa, Tunisia. Finding the town lightly defended, the Rangers passed through to regain contact with the enemy. Once contact was restored, they were to determine the enemy's strength and disposition and maintain themselves in the area of contact, while attempting to identify enemy units.

Information obtained from these operations was vital for Patton's planned attack on Italian forces at El Guettar, Tunisia. Darby was told to act aggressively, but not to commit himself to actions from which he could not withdraw. The Rangers were now ordered to infiltrate enemy lines and attack the Djel Jel Ank Pass from the rear while the 26th Infantry Division attacked from the front. Patrols mapped out a route to the rear of the Italian positions, and Darby personally carried out a daylight reconnaissance against the north wall of the pass. Night reconnaissance continued, enabling the Rangers to map a tortuous ten-mile route to an unguarded rocky plateau overlooking the enemy positions.

As the Rangers overran the Italian positions in the mountains, the 26th Division entered the pass. A little before noon, division operations directed Darby and the infantry to clean up what resistance remained, and take the high ground further on. As the attacks continued toward the east, the Rangers were returned to El Guettar.

Invasion of Sicily

When Patton's 7th Army landed in Sicily on 10 July 1943, the Rangers landed with the lead elements of the invasion forces on the beaches near Gela. The Ranger Force consisted of the 1st, 3rd, and 4th Ranger Infantry Battalions. They captured the town, and defended it against counterattack. Their mission included the destruction or neutralization of the coastal defenses located on high ground northwest of Gela. Once secure in Gela, the

Rangers seized the high ground surrounding the town.

Ranger units also landed with the 3rd Infantry Division on Green Beach, where they destroyed enemy installations before moving to the southwest to seize and hold strategic ground until relieved. From these positions the 3rd Ranger Battalion moved inland. Patton now employed the Rangers in his armed reconnaissance to Porto Empedocle. Ranger units penetrated thickly defended areas. On their approach to the city, they ambushed an Italian motorized company. Many of the enemy were killed and so many prisoners were taken that they had to be sent back to the 7th Army lines. On 17 and 18 July, the Rangers entered the town and moved to take the port, afterward setting up a perimeter defense around the city. Ranger units moved toward Messina, and also participated in taking that city.

Invasion of Italy

Following the fighting in Sicily, the Rangers prepared for the invasion of Italy. When the Allies came ashore, the Rangers participated, landing about twenty miles west of Salerno. Their objective was to capture Salerno and destroy nearby coastal defenses. Moving inland, they seized the Chiunzi Pass and prepared to operate against the rear of the enemy. By midmorning, their mission was accomplished. They soon found themselves involved in regular infantry actions, where they sustained more than seventy men killed or wounded.

Operations in Italy reached a stalemate, and a plan to outflank the Germans was devised. It was hoped that with the Allies landing at Anzio, the Germans would be forced to withdraw northward while keeping out of the Alban Hills. The Rangers were taken out of combat to prepare for the landing.

The extensive combat operations in North Africa and Sicily had resulted in Ranger casualties, and the training received by Ranger replacements was apparently not as complete as for the first volunteers. Evidence of this came on 17 January 1944 during a practice landing west of Naples.

After landing, umpires noted that some units made excessive noise and moved when flares were fired, making them more visible than if they had stayed still. Men of the 1st Ranger Battalion established themselves in indefensible positions and failed to send security forward when necessary. Moving inland the 4th Ranger Battalion traveled up a road in column without an advance

Camp Eagle, Republic of Vietnam, 1971. The Ranger companies in Vietnam deployed out of base camps like this one. Conditions were often little better at camp than out in the field. US Army via Col. David Grange

2nd Platoon, L Company Rangers return to Camp Eagle after an interdiction operation near the Ashah *Valley in Vietnam. Not all of the headgear is regulation.* US Army via Col. David Grange

guard and moved through a defile without proper reconnaissance. Either of these actions could result in an ambush.

Anzio Landing

In the early morning hours of 22 January 1944 the Allies put Sixth Corps ashore on the beaches of Anzio, Italy. The town lay in the middle of the invasion area, and was secured by Darby and his Rangers. To the east of Anzio, the US 3rd Infantry Division, reinforced by the 504th Parachute Infantry Regiment, landed near Nettuno. To the west of the Rangers in Anzio the British 1st Division came ashore. The beachhead was established, but the Allies were too weak to take advantage of the surprise.

The ranger Force consisted of 1st, 3rd, and 4th Ranger Infantry Battalions with assorted units attached, including the 83rd Chemical Battalion, and a cannon company. The Rangers remained in the front lines until shortly before the planned attack out of the beachhead was to take place.

At 0100 hours on 30 January 1944, the Rangers began their movement toward the town of Cisterna di Lattoria, which they were to seize and hold until relieved, after which they were to occupy the ground to the immediate northwest. The 1st and 3rd Battalions crossed the line of departure first, moving along a ditch that offered some concealment. Third Battalion became lost, and then contact between the two units was broken. Radio contact with Darby at his command post was interrupted as it became obvious German troops and armor had infiltrated in and around the advancing Rangers.

The Rangers had to fight their way to Cisterna and arrived at dawn only to find Cisterna garrisoned. In this situation the plan called for support from the 4th Ranger Battalion, but the battalion's forward movement had been stalled by heavy resistance. Fierce fighting continued throughout the area. For those Rangers still in the Pantano ditch, the fighting was brutal. The Germans drove their tanks to the edge, lowered their guns, and fired.

Carlo D'Este, in his *Fatal Decision*, says some Rangers were "deliberately spared, pulled from the ditch and formed into a ragged column," to shield the Germans as they moved toward American lines. Incoming fire killed several prisoners and a witness reported "the Germans machine-gunned and bayoneted some of the helpless prisoners in the column. They had already shot the wounded men left in the ditch."

Very few survived. Of the 767 men who reached the town, only six made their way back to American lines; the rest were killed or captured.

Despite the failure at Cisterna, the Rangers inflicted 5,500 casualties on the Germans, forcing them to commit their reserves and postpone their attack for two days, giving the Allies time to prepare.

First Special Services Force

Those Rangers who survived either were transferred to training units in the United States or were incorporated into the First Special Services Force (FSSF) which was in the area. The FSSF was an American and Canadian unit developed at the urging of British Prime Minister Winston Churchill. The unit was never used in Norway, as originally planned, but was used in the Aleutians and later in Italy.

Though not usually considered a Ranger unit, its training and operations were in the Ranger tradition. Airborne training was completed in six days as opposed to three weeks. Cold-weather training included skiing, rock climbing, mountain walking, use of ropes, and basic cold-weather survival training.

During the many nights spent in mountains during the winter, basic infantry skills were stressed. Training included marksmanship, small arms and automatic weapons, bazookas, mortars, flamethrowers, demolition training, and the use of captured German weapons. Training was so realis-

Members of 2nd Platoon, L Company Rangers, extracted after a reconnaissance patrol in Vietnam, 1971. The machine gun in the right background is part of the armament of the UH-1 helicopter that extracted the Rangers. US Army via Col. David Grange

tic that bayonet training was done with bare blades.

Training continued near Norfolk, Virginia, where they practiced amphibious landings. Further training continued in Vermont in the use of rubber boats, scouting and patrolling, raiding, and demolitions.

On 15 August 1943, under cover of darkness, the unit landed on the island of Kiska in the Aleutians. The raiders found the island evacuated.

General Eisenhower wanted the FSSF in Italy, where it was assigned to the 5th Army in November of 1944. While in Italy, they participated in several attacks through mountainous terrain. In their assault on Mount de la Difensa on 2 December 1944, the FSSF climbed the face of a sheer cliff believed to be unclimbable. This accomplishment in fog and drizzling rain completely surprised the Germans.

The FSSF continued to operate in this forbidding terrain, often moving through sparsely settled areas in separate columns capitalizing on stealth and night fighting capabilities. On 30 January 1944, the unit was ordered into the Anzio beachhead, where they held a portion of the line. During this time they aggressively patrolled the area to their front so successfully that the Germans were forced to pull back their lines. In the final breakout the FSSF accompanied the US Army to Rome, where it occupied strategic bridges over the Tiber River. Passing through the city, they continued to scout while clearing resistance and posting signs for the main body, thus allowing the 5th Army to move past Rome with some degree of security.

The FSSF's last major operation was to secure two strategically placed islands off the coast of southern France during Operation Anvil, the invasion of southern France. The terrain on both islands was formidable, and landings were made on beaches where the cliffs rose from the sea. The FSSF was disbanded on 5 December 1944.

D-day

On 6 June 1944, the Allies landed on the beaches of Normandy, France. The Rangers landed with the assault troops at Pointe du Hoe, four miles west of Omaha Beach. Here the Allies believed the

The total security force for the Desert One hostage rescue attempt. Company C, 1/75, rehearsed under conditions similar to the actual mission. For a deliberate-response operation such as Desert One or Operation Just Cause (Panama), the Rangers meticulously go over every detail beforehand. For quick-response operations such as Grenada, when there is no time for rehearsals, the Rangers rely on their combat-oriented training for success. US Army via Col. David Grange

Germans had emplaced heavy guns that could fire on the beaches.

Sheer cliffs rose from a narrow strip of beach some 85 to 100ft above sea level. Once on the cliff, the Rangers would be in an area mined and criss-crossed with barbed wire. German supporting positions on the flanks consisted of machine and antiaircraft guns.

To accomplish their mission the Rangers were equipped with specialized equipment. Their landing craft carried rocket launchers at the bow, amidships, and in the stern that could be fired either in series or in pairs from one control point at the stern. The rockets would carry $3/4$in ropes and light rope ladders to the top of cliffs. Ropes and ladders had grapnels to secure them to the cliffs. Extension ladders, with Lewis machine guns attached to the top, were also carried.

Rangers carried an assortment of infantry equipment, including two hand grenades, an M-1 rifle, and D-bar rations. Some carried pistols or carbines. Heavier weapons included Browning Automatic Rifles, light mortars, and thermite grenades. After the assault wave, more ammunition and heavy mortars were scheduled to land.

On D-day all did not go as planned. High seas soaked the Rangers and their equipment. They realized at the last minute that they were heading for the wrong beach and had to change direction, delaying their attack. Some of the Germans had recovered from the naval and air bombardment and were ready to oppose the Rangers as they scaled the cliff. The beach contained no cover, although the shell holes produced ready-made foxholes. Some fifteen Rangers became casualties on the beach.

The high seas not only soaked the Rangers but also their equipment. The ropes, saturated with water, were too heavy for the rockets to boost to the cliff above the beach. A hand-held launcher finally succeeded in hauling a rope to the crest. The wet Rangers and their ropes produced slippery mud as they struggled to reach the top, where the defenders fired or threw grenades at them.

Once on top, the Rangers found the area desolate, all landmarks gone. Eventually, assault teams neutralized or destroyed the fortifications. To their surprise, the German howitzers were gone but were found later some distance away and destroyed by thermite grenades. Ranger units that had moved inland were attacked during their first night in France, and eventually pushed back to the cliff above the water. Naval gunfire helped the Rangers maintain their positions, and by $D + 2$ they were relieved.

As the 2nd Ranger Battalion was delayed getting ashore and had trouble scaling the cliff, the 5th Ranger Battalion landed in the Vierville sector behind the 116th Infantry Regiment. Working their way toward Pointe Du Hoe, together with the engineers, they knocked out strong points flanking Omaha Beach.

Following D-day, the Rangers moved inland. The 2nd Ranger Battalion received replacements during July 1944, and with the 5th Ranger Battalion participated in the fighting for the port city of Brest (August-September 1944). In the assault, the 5th Ranger Battalion destroyed several pill boxes with explosive charges and twenty gallons of petroleum oil, which burned for forty minutes. Many Germans surrendered similar positions the next day.

The 2nd Ranger Battalion moved eastward to the Heurtgen Forest, Germany. In December 1944, they were ordered to move to an area overlooking the Schmidt and Roer dams. The Rangers were used to assault a hill that regular infantry had failed to capture. Despite counterattacks, the Rangers held. They were relieved on 9 March.

Toward the end of the war, the 5th Ranger Battalion was employed in a long-range penetration. On 23 February 1945 they were relieved from duty with the 3rd Cavalry Division and given a new mission. They were to pass through the division bridgehead and infiltrate enemy lines, finally establishing a blocking position across the Irsch-Zerf road in Germany.

Several small engagements were fought on the way to the objective. Some Germans were captured, and the objective cleared of enemy troops. The Rangers set up a perimeter that included antipersonnel mines. When the Germans realized the potential of the blocking position, they attacked. Despite orders to fight to the last man, many Germans surrendered. The mission lasted longer than expected; attempts were made

The battle at the Commendancia, Gen. Manuel Noriega's headquarters in Panama City. This was the fiercest fighting in the city during Operation Just Cause. US Army

to supply the Rangers from the air, but gunfire kept the aircraft at 1,500ft and the supplies landed outside of the perimeter. Friendly armor reached the Rangers on 26 February and passed on through the block. The final action was an ambush of German troops in enveloping fog. The Rangers killed an estimated 299 enemy soldiers, taking 328 prisoners, during an operation lasting five days. Afterward, the Rangers were used as regular infantry, a role for which they were not suited.

Philippines Invasion

In the Philippines, the 6th Ranger Battalion took part in preinvasion landings on strategically located islands, guarding the entrance to Leyte Gulf. Going ashore on 17 October 1944, three days before main units landed, they destroyed radio facilities and anything else of military value.

With US forces storming into the islands, the US high command was concerned that the Japanese would move prisoners from the camp at Cabanatuan. The camp was located behind enemy lines, in the mainstream of enemy troop movements, and was a resting place for retreating troops. The main road in the area was used by Japanese trucks and tanks.

A plan was developed to send the Rangers behind enemy lines, free the prisoners, and move them safely back to American lines. The route passed through heavily forested areas, open grasslands, and rice paddies. The Rangers crossed the Talavera River at midnight, and later that night crossed the Rizal road. Guerrillas gave support in the form of intelligence and established a road-block on the main road. Despite the long route to the objective, and the presence of Japanese forces on the road, the Rangers arrived safely at the camp. Their attack was a surprise. Having freed the prisoners, they now had to escort them to safety. This part of the mission was completed when the group reached a patrol of the 6th Army.

Merrill's Marauders

At the Quebec conference (August 1943), the United States agreed to form a long-range-penetration unit, similar to the British Chindits, for use in Burma. On 1 September 1943, the unit's size was fixed at a battalion. The Army wanted at least 300 rugged, physically fit volunteers from the Southwest Pacific. Seven hundred more were required from the South Pacific, and more than 1,000 were taken from the Caribbean Defense Command and Army in the United States. Among the volunteers were veterans of Guadalcanal, New Guinea, and other Pacific battlegrounds.

These men were brought together under the command of Gen. Frank D. Merrill and were popularly known as Merrill's Marauders. After arriving in India they began training in the tactics of long-range penetration. Locations for jungle training were chosen; but in several of them, conditions, particularly sanitation, were bad. This training lasted for slightly more than two months during which marksmanship, scouting and patrolling, map reading, jungle navigation, calisthenics, and marches with packs were part of the course.

Platoon tactics were stressed, as well as combat team and battalion level movements. Rifle platoon leaders and NCOs were trained to direct mortar fire, and all were taught the rudiments of voice radio. In general, heavy weapons, intelligence, reconnaissance, pioneer, demolition, and communications specialists were already trained, but were further hardened by training with the group.

Rear echelon units included parachute riggers and so-called kick-out units whose job was to deliver supplies to the unit from aircraft. These units prepared adequate supplies in advance so they were ready when the long-range patrols needed them. The pilots were carefully trained, especially for low-level drops into small clearings. All of this was made more difficult by poor flying conditions over Burma.

Facilities were set up for supplies, and arrangements made for radio communication with the units to be supplied. Merrill was in contact with forward units by radio. Long- and short-wave radios were carried in order to coordinate movement of columns and to contact higher headquarters. Long-range radios were carried on mules. Units also carried SCR-300 walkie-talkies with a range of about three miles—a ten-mile range in level terrain, rare in Burma.

On 8 January 1944, the unit, officially known as 5307 Composite Unit (provisional), or Galahad, was assigned to Gen. Joseph Stillwell's command in northern Burma. This was an extremely difficult area in which to operate because it was criss-crossed by rugged hills, high mountains, and deep valleys cut by numerous rivers. A good part of the area was covered by thick jungle, in which strands of bamboo grew so thick that tunnels were cut through them. Troops crossing rivers often emerged covered with leeches. During monsoon season, the area became almost impassable. Mountainsides became so muddy that men and animals slipped and stumbled in the mire, and some areas were so steep that men carved steps in the slopes. Added to this were rain, high humidity, and temperatures producing heat prostration. Mosquitoes and mites carried diseases including common malaria and scrub typhus—and some more exotic.

Galahad was noted for rapid movement and ability to move over what seemed impassable terrain. Its reconnaissance and intelligence platoon always moved ahead of the main body, sometimes by as much as several miles, and one of its rifle platoons formed the first element of the main body. A rifle company with half of the heavy weapons platoon was next in line. The middle of the formation contained the column headquarters, transport, and medical detachment. The rear consisted of a rifle platoon and the rest of the heavy weapons. On occasion, some columns separated the combat elements from support elements so they would not delay the tactical deployment in case of combat.

In the field, the wounded were first treated by medical corpsmen and surgical teams traveling with the unit. Once initial care was given, casualties were removed to the rear by light aircraft which landed on nearby dry riverbeds, rice paddies, and gravel bars along rivers. They were then taken by transports to a hospital equipped to handle them. These aerial ambulances were stationed at Ledo.

On 24 February, Galahad began a series of operations in conjunction with Chinese troops. They were sent on a wide encircling movement east of Chinese forces, where they were to block trails and cut Japanese supply lines when possible. For several weeks the men marched through the jungle, blocking Japanese movements and destroying whatever supplies they could find. Unfortunately, part of Galahad was trapped at Nhphum Ga, where they suffered from combat and disease, and as the official history reports, "The fighting edge of the most mobile and most obedient force that Stillwell had was worn dull" (Romanus 1956). No compensating damage was done to the Japanese, who moved to the defense of Myitkyina airfield, Burma.

The remaining Marauders followed the Japanese to attack Myitkyina airfield. Moving swiftly, they arrived at the field before the enemy realized

The men's room at the Panama City International Airport after a firefight between Rangers and Noriega's forces. This battle encompassed the heaviest fighting at the airport. US Army

28

they were there. In a quick daylight attack, the field was taken. Stillwell now ordered Galahad to take the town of Myitkyina, a mission for which the unit was not suited and was physically unable to perform.

Galahad now had some 1,000 men out of the original 3,000. Most of their casualties resulted from disease and exhaustion. All were undernourished. One survivor said, "We were perpetually famished" (Ogburn 1959). K-rations lacked bulk and "every fourth or fifth day we ran out of them" (Ogburn 1959). Men would pick up and eat the maltose and dextrose tablets discarded by others. Two conditions existed: "One in which we felt unfed, the other in which we *were* unfed" (Ogburn 1959).

As hunger increased the men engaged in eating rituals which included the precise cutting of a bar of chocolate. Closing one's eyes and "chewing [a cocoa bar] together with [a] soft biscuit gave [the] illusion of eating a chocolate cake" (Ogburn 1959). Unfortunately, after an hour men were once again hungry; and when asleep, hunger returned, as "after midnight [there was] constant waking up to gnawing in belly" (Ogburn 1959).

Having taken the airfield at Myitkyina, the men believed they would be relieved, as they had been promised. Morale plummeted, and Galahad began to lose cohesion. This was compounded when hospitalized men were ordered to return to the front, including many who were not fit for service. In one incident, doctors took sick men off aircraft heading for Myitkyina and sent them back to hospitals. Once relieved and in the rear, discipline was difficult to maintain, and most of the men were unfit for further action.

From the start Galahad seemed doomed. Men from the Pacific already had malaria, other chronic diseases endemic to the area, and psychiatric complaints. Blanket malarial treatment was ordered for all of the 3rd Battalion of Merrill's Marauders. Daily suppressive Atabrine treatment was ordered, but men had to be checked regularly to see that they complied. When morale dropped, this became difficult. Even after periods of rest, the men failed to regain their strength. Improved rations did not help and "the men continued to decrease in strength and endurance and their physical and mental lassitude and exhaustion continued to increase until the very last" (Stone 1969). Doctors reported that "never before has severe exhaustion syndrome been so manifest on such a large scale. . . . Before the third month of combat, evidence of marked adrenal insufficiency began to be noticed in the men" (Stone 1969).

Stillwell's command, and those who failed to see that Galahad could no longer function, were responsible for the unit's deterioration. Merrill stated that promises of relief after three months had been made, and that when asked to move to Myitkyina the men had been told this was the last mission. Unfortunately, Merrill's poor health—he was evacuated twice because of his heart—meant there was no one to fight for the unit at Stillwell's headquarters. The unit was later reconstituted and operated for the rest of the war as Mars, ending the war in China.

At the end of World War II, Ranger units were disbanded. Successful in many of their operations, Rangers were often committed to operations for which they were neither trained nor equipped. In large measure this was because combat troops were scarce, and it was often impossible not to commit the Rangers to battle.

Korean War

Shortly after the end of World War II, the United States and the Soviet Union agreed to partition Korea at the 38th parallel. On 25 June 1950, the North Korean Army attacked across the 38th parallel, pushing deep into South Korea. The United States, with United Nations (UN) support, moved to counter this attack, and American air and ground troops were committed under the command of Gen. Douglas MacArthur. Following MacArthur's brilliant landing at Inchon, South Korea, 15 September 1950, US troops stormed into North Korea, some units reaching the Yalu River, Korea's border with China. Chinese troops entered the war, fighting UN forces to a stalemate, as neither the United States nor its allies desired more than a limited war fought for limited purposes. In the early phases of the war, while the fronts remained fluid, Ranger units were trained and committed to combat in Korea.

Gen. J. Lawton Collins, US Army chief of staff, impressed by the success achieved by infiltrating Communist units at the beginning of the war, sent a memo to Army Operations in Washington, D.C., asking that one company of Rangers be attached to each division, where they would be used to "infiltrate through enemy lines and attack command posts, artillery, tank parks, and key communication centers or facilities" (Lanning 1988).

Eventually, six Ranger companies would be sent to Korea, attached to the 8th Army. Rangers would be attached to the 1st Cavalry, and the 2nd, 3rd, 7th, 24th, and 25th Infantry Divisions, where they would fight in almost all the major battles from their arrival in late 1950 until their deactivation in the fall of 1951.

In the Far East, requests for volunteers were circulated for a unit designated Raiders, but to be known as the 8213 Provisional Company. They were activated in August 1950 and saw action with the 25th Infantry Division until the arrival of the 5th Ranger Company from Fort Benning, Georgia.

Training of Ranger companies began on 2 October 1950 at Fort Benning, Georgia. During this period entire companies trained as units. The original companies were all white, but on 9 October, Fort Benning received a company of black airborne volunteers. Initially designated the 4th Ranger Company, but operating as the 2nd Ranger Company, they were the only all-black Ranger company in US Army history.

The Ranger Training Command was set up at Harmony Church, Fort Benning, where the companies proceeded to pass through the training cycle. The initial cycle lasted six weeks, but the cycle period soon went from a forty-eight-hour week to sixty hours. Training included demolition, sabotage, land navigation, hand-to-hand combat, and communications.

Each training day began with a five-mile run, calisthenics, and long-distance marching with full equipment. The goal was "to prepare a Company to move from forty to fifty miles cross-country in twelve to eighteen hours, depending upon terrain" (Black 1989). Each company was thirty percent overstrength to allow for men who would fall out of the program.

Cold weather training and mountain training were given in a four-week course at Camp Carson, Colorado. Everything was difficult in the mountains of Colorado where the air was thinner and the temperatures low. Equipment issued included special boots for better traction, thermal underwear, fur-lined pile caps, and parkas. Special mittens, called trigger finger mittens, were issued along with shoe packs, rucksacks, and pack boards. Two-man mountain tents with white interiors that allowed the tent to be heated with a candle were used.

In the mountains, men learned how to cross swiftly flowing streams, and to move through draws, ravines, and canyons. Movement through snow and ice was facilitated with ice axes and pitons. Rappelling and snowshoe walking were practiced, along with tactics and techniques previously learned at Fort Benning in better weather.

Cold weather rations included one meal bar, ten cigarettes, one soup packet, and packets of tea, coffee, cream and sugar. These rations were supplemented by extra iron and necessities such as matches and toilet paper. Following mountain and cold weather training, the Rangers were marched to a corral where they were taught to work with mules.

In Korea, Ranger units were used for reconnaissance, sabotage behind enemy lines, and blocking enemy movements. As in previous wars, they were used in operations for which they were not equipped, such as spearheading infantry attacks or holding vulnerable positions of the line.

In March 1951, eleven Rangers were dropped behind enemy lines to blow up a railroad tunnel in the Wonsan area, but failed to do so. They were hampered by deep snow, and Chinese troops were present in large numbers. The Rangers' SCR-300 radios failed to operate until it was too late. Three Rangers were eventually evacuated by helicopters, but the rest were killed or captured. Later in March the Rangers were again used in an airborne operation, Tomahawk, to block enemy troops retreating from the area around Seoul. The operation began on 23 March 1951, with the 2nd and 4th Rangers working with the 187th Airborne Regimental Combat Team. The Rangers seized several

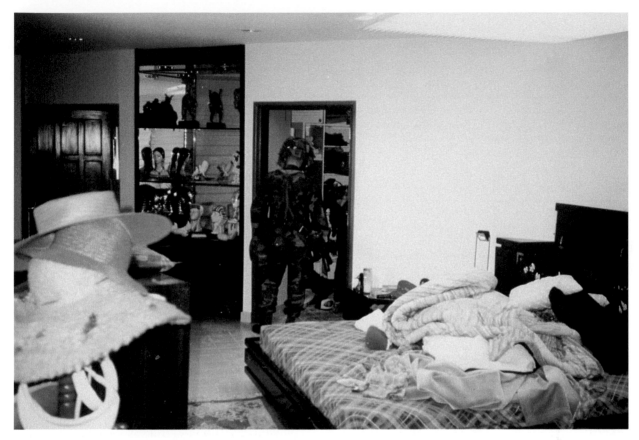

Bedroom of Noriega's beach house, searched by Rangers after the airfield at Rio Hato was secured. US Army

hills and, supported by aircraft and mortars, cleared and captured a village.

These operations are illustrative of the missions carried out by Ranger units in Korea. By the middle of August 1951, the front lines had begun to harden, and pressure mounted to deactivate the Rangers. This process began, officially, on 10 July 1951, when the Department of the Army issued message 95587 directing the inactivation of Ranger companies in Korea. General order 584 was issued on 25 July 1951 declaring that the 1st, 2nd, 3rd, 4th, and 5th, and the unit known as the 8th Army Rangers, were to be inactivated, and that this should occur on 1 August 1951. Those personnel rated and designated as parachutists were to be

reassigned to the 187th Airborne Regimental Combat Team which would ensure that the unit would have a full complement of men.

Many forces worked against the Rangers at this time. Many division commanders with attached Ranger units complained about their austere organization, and especially that they could not supply themselves. Some argued that Ranger companies drained desperately needed elite troops from regular units, and that the concentration of superior leaders in a few units was a luxury the Army as a whole could not afford. The final blow to the Rangers in Korea was the static nature of the war in its last years, for units now would have little opportunity to operate successfully behind North Korean and Chinese lines. The argument was advanced that the mostly Caucasian Rangers would find it difficult to operate effectively in areas populated by Asians, an argument that ignored the history of Galahad behind Japanese lines in Burma.

The Ranger training program was to continue, though. Ranger Training Command was inactivated, but immediately reconstituted as the Ranger Department of the Infantry School. This organization would be responsible for training in doctrines, tactics, techniques, and organization. The course would be established so as to provide infantry officers and NCOs assigned to infantry units with training in Ranger operations. The new situation was stated in the last entry of the Diary of Ranger Training Command: "Selected individuals will receive a course of instruction in Ranger tactics and will return to their parent organization to serve as Ranger Instructors therein" (Black 1989).

Vietnam War

At the end of the Korean War no Ranger companies, battalions or regiments existed in the US Army, and this situation continued until the 1970s. In 1969 the Long Range Reconnaissance Patrols (LRRPs)—which had a similar mission and organization but were identified as separate companies and detachments—were designated as Rangers. Pressure to do this was applied by many, including the Merrill's Marauders Association. They felt that the Rangers should have a place in the Vietnam-era Army, and LRRPs were doing Ranger-type operations.

On 16 January 1969, the Department of the Army issued a message designating LRRPs as letter companies of the 75th Infantry Regiment to become effective 1 February 1969. Two new Ranger companies, A at Fort Benning, Georgia, and B at Fort Carson, Colorado, were to be formed. On 7 March 1969, the Department of the Army issued a field manual titled *Long Range Reconnaissance Ranger Company*.

A typical LRRP mission in Vietnam lasted from five to seven days; a mission lasting more than a week was unusual. Missions were limited by human and logistical considerations, for men slept little while in the field, and everything needed was carried on the men's backs.

It was common practice for a team to be assigned a four-square-kilometer zone in which to operate. On the fifth or sixth day of the mission an ambush site was chosen. The team would remain in this position for twenty-four to forty-eight hours. Once an ambush was initiated, they would move immediately to the landing zone (LZ) for extraction.

Each team was composed of six men. This number of men provided enough firepower for security and offensive actions against small enemy units, but they were small enough to move without too much noise, and large enough to divide into two three-man teams. Units this size could conceal themselves along trails, but there would still be enough men to care for the wounded and to continue the fight. Also, larger teams would have needed more than one Huey helicopter for transport.

Planning for each mission lasted two or three days. Before a mission, available intelligence was reviewed. This included maps, aerial photographs, weather and light data, after-action reports, ground and airborne sensor data, agents, and any prisoner interrogations available. LRRPs kept their own files collected from previous missions complete with maps and overlays.

Insertion was accomplished by boats, truck, foot power, and helicopters. On the way in, helicopters might make false approaches to several LZs, or order false artillery barrages. After insertion, units moved in several hundred meters, where they would sit quietly for about an hour, listening. When sure they were not spotted, they would make a quick communications check and then move out on the mission. The time between missions would usually be three to four days for rest and essential planning for the next one.

In 1973, perhaps with the Yom Kippur War in mind, the Pentagon became concerned with the lack of mobility of US Army infantry units. A need was perceived for light infantry which could be moved quickly to any trouble spot in the world. Thus, in January 1974, Gen. Creighton Abrams ordered the formation of Ranger battalions. "This elite unit is to be composed of highly trained and motivated Airborne, Ranger qualified personnel" (Lanning 1978).

On 25 January 1974, the Army ordered the activation of the 1st Battalion (Ranger), 75th Infantry, which would be effective on 31 January 1974, to be stationed at Fort Stewart, Georgia. This was followed on 1 October 1974 by the activation of the 2nd Battalion (Ranger) at Fort Lewis, Washington. Companies A and B were disbanded, since the Rangers would now be doing much more than reconnaissance. The Rangers were now dedicated not only to battlefield missions, but also to "national strategic objectives" (Lanning 1978). The 3rd Battalion (Ranger) would not be activated until after Grenada, on 3 October 1984.

Desert One

The ill-fated attempt to rescue the American Embassy personnel held hostage in Teheran, Iran, code-named Desert One, was primarily a Special Forces operation. It is not generally known that Rangers were also to take part. While 1st Special Forces Operational Detachment—DELTA—was to perform the actual rescue, Company C, 1st Battalion, 75th Ranger Regiment (1/75), was to provide security for the men and equipment.

The rescue force assembled in Egypt on 21 April 1980. Three days later, a fleet of C-141s carried the 120-man force to Masirah Island, off the coast of Oman, where they transferred to three MC-130s accompanied by three fuel-bearing EC-130s. They

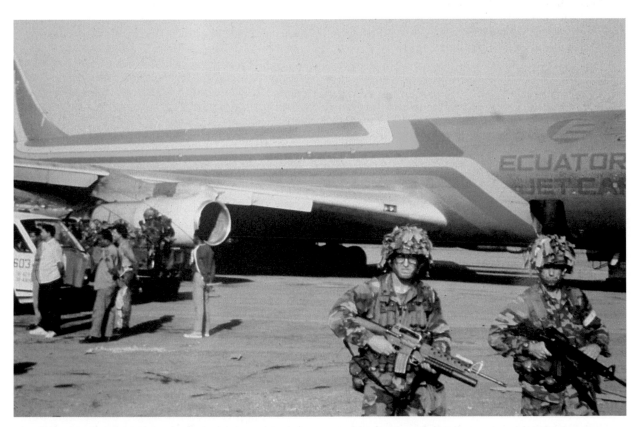

Rangers guarded civil aircraft of many countries after securing the Panama City International Airport. The Rangers not only protected the aircraft from harm, but helped prevent false damage claims against the United States by photographing what they were guarding. US Army

landed 200 miles southeast of Teheran at 2200 hours and waited for the arrival of eight RH-53D Sea Stallion helicopters from the aircraft carrier *Nimitz*. A twelve-man road watch team, composed primarily of Rangers, was along to secure the landing site while the helicopters refueled. The team would return to Egypt on one of the MC-130s.

DELTA was to be flown to a hidden shelter (HIDE) site before dawn on 25 April by the RH-53Ds, which would remain at their own HIDE site until the assault on the compound where the hostages were held. The plan was to use the helicopters to ferry the hostages to waiting transport.

The task of Company C, 1/75, was to secure a landing area for the transports. The Rangers were to fly from Egypt to Manzariyeh, Iran, and take the airfield there. They would land, if possible, or jump if resistance was offered. Once the airfield, which was thirty-five miles south of Teheran, was secure, the Rangers would hold it while C-141 StarLifters arrived to airlift the hostages and their rescuers to Egypt. The Rangers would then "dry up," or remove all signs of their presence, render the field useless, and be airlifted out themselves.

Taking and securing a hostile airfield within enemy territory is one of the primary components of the Ranger mission. They were prepared to hold the field as long as necessary if there were not enough transports to take everyone out in one trip. During training, the Rangers worked out all probable scenarios on a mock-up of the type of airfield in Iran.

Desert One was aborted at the first stage when two Sea Stallions crashed into each other on landing, killing their crews. One helicopter had aborted before leaving the carrier. It had been decided that at least six helicopters were necessary for the mission to succeed. Fewer than six automatically cancelled the rescue attempt. Company C, 1/75, never left Egypt. The Rangers in the road watch team returned with DELTA.

Grenada Invasion:
Operation Urgent Fury 25-28 October 1983

The Rangers had little time to prepare for their role in Urgent Fury, the invasion of Grenada. Within hours of receiving orders to move, Ranger units were marshalling at Hunter Army Air Field, Alabama, prepared to board C-130s and MC-130s for the ride to Grenada. Their first objective was Salines airfield, located on the island's most southwestern point. While securing the airfield, Rangers were to secure the True Blue Campus at Salines, where American medical students were in residence. As quickly as possible, Ranger units were then to take the army camp at Calivigny.

Things started to go wrong as the operation began. A Navy SEAL team was unable to get ashore; they were to have provided intelligence on the airfield at Salines. H-hour, originally scheduled during darkness, was moved several times until morning twilight. In the lead MC-130s there were problems with the inertial navigation equipment. Since there were no hatch-mount antennas on the cargo doors of the aircraft, communications to Ranger units would be delayed while passing through Air Force communications.

While in the air, the Rangers were notified of photographic intelligence indicating obstructions on the field. Instead of landing, the majority of transport would have to drop all the Rangers at Salines so the runway could be cleared.

In some aircraft the men were told to remove their harness, rucksack and main and reserve parachutes. These items were placed in kit bags and moved forward to facilitate off-loading troops and cargo. Before long, the loadmasters were yelling, "Only thirty minutes fuel left. Rangers are fighting. Jump in twenty minutes."

These Rangers now had to re-rig for the drop, unpacking nonessential equipment and pulling on parachutes. Rucksacks had to be hooked under the reserve pack and weapons strapped to the left side. Under these conditions it was not possible for the jumpmaster to check each man, so buddy rigging was employed.

Aboard the lead MC-130, navigation equipment failed and the pilot reported he could not guarantee finding the landing zone. Rain squalls made it impossible to employ a lead change, so both lead aircraft pulled away to the south. As the Rangers approached the target, the aircraft were out of assigned order and the planned order of arrival was no longer possible. This meant that the runway clearing team would not be the first on the field. The Rangers then requested a mass parachute assault, a contingency previously planned, so that only the order of exit from the aircraft would be affected. But the Air Force would not conduct a mass drop.

At 0534 the first Rangers began dropping at Salines: a platoon of B Company and the Battalion Tactical Operations Center (TOC), followed almost twenty-five minutes later by part of A Company, 1st Battalion, 75th Rangers. Over a half hour later the rest of A Company, 1/75, minus seven men were over Salines. It was now 0634, but the remaining men of the 1/75 would not be on the ground until 0705.

Men of 1/75 assembled on the east end of the runway. They were short C Company, which had been sent with about sixty Special Operations Forces troops to take the Richmond Hill Prison. The Ranger battalions were already operating below strength. One reason for this seems to have been the fact that a limited number of aircraft and aircrews were trained for night operations.

Over one and a half hours elapsed from the first drop of the 1/75 until the last unit was on the ground shortly after seven in the morning. These men jumped from 500ft so they would be in the air between twelve and fifteen seconds. Their drop zone was very narrow because there was water on the north and south sides only a few meters from the runway.

At 0707 the 2nd Battalion (2/75) began to drop. For several hours their aircraft had orbited, waiting to unload and refuel. They dropped in a much shorter period, and all but one man was safely on the ground. One Ranger broke his leg, and one Ranger's static line became tangled as he exited the aircraft, dragging him against the tail of the plane before he was hauled back aboard. The 2/75 assembled on the western end of the runway.

Once on the ground, the 1/75 was not under effective fire, and thus could begin to clear the runway of blocking trucks and bulldozers. Some of the vehicles had keys in them; others were hot-wired and removed. A Cuban bulldozer was used to flatten the stakes that had been driven into the ground with wires between them, and to push aside the drums placed on the runway. For fifteen minutes there was no enemy fire, and the Rangers worked without interruption.

By 1000, A Company, 1/75, had its second platoon at the True Blue Campus and its first and third platoons had moved north of the runway. In the center, B Company, 1/75, had moved north and was holding the high ground not far from the Cuban headquarters. On the left, to the west, units of 2/75 had cleared the area to the west of the airfield as well as the area north of their drop zone to Canoe Bay. The airfield was secure, and the C-130s, which had gone to Barbados to refuel, returned to unload equipment not dropped—which included jeeps, motorcycles, and Hughes 500 Defender helicopters.

Eight hours after landing, the commander of B Company, 2/75, was notified that two Rangers were missing near their positions. The company commander decided the missing men must be near a building which lay between B Company and the Cuban positions. A Cuban construction worker was sent forward with an eleven-man Ranger squad under a flag of truce. While the Rangers remained outside, the Cuban entered and spoke with those inside, who agreed to a truce if the Rangers would treat the Cuban wounded. Two Rangers and seventeen wounded Cubans were evacuated. Afterward, the Ranger commander called for the Cubans to surrender, and eighty to 100 did so. The remainder surrendered later, after a brief fight, to the 82nd Airborne.

At 1530 that afternoon, a counterattack was launched toward A Company, 1/75, consisting of three BTR-60s, which moved through 2nd platoon's positions, firing toward the runway. The Rangers countered with rifles, M60 machine guns, light antitank weapons, and a recoilless rifle. Two of the BTRs hit each other when the first one halted. Both were disabled. The third began a hasty retreat and was hit in the rear. It was finally destroyed by an AC-130 Spectre gunship.

The last action of this first day took place east of True Blue Campus, where Rangers came under fire from a house on top of a prominent hill, 1,000 meters east of the runway. No Spectre gunship was available, so an A-7 attack plane finally destroyed the house, but only after several duds landed alarmingly near the Rangers.

A medical evacuation exercise during preoperational training before Desert Storm. Ranger medics carry weapons. Only the platoon medic receives his medical training before he becomes a Ranger. The squad medics and all team, squad and platoon leaders receive basic emergency medical training from the Regiment. US Army via Col. David Grange

36

At the end of this first day in Grenada, the Rangers had secured the airfield and True Blue Campus at a cost of five dead and six wounded. Unfortunately, C Company, 1/75, had run into a more difficult situation. When their Black Hawk helicopters arrived at the prison, the local defenses were active. Perched on a high ridge whose sides were almost vertical and covered by dense foliage, the prison was surrounded by walls twenty feet high topped with barbed wire and watchtowers covering the area. Intelligence had failed to report the presence of two antiaircraft guns on a ridge some 150 feet higher than the prison, which brought the Black Hawks under fire. It was impossible to use ropes to lower the Rangers. The helicopters had to remain steady during this operation, making the Rangers and the crews easy targets. No air support was possible at this time, since all aircraft were engaged at Salines.

At least two attempts were made to bring the Black Hawks in to unload the troops, but antiaircraft fire hit pilots, crew and the attacking troops. Suppressive fire from the Black Hawks was ineffective because of their violent maneuvers. Although some Rangers walked away from the crashed and damaged Black Hawks, others were badly hurt and were not immediately evacuated. Part of the evacuation problem seems to have been that Army pilots could not land aboard Navy ships because they were not qualified to do so, although this was eventually waived.

Intelligence failed at the prison and also when the Rangers were not informed until 1030 on the morning of 25 October that there were still students at the second campus at Grand Anse. Students reported guards in the area, but the Rangers thought they could bring the students out. A heliborne operation with Marine airlift from the *Guam* was planned. Marine Helicopter Squadron 261 was to provide the helicopters, with supporting fire from USAF C-130 gunships, ships off the coast, and the Marines' two remaining Cobra attack helicopters. American suppressive fire would continue until twenty seconds before the Rangers were committed.

The Rangers would fly to the objective in three waves, each composed of three CH-46s. Each wave of three would carry a company of Rangers, about fifty men. A Company would go in first, followed by B Company, which was to cordon off the campus to prevent outside intervention. C Company would then arrive, its mission to locate the students and pack them into the four CH-53s waiting offshore.

During lift-off the order of aircraft somehow became confused. Instead of the lead flight having three CH-46s carrying A Company, the first wave had one from A Company and two from B Company. Consequently, the second wave had two from A and one from B. The first three aircraft missed the designated beach in front of the campus. There was sporadic small arms fire, but the only serious damage came from overhanging trees. One helicopter shut down and was abandoned in the surf, but the Rangers scrambled out as water poured in. Later, a second machine was damaged by a tree.

The orbiting Sea Stallions were now brought in to remove the students. The CH-46s returned and extracted the Rangers, completing the entire operation in twenty-six minutes. After leaving the beach, they realized that eleven men sent up the beach as a flank guard had not returned. By radio these men were told to move toward positions held by the 82nd Airborne. The Rangers were not sure they could safely enter those lines, so they decided to use one of the inflatable boats from the disabled helicopter. However, the rafts had been damaged during the air assault. The Rangers soon had to swim alongside their damaged boat. Having battled surf and tides for some time, they were spotted, picked up at 2300, and brought to the USS *Caron* lying off the coast.

One of the Rangers' initial D-day objectives, Calivigny Barracks, had not been secured. Lying about five kilometers from the airfield, the barracks reportedly housed and trained troops. On 27 October, under the command of a Brigade headquarters from the 82nd Airborne Division, a full-scale attack was carried out by Company B, 2/75, reinforced by Company C, 1/75.

Four waves of four Black Hawks, each carrying a company to assault the camp, were to fly out to sea before heading to the beach, flying low over the water at about 100 knots. Support was furnished by Spectre gunships and Navy A-7s. At

Salines the Army had seventeen 105mm howitzers, and at sea the USS *Caron* would supply fire support. A Company, 2/75, was to land at the southern end of the compound, on the left, and on the right, C Company, 2/75, was to set down. B Company, 2/75, was to land in the southeast, assault suspected antiaircraft guns, and rejoin the other companies in the north. In reserve was C Company, 1/75, which would also hold the southern end of the perimeter.

The Black Hawks came in over the waves, climbing sharply to the top of the cliffs. Quickly, the pilots slowed down in order to find the exact landing zone inside the perimeter. Each Black Hawk came in rapidly, one behind the other. The first helicopter put down safely, near the southern boundary of the camp, and was followed by the second. Rangers began to dismount. The third Black Hawk suffered some damage, and spun forward, smashing into the second machine. In the fourth Black Hawk, the crew saw what was happening and veered hard right; the aircraft landed in a ditch, damaging its tail rotor. Apparently not realizing that the helicopter's rotor was damaged, the pilot attempted to move the Black Hawk, which rose sharply, seemed to spin forward, and crashed. In twenty seconds three machines were down. Debris and rotor blades flew through the air, badly wounding four Rangers and killing three who, sadly, were the only deaths in the 2/75.

A Company regrouped as C Company landed on large concrete pads on the edge of the compound. B Company also landed safely, and moved on its objective. C Company, 1/75, also landed without incident. Contrary to expectations, the barracks were deserted. The Rangers found nothing. That night they slept in the rubble caused by the intense bombardment. This was their last action before returning to the United States.

Panama Invasion

The Army learned much from the confusion in Grenada. Special Operations Command (SOCOM) was established in 1984 to coordinate special operations. Air assault missions similar to the invasion were practiced and planned for several years before it took place. On 17 December 1989, Gen. Karl Steiner alerted specific units to prepare for an operation. Cargo planes began to arrive at Pope Air Force Base, North Carolina. On 18 December the Rangers moved to Green Ramp at Pope, where they were isolated to prevent information leaks. Other airborne units also arrived at Green Ramp. On 19 December, General Steiner flew to Panama.

The Rangers were to secure Torillos International Airport, Rio Hata Military Airfield, and then Noriega's beach house. Rangers who dropped into the International Airport later moved into Panama City, where they took the military headquarters of the Panamanian Defense Forces.

The jump into Rio Hata airfield was made under fire at an altitude of 500ft. Heavy antiaircraft fire was encountered and one Ranger was hit in the back of the head while still in the airplane. He survived, but four Rangers were killed in this operation. The Rangers secured the perimeter of the field before the Panamanians began to test the defenses. At Rio Hata the Rangers were supported by AC-130 Spectre gunships, whose target acquisition cameras found targets in the dark. Two hours after the drop at Rio Hata, the airfield was secure enough for transport aircraft to begin landing with supplies and additional equipment for the Rangers.

Once the airfields were secure, the Rangers moved against the Panamanian special forces, the Mountain Troops. Rangers moved from house to house in the compound, and at the village where the families of the soldiers lived. Many of the Mountain Troops were caught while trying to shave off their distinctive beards. On the fifth day of the operation the Rangers were sent to secure Calle Diez, an area some twenty to twenty-five miles from Panama City, held by the "Dignity Battalions."

Rangers took many pictures of Panamanian and foreign property, aircraft, shops, and houses to show that property was still intact and protected by the US Army. This prevented false claims and probably saved the United States many hundreds of thousands of dollars. Rangers also guarded buildings—such as the Vatican Embassy where President Noriega took refuge—to see that no damage was done. Twenty days after the start of the operation the Rangers left Panama.

Desert Storm

Very little is known about Ranger participation in Desert Storm, 1991. Delta Company of the 4th Ranger Training Battalion sent a squad to train members of the 24th Infantry Division (mechanized) to carry out long-range surveillance (LRS) operations in the desert. One incident proved the effectiveness of the training. Two teams in surveillance holes about 125 miles behind enemy lines the second day of the ground war spotted a squad of Iraqi soldiers with an armored reconnaissance vehicle approaching. For forty-five minutes the Iraqis surveyed the area, coming as close as ten feet to the camouflaged holes. The LRS teams were not detected and the Iraqis moved on.

Company B and one platoon of Company A, 1/75, took part in special operations in the desert. We can only surmise that they carried out missions against radar and communications installations, and hunted Scuds, especially after the attacks on Israel. The Rangers may also have secured airfields in Iraq for use by other special forces. All these missions are consistent with Ranger training. The rest of the Ranger Regiment was held in reserve for contingency operations.

In December 1991, Company C, 1/75, and the Regimental Headquarters Company deployed to Kuwait for a routine training exercise. The Rangers jumped into Kuwait during daylight hours, which is not typical, so television news cameras could record their arrival. The daylight jump also reminded Saddam Hussein that the United States was capable of quickly responding to any further threats to the security of the region.

Chapter 2

Ranger Training Brigade

The Ranger Department of the Infantry School at Fort Benning, Georgia, was established in 1951 to provide individual Ranger training to officers and noncommissioned officers (NCOs). Graduates earned the right to wear, on their left shoulder, a curved, yellow on black strip, or tab, that said "Ranger." Students were trained at Fort Benning in patrolling, ambushes, raids, airborne operations, and leadership skills. Physical training was also emphasized. Mountain training was moved from Colorado to Dahlonega, Georgia, and a jungle phase conducted at Eglin Air Force Base, Florida, was added. The first class to earn the Ranger tab graduated in March 1952.

The Ranger Department was reorganized in 1958 into three companies: 1st Ranger Company, Florida Ranger Division; 2nd Ranger Company, Mountain Ranger Division; and 3rd Ranger Company, Benning Ranger Division. Desert training was instituted in 1983, first at Fort Bliss, Texas, and then in 1985 at Dugway Proving Grounds, Utah. On 13 September 1991 the desert phase was moved back to Fort Bliss. The change was made because the Utah desert, which is a high plateau desert, becomes too cold in the winter to provide an environment similar to that of the Middle East.

On 5 August 1987, the Ranger Department was separated from the Infantry School and reestablished as the Ranger Training Brigade. The Ranger companies now became the 4th Ranger Training Battalion, Fort Benning; 5th Ranger Training Battalion, Dahlonega; 6th Ranger Training Battalion, Eglin; and the 7th Ranger Training Battalion, Fort Bliss. The training schedule was fifty-eight days before the desert phase and sixty-five days after. Starting with the class of 1-92, 14 October 1991, the training schedule was increased to sixty-eight days. The original training rotation was Fort Benning, Dahlonega, Eglin, and Dugway. With the 1-92 class, the sequence became Fort Benning, Fort Bliss, Dahlonega, and Eglin, with about sixteen days at each phase. The rest of the time is devoted to travel and processing.

With the establishment of the Ranger Training Department in 1952, the emphasis of Ranger training shifted from the company level to the individual. The idea became to transmit Ranger training to the rest of the Army by training officers and NCOs who would return to their units and teach what they had been taught. The original goal was to have one Ranger NCO per platoon and one Ranger officer per company by graduating 3,000 Rangers a year. However, with the dropout rate remaining steady at approximately sixty-five percent, the goal was not usually met. In 1984 the Army investigated the idea of making Ranger training mandatory for officers. This was rejected because a mandatory program would reduce the enthusiasm and morale of the students and dilute the value of the Ranger tab. The honor associated with the tab, and its utility in career advancement, would keep high the number of volunteers.

The goal of Ranger training, according to the commander's brief, is "to produce a hardened, competent, small-unit leader who is confident he can lead his unit into combat and overcome all obstacles to accomplish his mission" by requiring them to "perform effectively as small-unit leaders in tactically realistic environments." Upon graduation, the student knows that, when necessary, he can reach down into himself to do whatever is required to get the job done and get his men out alive. When you've earned your Ranger tab, as one sergeant put it, "you know you'll be able to do anything, even if it's something you've never done before and know absolutely nothing about. That doesn't matter. You're a Ranger, you can do anything!"

To produce a realistic environment, the stress of combat is simulated by hunger, lack of sleep, constant pressure, and a grueling physical setting. The long training day, usually from 0500 hours to 0200 hours, makes judgment difficult, similar to when in battle. The short rations—one or two MREs (meals ready to eat) a day after the Fort Benning phase—add further problems. The average weight loss per student is thirty pounds. Live fire exercises were stopped in early 1991 because the students come from all of the armed forces and do not have enough training as a unit to be sure of each others' responses when shooting live ammunition. The students are expected to go from squad to platoon to company level operations as they get physically weaker and mentally confused. By the end of the course, the student is in the worst physical shape of his life.

While the Ranger school trains individuals, teamwork is essential to pass. The concept of working with your Ranger buddy is constantly emphasized. All tasks are done by two-man teams. If your buddy has trouble, you don't continue until he is ready. Cooperation within the platoon is also stressed. Passing the course does not depend on the failure of others. Those platoons with the most cooperation have the highest rates of graduation. Within the course all students are equal regardless of rank and all have the same chance of success or failure.

All male officers and noncommissioned officers (sergeant and above) from American and allied services are eligible to apply for Ranger training. Anyone below these ranks must obtain a waiver from the first colonel (O6 grade) in his chain of command. All applicants must be in good

Students jump into the Ranger Training Camp at Dugway Proving Grounds, Utah, for the desert phase of training. The camp was moved to Utah in 1985, but in 1991 it was returned to Fort Bliss to take advantage of the fort's better support facilities. US Army

41

health and top physical condition. Certain conditions such as any hypothermia injury are grounds for disqualification. Airborne qualifications are desirable but not required. Students come from all branches of the armed services of the United States and allied countries. Approximately sixty percent come from the US Army, twenty percent from other US services, and twenty percent from foreign countries.

4th Ranger Training Battalion, Fort Benning, Georgia

Training is conducted at Fort Benning in two phases. The first five days of training, mainly processing and testing, occur at Camp Rogers, named for Robert Rogers of Rogers' Rangers fame. This is a garrison in which the students live in barracks and eat in the mess hall. The Ranger Training Brigade and the 4th Ranger Training Battalion are headquartered here.

For the remainder of the Fort Benning phase, ten days, training is conducted at Camp Darby, named for William O. Darby, the founder of the modern Rangers. The camp, with few permanent structures, is located deep in the wooded hills of Fort Benning. Each company has its own rudimentary facilities in quanset hut structures. The students live and eat in the open.

Under the eyes of a Ranger instructor (RI), new students demonstrate their ability to maintain an M16 rifle. The Ranger Stakes were instituted in 1991 to test the students' familiarity with light infantry weapons and communications. Seven of the eleven tasks must be successfully completed to pass. The students get two tries at each task. The RIs retrain and retest those who fail the first time. A second failure counts.

Besides the "prisoner of war" camp, there are five permanent sites used for field training exercises. The largest is Cinder Block Village, which, as its name implies, contains two bare, partitioned buildings and a wooden tower, completely surrounded by a chain-link fence. The other sites, some of which contain small bunkers, simulate objectives such as missile installations and communications facilities. The Darby Queen obstacle course is the only other permanent installation.

The new student reports to the Ranger Training Brigade with his medical and military records, but without his rank or service insignia. After the in-processing paperwork is completed, each stu-

dent takes the Army Physical Fitness Test—fifty-two push-ups, sixty-two sit-ups, and a two-mile run in running shoes in less than fourteen minutes and fifty-five seconds. He must also do six chin-ups. The majority of entering students pass without problems.

The next test facing the student is the combat water survival test which consists of three events. The first, the fifteen-meter swim, must be completed wearing fatigues, boots, and web equipment such as canteens and ammunition pouches, and carrying a rifle, without loss of rifle or equipment —and without showing undue fear or panic. Next, the student must submerge and remain underwa-

Retesting a student on his ability to load an M60 machine gun. If the student fails again, this stake will be a no-go. If the student fails five stakes, he is dropped *from the course. He may recycle in the next class if he wishes.*

Students prepare M18A1 Claymore mines for detonation. They will run the wires back to positions about twenty-five yards in the rear and then detonate the mines. Knowledge of mines is important for many Ranger-type missions.

ter while discarding rifle and equipment and swim to poolside—again without undue fear or panic. Finally, the student, while blindfolded, must walk off the end of a three-meter diving board, remove the blindfold, and swim to poolside without loss of equipment or rifle. While some fear or panic is normal, an undue amount results in an automatic drop. Undue or unusual fear or panic is defined as more than the average, intelligent man feels. The students are then assigned to the three companies of the 4th Ranger Training Battalion. The rest of

the first day is taken up with equipment issue and more paperwork.

The students are now assigned buddies. A pair of Ranger buddies works together throughout the training course. If one falls behind, the other is expected to help him. No Ranger does anything alone. He and his buddy work as a team. This concept goes back to the "Me and My Pal" training of Darby's Rangers during World War II. Ideally, Ranger buddies stay together until graduation, but many change buddies at least once because of

Ranger students returning from a predawn run. During the Ranger Assessment Phase (RAP) at Fort Benning, students must complete the five-mile run to continue the course. The runs, as well as all other activities, are conducted by companies. Each student, *upon arrival, is assigned to A, B, or C Company of the 4th Ranger Training Battalion. During later phases of training, runs are not graded separately but are part of overall training.*

medical drops and failures. Ranger buddies often remain friends for life, regardless of rank.

The first five days of the Fort Benning phase of the Ranger Training Course are known as the Ranger Assessment Phase (RAP). Previous to the class of 1-92, students would begin training conditions almost immediately, including twenty-hour days and grueling physical training (PT). While PT is still stressed, the new RAP schedule calls for a more relaxed environment while testing the students in a five-mile run in forty minutes, day and

night land navigation, and a new series of tests known as the Ranger Stakes.

The Ranger Stakes was added because many of the students from other services and countries may not be familiar with US Army equipment and weapons. The Ranger instructors (RIs) found that it was too time-consuming and too distracting to teach the proper use of weapons and equipment at the same time as carrying on Ranger training. The Ranger Stakes provides a quick test of students' abilities and an opportunity to remedy any deficiencies on the spot. Those who fail are trained immediately and retested. Most students pass the retest.

The Ranger Stakes consists of eleven tasks, grouped into five parts, that test students on their ability to handle communications and light infantry weapons.

The first three Stakes tasks test ability with the M60 machine gun. A student must show he can maintain an M60 by taking it apart and putting it back together in a reasonable time. The time is determined by the RI in charge. A student from an Army unit is expected to be quicker at this task than someone from another service that does not regularly use the M60. The second task is to load an M60. The third task is to prepare a range card for an M60 machine gun. To prevent accidents to one's own troops and to cover every field of fire,

M60s and similar weapons are usually sighted to fire within an arc of several degrees. A properly prepared range card allows the gun to be manned by more than one person if necessary. The card shows the angle the gun is set at from the position of the operator.

Task number four is to employ an M181A1 Claymore mine. The mine is detonated electrically using a wire. Students must set the mine and then run the wire back about twenty-five yards, connect it to the electric detonator, and set it off. Of course the whole process is a simulation.

Tasks five and six involve communications. Students must send a radio message and encode and decode a message using the standard KTC 600 operations code. Foreign students who are not proficient in English sometimes have difficulty with these tasks.

Students negotiate the infamous worm pit before dawn on the confidence course. They crawl on their backs and on their bellies under knee-high barbed wire through a *pit of mud. The RIs keep the mud soft with generous applications from a garden hose.*

The next three Stakes involve the basic weapon of the Army and of the Rangers—the M16 rifle. Tasks seven and eight are to demonstrate the ability to maintain and correct malfunctions of an M16. Number nine is to perform a functions check on an M16. A Ranger is expected to maintain his M16 in good condition at all times. During training exercises, students do not rest before cleaning and checking their rifles.

The last two Stakes involve grenades. Number ten is to employ hand grenades and number eleven, the ability to maintain an M203 grenade launcher.

The Ranger Stakes are held the morning and afternoon of the second day of training. Students must pass seven of the eleven tasks to continue. Those who fail are immediately given training by an RI and retested. A second failure of a task is final. Over ninety percent pass the Stakes on the first or second try. Those few who fail more than four Stakes may recycle with the next class and try again.

The morning of the third day, after the predawn run, which is held every day at a pace of eight minutes per mile, the students tackle the confidence course which builds agility and endurance. The students first climb a four-meter-high log fence without the aid of ropes. Then they enter the worm pit, a shallow, muddy 25m length area covered by knee-high barbed wire. The students must crawl on their backs and bellies *under* the wire while the RIs keep the mud fresh with water from garden hoses.

Next, the students must cross another mud pit by going hand-over-hand on the rafters in the roof of the five-meter-long pit. Falling, even at the end, means you have to do it over again. The rafters, 10ft above the pit, become so slippery with mud that the last few students across are allowed to use their legs as well as their arms.

The last obstacle is loosely rigged rope netting. The students climb the netting and then slide down a rope on the other side. The companies that finish first usually do push-ups or run in place until the others are finished. Even in the coldest weather, the students are only too glad to wash off under the outdoor faucets and change into dry uniforms.

The students are tested on their map-and-compass navigation skills the third and fourth days. They are marched or trucked to an area away from Camp Rogers and then given a few hours to reach a coordinate on their maps. Only one compass per student is allowed. Any student found with more than one compass is immediately dropped from the course. The compass must be standard issue. Students may not use any other type. There is one daylight land navigation test and one night test. Those who fail are retested. Those

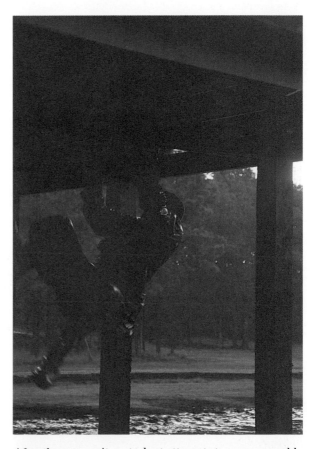

After the worm pit, a student attempts to cross a muddy pool by swinging from rafter to rafter. If he falls into the mud, he has to start again. The last company of students coming through is allowed to use their feet to stay aloft because the rafters usually become too slippery to grasp.

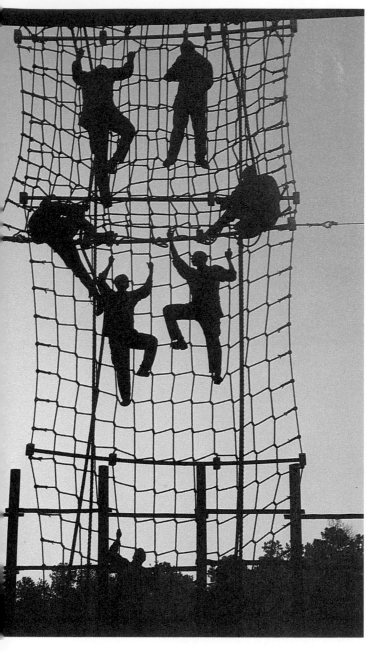

Students on the netting, which is the last part of the confidence course. While it is not one of the critical tasks that must be passed, the confidence course is not taken lightly. If he fails, a student is sent to take it over and over until he passes.

who fail the retest are dropped but may recycle in the next class.

Those students who fail any phase of Ranger training and decide to recycle may remain at the headquarters where they failed and join the Gulag. While waiting to join the next class, the members of the Gulag receive remedial training. They also perform routine tasks such as ground and building maintenance and improvements. The Gulag also aids the opposing forces (opfor) when necessary during field training exercises. Camp Rogers has the largest Gulag because it has the greatest number of students in a class and thus the largest number of medical and training drops.

The Ranger Assessment Phase ends with the water confidence test. The students climb a crude ladder, walk across a log thirty feet above the ground, and then drop from a rope 35ft into Victory Pond. Immediately afterward, the students climb up a 60ft tower and slide down a 200ft inclined rope back into the water. The water confidence test is conducted summer and winter unless the water temperature is less than 39deg Fahrenheit or the air temperature and wind chill are lower than 38deg Fahrenheit.

The RIs believe that the way a student walks across the log indicates the way he will behave in a combat situation. Those who walk firmly and without hesitation will do well. Those who hesitate or show fear may not. Occasionally, a student will try to show off for the RIs. One student who jumped over the two steps in the middle of the log was told to repeat the jump at least twice more for the benefit of those who didn't see it. The RI in charge then made the student hang from the rope longer than the others before being allowed to drop. Showoffs may be fun to watch, but they can be dangerous on a mission.

During the first five days of Ranger school, the students practice unarmed hand-to-hand combat in the evenings. Compared to more formal and stylized systems, Ranger methods may seem crude, but they are efficient. The students learn to use their fists, elbows, knees, feet—any part of the body that can be effective against an opponent. Working in pairs, the students practice for three or four hours at a time. During rest breaks, the RIs show how it's done and talk about what the students can expect in training. Some RIs like to play inspirational music during breaks; the scores from the movies *Apocalypse Now* and *Patton* are popular choices.

The Camp Darby phase of Ranger school begins with a parachute jump from helicopters into a clearing near the camp's permanent structures. Those students who are not airborne qualified are trucked to the clearing. This jump was instituted with the 1992 curriculum to familiarize the class with the type of airborne operations usually conducted by Rangers.

For the first three days the students receive classroom instruction in the fundamentals of patrolling, advanced land navigation, troop leading procedures, and leadership responsibilities.

RIs also conduct battle drills. Physical training continues daily. Runs at an eight-minute-per-mile pace are included, but are not graded separately from the other training.

On the fourth day, the students tackle the Darby Queen obstacle course: twenty obstacles strewn up and down a densely wooded hillside. They crawl, run, jump, climb, and slide through the obstacles with their Ranger buddies, helping each other where necessary. If your buddy doesn't make it over an obstacle, you don't continue until he does. In between the obstacles, the RIs usually have the students do push-ups, the most common activity in any phase of Ranger training.

The afternoon is devoted to survival training. The class learns how to catch and cook rabbits and

A company of Ranger students engaged in the most common activity in all phases of Ranger school.

Frequent push-ups are part of the physical conditioning program.

other fauna when no other provisions are available. The RIs deliberately did not allow the class to eat anything earlier that day so the students will not hesitate to eat their catches.

The remaining time at Camp Darby is spent on reconnaissance field training exercises using the crawl/walk/run method. The RIs first demonstrate the techniques and then guide the students through them. This is the crawl stage. During the walk stage students practice under the observation of the instructors. The run stage is a field training exercise which is graded. Crawl/walk/run training is an effective way to develop skills quickly.

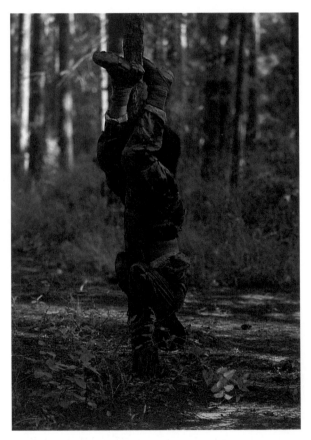

A Ranger student tries to do push-ups in the "koala" position. Push-ups, especially in awkward positions, are common as a disciplinary measure.

The opfor for the field training exercises are played by the Merrills, a platoon of the 4th Ranger Training Battalion Headquarters Company. The Merrills use captured Eastern Bloc or non-standard weapons and equipment to simulate a realistic enemy force. They occupy the various sites used during the exercises, patrolling and setting guards to detect intruders. Any students caught during missions are interned in the prisoner of war camp, which is also as realistic as feasible. The Merrills are the largest opfor at any of the training battalions because the 4th has the largest number of students at any time.

The students are given operations orders by squads and conduct day and night reconnaissance missions the last four days. If they are spotted, they run the risk of being "killed" or captured. During the field training exercises students receive only one MRE per day, two in the winter cycle, and a bread supplement. On the sixteenth day of Ranger school, the class flies out to Fort Bliss, Texas, for two weeks of desert training.

7th Ranger Training Battalion, Fort Bliss, Texas

The second phase of Ranger school, the desert phase, begins with in-flight rigging for a parachute jump upon arrival. Those students who are not jump-qualified join the rest of the class when the transports land. The garrison part of desert training, which lasts five days, begins the next day. During this phase, students receive three meals a day and get about five hours of sleep a night. The Ranger camp, located on the McGregor Range at Fort Bliss, will be named Camp Schocklee for the command sergeant major of the 7th Training Battalion killed in a parachute accident at Dugway, Utah.

The students learn desert-survival techniques such as water procurement and preservation. The RIs conduct classes reviewing leadership responsibilities and standing operating procedures for platoons. Each company of students spends one day practicing reconnaissance techniques and ambushes after classroom reviews.

Another day is spent practicing some battle drills important for Ranger operations. The drills are coordinated movement patterns such as flanking actions or turns that are usually executed as a reaction to enemy action. They are standard throughout the US Army. These include reacting to contact with the enemy, reacting to indirect (unobserved) fire, and reacting to ambush. The RIs also conduct platoon attack drills.

7th Ranger Training Battalion support personnel act as the opfor for these and all other exercises. During the garrison phase the members of the opfor who are killed in action are predetermined. This ensures that there will be bodies to search for booby traps and secure captured weapons and equipment. During the field exercises, casualties among the opfor and the students depend on the circumstances.

During the first week of desert training, students learn how to penetrate barbed wire without injury with wire cutters, or with makeshift ladders when necessary. They learn how to clear a trench line, working in two-man teams, each covering the other. They are also taught how to assault a fortified bunker.

The RIs teach how to ambush men and vehicles. The students alternate classroom lectures with walk-through exercises. The instructors stress the importance of mastering a technique until it becomes second nature. Only then should a leader try out other ways of ambushing. This holds true for any activity that is not a battle drill, which can only be executed one way.

All training is conducted with METT-T factors emphasized. M(ission) E(nemy) T(errain) T(roops)-T(ime available) must be taken into account whenever an operation is conducted. Even the most foolproof plan will not work if these factors are neglected. Throughout the remainder of training phases, the students will be constantly urged to remember METT-T when planning their field exercises.

On the afternoon of the sixth day of desert training, the field training exercises begin. The students will carry out reconnaissance, conduct raids, and mount ambushes. The class will participate in an airborne operation, parachuting to the target. There will also be an air assault from helicopters. The culmination of desert training is an airborne assault with full class participation. Students who are not airborne qualified are

Two RIs demonstrate hand-to-hand combat. The man on the ground appears to be defeated, but in a moment he will throw his adversary by pulling on the upper arm and kicking upward.

trucked to the jump site to take part. Meals are now reduced to one MRE a day.

Except for the night before a parachute jump when five hours sleep is mandated, most students get only one or two hours of sleep during field training exercises. Those who do their assigned tasks, including maintaining their weapons, more efficiently can grab a little more rest. The company, platoon, and squad leaders for each exercise who must plan the mission get the least sleep. By the fourteenth day of desert training, after six days in the field, the men are operating on instinct and training.

When the desert phase ends, on the thirty-third day of Ranger school, the class flies back to Fort Benning for the bus ride to Camp Merrill, Dahlonega, Georgia. Only about sixty percent of the original class will go on to mountain training. The remaining forty percent will have dropped out for medical reasons such as injury or illness. Some will have failed critical tasks or leadership evaluations. Those who wish may join the next class after recovery or retraining. This option is available at all phases of training.

5th Ranger Training Battalion, Dahlonega, Georgia

The mountain training phase is divided into lower and upper mountaineering, mountain techniques, and tactical operations. The first three days are spent in and around Camp Frank D. Merrill, named for the leader of the Marauders. Again, during the garrison part of training, students receive two hot meals and one MRE a day, and around five or six hours sleep a night.

The students learn various knots needed to secure ropes and climbing equipment. The knots are also important for securing explosives and rigging fuses. Rope handling and belaying (stopping movement on a climb) are taught on level ground.

A 20ft wall built of wooden slats is used to teach rappelling, including the Australian method where the climber appears to be walking straight down the slope face forward. Students learn how to secure their lines to a fixed point above the wall or to insert metal rings where no other anchor is available.

Next, students practice rappelling down a sixty-foot cliff, with and without rucksacks. They also learn how to carry an injured comrade while rappelling. To successfully pass this part of training students must perform three daytime rappels, including one with full rucksack, and one using only two bounces against the cliff. A nighttime rappel with full rucksack is also required. During the winter months rain and cold turn the cliff face

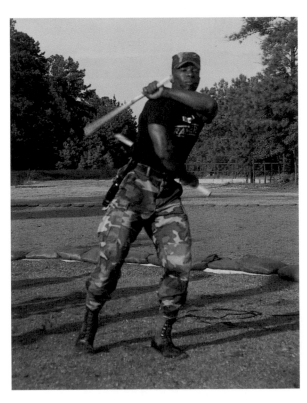

The RI in charge of hand-to-hand combat training shows off his skills with fighting sticks before the class starts. The use of such sticks is not taught to the students.

An RI throws his "enemy" into Victory Pond during a Rangers-in-action performance. Four or five times a year, on the morning of a Ranger school graduation, the instructors and opposing forces (opfor) at the 4th Ranger Training Battalion demonstrate the skills of Rangers to the incoming class and the public. The performance includes use of weapons and explosives, rappelling skills, and insertion and extraction by helicopter into a heavily wooded area.

into a sheet of ice. When this happens, a fixed rope descent is substituted for the night rappel. But the three daytime ones are still performed.

The fifth and sixth days of mountain training are spent on the top of Mount Yonah, the highest peak in Georgia. There, students learn how to climb, as well as descend. They learn how to use safety lines and transport equipment and all the skills necessary for mountain operations. The next two days are spent back at Camp Merrill.

During the time in garrison, physical training is not neglected. Every day begins with a run. Distances vary, but the pace is never less than eight minutes per mile—the Army standard. Often, the pace is quicker. Beside the ubiquitous push-ups, other calisthenics are part of the daily routine. One Ranger remembers during training that it "seemed we spent half our time in the flutter kick position and the other half doing push-ups."

The field training exercises in the mountains, which start on the eighth day, are tactical operations on the platoon and company levels. The students plan and execute reconnaissance, ambushes, raids, airborne operations, and air assaults as in other phases, but the mountains make these exercises more difficult. Movement along inclines and ridgelines is more difficult; rope bridges are sometimes needed. Helicopters must land in small mountain clearings completely surrounded by trees.

Airborne operations are more challenging. The drop zones for parachute jumps are the smallest throughout the Ranger Training Brigade. One, Garrett's Farm, is only 150 meters by 100 meters—with a stream and a Ẏ-shaped band of trees running through the middle. Not surprisingly, the RIs and support personnel carry special tools to extract men and parachutes from trees.

All these factors result in more medical drops due to injuries than in any other phase. Sprains, pulled or torn muscles, and dislocations are common. Every part of the body that can be broken will be. Even those who do not sustain more serious injuries collect scrapes and bruises. As in the other phases, students are allowed to miss a day of training to rest or recover from a minor injury. Anything requiring more time results in a drop, with the opportunity to recycle.

The field exercises follow a pattern throughout all phases of training. The company leader and the platoon leaders receive orders for a mission and then devise a plan to carry it out successfully. The squad leaders are expected to add their input to the plan. If weather or other natural factors prevent the completion of the mission or cause it to fail, the mission will still receive a "go" (pass) if the students have tried their best to continue. Leadership rotates among the students so that each may be evaluated at least once in every phase of training. A student in danger of failing is usually given more time as leader in the later phases so that he may improve his performance.

The members of the opfor at Camp Merrill live in the field for the eight days of the field exercises.

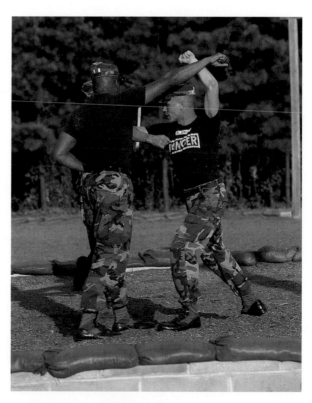

Two RIs rehearse before a hand-to-hand class. The RI on the right is parrying the attack with his left hand while counterpunching with his right.

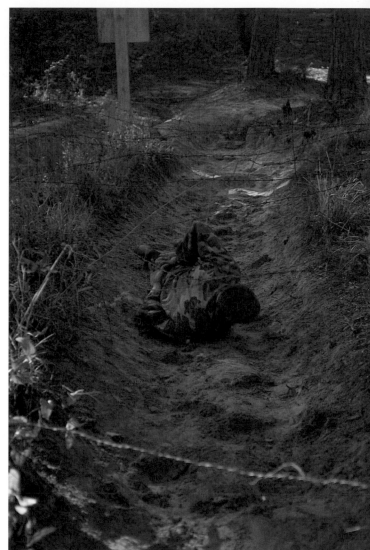

A student crawls under a barbed-wire obstacle on the Darby Queen. Ranger students seem to spend much of their time crawling through dirt and mud.

Another part of Ranger physical training—endless flutter kicks.

The trailer that impersonates a communications base during raids serves as the men's field quarters. Its interior sleeps eight on bunks that double as storage shelves. Battery-powered lights, food, water bottles, a small propane stove, and a few radios make life in the field as comfortable as possible. The men hope to hook up to an electrical source so they can add a television.

The opfor carefully plan their ambushes against the students for maximum effect. The students are attacked by a group in the treeline on a mountain landing zone as they exit the helicopters. To ambush a student company returning to camp for the mandatory sleep the night before a parachute jump, three or four men of the opfor conceal themselves among the bushes just past a bend in the road. They wait silently, often on wet and muddy ground on the side of the mountain, not moving for fear of revealing their position. After the advance squads of students pass, the opfor attack. The foggy evening adds to the confusion as the students scatter. A few squad leaders who manage to keep their men together and return fire receive positive spot reports.

On the forty-ninth day of the Ranger Training Course, the class travels by bus to Eglin Air Force Base, Florida, for jungle training. Less than half of the students have made it so far. At this point, students are totally immersed in the training. They are tired, hungry, and generally grungy. All thoughts of the soft, outside world have faded. Fast food burgers, the PX, movies, and the NCO club have been replaced by an M16, the rappelling ropes, and MREs. And the most grueling part of the training still lies ahead.

6th Ranger Training Battalion, Eglin Air Force Base, Florida

Camp James E. Rudder, on Eglin Air Force Base, is named for the commander of the 2nd Ranger Battalion who led the assault on Pointe du Hoe. Here, Ranger students learn to cope with a

During RAP at Fort Benning, students are taught the fundamentals of unarmed hand-to-hand combat. The students assume the basic stance for attack or defense. Pantlegs are rolled outside the boots to prevent injury.

An RI demonstrates the use of elbows and feet to fend off an opponent.

jungle and swamp environment. The high humidity of the north Florida coast adds to the rigors of training. To the physically and mentally tired students who arrive the night before the fiftieth day of training, the camp seems damp: hot and damp in summer and cold and damp in winter.

Students have a busy first day. In outdoor classrooms, they review patrol base operations and review the duties and responsibilities of platoon leaders and platoon sergeants. They go over the mechanics of zone reconnaissance. The cadre of the 6th Ranger Training Battalion demonstrate ambush and raid techniques.

For the first time in their training, the students are introduced to movement-to-contact tactics. The RIs and support personnel demonstrate how to move through terrain in expectation of encountering enemy forces and how to continue movement after engagement. This is taught only after the students have mastered patrolling and reconnaissance in the earlier portions of training.

The first day ends with another class. This one deals with reptiles—snakes and alligators—how to identify and avoid them. Students also learn first aid to treat snakebites. The 6th Battalion keeps a snake house and alligator pond at headquarters to facilitate training.

Days two and three are spent in the field, practicing raids, ambushes, and movement to contact. The companies, reduced by attrition to platoon size, spend the two nights in patrol bases. While these are not considered field exercises, the conditions are similar. Meals are MREs and sleep lasts a maximum of four hours. The days do not start with physical training.

The fourth day of training is devoted to stream crossings and small-boat operations. Until class 1-92, learning to use ropes to cross streams with men and equipment was conducted at Camp Rudder. Now, with the increase in field training exercises in Florida, rope crossings are taught at Fort Benning and Dahlonega. The cool streams are a welcome relief from the heat in summer, but are cold in winter.

The students practice on land first. Then, accompanied by RIs, they paddle squad-sized Zodiac boats to patrol bases in the swamp, where they will spend the night. During the field training

The defending student (on the left) ducks under the attacker's blow. The RI is commenting on their performance. Although Ranger techniques may seem crude, they are effective.

A student walks the log during the water confidence test. The log is thirty feet above ground over Victory Pond. The RIs say the way a man walks the log is the way he will behave in combat. Those who hesitate may also hesitate when on a mission.

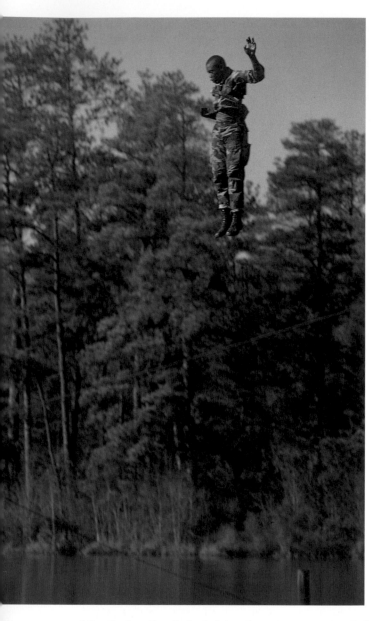

exercises, which start now, the boats will be used on rivers and in the open waters of the Gulf of Mexico.

During the field training exercises, the class conducts operations similar to the other phases: reconnaissance, raids, ambushes, airborne operations, and air assaults. Movement to contact and small-boat operations are now added. The three platoon-sized companies conduct separate and joint exercises. For the next nine days the students spend all their time in the swamps. Meals are limited to one MRE daily. Sleep is almost nonexistent. The only break is the night before a parachute jump, when they are allowed five hours sleep in the barracks.

The Florida phase is the most challenging. Ranger students, already exhausted and dazed, must expend whatever strength remains simply to move through the swamps and jungles. Thought becomes almost impossible, planning difficult. Those who will have hallucinations will usually have them in Florida. Students "see" all kinds of food. Bushes and trees become people. Students

A student slides down a 200ft rope into Victory Pond. At the RI's signal, the student will drop from the rope into the water. The red float on his back will enable a rescue team to haul him out if he sticks in the mud on the pond's bottom.

After the log, the students hang from a rope suspended thirty-five feet above the pond. They cannot drop into the water until the RI in charge says so. Sometimes, the RIs will make a particularly confident student untie his boots or place both hands in his pockets before giving permission. If a student drops prematurely, he is usually made to climb out and crawl through the mud to the next part of the water confidence test.

may walk in their sleep or even try to attack an imagined enemy. Students must rely on mental toughness to see themselves through. Those who lack it quit, even at the very end. Some students reach Santa Rosa Island at the end of the field training exercises and quit the course. They don't care that the only task left is graduation. They have had enough. Those who make it know that they have the strength to face anything.

The field training exercises and the Ranger course end with a predawn assault on Santa Rosa Island. Students start their preparations around 1600 hours. The zodiac boats are checked and loaded. Last-minute plans are reviewed. The three companies coordinate their attack. The boats set off at dark to cross the open stretch of water between the Florida Panhandle and the island. Around 0400 hours the boats reach the island. Suddenly, a barrage of flares, simulating supporting fire, lights up the beach as the Ranger students fight their way ashore. After the final after-action report, the only task left is to return to Camp

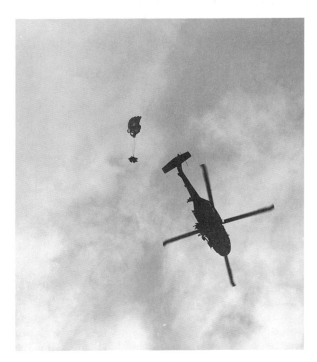

A student exits a Black Hawk helicopter. Those students who are airborne-qualified jump into Camp Darby to begin the next part of their training. This jump is the first one into Darby under the new curriculum. Previous classes did not begin the Darby phase with a jump. But as most Ranger activities usually involve a helicopter jump, the 4th Training Brigade added one at this point. After the jump, a student walks to his assigned assembly point.

A student jumps over a log while his buddy waits his turn. The Darby Queen obstacle course, located on a wooded hillside in Camp Darby, is one of the critical tasks required for graduation from Ranger school. The Darby Queen requires motor skills similar to those used in combat situations—running, jumping, climbing, and crawling. The men of the 75th Ranger Regiment negotiate the Darby Queen as part of their physical exercises.

The students negotiate the Darby Queen in pairs: if your buddy gets stuck at an obstacle, you don't continue until he does. Some obstacles such as the four-level platform cannot be negotiated without cooperation. The Ranger buddy system originated during World War II, when Darby's men trained in pairs.

Rudder and prepare for the trip back to Camp Rogers where it all started.

The next day, the sixty-eighth, the students return to Fort Benning, hungry and exhausted, to feast on steak and shrimp and get a rare full night's sleep. Those who have made it to this point will graduate in the morning. Graduation day is its own reward. Field music, parading colors, and admiring families all add to the fierce pride and esprit de corps the Army's newest Rangers feel as the long weeks of rigorous training culminate in the awarding of the coveted black and yellow Ranger tab.

A C-141 drops airborne-qualified students into the new desert training camp at McGregor Range, Fort Bliss, Texas, for the second phase of Ranger school.

Completing the Ranger Training Course

Less than thirty percent of those who begin complete the Ranger Training Course with the class they started. Half never earn the tab. There are many ways to fail. A student must receive one positive leadership evaluation in each phase. He must pass a minimum of one patrol each in the desert, mountains, and jungle, and a total of fifty percent of all combat operations (exercises) at each phase.

The student must pass twelve critical tasks: the Army physical fitness test, the combat water survival test, the five-mile run, the eight-mile foot march with full gear, the day and night land navigation tests, the Darby Queen obstacle course, the log walk/rope drop into Victory Pond, the suspension traverse, a 200-foot night rappel or a sixty-foot fixed rope descent in severe weather, eight of twelve knots, and the belay test.

The student must also undergo a peer evaluation at each phase, in which his fellow students rate his leadership qualities and Ranger skills. He must pass at least two of four to graduate. Failure to do so usually results in recycling.

Failure due to medical reasons, classroom and exercise performance, and peer evaluation is not final. The student may retrain at the phase where he failed and continue in the next class.

Students may not recycle if failure is due to negative critical incident (spot) reports or to a negative special observation report (SOR). Spot reports deal with good or bad conduct both in training and in attitude. Spots can be plus or minus, which can cancel each other out. Three minor spots equal one major. Four major minus spots at Fort Benning or three at the other phases are allowed. A cumulative total of five major minus spots results in a review of the student's status. Eight major minus spots mean an automatic dismissal. Students dropped in this manner cannot return to Ranger school.

SORs may also be positive or negative. One negative SOR approved by the brigade chain of command can result in a drop. An SOR as the result of lying, cheating, or stealing means automatic dismissal without chance of reinstatement.

The men who successfully earn their Ranger tabs wear them with pride in the knowledge that they have completed the most physically and mentally grueling training course in the US Army.

Delta Company: Long-Range Surveillance Unit Leaders Course

The 4th Ranger Training Battalion has two companies that do not train Ranger students.

A squad of the Merrills pose with their weapons. The Merrills, part of the 4th Ranger Training Battalion Headquarters and Headquarters Company (HHC), act as the opposing forces for the Darby phase of training. Reinforced, when necessary, by members of the Gulag, *the Merrills ambush students on exercises or defend an area under student-led reconnaissance. If discovered or captured, the unfortunate students are held in a prisoner camp until rescued or released.*

Rather, they provide specialized training to the rest of the Army. Delta Company conducts a Long-Range Surveillance Unit (LRSU) leaders course at Fort Benning designed to train selected personnel in those technical and operational skills enabling them to train and lead long-range surveillance units in support of corps- and division-level operations.

The course provides training in leadership, physical training, doctrine, organization, and identification of enemy tactics and vehicles. The RIs of Delta Company teach insertion, extraction, communication, and operational techniques. During Desert Storm, Delta Company provided on-the-spot training for the 24th Infantry Division in Saudi Arabia.

The LRSU leaders course is five weeks long. Although previously students had to have a Ranger or Special Forces tab, the expanding needs of the Army have made that requirement obsolete. There are not enough Ranger and Special Forces personnel to meet today's surveillance needs. However, airborne qualification is still required. The course is open to NCOs (sergeant and above) and officers who have been recommended by their units. Specialists 4th class and corporals may be admitted with a waiver.

Part of a squad assumes a defensive stance while listening to the RI during a lesson on patrolling. First, RIs lecture to the students in a classroom setting. Then, the students are walked through the lessons. The lessons are put into practice during field training exercises at Camp Darby, Fort Benning. The patrolling classes were formerly held during the garrison, or Camp Rogers, phase at Fort Benning. Beginning with the class of 1-92 in October 1991, all patrolling instruction takes place at Camp Darby.

Students learn about communications in the first week of training. They are taught to assemble and maintain communication equipment, encoding and decoding, and selecting suitable sites for their transmissions. The week ends with both a written and a hands-on examination. At night, the students bed down in hidden shelters they build.

The second week is devoted to field techniques. The class learns ingress and egress of an area by helicopter and boat. They practice infiltration by rappelling from a helicopter. To exfiltrate, the Special Patrol Insertion & Extraction System (SPIES) is used. Several men are hooked to a special rig on a line and pulled out by helicopter. One man calls it skiing through air. The class also trains in Zodiac boats, learning to approach by water and reconnoiter landing places. Once ashore, the students do a brief reconnaissance and return to the boats. Students must be careful to avoid splashing when entering and exiting the boats so as not to alert opfor trying to ambush students on the way back to the boats.

The students draw weapons and practice battle drills. They learn tracking, counter-tracking, and stalking. They are also introduced to canine operations. Part of the schedule is devoted to LRSU medicine, which is necessary when a unit is isolated in enemy territory. The instruction is similar to that given squad medics in Ranger units.

A squad on patrol at Fort Benning waits for the order to move on. The weight of the rucksack and rifle is usually over seventy pounds. Radiomen and heavy weapons squads carry an even greater weight.

A student company listens to a lecture on patrolling. While the Rangers follow standard infantry doctrine, their execution is more exacting. Staying awake is often a problem, but students are allowed to stand if they feel sleepy. Those who nod off are kept awake by doing push-ups until an RI tells them to return to their seats.

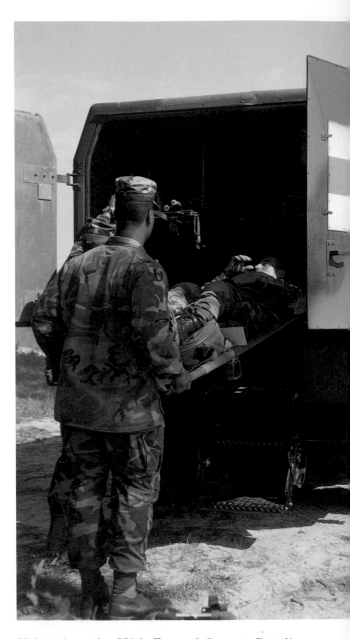

Medics from the 324th Forward Support Battalion treat an injured Ranger student after a jump. The medical bag is in the foreground. The Ranger Training Brigade does not have its own medical support. A medical team from the 324th accompanies each class throughout its training, except to Fort Bliss, which has its own medical battalion.

A Ranger student eats a chocolate cake sandwich. When the students are given hot meals, as opposed to MREs, the food must be eaten on the spot. Anything not finished in the allotted time, usually ten or fifteen minutes, must be returned. If there are seconds, they may not be taken until the first plate is finished. This leads to all sorts of interesting concoctions such as the above sandwich.

The second week ends with hidden shelters and surveillance classes. Students learn how to select sites and build shelters for surveillance and concealment. Usually shallow holes just large enough for three- or six-man teams to lie side-by-side, these hides are camouflaged to conform to the terrain. A team stays in concealment, observing such things as vehicle movement per hour or civilian population densities. The LRSU students spend the nights in hides they build. The hardest lesson learned is the self-discipline and patience required for this type of surveillance.

In the middle of the second week, one day is devoted to remedial training to bring the class up to standard. Any student in danger of failing practices with the help of the RIs those tasks in which the student is deficient. Because of the high caliber of the students, this day is usually regarded as a rest day. The RIs also teach a survival course similar to that given to Ranger students.

The students learn how to breach a wire obstacle by cutting through it. One uses a cutting tool while the other one prepares to thrust the wire aside using a piece of wood or his gloved hand. He has both of their rifles at his side, ready for use if needed. When the breach is wide enough, the cutter will go through and provide covering fire if required. The other student holds the breach open for the rest of the squad to pass through.

The third week is devoted almost entirely to classroom work. The students learn Russian order of battle and tactics. They become familiar with Eastern bloc vehicles and equipment, which are also used by many countries in the Middle East and Asia. This information is necessary in order to relay accurate intelligence from surveillance missions. Using slides and texts developed by the Pentagon and intelligence agencies, the RIs drill students until they can identify enemy equipment even when it is camouflaged. Some of this material is still classified because it may compromise the source.

The dissolution of the Soviet Union has not yet had any effect on this segment of LRSU training. Likely enemies such as Iraq and Libya still use Soviet weapons and tactics. This segment concludes with a written examination. The airborne parachute jump the end of the week is a welcome relief from sitting in a classroom.

The fourth week is spent on situational training exercises such as night insertions and night movement techniques. Patrol bases are established, from which surveillance sites are selected and occupied. Hide sites are built. Each student company conceals a cache of food and draws a map with coordinates indicating the location. The map is then given to another company for later retrieval. This week also ends with an exam.

Field training exercises are conducted in the fifth and final week of LRSU training. The exercises begin with an air assault by helicopter, followed by a SPIES extraction. After an airborne insertion, the exercise continues with movement through the area, surveillance, and evasion of the opfor, played by members of the 4th Ranger Training Battalion headquarters company. Survival tasks are carried out, including recovering the cache of food hidden earlier. If the company looking for the cache cannot find it, they do

An RI shows his students the blank explosives that will simulate grenades during the upcoming exercise. The RIs follow Gen. George S. Patton's dictum, "If you tell it to them dirty, they won't forget it." RIs generally specialize in one or more related skills. During the garrison portion of each phase of training, they teach classes and walk students through exercises. During field exercises, the RIs work twenty-four to forty-eight hours on, and twenty-four hours off. However, paperwork and evaluations cut heavily into off-duty time.

A fire team prepares for an ambush. One student will man the 90mm recoilless rifle, carried by the man on the left, while the other two will cover him and fire at the enemy. The team will not withdraw until the prearranged signal, usually the explosion of captured stores and weapons.

not get any other food. The field training ends with linkups with other units, extraction, and debriefing.

The skills and qualifications of the men who enter the LRSU leaders course ensures a high rate of completion—over ninety percent. Day thirty-five is graduation day.

Echo Company: Infantry Leader Course

Echo Company, 4th Ranger Training Battalion, conducts a training course at Fort Benning, developed by the Ranger Training Brigade for light infantry officers and NCOs to sharpen their skills and enable them to, in turn, train their units to US Army standard. The course also provides an environment which promotes cohesion among a unit's newly appointed leaders. The course length is twenty-eight days with an optimum class size of 118. Each year nine classes are held.

The usual class consists of all the new officers and NCOs of a regiment or division with rank insignia—unlike Ranger school, where rank insignia are not worn. Under the guidance of the RIs, students hone their skills at individual and collective tasks. The instructional process is the same crawl/walk/run method used throughout the training battalion.

An RI walks a student through a bowline knot. The RI will continue to work with the student until the knot is learned. Knot tieing is one of the critical tasks necessary to earn the Ranger tab.

Students at Camp Frank D. Merrill, Dahlonega, Georgia, learn to use the rappelling rope to belay—stop. The technique is important for safety on the mountains.

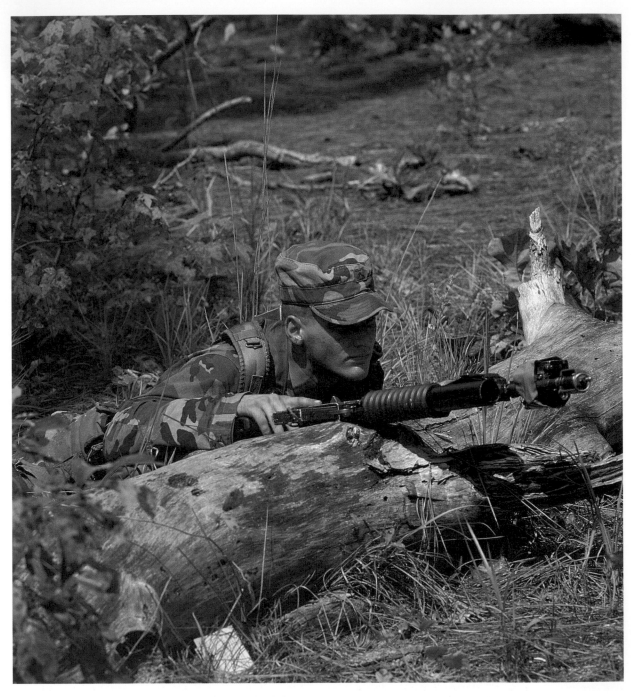

A Ranger on patrol covers a section of road while other members of his squad cross.

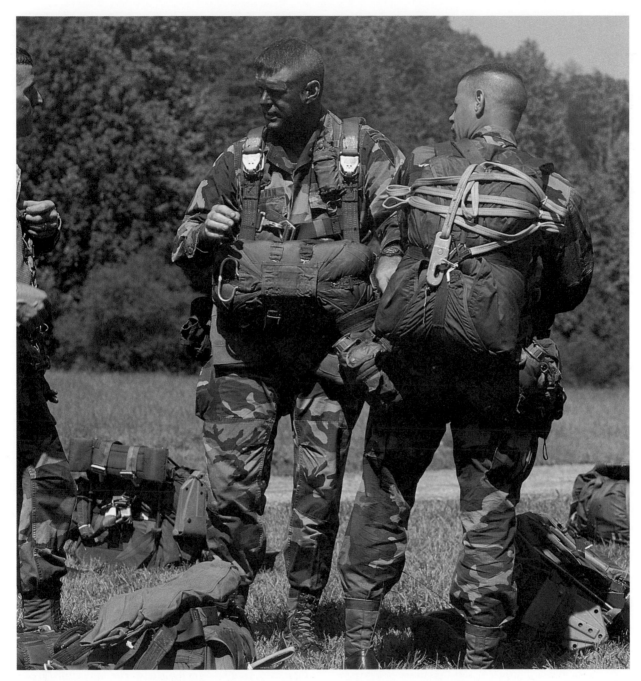

The commander of the 5th Ranger Training Battalion prepares to jump with his students. Battalion commanders are encouraged to spend time in the field evaluating students. Of course, commanders are delighted to leave their desks.

A Ranger student practices the Australian, or forward-facing rappel. Notice his gloved hands on the rappelling line ready to belay (stop) or slow his descent. The line passes through a snaplink on his belt. The wooden slat wall, which is approximately twenty feet high, descends to a dirt pit that cushions any falls.

A Ranger student rappels with full pack down a sixty-foot cliff. His right hand is positioned to slow or stop his descent. Students must perform three daytime rappels: one with rucksack, one without rucksack, and one using only two bounces against the cliff wall while descending. The rappel with rucksack at night is one of the critical tasks needed for graduation. Gloves protect the hands while rappelling. The number on his helmet is assigned at the beginning of the class at Fort Benning. By the mountain phase, there are far fewer than 286 students in the class. The mountaineering phase of Ranger training results in the most injuries and medical recycles, especially in winter, when the cliff face can become a sheet of ice.

The MRE, Meal Ready to Eat, is the staple of Ranger training. During field exercises, one MRE per day is usually the only food provided. It comes in a compact foil pouch, can be heated or eaten cold, and provides 3,000 calories. If the MRE is heated in boiling water, the water must be discarded afterward because toxic chemicals leach out of the wrapping. The kindest thing the men say is that an MRE won't hurt your ribs if you fall on it while landing in a drop zone.

A Ranger student learns how to carry his injured buddy down a cliff. Number 279 [the b/w photo] is the "injured" one. The rope around his body secures him to the line. The rescuer can easily lose his balance while rappelling. Fortunately, the student above recovered and completed the descent safely. RIs threaten to assign the smallest students to carry the heaviest ones. This threat is rarely carried out.

An "enemy" patrols at Camp Merrill, watching for a student raid. The opfors are made up of Rangers from the headquarters company who stay in the field during the entire exercise. Opfors wear older uniforms such as this World War II German officer's cap. The weapons are captured Eastern bloc equipment or reasonable facsimiles. Sometimes opfor uniforms are improvised by turning the standard uniform inside out.

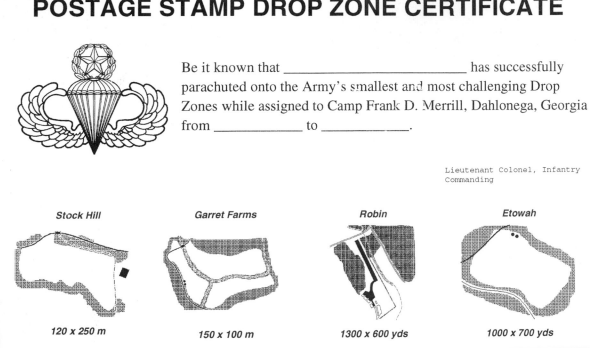

5th Ranger Training Battalion
POSTAGE STAMP DROP ZONE CERTIFICATE

Be it known that _____ has successfully parachuted onto the Army's smallest and most challenging Drop Zones while assigned to Camp Frank D. Merrill, Dahlonega, Georgia from _____ to _____.

Lieutenant Colonel, Infantry
Commanding

Stock Hill

120 x 250 m

Garret Farms

150 x 100 m

Robin

1300 x 600 yds

Etowah

1000 x 700 yds

The certificate given to RIs when they first jump into the drop zones at Camp Merrill. The students usually jump into Garret Farms, the smallest.

The students retrain in individual skills such as issuing orders in the proper form and coordinating with adjacent units. They conduct leader's reconnaissance and analyze terrain. Many tasks are map-related: navigating, locating targets, and orienting indirect fire. The leaders also learn how to conduct training to standard for these tasks in their units.

They go on to collective tasks (carried out by more than one individual) that are necessary for small unit, light infantry missions. They practice attacks, raids, ambushes, and movement to contact. They train in reconnaissance and security

procedures. They practice reacting to combat, breaking off contact, reacting to indirect fire. They conduct platoon attack drills and critique their actions. Some of the men have not performed any battle drills since their basic training. They must regain their own skills before they can expect to train their unit. The drills also afford an opportunity to observe the abilities of their fellows. Unlike Ranger school, food and sleep are adequate.

The last two weeks of the course consist of situational and field training exercises. Typically, a situational excercise will involve an attack on one of the objectives at Camp Darby, often Cin-

A Ranger student in a patrol base at Camp Merrill takes the opportunity to eat and attend to personal hygiene. A patrol base is usually located in areas near missions. However, it should be away from any area of value. This means that it is usually in uncomfortable and inhospitable spots. This patrol base can be reached only by climbing over a narrow ridge and down a steep slope. If opfors catch students in a patrol base, the base has to be moved and the platoon sergeant and platoon leader may receive a no-go for the exercise. After a mission, students still have to watch out for an ambush on the way back to base. Students spend the nights in the patrol bases for the duration of the mission.

A student who tangled his rifle in the lines of his main parachute deploys his reserve chute as a safety measure.

A jumper prepares to land near the smoke marking the drop zone. He has to avoid the trees all around him.

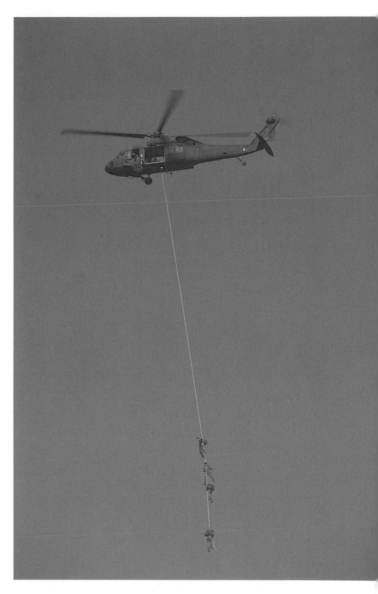

SPIES is used to extract an LRSU team. It is used to quickly remove three or four men from an area.

Black Hawks deliver students to a landing zone high in the mountains of North Georgia. They will have to survive the attack by the opfor and then continue on to their patrol base.

75

An RI at Camp Rudder, Eglin Air Force Base, Florida, shows a student how to secure the rope for a stream crossing. Rope bridges and stream crossings are now taught only at Fort Benning and at Camp Merrill.

derblock Village. The village and its surrounding bunkers are manned by Rangers from 4th Ranger Training Battalion headquarters company and members of the Gulag. The RIs of Echo Company observe the action. The leaders have to move toward the village, often crossing enemy lines and fighting if necessary. If there is contact with an opfor, the RIs receive an immediate after-action report, complete with casualty figures and ammunition expended.

The platoon and company leaders send out reconnaissance squads to the objective and then determine where to place their fire teams. If ladders for scaling or any such equipment is needed, they are built at this point. If artillery support is requested, the mission leader calls for it. Then comes the attack on the objective, which

A student crosses a stream by hauling himself along the safety rope. Once on the other side, he will join his squad to carry out the rest of the mission. If he is fortunate, he will be able to change into dry clothes before he beds down for the night. Even when a student is not in the water, he is always wet at Camp Rudder— hot and wet in summer, cold and wet in winter. The high humidity and swampy ground afford little opportunity for drying out. The major medical danger in

this environment is the constant threat of cellulitus. Hallucinations, especially about food, are not uncommon by the Florida phase. One student "saw" giant pizzas rolling along the ground. Students mistake bushes for their buddies. One student sleepwalked to the RIs' campfire and tried to attack the "enemy force." When he was awakened, he had no idea where he was or how he got there.

should be within a time specified by the operations order.

Things usually do not go smoothly in the early exercises. One group made so much noise trying to build scaling ladders, the defenders in the village could hear them coming almost an hour before the attack. One group couldn't find the village until two hours after the scheduled time for the assault. One hungry defender who had missed lunch joked he was going to find the attackers himself and show them the way. Sometimes, the attackers call down artillery on their own positions, knocking off most of their forces. The later exercises are more efficient.

After the battle, the final after-action report is given. An exercise that results in more than ten percent casualties is considered unsuccessful, even if the objective is taken. Unlike Ranger school, these exercises are not graded, only critiqued. The RIs guide the group in criticizing the action and making suggestions for improvements.

Field training exercises are conducted under combat conditions, but without live fire. Platoons usually participate as part of a larger unit. The field training exercises, using Military Integrated Laser Engagement System (MILES), involves movement to contact and raids, ambushes, and reconnaissance. A field training exercise usually

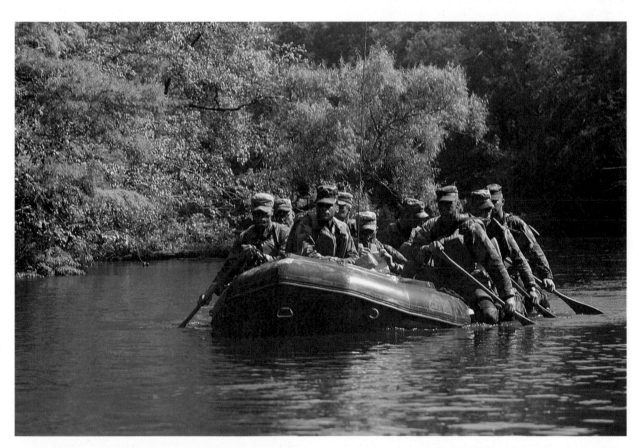

An RI in the prow of the Zodiac boat directs a squad of students along a river. Even on a trial run, the students carry full gear and wear camouflage paint. By this time, the original class of 300 students has dwindled to about 100. The three companies have become three platoons.

begins with helicopter movement to a landing zone a few miles from the first objective. The company moves through enemy territory, reacting to contact when necessary. They then establish and occupy an operational rally point (ORP), from which they set up an ambush. After the ambush, the company regroups and gives an after-action report to the observing RIs. Afterward, the company moves on to establish a patrol base where the men spend what is left of the night.

The next day, the company crosses a dangerous area where they are subject to indirect fire. Once past this area, they are resupplied by air and move to an ORP near their final objective. From there, the company reconnoiters the objective. The objective is then raided with the aid of fire support. After another after-action report, the company moves out to an area from which they are flown or trucked back to camp. The exercise ends with a final after-action report. The RIs

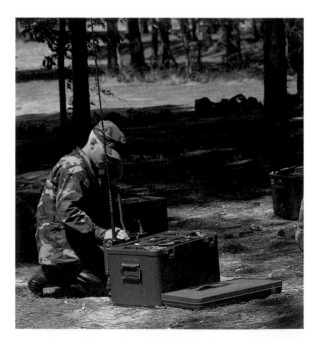

A student waits for the rest of his squad before proceeding deeper into the swamp.

A student studies the radio equipment Long-Range Surveillance Unit (LRSU) teams use in the field. He must be able to assemble and disassemble the radio rapidly.

An RI instructs an LRSU team in how to infiltrate by water. The boat is a zodiac.

An LRSU student crawls inland for a brief reconnaissance.

An RI checks out the exit door before takeoff.

LRSUs are often inserted into an area by rappelling from helicopters. This Black Hawk is inserting a team at Camp Darby.

and leaders analyze the exercise and comment on performance.

At the end of the course, students know more about the abilities of their fellow officers and NCOs. They have sharpened their own skills and are ready for the task of training their unit. The Rangers call the process "rebluing."

Echo Company: DEA Training Program

Echo Company conducts another training program that is not very well known. Agents chosen by the US Drug Enforcement Agency (DEA) are trained at Fort Benning to combat the drug trade in the jungles of South America. The eight-week program includes physical training, weapons training, and jungle and mountain training. The course is modified from the Ranger Training Course to suit the needs of the DEA agents. There is no sleep or food deprivation. Agents train in the sort of clothing they wear on the job, mostly t-shirts and camouflage pants.

The agents learn how to locate and raid a cocaine laboratory and return safely to base. To facilitate training, the Rangers have their own "lab" complete with fierce "drug dealers" to fight off the gringos. The men of Echo Company make most convincing enemies. Captured weapons and equipment are used to add to the realism. Only the cocaine is fake.

Part of the training is also conducted on-site in the mountains of Peru and Bolivia. There, the Rangers also provide training for the local forces as part of Operation Snow Cap. Camps and patrol bases are set up and used as in combat. The war on drugs is as real as any other war.

Members of the 10th Mountain Division run to board a Black Hawk while it is still in motion.

A defender in Cinderblock Village fires his M60 at the attackers. Note the Military Integrated Laser Engagement System (MILES) on the barrel. The defender is a member of the Gulag at Fort Benning. He will join the next Ranger school class as soon as he is medically fit. Meanwhile, he helps out by acting as part of the defending force for training exercises.

A student in the infantry leaders course rushes through the gate of Cinderblock Village during an assault. The smoke helps to conceal the attackers. The smoke can also act as a code for those in the rear: red smoke for danger, green smoke for clear.

Members of the Gulag at Fort Benning climb a tower at Cinderblock Village before an attack by the 10th Mountain Division members at the infantry leaders course.

Army Black Hawk helicopters at Camp Darby.

Students rapidly exit the Black Hawk and take cover.

The honor graduates are presented with their awards at a Ranger school graduation ceremony.

The new Rangers rush off the field after graduation ceremonies end. Most of them will rush right to the nearest restaurant. Some men report that after the end of the Ranger course, they had cravings for all sorts of food. For a few months, one student couldn't pass a convenience store without buying candy bars.

*Friends and family pin the hard-earned Ranger tab on
the graduates.*

Chapter 3

75th Ranger Regiment

Activation of 75th Ranger Regiment

The 1st Battalion (Ranger), 75th Infantry, was officially activated 8 February 1974 at Fort Stewart, Georgia, after training at Fort Benning. Its headquarters was at Hunter Army Airfield, Georgia. The 2nd Battalion (Ranger), 75th Infantry, was activated 1 October 1974 at Fort Lewis, Washington. The 3rd Battalion (Ranger), 75th Infantry, and Headquarters and Headquarters Company (Ranger), 75th Infantry, were activated 3 October 1984 at Fort Benning, Georgia. Subsequently, the three battalions and the headquarters and headquarters company were redesignated as the 75th Ranger Regiment. This was the first time that an organization of this size was officially recognized as the parent headquarters of the Ranger battalions. Not since Darby's Ranger Force headquarters has the US Army had such a large Ranger force—over 2,000 men.

Mission

The 75th Ranger Regiment is the nation's premier strike force, able to move across any terrain and endure any hardship necessary to complete its mission. It provides the United States the ability to move a credible military force to any region of the world in eighteen hours. Its ability to perform both light infantry tasks and special operations allows it to plan and conduct special forces missions as well as light infantry operations assigned to airborne, air assault, and light infantry battalions.

The Rangers can be deployed quickly to all types of terrain and weather conditions, infiltrating and assaulting by land, sea, and air. They conduct strike operations, including raids, interdictions, and personnel and equipment recovery. Ranger units perform specialized light infantry missions such as securing airfields, and destroying communications centers and command and control facilities. They also conduct short-duration reconnaissance. Ranger units usually operate three days in the field without resupply. Longer missions require resupply by whatever methods available. Limited operations are possible under nuclear, biological, or chemical warfare conditions.

Rangers can carry out quick-response operations such as they did in Grenada, or deliberate long-planned operations as in the case of Panama. In either case, Rangers are used in situations that require their unique skills. They should not be used for missions that can be accomplished by conventional forces.

The 75th Ranger Regiment fights as a light infantry force, following infantry doctrine and rules of operations, with special emphasis on METT-T factors. The typical Ranger mission requires initiative, depth, agility, and synchronization above that usually found in light infantry units. Detailed planning and coordination are most important to exploit the enemy's weakness and avoid his strengths. Rangers hold premission training briefings and rehearsals using all equipment and personnel needed for the actual mission. Individ-

Grant of Arms

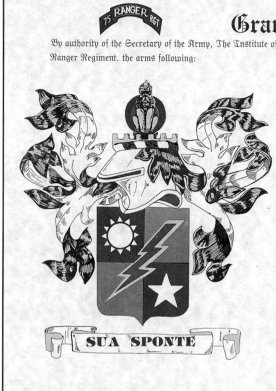

By authority of the Secretary of the Army, The Institute of Heraldry, United States Army, gives, grants and assigns unto the 75th Ranger Regiment, the arms following:

Blazon

Shield: Quarterly azure and vert, between the first and fourth quarters a radiant sun of twelve points and a mullet argent, a lightning flash coupled bendinisterwise gules fimbriated or.

Crest: On a wreath of the colors argent and azure, issuing in back of an embattlement of a tower with six merlons or a pedestal gules supporting a clinthe affronte of the third in front of a torteau within an annulet of the second.

Motto: Sua Sponte (of their own accord). The original Marauders, like today's Rangers, were all volunteers.

Symbolism

The colors blue, white, red, and green represent four of the original six combat teams of the 5307th Composite Unit (Provisional), commonly referred to as "Merrill's Marauders," which were identified by color. To avoid confusion, the other two colors, khaki and orange, were not represented in the design; however, khaki was represented by the color of the uniform worn by US forces in the China-Burma-India Theater during World War II. The unit's close cooperation with the Chinese forces in the China-Burma-India Theater is represented by the sun symbol from the Chinese flag. The white star represents the Star of Burma, the country in which the Marauders campaigned during World War II. The lightning bolt is symbolic of the strike characteristics of the Marauders' behind-the-line-activities.

Crest: The organization's service in the China-Burma-India Theater of World War II is represented by the clinthe (a gold Burmese lion). The blue annulet symbolized the Presidential Unit Citation awarded for service at Myitkyina, Burma, the "gateway to China." The gold embattlement in base refers to the unit's combat services in Vietnam while the six merlons represent six Valorous Unit awards; the two Meritorious Unit Commendations earned by elements of the Regiment are denoted by the scarlet disc at center.

Rangers Lead The Way

---

ual and unit initiative are encouraged to take advantage of changing battlefield conditions.

Surprise is a hallmark of Ranger missions. Operations conducted at night and during poor weather conditions tend to throw an enemy force off balance. Different methods of insertion and attack help prevent the enemy from discovering a pattern of operation. Deception, including using concurrent military operations as cover, and a willingness to accept risk to confuse the enemy are standard procedures. Coupled with the mobility, speed, and violence of execution, the shock effect of surprise often allows the Ranger unit to complete the mission before the enemy can react.

Using the normal infantry techniques of stealth and concealment, Rangers enhance their survivability. Taking full advantage of terrain allows Rangers to determine the time and place of combat. Rapidly departing the area by a different route after the mission is completed also helps keep casualties down.

The lack of organic combat support limits Ranger units to whatever support is available in the theater of operations. Limited air defense weapons and indirect fire support, and the lack of casualty evacuation capability, can further restrict the use of Rangers. However, the need to train replacements rather than simply reassign troops from other units is the most limiting factor of Ranger unit operations.

Organization

The 75th Ranger Regiment consists of three battalions, headquarters, and a headquarters company: 1st Battalion is located at Hunter Army Air Field, Georgia; 2nd Battalion at Fort Lewis, Washington; and 3rd Battalion at Fort Benning, Georgia. Regimental headquarters, also at Fort Benning, consists of the commander (a colonel) and his staff and contains five sections: personnel (S-1), intelligence (S-2), operations and training (S-3), supply (S-4), and civil affairs (S-5). The regimental commander also has a special staff that includes a communications officer, fire support officer, surgeon, and a staff judge advocate. A weather officer from the US Air Force and a tactical air control officer are also permanently assigned.

The regimental headquarters company consists of the company commander and his staff, including company S-1, S-2, S-3, S-4, and S-5, similar to headquarters. The headquarters company also contains the fire support element, communications platoon, reconnaissance platoon, medical treatment team, and the Ranger Indoctrination Program (RIP), which processes new recruits. Headquarters company provides support to the battalions when needed.

Each battalion consists of three combat companies and a battalion Headquarters and Headquarters Company (HHC). The battalion HHC

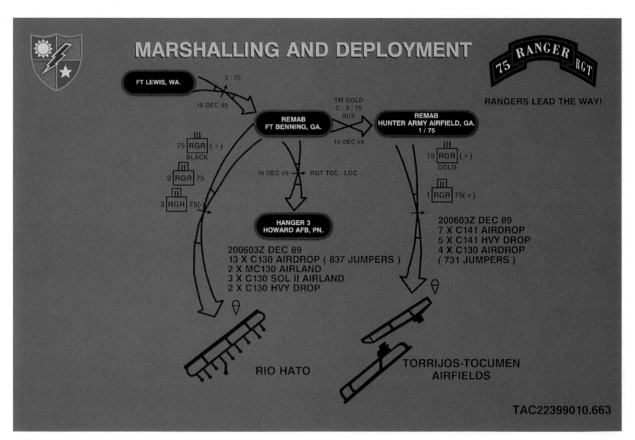

Deploying Ranger units. (RSE is Ranger Support Element, TOC is Tactical Operations Command, LOC is Logistical Operations Command, CONUS is Continental United States.) Ranger units can be deployed anywhere in the world in eighteen hours. One Ranger battalion is always on call as the Ranger Ready Force, with weapons and equipment packed for quick loading onto transports. US Army

includes company headquarters, a fire support team, the medical team, the communications team, and a support section that includes food service.

Ranger companies are heavy companies with three rifle platoons of about forty-five men each, and a weapons platoon of half that size. The rifle platoons are made up of three rifle squads of three teams each and a machine gun squad. All squad leaders are at least staff sergeants and team leaders are sergeants. Specialists—equivalent to corporals—who have the Ranger tab may also be team leaders when necessary. The heavy concentration of NCOs in Ranger companies allows a

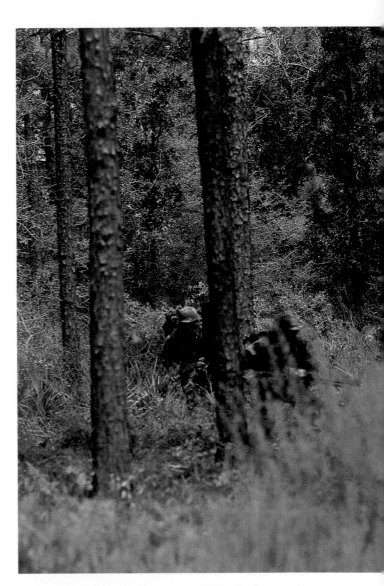

Members of the pre-Ranger course at Fort Benning prepare for the dinner break. Although the course is designed to prepare the men of the 75th for the Ranger school, there is no sleep or food deprivation. The men must be in top physical shape when they enter Ranger school.

A fire team from B Company, 3/75, checks out its surroundings on the way to a raid. The Rangers practice with MILES for live-fire exercises held throughout the year.

Men of the 3/75 move rapidly through a wooded area. Rangers must be fit enough to cover ground quickly, carrying everything they need. The total weight of weapons and supplies can be over 100lb per man. The Ranger Regiment is the only unit in the Army to mandate physical training five days a week, forty-eight weeks a year.

A squad from the 3/75 halts before moving on patrol. The squad is positioned to cover each other as well as the area. As a result of countless training drills, the men take the correct positions automatically.

Members of the 75th Ranger Regiment Headquarters Company Reconnaissance platoon with communications equipment. The platoon contains three teams that infiltrate enemy territory and remain on patrol for up to five days before returning. Using observation and electronic and photographic devices, the teams collect as much information as possible. The platoon's findings are reported by secure, long-range communications before the teams exfiltrate. The platoon operates for the regiment or for the battalions. US Army

Adverse Weather Aerial Delivery Systems (AWADS) and Station Keeping Equipment (SKE) aircraft formation. C-130s equipped with AWADS allow Rangers to make airborne insertions in virtually any kind of weather. The system uses a Doppler radar that calculates the ground speed of the aircraft and an AWADS computer programmed with flight route information, such as direction, airspeed, and route, to show where the aircraft is in relation to programmed checkpoints. Only a few C-130s have an AWADS aboard. The rest of the flight have SKE that tells the crew where the aircraft is in relation to the others in the formation. The two systems combine to allow Rangers to jump in poor visibility when an enemy force cannot track them. US Army great amount of individual initiative without sacrificing the level of performance. Ranger units also have the highest percentage of NCOs who later become officers in the Army.

Although Ranger units have no casualty evacuation capability, they can provide medical care in the field. All team, squad, and platoon leaders learn basic first aid and how to administer intravenous injections to prevent shock. Each squad has a medic who received emergency medical treatment training provided by the regiment. When necessary, they assist the platoon medics; otherwise, the squad medics carry a rifle.

The battalions rotate as the Ranger Ready Force. For one month the designated battalion must be ready to deploy anywhere in the world within eighteen hours. This means that supplies and ammunition must be secured on pallets ready

"The guards at a South American jungle drug lab lounge around, waiting for the cocaine to be trucked out." In reality, men of B Company are acting as the opfor for C Company, 3/75, during a rehearsal of a drug raid. The exercise, which will be evaluated, will take place the next night. The men of the 75th often train against each other; both sides benefit from acting against opposition.

Behind a cloud of smoke, the raid begins. Note the MILES on the webbing of the men.

A squad in the pre-Ranger course emerges from the woods at the end of the day. The v-shaped formation, which allows the men to cover each other, marks them as Rangers who carry out every small training detail as if in combat.

Two of the bad guys use the fallen branches as cover to attack a raider. The oncoming Ranger moves from tree to tree toward the drug lab.

for loading onto transports. The battalion must be able to recall its men from leave and assemble in a few hours prepared for combat. A longer period on alert tends to degrade the performance of the unit.

Recruitment and Training

Rangers say they volunteer four times in their careers: to join the Army, to go to airborne school, to join the Ranger Regiment, and to go to Ranger school. All Rangers in the 75th ("scroll" Rangers), officers and enlisted, are recruited from airborne units. The men who wear the 75th unit scroll insignia say that the Ranger Tab is a school. The scroll is a way of life.

Rangers are expected to train to standard and beyond. While their battle drills are common to all light infantry, Rangers perform them with an extra edge. They never let up. Every drill, every exercise, every alert is conducted as though they were in combat. Even returning to the barracks after days in the field, a Ranger unit will move in the combat V-formation. Such actions became instinctive.

Occasionally, training is more relaxed, as in a Hollywood jump where full uniform and equipment are not used. In those circumstances, while the clothing is not regulation, the procedure is. They may joke before and after, but during the parachute jump everything goes by the book.

All Rangers in a unit are expected to know the details of a mission so that if a squad, platoon, or company leader is put out of action, someone else can take over without loss of efficiency. Such rigorous training requires a great deal of self-discipline, but produces a confident soldier who can be permitted to use his initiative when needed.

Most Rangers do not spend their entire Army careers in the 75th Regiment. Some go on to the Ranger Training Brigade for a tour of duty and then return to the 75th for another tour. Only a handful manage to serve their entire careers in Ranger units. Often, Rangers of every rank find it difficult to adjust to other types of units. They find the training and discipline too easy. As one sergeant put it, "In the Rangers, the hours are lousy, but the action's great."

All enlisted recruits undergo a three-and-one-

A dead bad guy lies near the makeshift lab. The folded arms and crossed legs indicate the body has been searched. Those who are "killed" during a rehearsal are predetermined. The actual exercise will be more realistic.

half-week training program (RIP), designed to eliminate the weak or nonmotivated. Within a stressful environment, the new recruits must pass the physical training, operations, and procedures tests. In addition to passing the standard Army physical fitness tests, the recruits must complete an eight-kilometer run in forty minutes, and a twelve-kilometer road march with full rucksack and weapons. Recruits also must complete six-, eight-, and twelve-kilometer road marches with increasing rates of speed.

The recruits must pass day and night navigation tests and show their familiarity with the battle drills and procedures necessary to a member of a light infantry squad. Three jumps are conducted, with a tactical mission immediately following the last jump, which is a night jump.

Throughout RIP, Ranger lineage, history, and traditions are taught. The attrition rate varies according to weather and time of year, but averages about forty percent. Those who fail but show willingness and have the right attitude are allowed to try again.

After RIP, the new Rangers go to the battalions for operational training. The normal tour of duty is three years. Within six to twelve months, those who wish to earn the Ranger tab go to the Ranger school. With the exception of clerical staff,

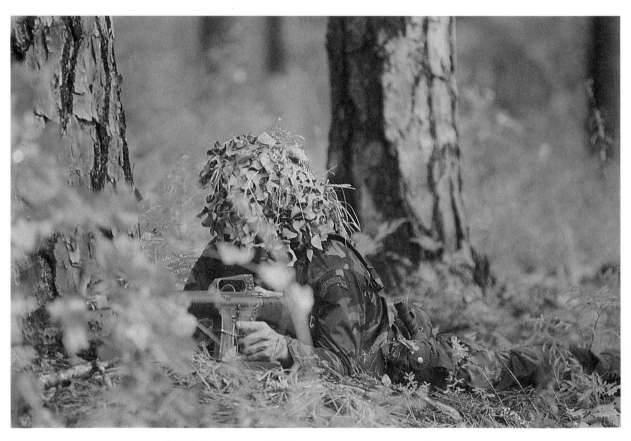

A Ranger wearing a camouflaged helmet guards the perimeter of the area after the raid. The camouflage on the helmet is made up of strips torn from a uniform.

A team searches the perimeter. Rangers always *work in pairs, ever since the days of Darby.*

cooks, and others in similar positions, those Rangers who want to be promoted to specialist and NCO must earn the Ranger tab. Entry in Ranger school is based on order of merit, seniority, and the number of places available. A clerk at 75th headquarters is one of only five clerks in the Army with the tab.

Those who go to Ranger school attend the pre-Ranger course one month before the start of their Ranger school class. Given by the RIP cadre at Fort Benning, the pre-Ranger course prepares the men for Ranger school by training and testing on the basics of Ranger skills such as raids, reconnaissance, patrols, and ambushes. Physical training requirements are reviewed. To prevent

physical deterioration before Ranger school, the men are not deprived of sleep and food. The program gives battalion Rangers a head start. Their attrition rate in Ranger school is less than ten percent.

All officers and NCOs recruited for the 75th must be graduates of Ranger school and airborne-qualified. Officers must have served at least one year in a leadership position in a non-Ranger unit. This means that an officer must be at least a first lieutenant before joining the Rangers. There are no inexperienced leaders in the regiment.

Officers and NCOs go through the Ranger Orientation Program before reporting to the battalions. In a nonstress environment they undergo the Army Physical Fitness Test and complete a five-mile run.

Ranger units have the most intense training schedule in the Army—forty-eight weeks a year. They train under tough, stressful, and often hazardous conditions, including live fire—as close to actual combat as possible. Field training exercises often set one unit against another, increasing the competitiveness of both. The opfor tries to be as authentic as possible. Often, an exercise will be repeated until each unit has played both sides.

All training is performance oriented. The level of proficiency is important, not the number of hours required. If a standard calls for certain hours of training, Rangers will do more if required. If proficiency is attained sooner, the unit goes on to other tasks. To this end, exercises are often evaluated and rated. These exercises are planned and rehearsed as if they were actual missions. Rehearsals are conducted during the day. However, most exercises are performed in darkness, as are most Ranger missions. Training is also conducted with other units at the Joint Readiness Training Center in Arkansas.

Each battalion holds a readiness exercise once or twice a year. Without prior preparation, the battalion must assemble men and equipment for immediate movement. Then, just as in actual combat, they are loaded into C-130s or other transport for a parachute jump into the target area. These exercises are usually graded for speed and efficiency. One must not be sacrificed for the other. These exercises are independent of the Ranger Ready Force rotation.

Rangers train in environments as close to real combat missions as possible. During a three-year

Cadre of the 4th Ranger Training Battalion board the OV-10 for a jump. Two or three jumpers and a jumpmaster fit in each OV-10.

The raiders give an ACE report to their team leader, who will pass it along to the squad and platoon leaders. The report details the amount of ammunition expended, the casualties suffered, and the equipment captured or destroyed.

Rangers inspect the OV-10 Bronco that will drop them for a practice jump.

period, each battalion trains at least twice in extreme cold and in amphibious operations. Jungle, mountain, and desert training are done at least once every year. Urban training is undergone every six months. Such environmental training includes critical skills and techniques necessary to each area.

Throughout the training cycle, physical training is not neglected. Rangers conduct physical training, including runs at a pace of at least one mile in eight minutes, five days a week. All other Army units usually conduct physical training one or two days in seven.

The results of this intensive and lengthy training schedule provide the finest light infantry regiment in the US armed forces, perhaps in the world.

Members of C Company, 1/75, in a desert training exercise in the United States. The Rangers train in a desert environment at least once a year. US Army via Col. David Grange

A Navy Ch-47 carries Rangers of the 3/75 for a water jump into Lake Eufala, Alabama. The jump is a "Hollywood" one; that is, it is not done with full uniform and gear.

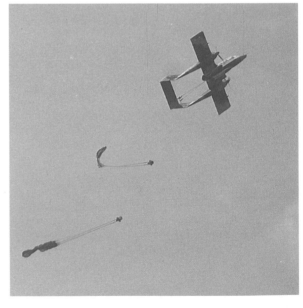

The jumpers slide out the back as the OV-10 pitches near vertical, but the jumpmaster stays in the aircraft.

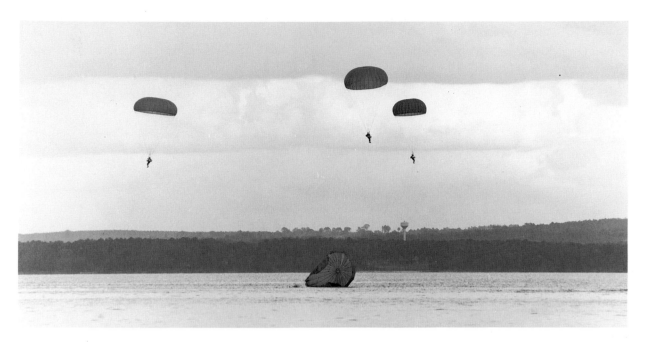

The jump into Lake Eufala. The men inflate their life vests as a safety measure before they hit the water. In case of a problem, the wet parachute would drag them under before they could use the life vest.

As part of the safety orientation, a Ranger learns how to extricate himself from a tangled parachute.

Capt. Chae, Col. David Grange, CW3 "Doc" Donovan (left to right) at Dekkar Airstrip, Fort Benning, during a Mangudai officers training exercise, November 1991. Mangudais usually begin with an air assault or jump, *followed by a patrol. The officers of the 75th train as hard and as often as their men. US Army via Col. David Grange*

75th Regimental officers on a run at Fort Benning, September 1991, following a three-day tactical training exercise with no food or sleep. Code-named Mangudai, the exercise provides periodic stress training for the 75th's officers. When in physical training uniforms, Rangers wear running shoes. US Army via Col. David Grange

The Ranger Creed

R Recognizing that I volunteered as a Ranger, fully knowing the hazards of my chosen profession, I will always endeavor to uphold the prestige, honor, and high "esprit de corps" of the Ranger Regiment.

A Acknowledging the fact that a Ranger is a more elite soldier who arrives at the cutting edge of a battle by land, sea, or air, I accept the fact that as a Ranger, my country expects me to move farther, faster, and fight harder than any other soldier.

N Never shall I fail my comrades. I will always keep myself mentally alert, physically strong, and morally straight and I will shoulder more than my share of the task, whatever it may be. One hundred percent and then some.

G Gallantly will I show the world that I am a specially selected and well-trained soldier. My courtesy to superiors, my neatness of dress, and my care of equipment shall set the example for others to follow.

E Energetically will I meet the enemies of my country. I shall defeat them on the field of battle, for I am better trained and will fight with all my might. Surrender is not a Ranger word. I will never leave a fallen comrade to fall into the hands of the enemy and under no circumstances will I ever embarrass my country.

R Readily will I display the intestinal fortitude required to fight on to the Ranger objective and complete the mission, though I be the lone survivor.

RANGERS LEAD THE WAY

Chapter 4

Weapons and Equipment

Each Ranger battalion is supplied with the latest light infantry weapons and equipment. These include laser range finders, infrared aiming devices, and all types of night vision aids. However, the Rangers will use whatever is effective for them, even if it is not the most up-to-date. They still use the 90mm recoilless rifle and are one of the last units to do so.

The Rangers can also call on support from other units throughout the armed forces. The Air Force Special Operations Command at Hurlburt Field, Eglin Air Force Base, Florida, supplies specialized transports such as the MC-130 Talons and helicopters when needed.

The Navy provides transport and fire support when asked. During Urgent Fury, the Navy provided helicopters for evacuation and fire support. Throughout the Vietnam War, Navy units provided boats for river ambushes. Ranger units often called on Navy gunners to cover an extraction from areas near the coasts.

Of course, the Army provides the majority of support to the 75th: most transport, indirect fire, antiaircraft fire, and other combat support. Medics to work with the Ranger Training Brigade come from the 324th Forward Support Battalion at Fort Benning and from units at Fort Bliss.

As light infantry, Rangers are issued all standard Army uniforms and equipment. Special equipment such as sniper rifles is used by those Rangers who have additional training. Only twenty-four such rifles are issued to each battalion. The basic weapon is still the M16.

Rangers tie items such as canteens and knives to their webbing so they can grab their rifles without losing time or equipment.

The Military Integrated Laser Engagement System, or MILES, is used with M16s and M60s. One part fits on the front of the gun barrel, and the other part is worn by the Ranger. When the gun fires a blank, the laser is activated. If the gun is aimed correctly, the receiver on the target beeps. More than one hit, the target is considered killed. The MILES is a valuable tool, but in deep foliage or heavy fog, the system will not work accurately. Of course, if the batteries run out, the system doesn't work anywhere.

An M67 90mm recoilless rifle. Not all the equipment used by the Rangers is up-to-date. If something has proved its worth, it is used until a better replacement comes along. The Rangers are virtually the only unit in the US military to still use the 90mm.

An M60 machine gun, the type used throughout the infantry.

An AN/PVS-4 night vision individual weapons sight. A second-generation starlight system, it may also be handheld for night observation. It mounts on the M14 and M16 rifles, M60 machine gun, M67 recoilless rifle,

M72A2 Light Antitank Weapon, and the M79 grenade launcher. Its range is 600 meters in moonlight and 300 meters in starlight.

A Ranger simulates the arming of an M18A1 claymore mine. Such mines can be set off by trip wires or remotely and are very useful in laying ambushes.

These AN/PVS-5 night vision goggles are lightweight and battery powered with a built-in infrared source for close-up viewing. They provide a forty-degree field of view with a range of 150 meters in moonlight and fifty meters in starlight, sufficient to spot a man-sized target at those distances. US Army

The latest version AN/PVS-7B night vision goggles provide improved night vision in lower light levels. The range is the same as the AN/PVS-5. Most of the Ranger missions take place at least part of the time in darkness, so such night vision devices allow them to move freely.

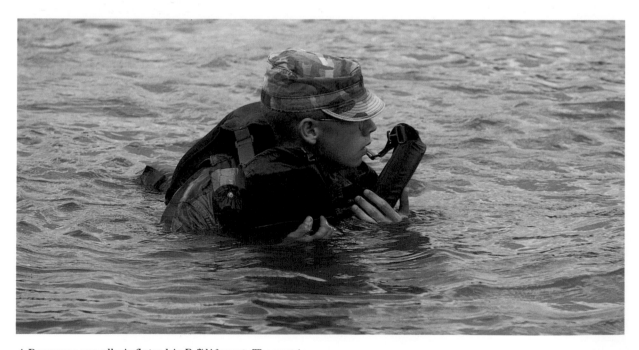

A Ranger manually inflates his B-7 life vest. The vest is standard equipment on any mission involving water other than stream crossings.

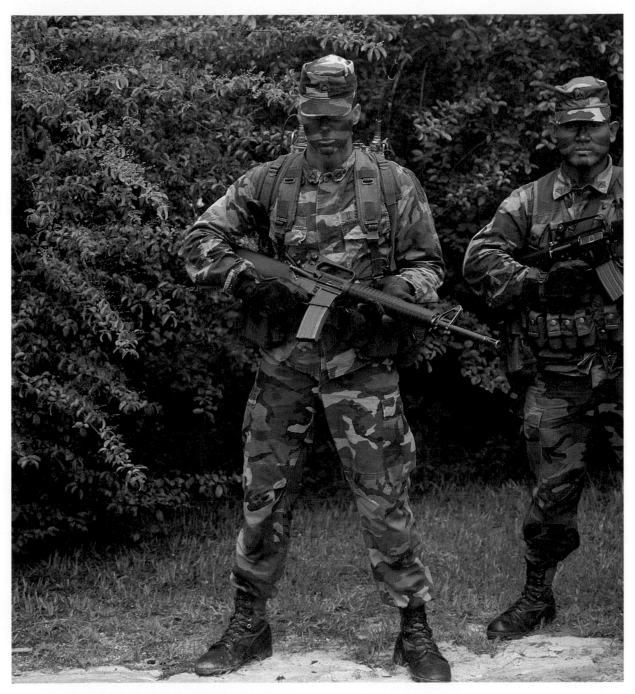

A Ranger holds an M16 rifle, the basic weapon of the US Army.

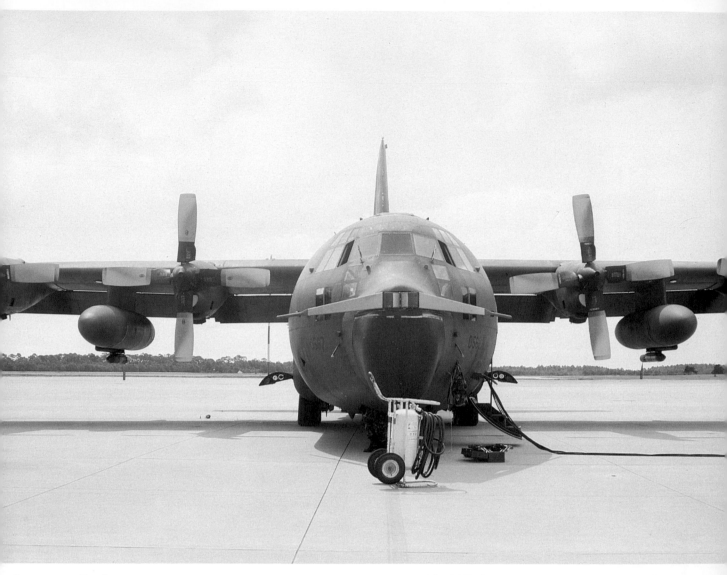

Previous page
An MC-130E Combat Talon II from the 8th Special Operations Squadron, 1st Special Operations Wing, Hurlburt Field, Florida. Like the Talon I, the Talon II is a Lockheed C-130E modified for special operations support. The electronics have been upgraded so that it is even more effective. The Talon II does not have the STAR yoke. It was determined that the STAR system would be more effective on helicopters.

An MC-130E Combat Talon from the 8th Special Operations Squadron, 1st Special Operations Wing, Hurlburt Field, Florida. The specialized aerial delivery equipment on the MC-130 enables it to locate small drop zones and make high-speed deliveries with great accuracy day or night into unfamiliar terrain. At fifty feet or above, the Talon can deliver personnel at 144mph, and equipment at 150 to 288mph. The yoke on the nose is the Fulton Surface-to-Air Recovery (STAR) system, which can recover two people or a 500lb package in less than ten minutes from land or water.

FIRST SPECIAL OPERATIONS WING

An MH-53J Pave Low helicopter from the 1st Special Operations Wing, Hurlburt Field, Florida. A version of the H-53, the Pave Low is considered the most sophisticated helicopter in the West. It has either three 7.62mm mini-guns or three .50ca machine guns and armor plating. It has a range of 600 miles and is capable of air refueling. The crew of six can carry thirty-seven passengers or 13,000lb of cargo. It can be used as an air ambulance, holding sixteen litters and four medical attendants. The electronics include the forward-looking infrared receiver (FLIR) for night vision, terrain following and mapping radar, Doppler radar for navigation, and a mission computer. Its electronic and infrared countermeasure systems make it a formidable support helicopter for special operations missions.

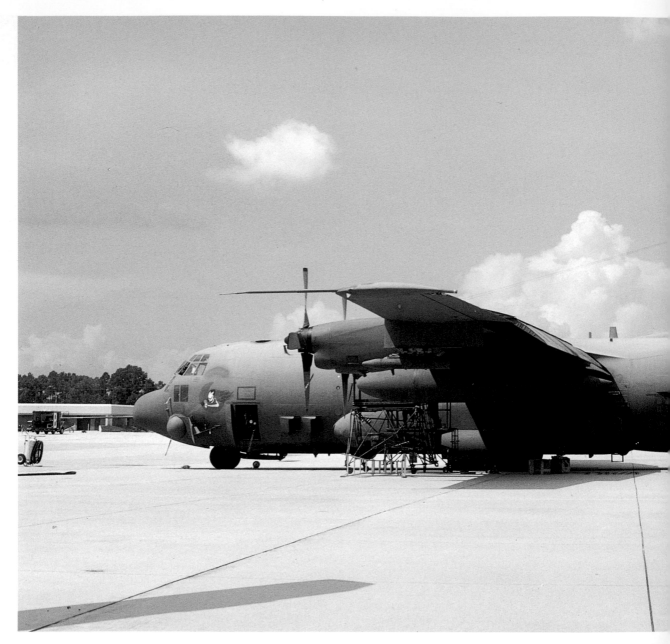

Previous page
An AH-64 Apache helicopter in flight. The Apache provides fire support with its advanced sighting and fire control systems. It has a 30mm chain gun automatic cannon under the fuselage and carries rockets or Hellfire missiles.

An AC-130H gunship from the 8th Special Operations Squadron, 1st Special Operations Wing, Hurlburt Field, Florida. The gunships provide fire support during jumps and landings into enemy areas.

Close-up of guns on an AC-130H gunship. Armament includes two 20mm Vulcan cannons, one 40mm Bofors cannon and a 105mm howitzer.

Next page
The bible of the Rangers. The pocket-sized Ranger Handbook *contains information on everything from combat orders to survival and first aid. A Ranger can refresh his memory on knots or explosives, or recall the use of map overlays or the different ways of laying an ambush. All the basics of Ranger training and operations are included. Issued in Ranger school, a Ranger keeps his handbook with him throughout his Ranger career.*

SH 21-76

UNITED STATES ARMY

RANGER HANDBOOK

RANGER TRAINING BRIGADE

UNITED STATES ARMY INFANTRY SCHOOL

FORT BENNING, GEORGIA

June 1988

---

(8) Munter hitch - Used for rappelling or in a mechanical belay. Loop is laid alongside a bight forming two parallel "windows." Snaplink passes through the windows (figure 15-13).

Figure 15-13. Munter hitch

---

b. Other Ambush Formations. The V, X and Z are all variations of the basic linear and L formations. They are more advanced ambush formations and the leader <u>must</u> be an expert in the basics before he employs these more complicated ambush techniques.

(1) V formation (figure 5-16). The V-shape attack force elements are placed along both sides of the enemy route so that they form a V. Care must be taken to ensure that neither group (or leg) fires into the other. This formation subjects the enemy to both enfilading and interlocking fire. When employed in dense terrain, the legs of the V close in as the lead elements of the enemy force approach the point of the V. The legs then open fire at close range. Fire must be closely coordinated and controlled to ensure that the fires from one leg do not endanger the other leg. Wider separation of the elements makes this formation difficult to control, and there are fewer sites that favor its use. Its main advantage is that it is difficult for the enemy to detect the ambush until well into the kill zone.

Figure 5-16. V-Ambush.

---

(2) L-Shaped Ambush. The L-shaped ambush is a variation of the linear ambush which employs flanking as well as infilade fires (figure 5-15). The short leg prevents escape or reinforcement. The L-ambush is formed with the base (bottom) of the L perpendicular to the expected enemy direction of advance. This is a good ambush for a road, trail, or any place where the ambush force can be sure of the enemy approach route. The L-ambush can handle an enemy coming from the expected direction (toward the base of the L) and from the front (stem of the L). It is less effective but usuable against an enemy formation that comes from the opposite direction than expected. In this case, the ambush must be executed when the enemy main body has cleared the base of the L. The flank security must protect the rear of the L base. In the L-ambush, weapons must be carefully sited to avoid direct or ricochet fire into friendly forces. Don't forget about the security elements when planning fire fans.

Figure 5-15. L-Shaped Ambush Formation.

Ranger Milestones

Three milestones in Ranger history occurred in 1992.

The first was the fortieth anniverary of the Ranger school, which occurred on 20 March, when the Ranger Training Brigade graduated Class 4-92. Members of the first class to earn the Ranger tab, Class 1-52, attended the ceremonies. To commemorate the event, the brigade announced the establishment of the Ranger Hall of Fame to honor and preserve the contributions of the most extraordinary Rangers in American history. All those who served in a Ranger unit in combat, or who graduated from the US Army Ranger Training Course are eligible for membership. The brigade hopes to induct a substantial number of men from each era in Ranger history by 1997. Brigade headquarters at Fort Benning will house the Ranger Hall of Fame until a suitable facility is made available.

The second was the tenth anniversary of the Best Ranger Competition—a multiday event for two-man Ranger teams from throughout the US Army, Navy, and Marine Corps—which occurred from May 1 through 4, 1992. Participants in the competition, named for Lt. Gen. (Ret.) David E. Grange, Jr., must be airborne- and Ranger-qualified, on hazardous duty orders, have no adverse personnel record, and assigned to a unit receiving a formal invitation to compete. The winning teams receive pistols and the runners-up, knives. Sixty-four teams took part in 1992.

To provide funds for the Hall of Fame, and also for the annual Best Ranger Competition and the Ranger Store which sells such items as T-shirts, the brigade established the Ranger Association Fund, a nonprofit organization. The fund allows the Ranger Training Brigade to receive private and corporate donations to support these activities. Contributions may be sent care of The Ranger Training Brigade, Fort Benning, Georgia.

The third milestone was the fiftieth anniversary of the creation of Darby's Rangers, which occurred in June. The 75th Ranger Regiment and the World War II Ranger Battalions Association hosted a celebration June 17 through 20 at Fort Benning. Beginning with a regimental airborne operation on the morning of June 17, the four days were filled with competitions and reunions.

A special Ranger exhibit was set up in the National Infantry Museum, Fort Benning, as part of the fiftieth anniversary celebrations. Items on display include Maj. Gen. Frank D. Merrill's uniform and decorations, battle flags from various Ranger battalions, and special equipment such as the "knuckle-duster" knife invented by a member of the 1st Ranger Battalion. The exhibit will remain in the "Ranger Room" on the third floor of the National Infantry Museum until such time as a permanent Ranger wing is added to the museum. Maintenance of the Ranger Room and the proposed wing is supplemented by private donations.

As part of the fiftieth anniversay ceremonies, ground was broken for the Ranger Memorial in Ranger Field on Main Post at Fort Benning. The Memorial will include a tree-lined walk leading to monuments to all Ranger units. The site will eventually host various official and social functions. Fort Benning was chosen as the location for the memorial because it is the headquarters of the modern Rangers of the 75th Ranger Regiment and the site of the Ranger Training Brigade, where all Rangers receive their training. The location and planned monuments will provide a dignified memorial to the fallen and an inspiration to all Rangers and those who aspire to be Rangers. The memorial and walk are funded entirely by private contributions. Tax-deductible contributions may be sent to:

The Ranger Memorial Foundation, Inc.
c/o NCOA Service Center
2029 South Lumpkin Road
Columbus, GA 31903

The Ranger Regiment Association welcomes both present and former Rangers as full members. Non-Rangers may become associate members.

The Ranger Regiment Association

TO SPONSOR AN ASSOCIATION WHICH REPRESENTS RANGERS CURRENTLY ASSIGNED TO THE 75TH RANGER REGIMENT, AND THOSE WHO SERVED UNDER THE CHARTER OF GENERAL CREIGHTON ABRAMS, SINCE 1974

TO GAIN SUPPORT WITHIN THE CIVILIAN AND MILITARY COMMUNITIES

TO PROMOTE THE LINEAGE OF RANGERS AND TO SUPPORT THE INTEGRITY AND IDENTITY OF EACH EXISTING RANGER ASSOCIATION

TO SERVE ALL RANGER ASSOCIATIONS; TO REPRESENT, SPONSOR AND SAFEGUARD LINEAGE AND HERALDRY, AND SERVE AS THE CUSTODIAN FOR DONATED HISTORICAL/MUSEUM ITEMS

THE RANGER REGIMENT ASSOCIATION IS ESTABLISHED TO BRING TOGETHER THE BROTHERHOOD OF RANGERS AND PEOPLE WITH A COMMON INTEREST IN SUPPORTING RANGER ACTIVITIES

TO PROMOTE THE VALUES ESTABLISHED IN THE RANGER CREED, TO HONOR RANGERS, THEIR FAMILIES AND FRIENDS

TO ESTABLISH A RANGER TRUST FUND THAT PROVIDES MONETARY ASSISTANCE FOR THE FAMILIES OF FALLEN COMRADES

TO PROVIDE AN INSTITUTION FOR MANAGING REGIMENTAL FUNDS AND SPONSORING ACTIVITIES WHICH ACHIEVE THESE MEANS

RANGERS LEAD THE WAY!

Selected Sources

A standard source for the colonial period, which discusses Rangers, is Lawrence H. Gipson, *The British Empire Before the American Revolution*, particularly vol. 6, *The Years of Defeat* (New York: Alfred A. Knopf, 1946-1947). For Braddock's defeat, we recommend Paul E. Kopperman, *Braddock at the Monongahela* (Pittsburgh: University of Pittsburgh Press, 1976), which contains a bibliography and differs with Stanley Pargellis, "Braddock's Defeat," *American Historical Review* 41 (Jan. 1936), 253-269; the same author's *Military Affairs in North America, 1784-1765* . . . (New York: D. Appleton-Century, 1936) has documents pertinent to a study of Rangers. That Braddock used Rangers is shown by Pargellis as well as by Franklin Thayer Nichols, "The Organization of Braddock's Army," *William & Mary Quarterly* 4 (April 1947), 125-147.

Indispensable for wilderness warfare, Rangers, and light infantry are Daniel J. Beattie, "The Adaptation of the British Army to Wilderness Warfare, 1755-1763," in Maarten Ultee, ed. *Adapting to Conditions* (Alabama: University of Alabama Press, 1986), 56-83, and Peter E. Russell, "Redcoats in the Wilderness: British Officers and Irregular Warfare in Europe and America, 1740 to 1760," *William & Mary Quarterly* 35 (1978), 629-652. Also useful are John K. Mahon, "Anglo-American Methods of Indian Warfare, 1676-1794," *Mississippi Valley Historical Review* 45 (1958), 244-275, and Edward Pierce Hamilton, "Colonial Warfare in North America," *Proceedings of Massachusetts Historical Society* 80 (1968), 3-15.

Burt B. Loescher's *The History of Rogers' Rangers: The Beginnings, 1755-1758*, published in California by the author, is not easily found. More generally available is John R. Cuneo, *Robert Rogers of the Rangers* (New York: Oxford University Press, 1959). These works were used to describe the attire and weapons of the Rangers. Rogers' *Journals of Major Robert Rogers* (New York: Corinth Books, 1961) describes their missions. Gary Zaboly has described "The Battle on Snowshoes," in *American History Illustrated* 14 (Dec. 1979), 122. Of interest and some curiosity is T. D. Seymour, editor, "A Ballad of Rogers' Rangers' Retreat, 1759," *Vermont History* 46 (Winter 1978), 21-23, detailing the disastrous retreat after the St. Francis raid.

George Washington's first Ranger unit is described by Sheldon Cohen, "The Death of Colonel Thomas Knowlton," *Connecticut Historical Society Bulletin* 30 (April 1965), 50-70. A. Theodore Steegman, Jr., "New York Rangers in the Hampshire Grants 1776-1777," *Vermont History* 51 (Fall 1983) 238-248, describes a rebel unit. For Tories, see Kenneth Scott, "Captain Christopher Benson's First Independent Company of New York Rangers 1777-1782," *National Genealogical Society Quarterly* 73 (June 1985), 132-134. Robert Rogers' attempt to set up British Rangers is detailed in John Cuneo, "The Early Days of the Queen's Rangers, August 1776-1777," *Military Affairs* 22 (Summer 1958), 65-74. Larry Ivers' short history, in manuscript form, of the Rangers covers aspects of the war in the north, and is available at the Donovan Technical Library, Fort Benning, Georgia.

For the south, see Jack Weller's "Irregular Warfare in the South," *Military Affairs* 24 (Fall 1960), 124-136, and "Irregular but Effective . . . ," *Military Affairs* 21 (Fall 1957), 118-136. For a detailed account of one organization, see Gary Olson, "Thomas Brown, Loyalist Partisan, and the Revolutionary War in Georgia 1777-1782," *Georgia Historical Quarterly* 54 (Nos. 1 and 2, 1970). Much the same ground is covered in W. Calvin Smith, "Mermaids Riding Alligators," *Florida Historical Quarterly* (April 1976), 443-464.

Francis Marion's military career is detailed in John Ferling, "Francis Marion," *Dictionary of American Military Biography* II (Westport, Conn.: Greenwood Press, 1984), 730-731; and George W. Kyte, "Francis Marion as Intelligence Officer," *South Carolina History Magazine* 77 (Oct. 1976), 215-226. A popular description is George J. Scheer, "The Elusive Swamp Fox," *American Heritage* 9 (April 1958), 41-47, 111.

Rangers continued to exist in the early national period, but information is sparse. Larry Ivers has written a short description of one unit in Florida in "Rangers in Florida—1818," *Infantry* (Sep.-Oct. 1963), 37. Otis E. Young has written "The United States Mounted Ranger Battalion, 1832-1833," *Mississippi Valley Historical Review* 41 (Dec. 1954), 453-470.

The rise and fall of Confederate Rangers is described by Carl E. Grant, "Partisan Warfare, Model 1861-65," *Military Review* 38 (Nov. 1958), 42-56. Andrew Brown's, "The First Mississippi Partisan Rangers," *Civil War History* 1 (Dec. 1955), 371-399, describes their activities and supports the view that such units were of little value to the Confederacy.

Grierson's raids are detailed in Edward Longacre, *Mounted Raids of the Civil War* (New York: A. S. Barnes), and Edwin Bearss, "Grierson's Winter Raid on the Mobile and Ohio Railroad," in *Military Analysis of the Civil War* (Millwood, N.Y.: American Military Institute, KTO Press, 1977).

Information on Darby and his Rangers may be found in Michael J. King, *William Orlando Darby: A Military Biography* (Hamden, Conn.: Archon Books, 1981), and from interviews with Darby before his death, *We Led The Way: Darby's Rangers* (San Rafael, Calif.: Presidio Press, 1980). James Altieri's pictorial history *Darby's Rangers* (Durham, N.C.: Seeman Printery, 1945), is hard to locate but worth the attempt, as is his *The Spearheaders* (New York: Bobbs-Merrill Co., 1960). The most recent, and in many ways the best, account of the Rangers at Cisterna appears in Carlo D'Este, *Fatal Decision* (New York: Harper Collins Publishers, 1991), chapter 10.

D-day and the Rangers can be studied in the war department's "Pointe Due Hoe (2nd Ranger Battalion, 6 June 1944)," part of the *Small Unit Actions* series published in 1946 and since reprinted. Short sketches of each Ranger unit may be found in James Ladd, *Commandos and Rangers of World War II* (New York: St. Martins Press, 1978). Michael King has written *Rangers: Selected Combat Operations in World War II*, Leavenworth Papers (No. 11, June 1985). King describes the prisoner of war raid in the Philippines, as well as Rangers in Africa, Sicily, and the Zerf operation in Europe.

Scott R. McMichael discusses the FSSF in *A Historical Perspective on Light Infantry* (Fort Leavenworth, Kan., US Army Command and General Staff College, 1987).

McMichael also discusses Merrill's Marauders, whose operations are traced in the Army Official Histories, such as Charles Romanus, *Stillwell's Command Problems* (Washington, D.C.: Office of the Chief of Military History, 1956), and in an Army monograph, *Merrill's Marauders Feb-May 1944*, published in 1945 and reissued in 1990. Controversy over the unit's treatment, especially by Stillwell's command, is highlighted in Charton Ogburn, Jr., *The Marauders* (New York: Harper & Bros., 1959), which describes the hunger and rituals surrounding meals. Following the war, the Army published "The Marauders: A Record of Righteous Indignation" in *Crisis Fleeting*, 293-396, compiled and edited by James H. Stone, which contains doctors' reports from the China-Burma-India theater. Published in 1969 by the Department of the Army, it in large measure supports McMichael. The debate is renewed in Scott McMichael, "Common Man, Uncommon Leadership: Colonel Charles N. Hunter with Galahad in

Burma," *Parameters* 16 (Summer 1986), 99-111. Several rejoinders appeared in a later issue of *Parameters* 17 (Spring 1987), 45-56. George McGee, Jr., has published *The History of the 2nd Battalion, Merrill's Marauders* (privately published, 1987); he is one of those who sharply disagrees with the doctors and McMichael.

For the Rangers during the Korea War, see Robert Black, *Rangers in Korea* (New York: Ballantine Books, 1989). Martin Blumenson has described a Ranger action in "The Rangers at Hwachon Dam," *Army* (Dec. 1967), 37-53.

Michael Lanning has a short history of the Rangers in his *Inside the LRRPs: Rangers in Vietnam* (New York: Ballantine Books, 1988), where he describes their missions and how the LRRPs became Rangers.

Ranger missions in Grenada are described in Mark Adkin, *Urgent Fury: The Battle for Grenada* (Lexington, Mass.: Lexington Books, 1987), which must be used with great caution. Rangers we interviewed who are knowledgeable about the Grenada action dispute some of Adkin's facts. Much information is still classified.

Some information on Rangers in Panama was found in Godfrey Harris, *Invasion: The American Destruction of the Noriega Regime in Panama* (Los Angeles, Calif.: The Americas Group, 1990).

Little or nothing is available on the Rangers in Desert Storm. One source is Ron Martz, "Behind the Line Teams Paid Off in Gulf War," *The Atlanta Journal/The Atlanta Constitution* Saturday October 19, 1991.

U.S. SPECIAL FORCES

DELTA
America's Elite Counterterrorist Force

Terry Griswold and D. M. Giangreco

Preface

This is another type of war, new in its intensity, ancient in its origins—
war by guerrillas, subversives, insurgents, assassins . . . seeking victory
by eroding and exhausting the enemy instead of engaging him.

President John F. Kennedy, 1962

The success of Fidel Castro's Cuban revolution in 1959 and rising tide of insurgencies around the globe made it clear to newly elected President of the United States John F. Kennedy that the focus of communist expansionism had shifted to the Third World. Kennedy firmly believed that the communist's ominous Cuban foothold in the Western Hemisphere could be countered by a program aimed at stimulating peaceful evolution instead of violent revolution. His response to the communists' challenge was the Alliance for Progress.

The Alliance for Progress was a serious effort to promote stability in Latin America through political reform, as well as economic and social development, and it served as a model for similar US commitments in other less–developed regions. Embryonic communist insurgencies threatened this evolutionary process, and Kennedy moved quickly to blunt their threat by devising and implementing a doctrine of counterrevolutionary warfare. More than thirty years later, the descendants

of his elite, unconventional warriors continue to assist dozens of potential or fledgling democracies while specifically tasked, direct–action arms of the Army, Navy, and Air Force stand ready to fight an insidious by–product of Third World instability and the recent Cold War: terrorism.

In the years following the Iran hostage crisis and disaster at *Desert I*, a great deal has been written on the 1st Special Forces Operational Detachment–DELTA. Most of the focus has been on the origins of the failed rescue attempt, the major players, technical problems, and in some cases, the strategic and tactical leadership of the units involved. However, the guts and backbone of DELTA and similar units is the individual trooper. For the most part, he is typical of those in the special operations community.

But there is more to the soldiers who make up DELTA. Each man is a self–starter who not only displays personal initiative but can work well when part of a team. They are mature individuals, confident in themselves and their unit, who are unquestioned experts in their craft. These qualities are more than just factors in what makes a good DELTA trooper, they are the essence of DELTA. And while most of the unit's officers stay around long enough to learn the art of counterterrorist (CT) operations, it is still the old hands, the highly professional noncommissioned and warrant officers, that keep DELTA on the straight and narrow. This story examines CT training and operations from their viewpoint: the elite special operations team members who must wade into the dirty business of counterterrorism to protect US lives and interests.

In a free—and financially strapped—society, there is immense pressure on units costing the taxpayer millions of dollars to produce and show results. Because of the clandestine nature of DELTA's mission, however, the full story of this extraordinary and sophisticated unit cannot be told no matter how important its unique capabilities are to the ongoing war against international terrorism. This relative anonymity makes DELTA an easy target for congressional budget cutters searching for a "quick fix" and the unit may well find itself as an expensive toy up for funding cuts in the austere future. Such actions would be disasterous.

The information in this book is based upon the research and experience of the authors and does not represent the positions or policies of any official, agency, or department of the United States government, British government, or any other government. The information was derived from unclassified publications and sources and is intended to neither confirm or deny, officially or unofficially, the views of those governments.

Uncredited photos in this book were taken by US armed forces personnel and are in the public domain. The names of current DELTA troopers are classified and, unless otherwise noted, all names given for soldiers below the rank of colonel are pseudonyms.

Chapter 1
Out of the Desert

The takeoff had to go right the first time. There would be no second chance. As the last item on the pre–flight list was checked off, the pilot revved up the EC-130E's Allison turboprops to gain maximum power. Releasing the already–straining brakes and pushing the throttles to the firewall, the pilot nursed his aircraft slowly forward out of the jumbled mass of wheel ruts furrowed deeply into the Iranian desert. The straining engines created a mini sandstorm that all but obliterated the ghastly funeral pyre they were leaving behind. Resembling some prehistoric bird of prey, the dark Hercules sluggishly lifted away from the makeshift desert runway and the disaster that Operation *Eagle Claw* had become.

This aircraft was one of the last special operations birds leaving Iran after the aborted rescue attempt to free American hostages in Teheran. The Ayatol-

RH-53D Sea Stallions from the USS *Nimitz* practicing low–level formation flying before the attempted rescue of American hostages in Iran.

lah Khomeini's Revolutionary Guards had held their fifty–three prisoners in the captured US Embassy compound for nearly six months and the half–dozen Hercules had been slated to play a key role in rescuing them. Now, as five heavily loaded aircraft flew into the early morning darkness, an EC-130E tanker and RH-53D Sea Stallion helicopter lay blazing in the desert. Through the swirling sand, passengers with portholes could clearly see what each had never believed possible: failure. Despite well–laid plans, the team's efforts had ended in an inferno of exploding ammunition and twisted, burning aircraft.

What happened at the refuel site code–named *Desert I* has been argued about and even embellished in a Hollywood adventure film, but the basic facts remain the same. The six special operations aircraft that penetrated Iran on the night of April 24–25, 1980 were configured either as tankers to refuel the Sea Stallion helicopters or as transports to bring in the assault teams and their ground support. After reaching the site, the mission was scrubbed

and the force had to prepare for exfiltration.

The decision to abort was made after three of the eight Sea Stallions either failed to reach *Desert I* or could not proceed because of mechanical difficulties. Not enough helicopters were available to carry out the mission, so there was nothing for the rotary and fixed–wing aircraft to do but return to their separate starting points. In preparation for the exfiltration, one of the RH-53Ds had to be repositioned. During that maneuver, the helicopter's main rotor smashed into the cockpit of a parked EC-130; both aircraft erupted into flame, and the explosions turned the stark desert night into a ghastly beacon. During the hasty evacuation of the site, the remaining Sea Stallions were left behind.

On board the EC-130E were members of America's newly formed counterterrorist unit known simply as DELTA. The unit had been activated in November 1977 but was untested or, as military professionals would say, "unblooded," and this was to be their first operational mission. But while the troopers anticipated that their baptism of fire would soon come in Teheran, they instead found themselves trapped in a terrifying inferno fed by thousands of gallons of aircraft fuel. As one of the survivors would later report, the DELTA Blue Team troopers and air crew from the stricken EC-130 struggled to "unass the muther" as best they could, bearing their injured with them.

Caught in the tanker's burning, smoke–filled cargo bay, Master Sergeant Leonard M. Harris was quickly overcome by smoke as he attempted to rescue an Air Force crewman. Luckily for both men, they were pulled from the burning plane by other members of DELTA.

Harris and the other survivors were loaded into various aircraft for the trip out. Now, as the last Hercules flew in a rough trail formation through the inky darkness toward the Indian Ocean and safety, Harris began to regain consciousness. Watery eyes fixed on a light on the cabin roof and then wandered down to scan the confusion around him in the crowded cargo bay. DELTA troopers, dressed in Levis, boots, and black field jackets, were interspersed with air crews, combat control team members, and other support personnel. Some sat in stunned silence, still wearing their woolen naval watch caps, while others were stripping off layers of body armor, web gear, and sweat–stained clothing. Checking his own physical condition, Harris was surprised that, despite his brush with death, the only damage that he was able to perceive, other than a raw throat from smoke inhalation, was a good singeing of his field jacket and a relatively minor burn across the back of his left hand.

Looking down at his recently black–dyed field jacket, he absently picked at the melted tape that covered the only insignia on the assault teams' tactical uniforms: a small American flag sewn on the right jacket sleeve. The troopers were to have displayed the flags after entering the Embassy grounds so that the hostages would readily follow them out during the exfiltration. After all, in their uniforms, the rescue team looked more like muggers in a New York subway than members of an elite counterterrorist unit.

Peering across the red–lighted cargo compartment, Harris realized that he and the rest of the passengers were sitting, lying, or in some other way trying to get comfortable while riding on the bouncing fuel bladder covering the length of the plane. While team medical personnel provided aid, others appeared to be sorting out what had happened to them. Regaining a sense of stability, Harris was

(Top) RH-53D Sea Stallions on the aft hangar bay of the USS *Nimitz* before launch and (left) a burned–out hulk at *Desert I*. Note the .50cal machine guns mounted in the cabin doors at the extreme left and right of the top photo. *Wide World Photos.*

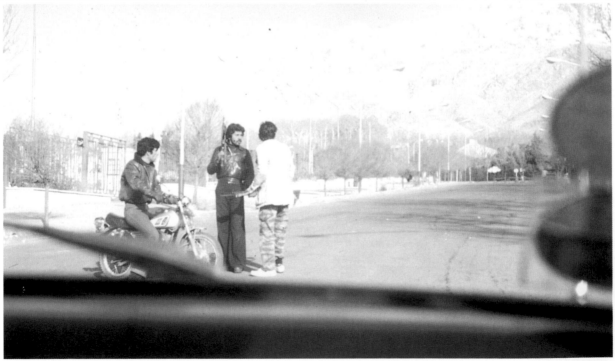

helped into a sitting position by another trooper. He noticed that his palms were wet with sweat, and not really knowing if it was from fear or just shock, he wiped them on his faded Levis. Leaning his head back against the cold metal skin of the Hercules, he muttered, "Good ol' Herky Bird." The vibration and steady hum of its engines made him think of his airborne instructors at Fort Benning, Georgia. "Damn if they weren't right," he thought. "The 130 *is* a living creature."

In the absence of the fear and pain that fatigue brings, he began to reflect on the events that brought him to this godforsaken situation. "How in the hell did I get in this mess?"

The Reception Committee

As the last of the special operations aircraft lifted off from the chaos of *Desert I*, another intense drama was taking place in the Iranian capital. From a clandestine communications site well outside Teheran, Dick Meadows, a highly decorated and skilled former Green Beret, received word of *Desert I*'s disaster. His vulnerable advance party of Special Forces soldiers had infiltrated the city only a few days earlier under various cover stories designed to hide all traces of their true identity and mission. Now, however, events beyond their control had forced them to immediately execute their own escape and evasion plans.

Nearly six months before *Eagle Claw*, on November 4, 1979, "subject matter experts" from all relevant military and civilian agencies were drawn to-

Revolutionary Guard checkpoints in Teheran surreptitiously photographed by Army personnel. They are armed with a variety of 7.62mm Heckler & Koch G3 rifles manufactured in Iran under a license obtained from the West German firm. (**Top**) A Revolutionary Guard is carrying several weapons to comrades up the street while, (**left**) the mountains ringing Teheran are clearly visible.

gether to form an ad hoc joint task force (JTF) charged with both the planning and execution of the hostage rescue. Like so often in the military, the "old boy" network was initially used to fill the JTF. This approach brought in many talented people whose broad range of expertise at first quickened the planning phase of the operation. Unfortunately, though, interservice and interdepartmental bickering soon created coordination problems. Despite later denials, virtually everyone either wanted a piece of the action or seemed intent on distancing themselves from the operation. The resulting problems—demonstrated by the initial lack of cooperation from the Central Intelligence Agency (CIA) and State Department officials—tended to frustrate rather than facilitate planning by the JTF's staff officers under the stewardship of Major General James B. Vought, a highly respected paratrooper who had much experience working with Rangers.

Ideally, CIA operatives would have already been in the "area of interest" providing current intelligence and would have been responsible for obtaining critical items such as "safe houses" and locally procured trucks in Teheran. However, at this time in its history, the agency was undergoing a number of reorganizations prompted by highly publicized criticism of its role in major incidents going back as far as the Bay of Pigs invasion of Cuba. Sensational reports of alleged assassination attempts on foreign leaders, Vietnam's numerous "black" or covert operations (including the unjustly maligned *Phoenix* program), and the increasing number of former CIA employees who turned into authors of "tell–all" books added to the growing public perception of a bumbling group of spies running amuck.

After Jimmy Carter assumed the presidency in 1977, he installed a fellow Annapolis graduate, Admiral Stansfield Turner, to oversee the restructuring of the CIA and the institution of his administration's "Georgia approach" to governmental man-

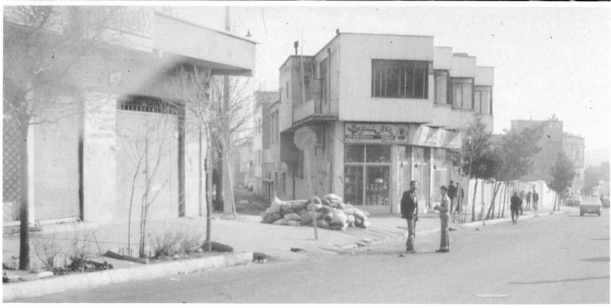

agement. Under Turner, hundreds of experienced personnel were laid off (referred to in the government's bureaucratic language as a reduction in force or RIF). The agency soon became heavily dependent on mechanical and technical means as the primary method of intelligence gathering instead of using them in conjunction with, or as a complement to, human intelligence collection, or HUMINT. By the time the Embassy in Teheran was seized, Middle Eastern operations were in a major decline; in fact, the last full–time operative in Iran had already slipped into the warm embrace of retirement.

Despite the CIA's reinfiltration of one of its agents into Teheran, DELTA's thirst for intelligence on a broad range of matters was not satisfied. The "black boxes" were clearly failing to produce the information required to carry out this delicate operation, and the *Eagle Claw* planners in DELTA began to look within the special operations community for HUMINT collection means to make up the shortfall. The search led them to Dick Meadows.

(**Top**) A mass demonstration at "Freedom Square" on Eisenhower Avenue about a half–dozen miles west of the US Embassy. In the unlikely event that Iranian mobs would react quickly enough to threaten the rescue mission, an orbiting AC-130H Specter gunship would perform "crowd control" around the embassy and prevent the armored vehicles based at an army ordnance depot to the north and the police headquarters near the Ministry of Foreign Affairs to the south from intervening. If the Specter found itself hard–pressed to keep the threats at bay, a second gunship covering Mehrabad International Airport to the west, would destroy Iranian F-4 Phantom jets, capable of chasing down the rescue aircraft, and assist at the embassy. (**Left**) A Revolutionary Guard bunker in central Teheran. The broad avenues which criss–crossed the capital, such as Roosevelt, which ran between the embassy and the soccer stadium and north to the army depot, were fed by an intricate—but well–mapped—maze of narrow streets fully or partially blocked by these randomly placed defensive positions.

This was not the first time that Meadows had participated in an effort to free US prisoners. Ten years before, he had been in charge of the compound assault team during Operation *Ivory Coast* (more commonly known as the Son Tay Raid), an airborne assault on a prisoner of war camp only twenty miles from Hanoi in North Vietnam.* Other exploits in Southeast Asia included the capture of North Vietnamese artillery pieces in Laos and the recapture of a major CIA outpost in that same country. He was an expert in what are referred to as "low–visibility insertions" and "takedowns."

Meadows had become a civilian advisor to DELTA after retiring from the Army, and his extensive background in clandestine cross–border operations, as well as his completion of the British Special Air Service (SAS) selection course, carried a great deal of weight in choosing him to enter Teheran ahead of the rescue force. Above all, the JTF planners knew he could be trusted to do his best to accomplish the mission—and, besides, he knew DELTA inside and out. This knowledge, however, could prove to be a rather negative aspect of his qualifications if he were caught.

Meadows' orders were to infiltrate the chaos of Teheran, establish a safe house, locally procure covered trucks to transport the rescue force, and guide the rescuers from the landing zone to their assault positions near the Embassy. In military terms, he was the reception committee and, on paper at least, this part of the operation was one of the less–complicated portions of the entire plan. One critical concern of Meadows was his cover and its associated background information and the story

---

*The over four dozen US prisoners were held at the camp but were moved shortly before the raid and remained in captivity until after the 1973 signing of the Paris Peace Accords. One side benefit of the operation, however, was an accidental attack on a nearby compound that apparently killed as many as 200 East Block or Soviet specialists involved in upgrading North Vietnam's air defenses.

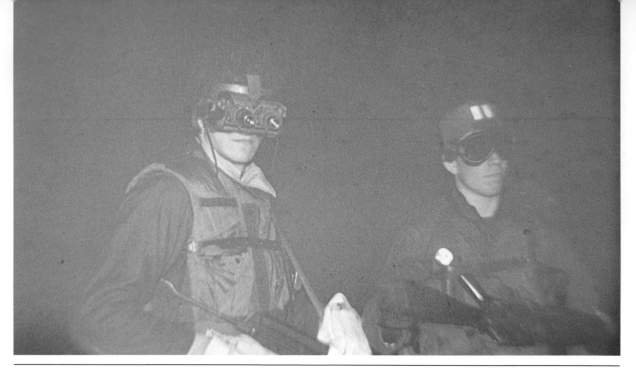

A force of a dozen US Army Rangers and DELTA members made up two teams to secure the road running through the *Desert I* refuel sight. (**Above**) Troopers armed with a Colt M16 assault rifle and Walther MP-L submachine gun peer intently through the night. The relatively heavy PVS-5 night vision goggles, used during the operation, could only be worn for about thirty minutes at a time before a pilot or trooper would have to hand it off to a designated partner to wear. Within minutes after they rode their Yamaha motorcycles out of the belly of the first MC-130 to land, the team captured a bus with forty–four Iranian civilians, blew up a gasoline tanker truck with a light antitank weapon, and ran off another truck.

Although *Eagle Claw* planners were later criticized for establishing the refuel site in a moderately traveled area, mission parameters left them little choice, and DELTA planned to fly any Iranians taken into custody back to Misirah Island on the returning MC-130s. The Iranians would then be flown back to Iranian territory and released at Manzariyeh Air Base the following night. There were never any plans to hold any detained Iranians in exchange for the US hostages (such a move would have had disasterous political repercussions), and if the mission were aborted after they had been flown from *Desert I*, the Iranians would be speedily turned over to the International Red Cross for repatriation.

fabricated to explain what brought a Westerner to this hostile land. CIA liaison officers supplied him with an Irish background, including all the necessary documentation and accessories, while the JTF provided additional backups and an enhanced language capability in the form of three sergeants recruited in Germany, two from a covert Special Forces unit and one from the Air Force.

Unlike Meadows, these men already had covers and were conducting their daily lives under that blanket of anonymity. All were foreign–born na-

tionals who had joined America's armed forces and were now US citizens. One of the men was a native of Germany and was intimately acquainted with the murky world of working with and supporting intelligence requirements levied on the Army by other agencies such as the CIA. Another of the operatives was born in the British Isles and was easily cloaked with the mantle of a Scottish background. The third (who had undergone no previous Special Forces training) was a native of the Middle East and was fluent in Farsi, the primary language of Iran. These men would provide Meadows with the additional skills required of the advance party.

When it was discovered, rather late in the planning, that three high–ranking hostages were being held in the Ministry of Foreign Affairs building six miles from the Embassy, an additional thirteen soldiers were recruited from a clandestine unit in Germany. Not enough time was available to change the basic plan as well as shift existing personnel to other targets, so it fell upon these men to fill the operational void created by the last–minute intelligence. Special Forces detachments like theirs had been preparing to fight potential Soviet invaders in the extensively built–up areas of western Germany since the late 1950s and were composed of experts in urban warfare.

Eagle Claw's mission profile called for the advance team to rendezvous with the DELTA rescue force staging out of a little–used airfield near Qena, 300 miles south of Cairo in central Egypt. Upon receipt of the execution message, the 132 men of the rescue force and additional support personnel flew on two C-141s from Egypt to an air base operated by British and Omani personnel on the large Arabian Sea island of Misirah. At the same time, the helicopter element located on the aircraft carrier USS *Nimitz* "patrolling" nearby in the Gulf of Oman prepared to launch its RH-53D helicopters to an isolated spot, code–named *Desert I,* in Iran's Dasht–e Karir (Salt Desert). While all this was taking place, a contingent of four AC-130E and H Specter gunships were readied for their launch the following night. They would fly directly from Qena to Teheran where they would support the rescue. The Specters would be refueled by KC-135 tankers as they passed over Saudi Arabia.

The next phase of the operation called for DELTA's surgical assault force, along with its security and support element, to take off from Misirah in EC- and MC-130Es of the 8th Special Operations Squadron. Their destination, *Desert I,* had already been surveyed by an Air Force Combat Control Team member who placed remotely operated infrared beacons along the "hasty" landing strip. After the force successfully rendezvoused at *Desert I* near Garmsar, 265 nautical miles southeast of Teheran, the assault element was to load onto the helicopters and fly on to *Desert II* in the rugged, mountainous region just southeast of the capital. Once there, the choppers would be hidden nearby, at a site codenamed *Figbar,* while the assault force linked up with the reception committee before dawn.

The assault force would settle in for the day while the DELTA commander, Colonel Charlie A. Beckwith would infiltrate Teheran along with a select group of twelve troopers who would receive the trucks gathered by Meadows' team near the city at a secure warehouse called the "Mushroom." It was their job to drive the small convoy out of the city on the second night of the operation and collect the rest of the rescue force from the hide site. After transferring to the six large, tarpaulin–covered Mercedes trucks and a Volkswagen van, 106 DELTA and Special Forces troopers would journey to the capital where final preparations for the impending rescue would be made. The plan called for the rescue force to depart from *Desert II* at 2030 hours and be in their designated assault positions by 2300 hours. Meadows would take Colonel Beckwith on a personal reconnaissance of the target before the attack at approximately the same time that the AC-130s were lifting off in Egypt.

The main assault group's three teams (code–named *Red, White,* and *Blue*) and Foreign Ministry assault group would use the principles of surprise, shock, and coordinated movement to take out the Ayatollah's Revolutionary Guards. As soon as the short, violent rescue operation erupted at the walled Embassy compound, the hidden RH-53D helicop-

(**Top**) An M151 roars over a a sand dune in Egypt. The soldiers given the mission of guarding the dirt road running through *Desert I* were not picked until after the main body of Rangers, slated to seize Manzariyeh Air Base, had arrived at Qena, Egypt. Intensive training was immediately begun for both the road–watch and airfield–seizure teams. (**Above**) Before operations could begin, Air Force ground personnel had to be flown into both Qena and the British–Omani air base on Misirah Island to set up communications and logistics for the thirty–four special operations tankers, transports, and gunships involved in *Eagle Claw*.

ters would emerge from their camouflaged position near *Desert II*. One would head for the large park surrounding the Foreign Ministry, while the rest would fly to sites at the rear of the Embassy compound and the Amjedeih soccer stadium across the street, where both hostages and rescuers would be picked up. If the compound site couldn't be cleared of obstructions in time, all extractions would be conducted from the stadium.

Throughout the ground phase of the operation, one AC-130 gunship would orbit over the target area providing fire support, and another would cover the two Iranian F-4 Phantom jets on strip alert at Teheran's nearby Mehrabad International Airport. Two additional Specters would orbit close by in reserve. All parties concerned were fully confident that the massive firepower the Specters could bring to bear on the surrounding area would be more than enough to suppress any Revolutionary Guards attempting to reinforce their Embassy security force and prevent the infamous Iranian mobs from interfering with the rescue.. As one of the gunship pilots was later to explain, the Specters' awesome firepower was the "best crowd–control measure" available.

While the AC-130s dominated the area, the helicopters would leave the chaos of Teheran for nearby Manzariyeh Air Base only thirty–five minutes away. Manzariyeh was to have already been secured by a seventy–five–man Ranger contingent and support personnel flying directly from Qena on four MC-130s. This elite light infantry unit was composed of experts in airfield seizure. Using M151s (commonly, if erroneously, referred to as jeeps) and commercial off-road motorcycles, they were capable of gobbling up the sprawling but lightly defended facility in a matter of minutes.

Throughout the exfiltration, F-14A Tomcat fighters and KA-6D Intruder tankers from the USS *Nimitz* would orbit over Persian Gulf waters—on call to knock down any hostile aircraft coming after the vulnerable transports, and gunships leaving Manzariyeh. If all went well, the entire force—Rangers, Special Forces, Meadows' team, support personnel, DELTA, and their newly rescued char-

Sea Stallions receiving preflight preparations on the deck of the USS *Nimitz*. The RH-53Ds had been freshly painted to mimic the look of Iranian helicopters and also carried green, white, and red Iranian identification roundels that could be added to further confuse prying eyes.

ges—would be quickly loaded aboard a pair of C-141s, which had made a quick dash from Dhahran, Saudi Arabia, and exfiltrate to Qena before the Iranians could take any effective countermeasures. There was no way to fly the helicopters out of Iran, and they were to be destroyed before the last Rangers left the airfield.

The catastrophe at *Desert I* changed all that. After Meadows received word over a clandestine radio to abort the mission, he notified the team, which dispersed from the safe house, and all made their individual ways to the passenger terminal at Teheran's Mehrabad International Airport. Security within the terminal was visibly increased. Unshaven and clad in an irregular mix of civilian and military clothing, the pride of Iran's Revolutionary Guard nervously paced back and forth near entrances, fingering their newly acquired Heckler & Koch G3 rifles. The menacing looks—as well as a healthy respect for the weapons' stopping power—caused Meadows to give each of the guards a grudging deference. Swallowing hard, Meadows entered the terminal entrance and walked directly to the Swiss Air ticket counter. Very deliberately, and somewhat slowly, he reached into the inner pocket of his corduroy jacket for the cash necessary to open the first of many doors to the waiting jet and freedom.

While being processed, he noticed that his "Scottish" comrade was in another part of the terminal area, being heavily questioned by a combination of Revolutionary Guards, customs officials, and men in soldiers' uniforms. Meadows later learned that the large amounts of US currency that had initially brought this unwanted attention to the Scotsman stayed in Iran with that "interested" group of officials. The newfound hatred of the "Great Satan" obviously did not extend into financial matters, and well-placed bribes of American greenbacks continued to do the trick.

Reaching down to retrieve his carryall, Meadows realized that despite the fact that word had been received about an "invasion" to the south, the security efforts within the airport remained disjointed and uncoordinated. Walking at a casual but determined gait toward the Swiss Air jet, he wondered what things were like at the Embassy.

Chapter 2
A New Game in Town

Kill one and terrorize a thousand.

Sun Tzu, 500 BC

Festering Arab resentment of America's direct and substantial support of Israel grew steadily after the United States became the Jewish state's chief sponsor in the wake of the 1967 Six Day War. By 1973, when massive American arms shipments played a critical role in blocking an Egyptian–Syrian victory in the Yom Kippur War, the United States was firmly planted on a collision course with the rising tide of pan–Arab nationalism. From now on, Americans would no longer be incidental victims of terrorist attacks. They would be the targets.

During the Six Day War, the sweeping successes of the Israeli military machine made it clear to the Arab world that change could not be guaranteed by conventional forces alone. One of the key audiences watching from the sidelines with a great deal of interest were the millions of Palestinians living in forced exile not only in the Middle Eastern countries, but also in Europe. Across the Atlantic, the United States was focused on the problems of the war in Vietnam, internal strife centered on the civil

rights movement, and there was growing unrest on college campuses. Against this background, the United States hoped that every effort would be made to solve the numerous long–standing issues in the Middle East peacefully. Failing that, preventing disagreements from boiling up into open warfare was the least that could be strived for. But as world affairs would have it, the Palestinian issue exploded to the surface, amid smoke and gunfire, in the Hashemite kingdom of Jordan.

When shoved into a corner by Soviet–sponsored, Syrian–armed Palestinian forces intent on using his country as a staging area for raids on Israel, King Hussein ibn–Talal used his army to drive the Palestinians into Syria and reasserted his authority. The king and his Hashemite followers had never enjoyed an easy relationship with the various *fedayeen* groups making up Yasir Arafat's Palestine Liberation Organization (PLO), and its military arm, the *Fatah*, which was openly encroaching on the country's control of the Jordan River Valley. One faction, George Habbash's Popular Front for the Liberation of Palestine (PFLP)—the largest and most anti–Hashemite of the *fedayeen*—had worked feverishly to undermine Hussein's throne

One of the terrorists holding Israeli athletes at the Munich Olympics relays demands to German negotiators in front of millions of television viewers.

Television crews and reporters line the balcony of the Beirut International Airport terminal during the nine–day hijacking of a TWA jet, June 22, 1985. The media was—and continues to be—one of international terrorism's most important weapons. *Wide World Photos*

long before the bloody confrontation.

The intense fighting for the capital of Amman and across northern Jordan in September 1970 caused a great deal of worry in the Western world, and supplies were sent in from a number of countries. Military forces were also alerted to move in and provide help, but the Jordanian Army succeeded without them. This stunning defeat of the *Fatah*–led Palestinians, however, laid the groundwork for the emergence of full–fledged terrorist organizations such as Black September, a radical group that operated as an arm of the "moderate" PLO until it split off on its own. The name itself commemorates the *fedayeen's* expulsion from Jor-

dan, and they took their revenge on the man who directed King Hussein's forces, Premier Wafsi Tal, by assassinating him the following year in Cairo.

While terrorists have never hesitated at murdering any Arab leader who was not in strict agreement with the dogma of their particular group, it is generally not considered socially acceptable to blame other "brother" Arabs for their numerous defeats to Israel. The fledgling terrorists saw the Western world as the cause of virtually all Arab problems––whether perceived or real––and several factors combined to make Western Europe an excellent target for their activities. Initially, these countries made particularly juicy targets because of their close proximity to the Middle East and the fact that their open societies allowed the terrorists a remarkable degree of freedom to carry out their activities.

These new terrorists were also a particularly media–savvy bunch who fully understood the rami-

The grand finale of the Palestine Liberation Organization's September 1970 hijacking of three civilian airliners. Their 300 passengers were held for a week and, after their release, the aircraft were blown up at an abandoned airfield near Amman, Jordan.

fications of the still–evolving revolution in global telecommunications. Recent advances in television technology allowed the terrorist networks to increase their range beyond the printed word of newspapers, and much of the world's population now lived with their acts as a daily fact of life. Ratings–conscious news agencies and the viewers themselves had enabled the television camera to become one of the terrorists' chief weapons.

The use or threat of violence against individuals to affect a much larger, related group is not a new phenomenon; what is call "terrorism" today is a tactic of warfare that has been employed throughout history. Bombing, hijacking, assassination, and kidnapping are simply facets of this type of warfare magnified a thousand–fold by the electronic media. In the early 1970s, the world was introduced to such new television stars as Black September* and the Baader–Meinhoff Gang. Their activities were caught on television in 1970 when several commer-

cial airliners were hijacked and taken with their 300 passengers and crew to Dawson Field, a desert airfield 40 miles from Amman that had formerly been used by Britain's Royal Air Force. After a week, the hostages were removed from the aircraft which were then blown up in full view of the world. But the event having the deepest and most far–reaching impact was the drama which unfolded at the 1972 Olympic Games in Munich, West Germany.

*One of the many organization names used by Sabri Khalil al–Banna (alias Abu Nidal) in an effort to sow confusion in the West as well as make the "armed struggle" against Israel appear larger than it is. In addition to Black September, other names used by the Abu Nidal Organization include: Fatah Revolutionary Council, Black June Organization, the Arab Revolutionary Brigades and Revolutionary Organization of Socialist Muslims.

Viewers were stunned by image after image of the wanton murder of innocents flashing across the screen, and governments in the West soon felt their power to control events slipping from their hands. Terrorist actions—or even the threat of such actions—were increasingly shaping policy decisions on major questions.

One ramification of these terrorist attacks not observed by the public was the new requirements

As an instructer looks on, a member of SAS takes position and returns fire against mock terrorists during a training exercise. He is positioned behind the engine block, which can provide adequate protection against most conventional pistol and rifle ammunition.

placed on international law enforcement and military forces. After the failure to negotiate or rescue successfully for the release of the Israeli athletes, West Germany's security needs were scrutinized from every possible angle with Teutonic efficiency. The findings were many, but the realists who would have to face the next round of fighting concluded that virtually every Western nation was now in the battle with this ancient form of warfare. The emergence of a new combatant—the counterterrorist—marked Western Europe's response.

Each country dealt with the new problem based on its own perception of how various political, economic, social, and, in some cases, religious factors affected security considerations. The Germans established a special unit within its border police—later presented to the world as GSG-9, short for *Grenzschutzgruppe 9*—and the French formed the *Groupe d'Intervention de la Grendarmerie National* (GIGN). The British turned to their old standby, the SAS, while the Americans took the approach of wait and see, or more typically, "This will not happen to us." Yet, as the world continued to spin through the early 1970s, it was painfully obvious that the terrorists were moving a step or two ahead of the various national security forces and could attack whenever or wherever it was to their advantage. The organizations established to blunt terrorist attacks would, however, soon prove that they were forces to be reckoned with.

In October 1977 at Mogadishu Airport in Somalia, the German GSG-9 took revenge for their country's embarrassment at Munich by accomplishing a difficult aircraft "takedown" in response to a hijacking. Unknown to the terrorists, the Germans had learned much from the tragedy of Munich, and, with the help of two SAS commandos who blew open the aircraft's doors, a thirty-man GSG-9 force stormed the plane during the early morning hours. Later, in May 1980, the SAS gained international fame by conducting one of the most daring and highly publicized hostage rescues, when Pagoda Troop of B Squadron, 22nd SAS Regiment, launched their spectacular assault on the Iranian Embassy in Princess Gate, London, as television cameras broadcast the action around the world.

Preceding these events was the most famous rescue operation of the period: the raid on Entebbe Airport in Uganda, conducted by the Israeli special forces. Launched from bases within their own borders, more than 2,500 miles to the north, the commandos of Unit 269 flew directly into the site where 103 hostages were held. In the early morning darkness of July 4, 1976, Operation *Thunderbolt* was

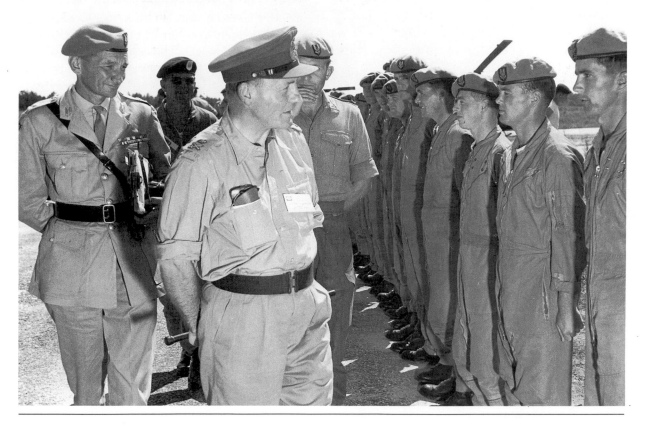

Great Britain's 22nd SAS and US Special Forces have enjoyed a long, close relationship which began in earnest during the late 1950s. (**Above**) Lieutenant General Sir Charles Richardson, Britain's Director General of Military Training, inspects an SAS unit during an exercise with 5th and 7th Special Forces Groups at Camp Troy, North Carolina, September 28, 1962. General Richardson's visit turned out to be a pivotal event for the SAS. While the conservative British military establishment had grudgingly conceded the regiment's value in certain situations, the unit was generally thought of as little more than a "private army" of ill–disciplined mavericks that skimmed some of Britain's best soldiers from the top of traditional regiments. A tour with the SAS could kill a young officer's career.

At Camp Troy and Fort Bragg, Richardson witnessed SAS troopers studying advanced demolition and field medicine techniques plus engaging in specialized training in foreign languages, as well as a worldwide assortment of weapons. He left North Carolina greatly impressed with what he saw, and the almost immediate improvement in the attitude of the British military establishment toward the SAS was credited to the general's glowing report.

The same month that General Richardson visited SAS elements training in the United States, the US Special Forces soldier who would later found DELTA, Charlie Beckwith, was leading a troop from A Squadron, SAS, in a combined exercise with the French "paras" of the *1st Bataillon de Parachutistes de Choc* in Corsica. Beckwith had been attached to the regiment as part of an ongoing exchange program and, in 1963, would ship out to Malaya with the SAS to take part in deep–jungle penetration missions against guerrillas along the Thai border. The tour nearly cost him his life but, upon his return to Fort Bragg, he pushed hard (very hard) to have SAS training and organizational techniques adopted by Special Forces.

Israeli commandos, circa 1960, are representative of the high degree of individuality commonly found in elite special operations units. Informally dressed in a variety of military jackets, coats, scarves, and sweaters, they are a diverse lot with members who might easily pass themselves off as Britons, Arabs, Frenchmen, or Americans. Indeed, they may have once been Britons, Arabs, Frenchmen or Americans before emigrating to Israel. Such elite troopers from Unit 269 were responsible for the successful hostage rescue at Entebbe. Note the use of personal weapons of different types and calibers attuned to the taste of the individual soldier. The soldier in the center is armed with the standard Soviet assault rifle of the day, the 7.62mm Kalashnikov AK-47, while the others carry 9mm Uzi submachine guns, which were based on earlier Czechoslovakian weapons but designed and produced in Israel.

carried out with clockwork precision. Keeping it simple, the rescue force landed in four C-130s (why jump your men in when they can be landed in a nice neat package?). The lead Hercules casually taxied to within 200 yards of the terminal building holding the hostages, and a black Mercedes sedan— the standard mode of transportation of all Ugandan officers from company commander on up—rolled serenely down the ramp. The sedan cruised up to the brightly lit building, followed by a pair of non-descript Land Rovers, and suddenly disgorged nine Unit 269 commandos.

Within minutes, the Israeli strike force had secured the terminal area and airfield perimeter, removing a potential problem by blowing up the Ugandan MIG fighter aircraft and then loaded up the rescued hostages. The rescue force commander, Colonel Jonathan Netanyahu, was killed, as well as the entire terrorist gang and an undetermined number of Ugandan soldiers protecting the hostage takers. All but one of the hostages, an elderly woman who had been taken to a hospital and was later murdered, were quickly freed and flown to Nairobi, Kenya, where casualties were transfered to a waiting jet airliner equipped for medical emergencies. The GSG-9 chief, Colonel UlrichWegener, had also accompanied the Israelis, probably because two West German terrorists were involved in the hijacking.

Americans Become Targets

The United States entered the CT arena as a very unwilling participant. The primary reasons were America's deeply engrained tradition of keeping military and police powers well separated and the resultant conservative approach of the US military leadership when dealing with what they felt was inherently a police problem. Neither the political nor military hierarchies originally supported the view, held by many in the lower echelons, of the increasing danger to the United States and its interests by media–savvy terrorists.

US intelligence agencies gained their first direct lessons from the *nouveau* terrorists during the September 1970 uprising in Jordan. It was feared that *Fatah* insurgents would seize the US Embassy in Amman, and US paratroopers were alerted to, if necessary, seize the International Airport, allow an armored force to land, race into Amman and retake the Embassy.

As with Operation *Eagle Claw* some ten years later, the Jordanian rescue plan was complicated, unwieldy, and fraught with unnecessary risks. For example, the 509th Airborne Infantry, which was selected to seize the airport, would have had to fly to Jordan via an extremely lengthy, circuitous route from their staging area in West Germany. Instead of taking the normal route over continental Europe to reach the eastern Mediterranean, their operational plan called for a flight out into the North Sea and Atlantic Ocean around Spain to the Gibraltar slot, and then travel the length of the Mediterranean. The force would have to take this roundabout route because the "allies" of NATO would not grant overflight rights—a situation unpleasantly similar to what F-111 pilots would find sixteen years later during a retaliatory raid on Libya for sponsoring a terrorist bombing.

American planners were faced with a number of similar situations over the next two years, and missions were not approved for execution. Either White House or State Department jitters prevented the launching of airborne or Special Forces units to counter terrorist assaults. Terrorist networks in the Middle East, however, could easily strike soft targets and continued to target Israeli citizens. Americans stationed in Germany, as well as West Germans, found themselves the targets of former antiwar students now turned terrorists. In May 1972, the Baader–Meinhoff Gang, also known as the Red Army Faction, finally forced the issue on the United States by conducting six separate bombings.

Their targets were such sacred areas as the officers' club in Frankfurt and the headquarters building of US Army, Europe, located in the sleepy university town of Heidelberg. The news media provided some coverage of these strikes but, understandably, only a fraction of the blow–by–blow reporting which characterized the debacle of that year's Olympic Games.

While the taking of American hostages was not yet a problem, perceptive military leaders realized that the United States needed to be ready and able to respond to terrorism, and units within the Army's Special Forces community were tasked to conduct rescues using what is commonly referred to as the "hasty option response." In lay terms, this means that if the hostage takers begin to harm their prisoners, the team attempts a rescue as quickly and efficiently as possible. The lives of the hostages are of utmost concern, but the hasty response does not allow for the meticulous planning, coordination, and rehearsals that are required to carry out the surgical strikes so often associated with the highly skilled CT units. The hasty response is the operation that all counterterrorists hope they never have to conduct. It is the option that makes a commander wake up at night in a cold sweat.

Due to command relationship conflicts and the numerous constraints on personnel and funds, which prevent in–depth training, the hasty option mission is still found in a number of Army Special Forces groups around the world. This approach, however, leaves little for the in–depth training required to perfect even the most fundamental aspects of aircraft or room entry techniques.

Soon after Munich, a number of American military and civilian advisors recommended that a suitable force be established to fight terrorism. But it was not until the increased threat was brought home to President Jimmy Carter and the feasibility of creating a unit like those who struck at Entebbe

The aftermath of a Red Army Faction car bomb explosion at Rhein–Main Air Base outside Frankfurt, West Germany, August 8, 1985. Over twenty people were injured and the blast killed one US airman and the wife of another. The explosives were packed into a car with forged US license plates and driven to the parking lot outside the headquarters of the 435th Tactical Air Wing. It is believed that the terrorist who drove the vehicle gained access to the base by using the identification card of a US serviceman murdered the previous night.

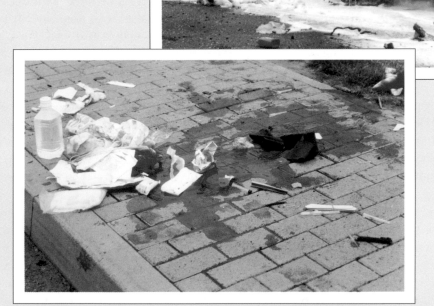

and Mogadishu that the United States acknowledged the need to establish its own full–time, state–of–the–art counterterrorist response unit. The success of Operation *Thunderbolt* further confirmed the idea that many US planners had been fostering. The United States needed to have a small, surgical force capable of carrying out such operations. It was their contention that, despite the claims of the airborne community, Ranger companies and battalions were neither trained nor equipped for hostage rescues.

From the smoke of military infighting and political intrigue, 1st Special Forces Operational Detachment–DELTA was formed in 1977. Its name is derived from standard Special Forces terminology. Six ALPHA detachments (A teams), commanded by captains, make up a company–sized BRAVO detachment (B team), commanded by a major. A CHARLIE detachment (C team) is a battalion–sized organization commanded by a lieutenant colonel. Since the 1st Special Forces Operational Detachment was commanded by a full colonel and structured along completely separate lines, following the squadron–troop structure of Britain's famed SAS, it became a DELTA detachment. Using the concept of the troop and the squadron as the building block or base, it initially trained to conduct counterterrorist operations. Recent activities in Iraq and Kuwait, however, reveal that DELTA's one–dimensional media image of a super–secret counterterrorist team falls well short of reality. The 1st Special Forces Operational Detachment is a multifaceted unit much like its counterpart, the SAS.

DELTA and *Blue Light*

Both DELTA's sponsors and opponents within the military held firm––and diametrically opposed—ideas on who should respond to the terrorist challenge. The majority of DELTA's sponsors were typical of America's military leadership. They were extremely conservative officers who were slow to respond to the terrorist threat, but once convinced that it was very real indeed, they were bulldogs in their support of the unit. And, like its sponsors, those who had worked hard to undermine or side-track DELTA (primarily because they didn't understand the nature of the threat) eventually gave it their full support when ordered.

At the top was Army Chief of Staff General Bernard Rogers. This astute Kansan and Rhodes scholar watched as the armies of Great Britain and West Germany rapidly took on what most American policymakers refer to as "police powers" normally kept out of the military's hands. After the Carter White House made it clear that they wanted a unit with specialized capabilities, Rogers gave his blessing for DELTA's formation. He told the relevant senior planners that he wanted the unit operational—and wanted it now!

The individual most instrumental in DELTA's birthing process was Lieutenant General Edward C. "Shy" Meyer. As the Deputy Chief of Staff for Operations, he was one of the most influential senior officers on the Army staff. It was from his office, that plans and policy for how the US Army would operate were issued. General Meyer took a direct, personal interest in DELTA. From the time that the need for a counterterrorist force was identified through its birth and Operation *Eagle Claw*, Meyer was always present in some form, providing guidance and support. The rest of the Army may have called him "Shy," but to DELTA he was "Moses" because he always seemed to be able to part the waters for them.

Next in the line of supporters came General William DePuy, commander of the Training and Doctrine Command. General DePuy was *the* expert in training; even though he was as conventional a soldier as any, he clearly recognized that a force was needed "like the SAS," as he was often quoted as saying during major policy meetings. He had to be won over before General Rogers and others could be addressed, but that proved to be easy after his inquiries about similar organizations in Europe demonstrated that an effective CT unit could be formed within the US Army. He would provide the training support.

The remainder of the cast were found at Fort Bragg, North Carolina. Fort Bragg has often been referred to as "home of the airborne" because of the vast numbers of parachute and related units based there. Bragg was also the home turf of the members of the US Army's Special Forces. The individuals making up these organizations possess unique skills, and it was from this elite body that DELTA's supporters and opponents would come.

The architect of DELTA was the commandant of the Special Forces School: a gruff veteran of the guerilla wars in Southeast Asia named Colonel Charlie Beckwith. Not only did "Chargin' Charlie" have a wealth of experience in the realm of unconventional operations, but he also knew who the power brokers were and how to use them. For example, in 1975, when General "Iron Mike" Healy was reassigned from his command at the John F. Kennedy Special Warfare Center at Fort Bragg, his replacement was Major General Robert "Barbed Wire Bob" Kingston. Kingston's association with Beckwith could be traced back to the days when Beckwith was an exchange officer with the SAS and Kingston was with the British Parachute Regiment. The two had also just served together at the Joint Casualty Resolution Center in Nakhon Phanom, Thailand, in 1973–1974. Kingston would work closely with General Meyer to establish an SAS–type unit.

It was during Colonel Beckwith's tour as commandant that the special operations community watched Europe's response to the outrages of various extremist groups. Located in an area known as "Smoke Bomb Hill," members of the Special Forces refined their traditional skills and added the hasty response to their repertoire. Special Forces, however, were responsible for carrying out a wide range of missions and could not dedicate much of their training efforts toward hostage situations.

Other soldiers who lent their guidance and support during this critical period were the commander of the 10th Special Forces Group, Colonel Othan "Shali" Shalikashville; General Frederick J. "Fritz" Kroesen, of Forces Command, who controlled all units stationed in the United States; and the XVIII Airborne Corps's chief of staff, Brigadier General James Lindsay. At one point during DELTA's shaky beginning, Shalikashville lined up all his senior commissioned and noncommissioned officers and told them flatly, "The job that Colonel Beckwith has to do is more important than the job we have to do. I would encourage anyone who has the desire to try out for this unit." As for Lindsay, when General Kingston's successor refused Beckwith's request to move DELTA into Bragg's underutilized post stockade, he saw to it that the unit would get it, reasoning, "Here we've got a nice stockade facility where we're keeping eleven bad guys. . . . Why don't we take the eleven and put them downtown in the Fayetteville jail? Your use of the stockade is better than the use it's being put to now. Colonel, you've got it!" Beckwith was obviously pleased that his problem had been solved so quickly but believed that the general would never see another promotion because he was just too practical. Ten years later, however, Lindsay would wear a total of eight stars on his shoulders and become the commander of the newly created Special Operations Command responsible for providing combat–ready special operations forces for rapid deployment to other unified commands around the world.

Still, support of the special operations community was not very strong at this point. Meticulously trained Special Forces units had conducted numerous missions during the Vietnam War, but now there was not a need for such specialists—or so the conventional leadership thought. And the conventional leadership controlled the Army and downsizing in forces that was taking place. Providentially, control of Special Forces fell to the commander of the JFK Special Warfare Center, and since General Kingston, his boss, was in control, Beckwith had the degree of freedom required to bring DELTA on line.

Charlie A. Beckwith of DELTA, circa 1979.

Complaints by the Rangers that DELTA would deepen their current manpower problems (partially true) and that the unit duplicated some of their functions (untrue) were brushed aside early on. Beckwith's only real opposition came from the commander of the 5th Special Forces Group at Bragg, Colonel Robert "Black Gloves" Montell, who believed that the shoot–from–the–hip hasty response was perfectly adequate. Montell was one of the Army's most professional and experienced officers. Always impeccably dressed, he wore what was commonly referred to as the "Bad Tolz" uniform. With pistol belt stripped and worn over olive drab jungle fatigues, spit–shined jungle boots, and an ever–present pair of black gloves topped off by the coveted green beret, he provided even the most hard–eyed professional with a source of pride in those days after Vietnam.

About the time that the DELTA program seemed to be a sure thing, Kingston was transferred to Korea, and Major General Jack "Bobo" Mackmull assumed command. No doubt Mackmull had received his marching orders from Washington to keep the program on track, but as a West Pointer and aviator, he was not very familiar with the missions and capabilities of this strange little unit under

his command and, unfortunately, made little effort to learn. Once DELTA was approved for activation, Mackmull was told to come up with a backfill unit until DELTA was certified for operations some two years in the future. Montell's 5th Special Forces Group received the nod.

To meet this requirement, Montell selected forty Special Forces troopers from within the community and trained them in hasty response techniques. This unit was code–named *Blue Light*. Operating under the principle that a bird in the hand is worth two in the bush, Mackmull threw his weight *Blue Light's* way regarding both funding and personnel. Despite reassurances from insiders, it appears that Beckwith feared that Montell's stalwart professionals would derail DELTA before it had a chance to prove its concept. If Beckwith lost his support in Washington, he would lose his unit. And DELTA was truly his.

As with most endeavors, it is not necessarily who is the best qualified, but who has the most support. Initially, that is what kept DELTA and its concept of a full–time, low–visibility CT organization alive. When General Rogers discovered that expected resources were being routed away from DELTA, he, as they say, "went ballistic." From that point on, through the support from the chief of staff on down the line, DELTA was allowed to gain the necessary breathing room to grow from nothing to a full–fledged force.

After 1st Special Forces Operational Detachment–DELTA was activated in October 1977, Beckwith had to select and train his new unit. DELTA troopers would have to be able to blend perfectly into the civilian world, when required, and possess unique skills that included everything from the relevant military arts to climbing the sides of buildings and hot–wiring cars. As luck would have it, DELTA had just completed their certification exercises. The date was November 4, 1979.

A

B

C

D

E

F

Weapons and Equipment

Pistols

In the special operations community, an oft–repeated comment on the controversy over which round is better, the .45cal ACP (automatic Colt pistol) or the 9mm parabellum, goes like this: "Opinions are like assholes, everyone has one." Stopping power, mass versus velocity, number of rounds versus weight—the argument seems neverending but, over time, weapons firing the 9mm (.38cal) round have become respected additions to DELTA's arsenal.

Modern conventional warfare generally calls for relatively light–weight, high–velocity rounds such as the Colt M16's .223cal/5.56mm or NATO's standard .308cal/7.62mm, that are effective out to ranges of several hundred yards. For the takedown of a hostage holding site, however, 100 feet is considered an extreme range. What the counterterrorist needs is a heavy slug that will knock a man down with as few shots as possible, and rounds smaller than .45cal have often proven themselves to be inadequate against a determined enemy. As early as the beginning of this century, Moro warriors battling US soldiers in the Philippines were not stopped by government issue .38cal pistols and, most recently, in the GSG-9 operation against aircraft hijackers at Mogadishu, Somalia, the German commander was forced to empty his snub–nosed .38cal into a psyched–up terrorist who continued fight even as six bullets ripped into his body. For this reason, many operatives prefer to have a bigger weapon.

A big (*very* big) round like that from the Smith & Wesson .44cal Magnum will drop a hijacker in his tracks but, unfortunately, the high–powered bullet is likely to go through its intended target as well as several seats and passengers before it stops. Moreover, the .44 Magnum's substantial kick when firing can delay reacquisition of the same or other targets—possibly with disastrous results. The .45 ACP round fired by the Colt or Springfield Armory M1911A1 and other automatic pistols has a great advantage over its famous friend during takedowns. An old joke among shooters is that the .45's bullet travels so slowly that, for an instant, you can actually see it speeding towards the target. With such a low muzzle velocity—at roughly 830 feet per second, it's almost half that of the .44 Magnum— hostage safety is greatly increased since there is more likelihood that the captors' bodies will stop the bullets.

But while this would seem to make the .45 the obvious weapon of choice for takedowns, many shooters have gravitated to the 9mm Beretta Model

(**A**) The basic Colt 5.56mm M16A2 assault rifle, (**B**) Colt 9mm submachine gun, and (**C**) Colt 5.56mm Model 733 Commando assault rifle. (**D**) The Mossberg 12–gauge Cruiser 500 shotgun; (**E**) the Remington 7.62mm M40A1 sniping rifle mounting a ten–power US Marine Corps telescope instead of the Redfield twelve–power telescope commonly used by DELTA; and (**F**) the Spring-field Armory 7.65mm M21 sniping system based on the M14 rifle. (**G**) The Beretta 9mm Model 92F pistol, called the M9 by the US Army and (**H**) the Colt .45cal M1911A1 automatic pistol. (**I**) The General Motors Guide Lamp Division .45cal M3 submachine gun often described as "a pleasant gun to shoot"; (**J**) the Walther 9mm MP-K submachine gun, which served as a useful bridge between the M3 and (**K**) the Heckler & Koch 9mm MP5 submachine gun. (**L**) The Heckler & Koch 9mm MP5 SD3 submachine gun with integral silencer.

When DELTA was formed, its armorers developed special lighting equipment that could be attached to weapons for night operations. Today, such devices can be obtained off–the–shelf from manufacturers or are integral to the weapons. (**Top**) A Hensoldt aiming point projector fitted to a Heckler & Koch MP5 A2 submachine gun and (**bottom, lower left**) a laser pointer built into the forearm of a Mossberg 12–gauge shotgun. Also note the Stabo rings attached to the soldier's tactical vest and the flash/bang grenade (an SAS invention) ready for use in his left hand.

92 pistol. The high velocity of its 9mm parabellum slug is easily brought below 1,000 feet per second by reducing the round's charge, and, depending on which variant of the Model 92 is carried into a fight, the counterterrorist can count on making almost twice as many shots before reloading than he would if he carried a conventional .45cal automatic.

The automatic pistol made by Colt and the higher–quality product manufactured by the Springfield Armory, normally fire from eight– and seven–bullet magazines respectively, and can each carry an additional round in the chamber, while the Model 92 and its variants have thirteen– and fifteen–round magazines. The tradeoff is that while 9mm bullets are indeed smaller, their size is *adequate* and the Model 92 has more of them. Moreover, the ammunition a DELTA trooper carries on his body and in his weapon is all that he can count on having available

The Heckler & Koch MP5 SD3 fires 9mm ammo and, with its collapsing stock and integral silencer, it is an outstanding weapon for the closein fight. The sound supressor is a two-stage external silencer. The first stage of the system will absorb gasses while the second absorbs the muzzel blast and flame. The bolt noise is absorbed by buffers made of rubber. If you use subsonic ammo, the report cannot be heard more than fifteen to twenty feet away.

to him during a takedown. If everything goes as planned, there will be very little shooting. If the operation "goes sour," its just Delta and the terrorists in a high–intensity shootout of unknown duration. A situation can easily develop where the first side to run out of bullets loses and, with a weight nearly half that of a .45cal bullet, 9mm rounds can be carried in great quantity without encumbering a trooper.

Submachine Guns

The same holds true, of course, for submachine guns. Although pistols are preferred in most hostage situations, submachine guns become a necessity when large target areas or many terrorists (four and up) are involved. Delta initially settled on the domestically produced .45cal M3A1 "grease gun," a World War II vintage weapon that went out of production in the early 1950s and was generally shunned by the US Army. Interestingly enough, though, the very features that made it unpopular with most soldiers, enabled it be an extraordinarily effective tool for room–clearing: a low muzzle velocity which allowed its heavy slugs to slam into— not through—a terrorist and a rate of fire slow enough to enable single shots to be squeezed off

without disturbing the shooter's aim.

Acquiring adequate replacement parts for the weapon was an armorer's nightmare, however, and the old friend soon made way for a variety of submachine guns. Selection of weapons is a personal choice that often revolves around such factors as weight, reliability, how often must you clean it between firings, amount of ammo per magazine, and accuracy after it has been beat up in a parachute jump. The Heckler & Koch MP5 and the less expensive, easily concealable Walther MP-K are both German arms that fire 9mm rounds, as does the Colt submachine gun that has many parts common to the M16 rifle. The compact Colt Model 733 Commando assault rifle also benefits from this commonality and can be used on missions requiring its higher velocity 5.56mm round.

Trooper in southeastern Iraq armed with a Colt Model 727 carbine. Note the troopers sterile uniform (no identification or other markings) and longish hair. A three–power telescopic site is mounted on the carbine.

Shotguns

Shotguns are also useful in a variety of situations but are most commonly associated with forced entry techniques. Heavy rifled slugs can be depended on to supply the pure smashing power needed to quickly and efficiently blow the hinges off most doors. Sabot rounds, on the other hand, allow deeper penetration of the target and are best employed against vehicle or aircraft engines and door–locking mechanisms. After initial entry has been gained at a hostage holding site, shotguns can be used to force additional doors or, if necessary, against the hostage takers.

A 12–gauge rifled slug (**left**) and 12–gauge sabot slug (**right**).

Ammunition

Terrorists cannot be reasoned with and will attempt to kill their captives if a rescue is attempted, so when choosing ammunition, CT specialists want a man stopper that will knock a terrorist down and keep him down. While the heavy .45cal remains an ideal round for hostage situations, the lethality of smaller slugs, like the 9mm, can be greatly enhanced by using "soft–point" bullets with hollow or flat tips. The unusual point causes the soft, lead slug to expand into a broad, mushroom–shaped projectile upon entering the body, often doubling in diameter and increasing its shock effect dramatically. In a war where the armed forces of one nation are openly pit-

(**Left** to **right**) Flat–point, hollow–point and conventional bullets.

ted against those of another, the rules of land warfare prohibit the use of such ammunition. DELTA troopers participating in a hostage rescue, however, are not subject to the restrictions of the Geneva Convention. Like their police counterparts, they can legally use hollow–point ammunition (or exploding rounds that shatter on impact) to subdue captors and save the lives of the hostages.

The actual weapons and ammunition used on a mission are determined by the nature of the target.

A takedown of an oil platform, for example, is a very different affair from that of an airliner cabin crowded with hostages sitting upright. Only the team members assaulting areas likely to contain the platform's captive crew need to worry about carrying weapons with limited velocity.

Advances in technology have also complicated matters for DELTA and other CT specialists by adding dangerous factors to the equation such as handguns and bombs with almost no metal parts. Initially, only law enforcement agencies and the military had access to the lightweight body armor made from Kevlar fabric (which, incidentally, does *not* set off metal detectors). Over the passage of time, however, this type of highly effective armor has greatly proliferated and, if not already in terrorist hands, can be easily obtained by third parties or simply stolen. When worn in thin, easily concealable layers, Kevlar will stop the low–velocity slugs normally required for passenger safety. Technology and tactics have provided solutions to these and other problems but the decades–old argument over the most appropriate weapons to use is something that will die harder than any flesh–and–blood fanatic.

Sniper Rifles

Nearly all DELTA weapons—whether old or new—have been "accurized" to some degree by the unit's own gunsmiths. Loose–fitting parts typically found even in quality mass–produced weapons are replaced by custom–built pieces with closer tolerances, specialized trigger mechanisms, and better sights. For example, before it was superseded by the heavy–barrelled 40XB sniper rifle (which was specially manufactured for DELTA by Remington Arms), modifications were made to the trusty old M14A1 to upgrade its already formidable performance as a sniper rifle.

Modifications typically included polishing and hand fitting of the gas cylinder and piston to improve operation and reduce carbon buildup. Barrels were always carefully selected to ensure correct specification tolerances and are bedded into the forearms with a fiberglass compounds. Trigger housing groups were carefully fitted and polished to provide a crisp hammer release and suppressors fitted to eliminate sound and flash which could give the sniper's position away. Receivers could also be individually fitted to stocks using a fiberglass compound. The US Army now purchases an off–the–shelf versions of this weapon from the Springfield Armory called the M21 sniping rifle. DELTA troopers often use this weapon during training and it also receives considerable reworking such as having plastic spacers added to customize the length of the stock. The M40A1 and M24 sniping systems,

Flash/bang grenades with no–snag caps in an Eagle Industries hip pouch. Center pockets hold thirty–round clips for 9mm Heckeler & Koch submachine guns.

Nomex balaclava

Goggles with shatterproof lenses

H & K 9mm MP5 A2 submachine gun

Eagle Industries Tac III assault vest

Kevlar vest

Flex cuff pouch

Nomex gloves

Spare thirty–round magazine clipped to engaged magazine

Flashlight pouch

Gas mask pouch

Gadget bags

Rappelling belt

Beretta 9mm pistol with extended magazine

Spare 9mm magazine

Additional 9mm pistol magazines

Additional 9mm submachine gun magazines

Flash/bang grenades with no–snag caps

Eagle Industries flash/bang pouch

Nomex coveralls

Assault boots

DELTA troopers (and all CT specialists) wear mission–specific gear. For example, while the man at left is equipped for an "average" take-down, the SAS trooper at right is set to operate in a chemical environment and wears the minimum possible gear around his chest and hips to help ensure that nothing will snag his climbing rope.

standardized versions of the 40XB, are also being acquired by the Army and Marine Corps.

Grenades

The famous "pineapple," more properly known as the Mk II fragmentation hand grenade, is what most people think of when this type of weapon is mentioned, but the long–obsolete pineapple was pulled from front–line service with the US Army over a decade before DELTA was formed. A cylindrical canister, about the size of a shaving cream can, is used for concussion grenades, chemical grenades (such as tear gas), and the flash/bang grenade (a description of the grenade's employment is on page 57). This design allows the grenade's user to gently role it a predictable direction and distance into a room, unlike the Mk II and its similarly shaped or round descendants which are designed for throwing and, if rolled, could wobble almost anywhere—including back up against the very wall that a trooper is using for shelter! Before the recent fielding of the flat–sided M560 series fragmentation grenades, if a mission profile called for use of an antipersonnel grenade with a predictable roll, an M57 or M61 would have to be soldered into an appropriately sized tin can to achieve the desired effect. Once the pin was pulled and the safety lever fell away, a nearly perfect roll could be achieved every time.

Nomex hood

Leyland and Birmingham respirator

Climbing rope

Leather protective glove

Rappelling harness

Figure "8" descending link

Snap link

Kevlar vest

Browning (*Fabrique Nationale*) 9mm High–Power Mark 2 pistol

Leather protective glove

Nomex coveralls

Rope bag

Climbing/assault boots

The figure "8" descending link not only prevents clothing from being dragged into the snaplink but also allows the climber to control his descent with only one hand while leaving the other free to fire weapons, throw grenades, or place charges. This mountaineering device was added after the operation at the Iranian Embassy in London where an SAS commando had almost been killed by his own explosives. The soldier had become stuck outside a window after a demolition had been emplaced and its fuse ignited. Only quick action by his buddies on the roof above saved his life.

Clothing

From the early days of hasty option operations, counterterrorist equipment has steadily evolved. Lightweight, highly rigid specialized clothing and equipment has now become a standard for CT teams. Several European units such as the SAS and Germany's GSG-9 found out through practical experiences at the Iranian Embassy in London and at the Mogadishu airport that general issue equipment is great for conventional forces but suffers from dangerous shortfalls when used during specialized operations. Much of the evolution in equipment has focused on the tactical assault vest and modular pouches attached to the upper torso and hips.

They incorporate such items as extra ammo, radio, and first aid pouches along with rappelling rings. Counterterrorist operations are very personal affairs. Despite the fact that the soldiers belong to teams, each man puts a great deal of faith in his individual gear. The equipment *must* be capable of accommodating number of modifications to handle, for example either flash/bang or gas grenades; MP5 magazines or Colt 733 Commando magazines. The problem was solved by creating a basic vest capable of handling interchangeable sets of pouches and holders for the problems specific to a given mission.

Chapter 3

The Making of a DELTA Trooper

In the 82d Airborne, I was better than any guy in my company. Over here I gotta hustle just to keep up.

a DELTA trooper

Joining a counterterrorist unit is very similar to breaking into the big leagues of pro sports. There are a few differences, however. Major league ball clubs have quite a few rookies on the squad, whereas the CT arena requires that units be composed exclusively of veterans with basic special operations skills already refined to a razor edge. And an error in the major leagues won't cost you your life or the lives of your team members.

CT units are composed of senior noncommissioned officers (NCOs) and several rather well–qualified officers. Continuous assignments in such units have not always been career enhancing, and despite the Army's recent elevation of Special Forces to full branch status, few officers stay around for more than one or two tours with the Special Forces groups. Those who do are usually *extremely* dedicated to their units, its troops, and the basic

US and German counterterrorists conducting a joint exercise involving rappelling, door–busting, and room–clearing techniques.

idea that the worldwide terrorist threat and its network of supporters should be met head–on and eliminated. They usually hold the respect of their fellow team members, who are not as concerned with an officer's rank as they are with his ability to shoot straight and back up his team.

Counterterrorism is only one of the missions assigned by law to the special operations community. The men who are charged with carrying out these low–visibility operations are chosen from a wide range of backgrounds and spheres of our society. Each is selected based on his talents and the unit's need to fill particular slots within its ranks. The question, "How does the whole process start?" begins with this fundamental requirement to fill open positions.

Selection and Training

Special operations units, and especially the close–knit counterterrorist outfits, recruit in several different ways. Special attention is given to the "old' boy network." As with any other business or

167

All DELTA trainees are jump qualified, and previously acquired skills, such as scuba diving are further refined during training. Troopers are assigned to specialized teams containing soldiers with the same skills. Many teams and elements are multidisciplined.

occupation, word of mouth and vouching for someone are key ingredients in the selection process. A second method is to simply advertise the need for people. DELTA recruitment teams make the rounds of training centers, troop posts, and such facilities as the Command and General Staff College or NCO advance schools. These recruitment drives preceed DELTA's fall and spring selection and assessment courses. Recruitment letters are also routinely mailed from Army personnel centers and, more recently, as the unit has edged out of the black into a rather dark grey, volunteers have been openly solicited in Army journals.

DELTA's rigid entrance requirements are clearly spelled out for career officers and NCOs who may be enticed to leave behind the warm comforts of their current postings for a new adventure. The pitch is always straightforward and unambiguous:

"ASSIGNMENT OPPORTUNITIES are available in the 1st Special Forces Operational Detachment–DELTA. DELTA is the Army's special operations unit that has been organized to conduct missions that combine rapid response with the surgical application of a wide variety of unique skills and the flexibility to maintain the lowest possible profile of US involvement. . . . DELTA gives commissioned and noncommissioned officers unique opportunities for professional development. . . ."

A fourth and less–known method is for soldiers to be individually sought out by recruiters, based on a screening of their official records. This method may also be used with word–of–mouth recommendations. Recruiters are usually looking for specific assets, such as language skills, key past assignments, military qualifications, or schools attended. From the compiled list of likely candidates, individuals are contacted and asked to volunteer.

Drawn from the Active Army, Army Reserve, and Army National Guard, all DELTA members must pass a background security investigation, be at least twenty–two years old, male, and a US citizen. Each soldier's records are screened for psychological abnormalities or recurring discipline problems, and those accepting the challenge receive very thorough physical and eye examinations. Commonly referred to as the Scuba/HALO physical, it is akin to the in–depth exams pilots receive.

After getting the thumbs up from the doctors, or "chancre mechanics," the prospective counterterrorist is subjected to a battery of tests to determine if he is psychologically sound. The last thing a unit in the midst of a mission needs is to find itself saddled with a would–be Rambo or a real–life psycho. The cost of not conducting extensive psychological tests was graphically displayed as early as the Munich incident in 1972. At one point, the terrorists moved into the sights of the German sharpshooters who then froze. The results were quite unsatisfactory from the Israelis' standpoint.

Approximately 100 prospective counterterrorists receive intensive physical testing every session and high scores are an absolute requirement. In DELTA's formative stage, its selection process closely followed the British SAS model. This was due to the fact that many of the individuals who had a hand in setting up the unit were the products of SAS–Special Forces exchange programs and the close working relations these units have always had. This aspect of the month–long selection process has not changed.

The candidate's ordeal begins with six grueling events which must be completed within a designated period and earning a minimum of sixty points each. The candidates are, of course, expected to do better than the minimum. Periodically, small modifications are made to the test; examples of what is expected of the volunteers include: forty–yard inverted crawl in twenty–five seconds; thirty–seven situps in one minute; thirty–three pushups in one minute; run, dodge and jump course in twenty–four seconds; two–mile run in sixteen minutes, thirty seconds; and 100–meter swim while fully clothed and wearing boots.

Following the test, the candidate has the opportunity to show how well he can accomplish a speed march. The route covers eighteen miles, and the

Soldiers using the Stabo technique to land on a Fort Bragg rooftop. Hanging free from the helo during their approach, the men land simultaneously instead of one at a time. The target area is framed with a two–by–four barrier in case any of the soldiers loses his footing.

individuals must traverse it as rapidly as possible. Since this is one of the psychological problems to overcome, the passing times are never published. However, most of those who have passed it seem to agree that ten–minute miles are almost too slow!

Those who have made it this far into the selection process now receive a real treat. Just like in the SAS course, the candidates now are asked to really show what they are made of and are taken to one of several sites for a combination speed march, compass course, and survival exercise. Tests were originally conducted near Troy, North Carolina, in the Uwharrie National Forest, but are now done on the even more rugged terrain of Camp Dawson, West Virginia; recently, a test site has been added in the secured areas of Nellis Air Force Base, Nevada.

The Freedom to Fail or Succeed

If you were one of the few candidates to reach the forty–mile land navigation exercise, you'd find that the basic scenario goes like this: With all the ceremony of going off to a maximum–security prison, you and the other candidates are trucked out to the test site, where each is dropped at separate starting points. As dawn begins to break, you are given a set of instructions that amount to little more than a compass heading and a point on the map marking the final destination perhaps a half–dozen miles away. You are to pick out your route, keeping in mind that the object is to get there as quickly as possible.

Off you go. As soon as you leave the gentleman who gave you the instructions, your thoughts run the gamut of, "What the hell am I doing here?" to "I hope I can pull this off." Even though you made some rough calculations at the starting point, you drop off to the side of the trail to double check the situation and ensure your initial calculations are correct. (Besides, you didn't want to look indeci-sive in front of the guy at the drop–off point.) Squinting more closely at the map, you find that the contour lines are so close together that they look like some gigantic drunk worm. In other words, it is all up and down, with a few nice cold creeks in between. Off again, you settle into the comfortable trot the old hands taught you back at Bragg's Smoke Bomb Hill or Fort Benning. As usual, it starts to rain a little, but for the average Airborne, Ranger, or Special Forces type, rain is not a stranger. Checking your compass to keep oriented, you now settle into the routine. In most cases, the trial would be more enjoyable if you didn't remember that this was much more than just an exercise. You are here to show someone that you can hack whatever it takes to be part of that group called DELTA.

As you navigate along the trail, the shoulder straps of your fifty–five–pound rucksack begin to make themselves known to you—especially as the ruck gets wetter. Sweat trickles down your armpits, gets in your eyes, and seems to find refuge in your already chaffed crotch. After about the first hour and a half, the experience factors of Ranger School and the Special Forces qualification course, along with the numerous Special Forces Group exercises, take over. So it's time to stop, take stock of the situation, and drink some water. Pausing along the trail, you look around the dense hardwoods that make up much of the terrain along the mountains. Sensing something in the underbrush near your left jungle boot, you slowly retreat a few steps as "Jake no shoulders" decides to rattle a friendly greeting. Your mind comprehends the danger, but in some ways you really do not want to think about what could have happened, especially if he got upset as you were sitting down to check your feet.

Moving down the trail, you find a better place to get out of the drizzle and change your socks and apply some Vaseline to your sensitive areas. You get your bearings one more time and are off. Whether you are running the selection course in the mountains of Appalachia, with its forests and numerous streams, or driving on in the Sierra Nevada wastelands, the expected results are the same. Just like General Forest, get there "firstest with the mostest." In your case, get there fastest—period.

You've been at this all day, the sun dipped below the wooded hills uncounted hours ago, and at each rendezvous, you hope that it will be the one site where you will be told to throw your ruck into the truck and get aboard. But for some bizarre reason, the only words you hear at each brief stop are the location of your next rendezvous. After about a dozen hours of this, many volunteers begin to rest too long or slow down so much that they are unable to make the twenty–hour time limit. Even good soldiers begin to look for excuses to quit, and many inevitably find them. But not you. Cold, wet, and numb with exhaustion, you move off again, continuing in search of whatever you are out here for until well after midnight, when you are unceremoniously informed that the exercise is over. The survivors rarely remember exactly where they've been and, as with the speed march, even know how far they went or how long it took.

By now, the steady attrition of volunteers has weeded the field down to perhaps a dozen or so survivors. Many of those returning to their home units have been cut because they were unable to

An exhausted instructor from the John F. Kennedy Special Warfare Center training group, after negotiating a demanding confidence course like DELTA's. He is indicative of the highly motivated, professional soldiers in the US special operations community.

meet the tough physical and navigational challenges, while others were sidetracked for other legitimate reasons, such as knee, ankle, or back injuries. Some, however, drop out because they simply were not mentally prepared to follow the course through to the end without the accustomed "you can do it!" prodding that had been an integral part of all previous training. The NCOs overseeing the selection course steadfastly refuse to provide this encouragement. In any event, DELTA makes a great effort to ensure that those not selected know that they are

A trainee negotiates stairsteps to a room mock–up during entry technique training at the SOT. The object is to engage the pop–up silhouette targets from uncomfortable angles while in motion.

not failures. Each candidate receives a certificate of training and is simply told he was not selected.

Looking back at the physical side of the selection process, a key aspect becomes crystal clear: It is structured to put the maximum psychological pressure on those being tested. The individual is provided the freedom to succeed or fail on his own. A candidate not only must know his physical, mental, and emotional makeup, but must be able to use it to his advantage. In the CT arena, there are many occasions where individual actions are required, and in those life–and–death situations, you get only one chance to succeed. As Sun Tzu pointed out

so long ago, you have to know yourself as well as your enemy. If you are not ready to run in seemingly aimless directions for hours through the dark, wet, torturous terrain of overgrown, forested mountains, the cross–country land navigation exercise is not for you. If you are not ready to know what real fear is, to meet it head on and beat it, DELTA is not for you.

The trip back to Fort Bragg takes on an unreal atmosphere after what has occurred. Every selection course will have a variable number of thoroughly exhausted candidates who will go on to face the final and, according to some, hardest part of the selection process: the interview. A board of DELTA veterans grills the survivors and determines who goes on for training.

"So you're infiltrating an unfriendly area prior to taking down a terrorist hideout. Say you come across two little girls. You can't leave them. Do you take them along, tie them up, or do you kill them?"

"Tell us a little about Machiavelli."

"What were the arguments for and against our acquiring the Virgin Islands during World War I?"

"Was President Truman right or wrong to fire MacArthur?"

By this point in the four–hour grilling, some volunteers have taken on the look of frightened animals. The questions are asked seriously, and the DELTA veterans expect serious answers.

"Well, Sergeant, you've given a fine performance so far. Now tell us what you tend to blow it on."

"Why should we take you? What can you offer DELTA?"

"You're a good soldier!? So what!? Sergeant, we're up to our ears in good soldiers. Tell us about your unique skills, what you're really good at that's not military related."

In this tension–charged atmosphere, there are few right or wrong answers. The board is looking at the individual as a whole: his values and how he is able to handle himself in this situation.

The objective of the selection course is to find individuals who can both work with the team and yet operate independently without orders. In the end, only about ten percent or fewer of the initial candidates actually make it into DELTA; and a rumor circulating through the special operations community contends that one group moving throughout the selection process lost virtually every man before the assessment was finished. While such an occurrence could certainly wreak havoc with the manning levels of a small, highly specialized organization, such problems can be ironed out if they are not persistent. Moreover, the nature of DELTA necessitates that its emphasis must remain focused on the quality, not quantity, of personnel entering the unit.

The SOT

As the new DELTA trainee drives along Gruber Road past MacKeller's Lodge, he thinks back to the recent events of the selection course. Now the staff sergeant is at Fort Bragg, reporting in for some of the finest—and toughest—training in the world. To his right, he sees a high cyclone fence and dirt road used by the security force who patrols it. Beyond the fence and nestled within the rough horseshoe formed by Gruber, Lambert, and Manchester Roads is the secure training facility constructed for the training of America's elite CT units and the home of DELTA. Called the Special Operations Training Facility (SOT), the multimillion–dollar complex became a reality through the increased support from congress and the president for the war on terrorism in the early 1980s.

Almost as if the world has opened up its secrets, the SOT unfolds in the form of large two– and three–story buildings and training areas for heli-borne insertions. The staff sergeant is immediately struck by how easy it is for virtually anyone to get a look at this surprisingly well–publicized facility. With counterterrorism such a security–conscious business, this visual access seems odd, but he writes it off as the price DELTA must pay for being on an "open post" like Fort Bragg and chuckles to himself when he remembers what started the whole process that led him to Gruber Road today: a public announcement in his branch journal, *Infantry*, that "assignment opportunities" were available in DELTA.

The newcomer passes the SOT's entrance and continues to drive north toward Manchester Road. He is rewarded with a clear view of numerous open–aired and enclosed ranges he'll be seeing a lot of over the next two years. A thrill rushes through him. This is going to be the ultimate adventure! Coming back to the reality of the moment, he makes an unauthorized U turn and pulls up to the brick guardhouse at the gate. His identification is scrutinized

A trainee practices pistol shooting at multiple targets at one of the SOT facility's numerous ranges. Note the semi–crouch stance and two–handed pistol grip.

against the incoming roster for the day, and he is directed to park and await his escort. The games, as they said in ancient Rome, are about to begin.

So far, everything the trainee has seen speaks well of the command emphasis placed on the Army's counterterrorist mission, from the White House down through the major subordinate headquarters, the Joint Special Operations Command (JSOC). In military terminology, it is a "high–speed" operation. As DELTA's newest recruit waits for his escort, he is startled to see an MH-6, bristling with darkened human figures instead of gun pods, zoom overhead. Along each side is a trio of soldiers buckled into special side platforms for rapid egress. Unseen by the trainee, the six commandos slip wearily from their "Little Bird" just a moment later at a helicopter pad near Lambert Road.

This specially modified Hughes chopper belongs to another important part of the team, the 160th Special Operations Aviation Regiment (Airborne), or SOAR. This unit is a result of the many problems experienced during *Desert I* and objectively outlined in its after–action review. Commonly referred to as the Holloway Report, it pointed out that a major area to restructure, if future missions were to stand a chance, was helicopter operations, and the covert aviation unit was duly formed at Fort Campbell, Kentucky. Originally named Task Force 160, it soon became the major US Army aviation support element for DELTA.

The commandos clearing the aircraft have darkened faces and wear a patrol, or "Ranger," cap. Clad in sturdy, olive drab jungle fatigues plus a wide assortment of specially made vests and other web gear, they also carry rappelling gloves, snaplinks and nonstandard Heckler & Koch MP5 submachine guns. As the SOAR 160 bird rises back into the sky, its stubby, rounded frame gives it the appear-

American counterterrorist team practicing pistol shooting from several different positions. Ranges such as this one provide enclosed areas to practice room–clearing methods out of sight of prying eyes.

ance of an overweight bumblebee or lethargic beetle attempting to gain flight.

Most CT operations require lightning fast entrances into the target area, along with shock effect and disorientation of the hostage takers. Carrying out such complicated maneuvers requires a great deal of training, teamwork, and the building of mutual respect for each member's abilities. That is what the new recruits are to learn during DELTA's five–month operators course at the SOT.

The facility's mission is to teach new methods and refine old skills in the art of counterterrorism. Many writers and observers have referred to the skills of eliminating a terrorist situation as antiterrorism. This, however, is incorrect. Antiterrorism is a term that refers to skills and techniques used by people or organizations which will help *prevent* them from becoming the victim of a terrorist attack. There are schools and courses where basic antiterrorist methods and tactics are taught, but the SOT addresses the final options of dealing with a terrorist incident that has *already occurred*. This is where DELTA comes into play: the counterterrorist arena.

Whenever the complex subject of counterterrorism is raised for discussion or debate, the argument that a specialized unit for CT operations is too expensive in terms of manpower and money usually comes to the fore. Regardless of whether this view is correct, it is undeniable that the political impact of a successful terrorist attack is often immense; the economic costs alone can run into the tens of millions of dollars, and priceless, innocent lives are put at risk or even lost. That is why dedicated units tasked to conduct CT operations are a must. How such units are configured is the decision of each country that fields them. Yet, one piece of the equation remains firm: Counterterrorist skills are highly perishable and must be kept at razor's edge if the team hopes to succeed. Appropriate training and constant studying of the enemy's methods, personnel, and organizational structure are an absolute necessity. The required skills and support apparatus are manpower– and resource–consuming, but countries employing counterterrorist units must be prepared to accept the costs. In the long run, it is a low–budget affair when compared to the economic and human costs of a successful terrorist strike.

A CT operation is composed of several distinct phases. First, the unit must get to the area of operations— possibly many hundreds or even thousands of miles away— by reliable, secure transportation. Simultaneously, immense amounts of intelligence must be collected, analyzed, and disseminated by a number of supporting agencies. A critical issue at this phase is who is in charge. The Army's Special Operations Command (SOCOM) supports the DELTA's training and related operational requirements but, in time of crisis, JSOC bypasses the SOCOM link and directs the unit and the nation's other CT assets. Once deployed, the State Department is the key desision–making element for foreign operations, while the Justice Department deals with problems within the United States. This clean, simple chain of command allows a "stovepipe" of direction and support to the unit and cuts out a number of middlemen who would unintentionally hinder the execution of a mission.

After arriving at the site of the "incident," the next phase deals with preparation. In its simplest form, this means that target surveillance is begun; outer and inner security rings are checked; command, control and liaison functions are established; and incoming intelligence is analyzed. After all the players are satisfied (or the situation forces the issue), the next phase is the assault, or "takedown," of the objective. Closely on its heels is the swift withdrawal of the force back to their homebase.

With this as background, where does the new trooper fit in? He is likely to fill a number of roles or positions, and his titles may be many. As he progresses within the organization, he will use his past skills and experiences to benefit the team he is assigned to. For example, he may be a sniper because he went to sniper school while assigned to a Ranger battalion. If his demolitions background is good, he may find himself dealing with some very exotic toys designed to blow off the smallest locks or take down the entire wall of a room with minimal disturbance to the occupants of the next room. As a "door kicker" or "shooter," his skills will be fine–tuned in the art of lockpicking, room entry, and target identification. Common phrases often associated with the skills or strengths of these unique professionals include the "double tap," "happiness is a head shot," and "reach out and touch someone."

The SOT provides troopers with various methods of entry, seizure, and exit of terrorist situations. They learn to rappel into second– and third–story windows to get at the terrorists and their victims, as well as how to most effectively kick open a door, use specially manufactured stun grenades to disorient the terrorists and then closely follow the blast into the room. Each member of a four–man team must know not only where he is going, but also precisely where his teammates will be and in which direction their fields of fire are directed.

In this closely orchestrated ballet of death known as close–quarters battle, the troopers learn to pick their targets quickly and then instantly

National Command Authority → Chairman Joint Chiefs of Staff → JSOC → SOCOM → DELTA place a minimum of two shots in an eye socket–sized kill zone from as far as fifty feet away. This technique is known as the double tap. Moving quickly through the area, the team learns to secure everyone (regardless of who they are) with plastic flex cuffs and leave the sorting out and medical treatment to the follow–on police forces. These strong, yet pliable, restraining bands not only are easy to use, but a large number can be carried by one man.

It is this type of assault that most people associate with counterterrorist forces. During a takedown, terrorists and hostages alike see only dark apparitions, akin to *Star Wars'* Darth Vader, entering behind the stun or flash/bang grenades. From the top down, every trooper is clad in a modern array of sophisticated armor. Heads are protected by a dark gray or black Kevlar helmet identical to current military issue. Under his "Fritz" helmet is fitted a flame–resistant Nomex balaclava. An earphone and/or microphone provides him instant tactical communication with the rest of the unit. The principle is that everyone involved in the decision–making process and execution must be provided with real–time information in order to control the unfolding operation.

Depending on the situation, a trooper is wearing eye protection in the form of either shatterproof goggles or a protective chemical mask which also provides a degree of eye safety. His upper torso is encased by a Kevlar vest, for gunshot and blast fragmentation protection, over a dark Nomex coverall or a tactical battledress. Over this, a variety of general equipment is worn, along with items that will support his specific tasks. Some troopers will have ammunition and myriad survival aids, such as powerful miniature flashlights and radio receivers. Others will have a variety of grenades, different types of ammo and first–aid equipment or knives. When medical assistance is not likely to be immedi-ately available, CT teams carry a medical pouch containing assorted dressings, IV tubing, saline solutions, and tourniquets.

As with everything else, individual weapons are dictated by the situation. Of course, everyone has a particular favorite, but training on all available CT weapons is a must. Most room entries begin with the lead man using a submachine gun or a semiautomatic pistol. To expedite door–kicking procedures, shotguns firing a sabot or lead slug will be used to blow off the barrier's hinges. Many team members will insist that a submachine gun or shotgun, which can be carried in one hand, is the ideal weapon, and some even mount laser pointers or mini flashlights on their weapons for operations in buildings or dimly lit areas. Plenty of ammo is always strategically placed around his uniform.

Regardless of how much equipment the team member has, each man is aware that one lucky shot or a well–placed booby trap can ruin the best–laid plans. From the soles of his Gore–Tex assault boots to the crown of his Kevlar helmet, a team member's equipment is constantly reviewed and updated. A takedown is an affair that one must come properly dressed for.

Training generally falls into two categories. First the FNG (f——ing new guy) will go through individual skills training designed to break old habits that come from the conventional side of the Army, such as not shooting outside of the prescribed safety limits, and much emphasis is placed on individual action and initiative. New habits, like the double tap, are instilled in the FNG. These come from lessons learned through both successful missions and failures. In the case of the double tap, a pumped–up terrorist in the midst of a takedown cannot be reasoned with or talked into surrendering.

Once this basic training is completed, the FNG enters the team training phase where he is taught how to handle himself in any close–quarters battle,

(**Above**) A CT operative demonstrates how to use a shotgun during a window entry. (**Above right**) A close–up of a "best–case" anchoring system, with abundant safety features. In the heat of a fast–paced takedown, such fine points often have to be bypassed. (**Right and below right**) An assault team conducting a forced entry and room–clearing demonstration of a "hotel conference room." Lock picking is conducted with a charge of C4 plastic explosives. Also note the 360–degree protection and the Walther 9mm P5 pistol and MP-K submachine gun, protective masks, and ballistic (bulletproof) helmets. Expertise with personal weapons while wearing a variety of different equipment combinations is a requirement. (**Below**) If you can't go through the door or a window, go through the wall! Like high tech termites, two US operatives prepare to follow the blast into the next room.

or CQB, whether it is conducted in a building, train, or aircraft. For example, the trooper will be given his first taste of an aircraft takedown at a large mockup of a generic civilian passenger liner at the SOT before training on a great variety of actual aircraft happily supplied by the major carriers at various sites around the country.

Additional CT training is also conducted to teach numerous infiltration methods for moving into isolated target areas. These include parachuting into the area using high–altitude, low–opening (HALO) or high–altitude, high–opening (HAHO), underwater rescue operations using Scuba techniques and miniature submersible vehicles for long–distance travel, and rappelling and fast–roping from helicopters. Teams may also have to learn techniques for driving various types of all–terrain vehicles. Lock-picking is also taught.

Upon completion, the FNG is assigned to a team, and maintenance of his new skills is begun within his troop. Regular cross–training will now occur with related foreign and domestic CT units, such as Britain's SAS or our own Navy SEAL (Sea–Air–Land) teams. Some DELTA troopers will also find themselves temporarily assigned "personal protection duty," providing security to key US personnel, such as ambassadors in Central America and the Middle East.

The Killing House

Take a break you heroes."

The team sergeant chuckles to himself every time he uses that line. If everything is going as it should, his jibe would either cause a rush of sarcastic curses and catcalls or receive a deep–throated moan from the assembled trainees. This time, the muted response indicates that the humid North Carolina weather is having an impact on the strength of the team. More importantly, it was a good indicator of the amount and type of training that should be con-

ducted for the remainder of the day. Based on his observations, the team sergeant decides to deviate from the published training schedule and walk through a room–clearing exercise without the required live ammunition. Training accidents are acceptable in this business but are not sought after.

Fifty meters to the west of this training area, a second and much more experienced team is also working its way through the day's training. Having just finished with their own room–clearing exercise, the men are given one of the most beloved commands in the lexicon of military language: "Take a break."

The break is planned for thirty minutes, but to the team members, it should be longer. Sprawled in various positions underneath the pines, each trooper brushes pine cones out of the way and tries to find a comfortable position while attempting to keep equipment from becoming too dirty with grit and sand. Small rivets of sweat trickle down grimy faces as nomex gloves are removed and calloused hands reach up to brush the sweat away from bloodshot eyes. Each team member wears an assault suit of black Nomex, and some of the team had already removed their black Kevlar helmets and flashproof balaclavas. Goggles, used to provide protection from flying debris, lay in the crown of the helmet, along with sweat–soaked gloves and face masks. Sensitive individual communications earpieces and microphones are inspected to ensure they were switched off.

Each trooper wears body armor, designed to protect throat and chest areas, and "armored shorts" to protect vulnerable groin areas. Some troopers have also added knee and elbow pads under their assault suits, while shin protectors are pulled on by some of the veterans who have grown tired of the bruises and cut shins received in the furniture–cluttered "killing house." Individuals are equipped with either a special–purpose Mossberg automatic shotgun

"Walk–throughs" of room–clearing operations are run with troopers wearing progressively more equipment so the men will gain a clear idea of how different protective sets restrict vision and movement. They must attain extreme levels of proficiency while wearing all combinations of gear. (**Above**) Troopers in coveralls prepare to enter a SOT "killing house" and (**opposite**) perform their ballet of death. Note the mannequin terrorists and hostage in closet.

or a 9mm Heckler & Koch MP5 submachine gun. Most of the free world's CT forces swear by this weapon, and some even argue that it is the best export the Germans have had since *Fräuleins*, Mercedes and beer. In addition to the MP5s, the sniper teams on this exercise are equipped with M24 sniper rifles. Though there are more advanced systems, the accurized Remington 700 bolt–action rifle with five–round fluted, detachable magazine is still the favored standby. Its stainless–steel barrel, and hefty .300 Winchester Magnum round provide this team with the power required to "reach out and touch

someone." All members of the sweeper team carry 9mm Beretta Model 92F pistols: the standard side-arm of the US Army.

While some troopers "smoke and joke," others inhale nourishing liquids from canteens and jugs. Like the fondness each man has for his individual weapons, team members also have a distinct enjoyment of anything liquid. Gatorade, bottled spring water, juices, or just plain H_2O is found in the individual backpacks. Unlike what Hollywood would have one believe, hard–drinking troopers are not the norm. The shakes are not conducive to good teamwork. And to the experienced eye, the soldiers are an organized and tightly knit group of professionals, men who can easily operate as either individuals or a team, making decisions that could have far–reaching impacts at world levels.

"Saddle up, you assholes."

Staff Sergeant Dawkins hated it when the sergeant major tried out his hard, John Wayne voice, and comments sarcastically, "I really wonder if John Wayne ever called anyone an asshole." A number of other uncomplimentary thoughts are voiced as the troopers slowly rise to their feet and adjust their equipment. Gathering around the team leader, Sergeant Major Greg Tusconey, the men fall in to form a loose formation facing their boss.

Looking up from his notebook, Sergeant Major Tusconey begins with an in–depth critique of the morning's past exercise. He cites their strengths as well as their weaknesses. When finished, he faces his soldiers and says in a matter–of–fact tone, "OK, girls, let's get our shit together and try it again." The resounding reply to the implication that there is a collective lack of masculinity within the unit is indicative of a team who can give as much as it can take.

Sauntering back to their briefing area, the team members arrange themselves on wooden benches placed in front of a graphic representation of the

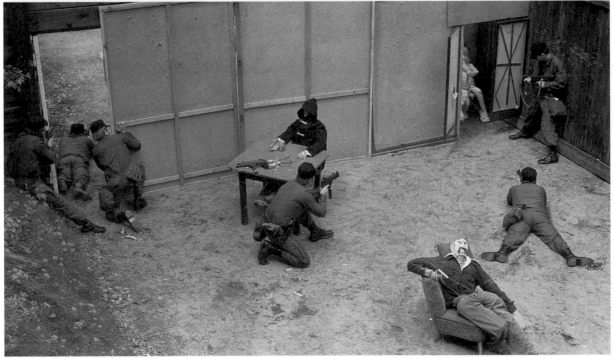

rooms within the killing house. A key factor in these exercises, as well as an actual assault, is the need for critical, accurate, and up–to–date information about the physical layout of the passenger aircraft or building, as well as the locations of the hostages and their terrorist keepers. Stepping up in front of the diagram, the sergeant major begins to describe the mission for the team in clear, concise, and pointed terms:

"At 1730 hours last night, terrorists assaulted the US Embassy, and took sixteen State Department employees as hostages. Two US Marines were killed during the initial assault. We are to prepare for a deliberate takedown of the building on order from higher." Stopping to scan the team for questions, he continues. "Outer security has been established by the local police, and inner security has been established by the hasty response team from the 10th Special Forces Group until after we arrive and take over responsibility for the mission. Recon of the building has been conducted, along with a debrief of our people and the locals who have solid, current intel."

Tusconey proceeds to outline the rehearsal schedules and timetables, who is responsible for what, and how he envisions the takedown will be accomplished. After the thorough briefing is completed, individual troopers are quizzed and then individual and team rehearsals are begun. As the last rays of the fading sun are engulfed by the approach of a cool, wet front, the last preparations are wound up. For this exercise, the chopper support for the takedown will come from "the Task Force" as the 160th SOAR is usually referred to.

The team is divided into sniper and assault elements, which coordinate the operation's precise timing, and move out. The two sniper teams each consist of a spotter and a shooter. They are linked together with the assault team, sweeper team, and command center by radio. Each sniper team moves along individual routes previously reconned and takes positions offering vantage points overlooking the target area. The assault element, meanwhile, is moving toward their pickup zone, or PZ, to rendezvous with an inbound chopper. The word circulates that the order has been received. The mission is on.

Because the operation will take place at night, infrared reflective tape is added to each member's equipment. Strips are applied around the chest, wrists, ankles and helmet. Using AN/PVS-7 night vision goggles (NVGs), all assault members will be easily seen in the heat of night combat. The sun has long ago set, and a steady drizzle falls through the tall pines as the team divides evenly and prepares to board the chopper. Right on schedule, the air is disturbed by the pounding of rotor blades beating the heavy night mist. Like a giant dragonfly, the MH-60 Black Hawk glides into the PZ, where the team immediately loads through the side doors. The pilot's eyes are unaided but his copilot wears aviator's AN/AVS-6 NVGs. Immediately, the team leader places the spare set of headphones over his ears and communicates with the pilot.

"Evening," says the pilot in a slow, Southern drawl.

"How's it going?" replies the sergeant major.

Formalities exhausted, Tusconey quickly briefs the aircrew on how the team will carry out the infil as the aircraft nears the target. Due to the lousy weather, the landing zone, or LZ, will be the building's sloping rooftop, and the team will drop onto a very small area at its peak, where a flat space had been located during photo recon analysis. Normally, the team would rappel or fast–rope in, but the wet weather and reduced visibility give them an added advantage and they'll be able to get closer to the target. With clockwork precision, the Black Hawk angles into the rooftop LZ and flares out level and steady. Looking through his NVGs, Tusconey sees that everyone is ready and in a low, distinct voice says, "Stand by, stand by." Prompted by his warning, the sniper teams report in: "Sniper One, ready. Target sighted." "Sniper Two ready. No target." At his hand signal, the lead team members prepare to exit. Taking a deep breath, he gives the command, "Go!"

The soldiers leap onto the mist–shrouded roof and fan out across its tricky incline in a predetermined (and well–rehearsed) pattern. Almost as quickly as the bird arrived at the LZ, it disappears into the gloom. Two team members attach green nylon climbing ropes to anchor points, drop them over the sides of the building along predetermined entry sites, and kneel in anticipation after attaching their snaplinks. Six other men move to a rooftop door and, after determining that it is locked, move into a tight file along the outside wall. The door hinges will have to be shot off.

The Number One man, armed with a Mossberg 12–gauge shotgun, prepares to blast the offending hinges off the wooden door. Despite the fact that every soldier is in communication with the rest of the team, discipline is absolute and the only sound breaking the silence is the constant hiss over each man's earpiece.

It has been ten seconds since the team landed. At the command, "Go!" the hinges disintegrate in a shower of sparks and splinters as the shotgun's solid lead slug crashes into each hinge, starting with the top and working down. Yanking the door to the side, the Number Two trooper rapidly steps into the doorway, where he immediately places his back to the dimly lit stairwell wall. Sweeping the staircase with his NVG, he breathlessly alerts follow–on troopers to the situation he is observing. Number Three now bursts through the doorway and in calculated steps moves down the stairs and secures the top floor stairwell. Peering down the hallway, he speaks in clear, crisp, and rapid tones into his micro-

phone: "Number Three, hallway clear." Trooper Number Four is immediately at his side, having followed his partner down the stairs. As Number Three moves to the right, Number Four moves left and blends into the darkened hallway. Both troopers' H&Ks move in measured arcs: ceiling to floor, left to right. Whenever a trooper's eyes move under their NVG, the stubby barrel of his MP5 follows, ready to spit out a lethal three–round burst along that same visual arc.

The second assault element of four men moves along the right side of the hallway toward a door on the right. The lead man (Number Three) senses motion in the room. Reaching down along his left thigh, he extracts a pop can–sized flash/bang grenade from his leg pouch. Bringing it up to his right hand, which still clutches an MP5, he slides the grenade's pullring over his right hand's gloved thumb. While holding the safety spoon, he pulls the ring. Gently rolling the grenade into the room, he flattens himself against the wall as he warns his teammates. "Grenade" reverberates through the soldier's earphones and, almost immediately, "Go!" is commanded before the nonlethal grenade has expended its package.

Number Five slides into the left side of the doorway as the room erupts in multiple flashes and explosions designed to disrupt, disorientate and illuminate. As he moves through the door, Number Six follows and slides into the black, smoke–filled room along the doorway's right wall. He is followed by Numbers Seven and Eight who had entered the floor through windows on the other side of the building. Number Seven backs Number Five by taking on any targets from his twelve– through three–o'clock (the right hand wall). Number Five already has acquired a target through his NVG in his twelve–through nine–o'clock area along the left wall.

A masked terrorist is wildly trying to bring his Polish–made AK-47 assault rifle to bear on a young

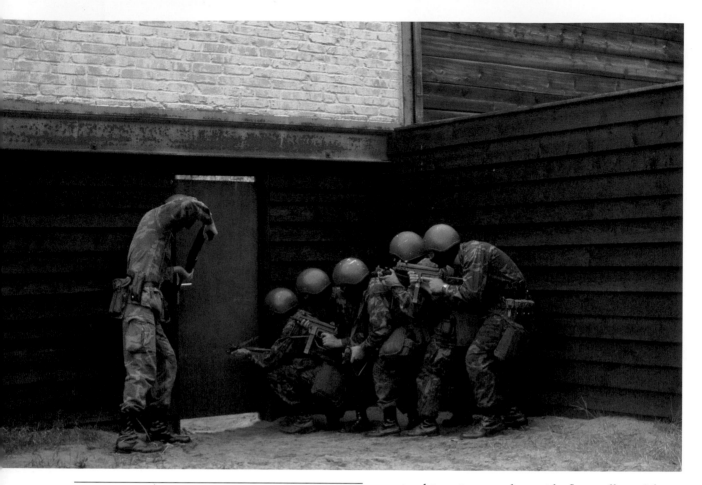

(**Above**) A team wearing ballistic helmets takes up position along the wall, to avoid being silhouetted against an open door, as their shooter takes aim at a European–style door latch with a pump shotgun. (**Opposite**) After entry, the team fans out along the walls before picking targets.

woman strapped to a chair near the center of the office. Number Five squeezes a three–round burst into the throat of the terrorist, who goes down in a spasmatic heap.

As Number Seven checks the terrorist for other weapons and vital signs, Number 5 maintains a steady aim on the lifeless corpse. Flipping the terrorist over on his stomach, Number Seven expertly

pins his wrists together with flex cuffs. After a quick check of the room, Numbers Six and Eight now check the bound female for booby traps. More than one rescue has ended in disaster when the rescuers failed to check for explosives secreted somewhere on a hostage. A grenade or stick of dynamite can turn a rescue into a sticky affair. After the check is completed, the team exits the room. Eight seconds have passed. As the leader leaves, he announces "Number Two, one terrorist down, one hostage secured, main room, top floor" to the command post and the other team members. Now it is up to the sweepers and backup police forces to take charge of the room.

This ballet of death will continue until the "embassy" is cleared of terrorists and all the hostages are accounted for. After the team exits the building, they move to an assembly area and are whisked away for an in–depth debriefing. If this had been a real takedown, actual terrorists and hostages would be considerably more unpredictable than the mannequins and pop–up targets the team had to deal with. Local police and medical personnel, as well as the sweepers, would have also been moving simultaneously through the building to deal with the carnage left behind and make a complete record of what happened. It may have to be used later as evidence.

This is a typical exercise.

During such exercises, the trooper is trained not to fall into the Rambo approach to CT operations: Never fire from the hip and always extend your folding stock. Fire at close range and don't waste ammo. You learn how to move: dropping to a crouch, firing, dropping and firing again, and moving to the next position. You learn to move quickly through doorways and get in position and maintain proper trigger control.

Chapter 4
Decade of Frustration

General [Bernard] Rogers told me of a note from the President. It had surfaced in the tank earlier in the day [October 18,1977] and asked, "Do we have the same capability as the West Germans?" Much discussion ensued before it was decided that we did not. One of the generals present had said, "Well I'm not going over to the White House and tell him we don't."

Colonel Charlie A. Beckwith, US Army (Retired)

Throughout the 1980s, DELTA was beset by a number of events that might have caused lesser organizations to collapse. The troopers trained hard but were seldom deployed. They watched helplessly as Americans were whisked from streets and university offices in Beirut and seized in large groups in hijacked airliners and ships. Worse yet, the men found themselves gearing up for rescue operations that were cancelled time and again for a variety of reasons. During this same period, the unit also found themselves on the receiving end of a disturbing amount of unwanted publicity. In addition to a highly publicized financial scandal involving DELTA members, the easy visual access to the Special Operations Training Facility (SOT) may have been a factor in the media's knowledge of deployments during several hostage crises.

A US flag burns on the Rhein–Main Air Base perimeter fence during a period of mass left–wing demonstrations and terrorist strikes against American targets in Germany.

Although it's shocking to think that a unit on the cutting edge of America's war on terrorism was—and still is—in appearance at least, so vulnerable, it was only the tip of the weak links plaguing counterterrorism. In addition to the expected security problems associated with CT operations, numerous interdepartmental squabbles and convoluted command and control issues abounded. An excellent example concerned justification for CT operations within the continental United States. The Justice Department's Federal Bureau of Investigation is responsible for tackling terrorist incidents at home, yet DELTA had to provide badly needed assistance during both the 1986 Statue of Liberty centennial in New York City and the 1984 Olympics in Los Angeles in spite of numerous jurisdictional and legal problems.

When CT operations are planned for overseas, numerous diplomatic issues become critical elements in the military/political equation, and the State Department steps to the forefront. Probably

(**Above**) US and GSG-9 counterterrorists conducting joint training at a West German site. A classic procedure in building clearing is for a team to rappel to a roof from a helicopter, then work its way from top to bottom, outside to inside. Such operations require split–second timing and in–depth coordination. Note that this special ops UH-1N Huey, though painted black for night operations, is clearly marked as an American military helicopter for any German operatives taking part in a joint takedown. (**Right**) After rappeling down the building side, a US operative prepares to enter a window. His teammate has already successfully completed this tricky maneuver. During actual operations, there is always the risk that an unexpected greeting awaits the team. (**Opposite page**) "Steady as she goes." A US trooper gives a German counterterrorist a hand before he disappears over the edge.

the most basic question that must be asked before contemplating operations on foreign turf is: What sovereign nation wants to relinquish command and control to United States military forces conducting such highly visible operations on their soil? It has to be remembered that no matter how discreetly DELTA may conduct itself in the run–up to an operation, every hostage rescue is undeniably a high–visibility operation *after* its well–publicized conclusion. The implication for the nation hosting DELTA is, of course, that it does not have the re-

sources to take care of its own internal problems. The domestic, as well as international, political ramifications for a government can be enormous. Add to this mess the fact that the Joint Special Operations Command, the direct link between DELTA and the president (known as the National Command Authority) and the Joint Chiefs of Staff (JCS), can receive marching orders from both. The JCS is better qualified to oversee any operations involving DELTA, but common sense remained a missing ingredient in this war, as can be seen by the less–than–desirable results in Grenada.

Aftermath

The fallout from the inferno of *Desert I* was complicated and far reaching. Not only did President Jimmy Carter lose his bid for re–election, but Egypt's supportive president, Anwar Sadat (who was already on a number of hit lists for his part in the Camp David Accords), was now a principal target of Iranian–sponsored fanatics for allowing the "Great Satan" to launch Operation *Eagle Claw* from his country. He would soon die at the hands of Muslim fundamentalists.

JCS planners continued their work, and soon a new mission to rescue the hostages in Iran, code–named *Honey Badger*, was put together under the direction of the renowned and much–respected General Richard Secord. Armed with the proper special operations support—and the hard–learned lessons gleaned from *Eagle Claw*— he assembled a powerful force of special operations aviators, Special Forces and DELTA troopers, intelligence collectors, and agents who were prepared to go it again. But it was not meant to be. Some two minutes after Ronald Reagan was sworn in as President of the United States, the hostages were released.

To help dampen the firestorm of criticism that erupted after *Desert I*, a six–officer review group was appointed by the chairman of the JCS, General David C. Jones. It was chaired by Admiral James L. Holloway, and the balance of its membership consisted of generals from the Army, Air Force, and Marines who had experience in either special or clandestine operations.

These investigators came to the conclusion that *Eagle Claw* was plagued by untested operational methods, poor communications procedures, and a dangerously informal command structure lacking unity of command. Training for the mission, moreover, had been conducted by its various compo-

nents at different sites without a full dress rehearsal using all the assigned elements—something that would have highlighted the most glaring operational and equipment shortfalls. The commission recommended that "a permanent field agency" of the JCS be established with "assigned staff personnel and certain assigned forces" and that a "murder board" of military experts be formed to independently examine mission plans before execution.

As for Colonel Beckwith, he was asked by General Meyer to formalize an earlier proposal for a permanently operating joint task force that would fall directly under the JCS and combine dedicated Army, Navy, and Air Force elements during its training and planning. Beckwith and others had long voiced the opinion that this type of organization was needed, and Major General John Singlaub put it best when he stated *Eagle Claw* didn't work because "we tried to bring disparate units from all over the Armed Forces—from all over the world— and then put them into an ad hoc arrangement to

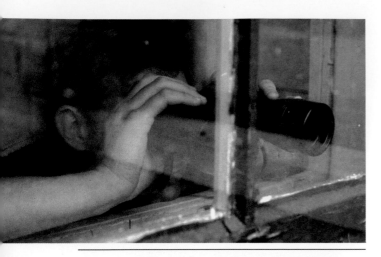

A key ingredient in CT operations is covert intelligence collection. Here, an intel specialist supports a DELTA training mission by conducting surveillance operations from a concealed site.

do a very complicated plan."

Beckwith's proposal to establish a Joint Special Operations Command (JSOC) was approved by Meyer in May 1980, and he was soon transferred from DELTA to the newly formed, independent organization he helped create. He badly missed the excitement of leading a combat team, though, and remarked that his staff billet "ain't as good a job [as DELTA]." He retired to the Lone Star State in 1981 and opened a security service. Harkening back to his days with Britain's Special Air Service, he gave his company the name SAS of Texas.

The establishment of the JSOC was one of many honest attempts to put teeth in America's counter-terrorist effort in the wake of *Desert I*. As expected, the new government programs became battle-grounds for interdepartmental squabbles. The major catalyst for this fighting was, of course, money since counterterrorism was now in vogue and took funding away from other programs.

DELTA's friends in high places went to even higher places, and the post–Beckwith organization

thrived during this period. The unit's strength before *Eagle Claw* of just over 100 men, making up two small A and B squadrons plus support, grew to a relatively stable force of 300 during the early 1980s— enough for three full–sized squadrons— with its selection and training as brutally efficient as ever. The unit also benefited greatly from production of *Task, Conditions and Standards for DELTA*, or, as it is more commonly known, "the Black Book." This document was produced only because General Meyer essentially grabbed Beckwith by the shoulders, pushed him down into a chair, and forced him to compose it.

Meyer, now the Army's chief of staff, was anxious that DELTA not reinvent the wheel with each new commander and wanted to ensure that it would retain its SAS–type structure, one that is unique within the US Army. Four troops of approximately sixteen men make up a squadron, with each troop able to reconfigure itself into eight–, six–, four–, three–, or two–soldier teams or elements. This degree of flexibility is one of the key ingredients in DELTA's ability to handle virtually any terrorist scenario.

DELTA also moved its headquarters from the old post stockade to the new, state–of–the–art SOT, appropriately nicknamed "Wally World" after a lavish theme park in the *National Lampoon's Vacation* movie. But, in a sense, it wasn't just DELTA that came up a big winner from the increased awareness of the terrorist threat. The whole military benefitted because it was identified as the obvious candidate to receive the now readily available funds. And the funds did flow: to Air Force special operations, Navy SEALs, Army aviation, Rangers, and Special Forces, as well as a large supporting cast in the various services, such as the Army's Intelligence Support Activity (ISA).

The State Department, however, was soon to emerge as the biggest winner. Being in the best position to judge the political ramifications of US actions on a host nation's territory, it received the responsibility for overseeing all overseas counter-terrorist operations. But despite the fact that the United States now had its CT apparatus well–organized and in place, the future proved to be not so rosy as the optimists hoped.

Operation *Urgent Fury*

After Ronald Reagan assumed the presidency in 1981, he "let it be known to friend and foe alike" that he had learned from the hard lessons of his pre-decessors. Surrounded by capable and, in some cases, hawkish advisors, President Reagan was de-termined that, like the sheriffs of the Old West, he would clean up the world and make it safe for wom-en and children. All he needed was a place to start and the force to sweep up the mess. He didn't have long to wait. At the southern end of the Antilles chain lies the beautiful Caribbean island of Grena-da. A former ward of the British Empire, this idyllic eight– by fifteen–mile island was to be the testing ground for the new president and the changes that had been made in the special operations communi-ty since *Desert I*.

On October 19, 1983, Grenada's Marxist prime minister, Maurice Bishop, and several cabinet mem-bers were lined up along the walls of old Fort Rupert and executed by former associates who formed an even more radical "Revolutionary Military Coun-sel." Bishop had aligned himself with the Soviets and their Cuban surrogates, who had, among other things, constructed a large military communications facility, a 10,000–foot runway capable of handling long–range transports, and extensive airfield sup-port facilities, ostensibly to support its meager tourist industry. While a single air base would not allow a hostile force to control the entrance into the southern Caribbean during a war, it would pro-vide an excellent stopover for aircraft bringing in material and personnel support for "peoples' revo-lutions" in Central and South America.

MH-6 Little Birds of the 160th SOAR operating in the Persian Gulf. Among other operations they took part in was the September 1987 capture of an Iranian mine–laying vessel that threatened oil tanker traffic.

With the execution of the genuinely popular leader, widespread protests broke out on the island, and when the military opened fire on the demon-strators, the die was cast. The threat to the region caused an uproar among the neighboring Caribbean nations, and the Reagan administration believed that a radical, Marxist government (that thought nothing of shooting its own citizens) would, sooner or later, get around to using the roughly 600 Ameri-can students at the island's medical school as pawns in a dangerous game to keep the US military from closing down the airfield. The young students were a hostage situation waiting to happen, so the United States moved quickly to launch Operation *Urgent Fury*.

Leading the assaults were several of the US mili-tary's elite as well as (until then) classified units. UH-60 Black Hawks of Task Force (TF) 160 flew directly from the United States to a nearby island launch site, with the help of additional internal fuel tanks, while MH-6s were brought in by Air Force cargo planes. During the early morning hours of

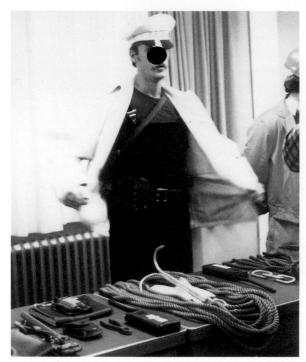

Counterterrorist specialists must be able to use any ruse or disguise to get close to hostage holding sites, such as an aircraft or buildings. Here, US Army CT operatives display equipment and various disguises during a briefing for General Bernard Rogers, Supreme Allied Commander, Europe, in the early 1980s. (**Left**) One of the typical "European businessmen" holsters his 9mm Beretta pistol and (**right**) a "street cleaner," standing beside a "municipal worker," shows off his protective vest and ammunition belt. Note the equipment on display.

ZSU-23-2 (twin 23mm) antiaircraft guns. In both cases, men and aircraft were lost (some figures are still classified). The lack of timely, on–the–spot, intelligence had again raised its ugly head.

October 25, the expert aviators of TF 160 ferried their ground counterparts, DELTA, to targets near the airfield at Point Salines, where they were to carry out a direct action mission ahead of two Ranger battalions parachuting in at dawn. Their target was the airfield control facilities which, it turned out, were heavily ringed by misplaced, but marginally effective, automatic weapons. A second mission entailed the takedown of Richmond Hill Prison, where one Black Hawk was lost to Soviet–made

Several members of the elite Navy SEAL Team 6 have privately related that they had an especially rough time as DELTA and the TF 160 units were running into their own problems in the south. One deadly incident occurred when four of their members parachuted into rough seas to conduct a linkup with a surface vessel that was to take them in close for a water infiltration. The drowning of these four men did not stop the mission, but it did tragically demonstrate that even the best of the best are sometimes incapable of overcoming the odds.

A major concern during *Urgent Fury* was the safety of the British government's representative. Tasked to keep the gentleman from falling into the hands of the Grenadan "Peoples' Revolutionary

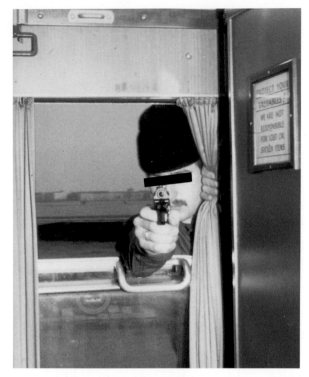

(**Above**) Unlike situations depicted in movies, actual aircraft takedowns must be accomplished quickly, violently, and with surgical precision. Here, a suspected hijacker in a mock airliner cabin is controlled the best way: with a pistol to the head. (**Right**) "Tickets please!" A terrorist's view of a US operative taken during a train–clearing exercise in Europe.

Armed Forces," twenty–two other members of SEAL Team 6 flew in by chopper, fast–roped onto the rooftop and grounds of the governor's residence, and took control. A stunned Grenadan defense unit located nearby summoned help from two Soviet supplied BTR-60 armored personnel carriers mounting multiple machine guns. The sudden appearance of substantial hostile elements forced the planned evacuation of Government House to be hastily cancelled. They were, as one SEAL member later described, "in a world 'a shit" and had to fight in place. With neither antiarmor weapons nor good communications, the team held out as best they could until a Specter gunship came to their rescue and eliminated the problem. But even with the help of the AC-130's massive firepower, up to half of the rescue party is reported to have been wounded by the time Marines reached them on the second day of *Urgent Fury*.

Months later, a veteran SEAL discussing the operation sighed after draining his beer and said, "Thank God it was just the Grenadans." When pressed, he continued, "Every time some nonqualified son of a bitch plans or directs our operations, we get our asses handed to us on a silver platter. It just ain't right." Right or wrong, the end result from the problems of *Urgent Fury* was that closer control over the planning of special operations would, at least for a while, be handled by people who "had been there," which means thoroughly qualified in special operations planning.

An interesting wrinkle on special operations on Grenada came from the media's coverage of *Urgent Fury*. Although the Army had refused to either confirm or deny the use of special operations forces for nearly eight years, ABC News was able to extract a concession that one TF 160 captain was killed and eleven DELTA troopers injured after broadcasting footage of the downing of his Black Hawk— an event previously unaccounted for in the Pentagon recap of the operation. An American resident of Grenada had shot the film; other footage showed MH-6s, aircraft for which no procurement information had been publicly released. They were identified by ABC News as Hughes 500 helicopters, its civilian designation.

After the operation, increasingly bitter complaints over the "veil of secrecy" surrounding special operations were heard from some quarters of the media. Also being made was the highly dubious claim that only the American public was being denied access to information since the Soviets supposedly already knew all about such activities. While this is a subject that will certainly never be concluded to everyone's satisfaction, it is an undeniable fact that even relatively low losses can have a severe impact on the capabilities of a small unit. And if the small unit performs a mission of vital strategic importance, that loss may be magnified a hundred-

fold. Not only do Western intelligence agencies monitor terrorist networks, but the terrorists themselves monitor CT organizations, with the assistance of various friendly governments that track Western units and capabilities largely through press reports and, occasionally, espionage. It is not in the best interests of the United States to reveal losses in key covert units within days—or even months— after they were suffered. In this case, freedom of information must take a back seat to security

Trouble in the Mediterranean

Almost immediately on the heels of *Urgent Fury*, members of Italy's own homespun terrorist organization, the Red Brigade, abducted an American one-star general named James L. Dozier from his apartment on December 17, 1982. Authorities were later to learn that Dozier was not the intended victim, but, instead, a Navy admiral had been the group's actual target. Regardless of who was snatched, the impact all over Europe was the same: NATO military facilities soon became prison camps for the Allies. Virtually every senior officer seemed to see himself or his family as a prime target for the terrorists.

Against this background of confusion, the experts from various special operations units converged on Italy. Much to their credit, the Italians told everyone to kindly go home since this was their turf. But while all door kickers were sent packing, they did keep some special operators who could assist with such exotic needs as radio and telephone intercept.

When the alarm was sounded, one of the units offered was the European Command's own hasty response detachment. Its commander found himself on the first plane into the area. He was also on the first plane out. The Italians recognized incompetence when they saw it, and had enough problems of their own without having to wet–nurse a rookie counterterrorist in addition to the US State Department. With the help of the US signal intercept folks, the Italians found and rescued the kidnapped general, and American CT "experts" learned one

General Dozier's kidnappers erected a tent inside a safe-house room to hold their prisoner. (**Opposite**) Dozier displays a diagram of the tent and nearest guard position after Italian counterterrorists forcibly freed him from the Red Brigade. (**Above**) Lebanese rescue workers and US Marines gather outside the flattened Marine barracks in the aftermath of a terrorist truck bombing. The suicide driver had driven directly past Marine guards, who had been ordered not to carry loaded weapons. There were lessons to be learned: Listen to the warnings of counterterrorist specialists, plus shoot first and worry about CNN later.

more lesson in dealing with the real world.

In 1982, Iran had sent roughly 2,000 of their fanatical Revolutionary Guards to the Lebanese free–for–all civil war as "volunteers." While a good number of them would go to paradise after falling in regular combat against Christian militiamen (and leftist Shiites and Druz militiamen and renegade Palestinians and US Marine snipers, as well as Israeli, Lebanese, and Syrian soldiers), a select few were destined to meet Allah in a less conventional man-

195

The television image of a TWA pilot being prevented from talking with reporters by an armed hijacker at Beirut airport in June 1985.

ner. These "martyrs" drove explosives–laden trucks into barracks, embassies, or other high–priority targets. On the night of April 18, 1983, forty French paratroopers and 241 US Marines were killed by a pair of these truck bombers after failing to heed the lessons of a similar attack earlier that year on a US Embassy building.

Another incident in late October of that year concerned members of the 10th Special Forces Group who were billeted in a downtown hotel while training and advising the Lebanese Army. The group's commander, Colonel Richard Potter, was warned by associates with connections to the Shiite fundamentalists that the group's quarters were targeted for yet another suicide bombing. Potter, DELTA's former deputy commander and a veteran of *Desert I*, was not about to let such warnings go unheeded and immediately moved his force to a Lebanese Army base north of the city. In this case, the training of one man, along with past friendships nurtured over years of frustration, spared the wives of the 10th Special Forces a visit from a chaplain and the ever present survivor assistance officer.

On December 4, 1984, DELTA was sent to assault a Kuwaiti airliner hijacked on its way to Pakistan. Two American passengers were killed during the incident, and the aircraft was forced to fly to Iran, where both the terrorists and hostages were released before the unit could intervene. Six months later, on June 14, the unit was sent back to the region in preparation for an assault on TWA Flight 847, but the affair ended before they could be employed; one off–duty Navy serviceman on board was singled out and murdered. DELTA failed to come to grips

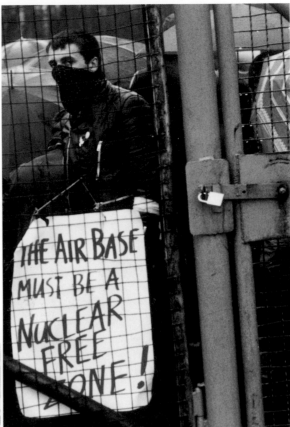

Throughout the 1970s and 1980s, terrorists in Germany were like fish swimming in a great sea of militant leftist/ Marxist/ecologist/misfit/nationalist extremists and sympathizers. (**Right**) A masked demonstrator protesting outside the US air base at Rhein–Main and (**below**), an arms cache believed to have been hidden by Germany's Red Army Faction. Terrorist groups rely heavily on hidden caches of arms and other supplies.

with terrorists again in October, during the *Achille Lauro* affair, and the resulting fiasco at Sigonella Naval Air Station, Sicily, pointed out that the Italians were not about to change their position on whether they or the Americans have jurisdiction on Italian turf. Members of SEAL Team 6 attempted to take the hijackers into custody and were re-minded that they were not the ones in charge.

The Palestinian extremists who commandeered the Italian vessel had been persuaded to leave it at Alexandria, Egypt, in return for safe conduct to friendly Tunisia, where the PLO maintained its headquarters. They boarded a commercial passenger jet and left Egypt immediately ahead of DELTA's arrival but was quickly intercepted by US F-14 Tomcat fighters, which diverted it to the US–Italian air base. Once the airliner was forced to land, it was quickly surrounded by the SEALs, who were, in turn, surrounded by Italian *carabonari*, who also blocked their C-141 with security vehicles. Since both groups were attempting to carry out their orders and

(**Above**) The unmarked limousine of General Frederick Krossen, commander of US Army forces in Europe, after a failed assassination attempt by Germany's Red Army Faction in September 1981. Only a month before, the general had finally heeded the advice of West German counterterrorists and obtained the special armored Mercedes that deflected the blast of the Soviet–made rocket–propelled grenade away from the car's interior. In the car was the general, his wife, an aid, and a German driver/ bodyguard. (**Right**) A West German wanted poster for known terrorists. As various fugitives were apprehended or killed, they were crossed off the poster by the US CT team that mounted it on their headquarters' wall.

apprehend the hijackers, a tense situation developed between the senior US officer present and Italian officers. The situation quickly degenerated and the *carabonari* loaded and locked their trusty Berettas and drew down on the equally well–armed SEALs. It was an Italian standoff until the diplomats intervened and determined that it was in ev-

eryone's best interest to let the Italians take charge.

Yet another incident occurred the following month, when a commercial airliner was hijacked to Malta by Palestinian extremists. This time, DELTA was on hand but not used. In fact, they were initially not even allowed to land. Since the hijacked aircraft was Egyptian, that country's commandos, trained by US special operations personnel, were allowed to conduct the takedown. It turned sour, and fifty–seven hostages lost their lives.

Troubles at Home

From 1970 through the mid–1980s, more than 1,000 Americans had been killed, taken hostage, or otherwise injured by foreign terrorists. Virtually all of these incidents had occurred overseas, but CT planners believed that America's luck might not hold out much longer: The upcoming 1984 Summer Olympics to be held in Los Angeles was an awfully tempting target. As part of the $1 billion effort to provide security from possible attacks, DELTA deployed to a nearby naval facility and stood ready to counter any terrorist situation. Along with DELTA was a massive CT force incorporating city and state SWAT (special weapons and tactics) teams and the Federal Bureau of Investigation's Hasty Response Team, commonly referred to as HURT. All were given varying degrees of responsiblity to counter threats, depending on their level of expertise and available manpower.

One interesting sidenote to DELTA's deployment at the Olympics was their use of a mobile command post disguised as a Budweiser beer truck for surreptitiously transporting a response team to the site of an incident. While mention of such a vehicle almost invariably brings snickers to the mouths of listeners accustomed to seeing similar tricks on scores of television cop shows and films as diverse as *Good Neighbor Sam* and *Stripes*, the fact remains that a vehicle camouflaged in this unconventional manner looks like it "belongs" and can move virtually unnoticed if that is what is required. Thankfully, the truck was not needed, but it had to be a comforting sight to those in the know.

Unlike the funds spent on producing the Budweiser truck, not all monies funneled through Army covert accounts were spent wisely or even legitimately. Army auditors discovered a number of irregularities in a covert account between 1981 and 1983. A disturbing amount of double–dipping had taken place and such items as a hot–air balloon and Rolls–Royce sedan had been purchased supposedly to support clandestine operations.

In a climate that one DELTA member described as "sheer hysteria," standard cost–accounting techniques were applied to ongoing covert operations and training. The result was dozens of reprimands and perhaps a score or more transfers resulting from nonjudicial punishments in lieu of court–martials. Some soldiers, however, were not so lucky. Nor did they deserve to be. In one case, an ISA lieutenant colonel, who supported DELTA set up a firm named Business Security International as a conduit for covert funds and misappropriated more than $50,000 in just six months. In a series of discreet courts martial and a civil criminal trial running through 1986, at least two officers were "assigned to the long course" and are still serving prison terms at Leavenworth Penitentiary.

For most DELTA troopers, though, life remained at its grueling, hurry–up–and–wait pace. Troopers continued their meticulous training and provided advice and support to CT units around the world as they did during the Los Angeles Olympics, when a team was quickly dispatched to Willemstad, Curacao, in the Dutch Antilles, to assist in the takedown of a hijacked Venezuelan DC-9. Both fanatics were killed and seventy–nine passengers were freed. Meanwhile, in Lebanon, kidnappings continued unabated and two of the hostages were murdered, CIA station chief William Buckley in 1985 and Marine Colonel William Higgins in 1989. Frequent changes in hostage holding sites and lack of solid US intelligence sources within the terrorists' camp prevented rescues from being undertaken, and at least one major operation involving DELTA and the SEALs was scrubbed. The professionals at DELTA were, in effect, all dressed up with no place to go. Sometimes, though, this was distinctly good news— as was the case when New York City's vulnerable Statue of Liberty centennial celebration passed without a hitch in July 1986.

On other occasions, events took care of themselves— as in San Salvador and Manila. On November 21, 1989, DELTA was dispatched to the Salvadoran capital of San Salvador to rescue Green

West Berlin police sifting through the rubble of the La Belle discotheque, a bar popular with American servicemen, where a soldier and Turkish woman were killed by a bomb. Intelligence analysts soon discovered that the explosives were planted by Libyan agents based out of their embassy in communist East Berlin.

Beret trainers trapped in the Sheraton Hotel during a guerrilla offensive. The trainers escaped unharmed, however, before the detachment could be put into action. Almost two weeks later, DELTA received another alert for a possible rescue attempt, this time in the Philippines. American citizens were again trapped, this time by an Army coup d'état, but emerged unscathed when the revolt fizzled.

Berlin presented a more interesting—and long-lasting—problem for US, as well as British and French, CT units stationed in the city's Western sectors. Along the seven crossing points through the Wall between East and West, Communist East German border guards, called *Vopos*, checked passports to prevent East Germans from passing into the West, while the British, French, and American guards allowed people to pass unimpeded both ways since they didn't, for political reasons, view East Berlin as a "foreign" territory. A situation was thus created where potential terrorists, finding some access restrictions from Western nations, could simply cross into the city from East Berlin, where the Syrians, Lybians, Iranians, and even the PLO, maintained diplomatic missions. A US hasty response team was always on a high state of alert and an active exchange program was conducted with DELTA. They operated in close conjunction with Berlin's other Western security organizations, but could not prevent terrorist attacks like the April 5, 1986, bombing of the La Belle discotheque, a club frequented by many American servicemen, in which two people were killed and 230 others were injured. The twilight world of terrorism and counterterrorism, espionage and counterespionage, did not end until the East German communist system finally collapsed of its own weight, bringing the Berlin Wall down with it.

Throughout it all, the frustrations and false starts, DELTA troopers maintained their high degree of professionalism and managed to keep their sometimes–irreverent sense of humor. All knew that the beeper clipped to their belts could sound its annoying electronic bleep at any time to signal a recall and they'd casually drop whatever they were doing with an offhand, "Looks like it's time to head on back to the Ranch,"* and disappear out the door for who knows how long.

*The affection of some shaggy–haired troopers for Levis, chewing tobacco, and cowboy boots led their original headquarters at Fort Bragg's old stockade to be called "the Ranch," and even after the unit moved to its new digs at Wally World, the name persisted.

(Top) The US Army's hasty response team in Berlin and several DELTA troopers pose for a group photo during a break in a training exercise. (Above) During antiterrorist training in West Berlin, an American serviceman is "snatched" by a group of mock terrorists.

Operation *Just Cause*

A public affairs release from Operation *Just Cause* stated simply that all units from the "special operations command participated" in the operation. DELTA's most publicized mission was the rescue of an American businessman and Rotary Club member held in Panama's notorious Modelo Prison. Kurt Muse was a resident of Panama and, in concert with fellow Panamanian Rotarians (dubbed the "Rotarians from Hell" by *Soldier of Fortune* magazine), had been causing Panama's strongman, Manuel Noriega, trouble by operating a clandestine radio station, filling the air waves with propaganda and, in some instances, reporting misleading or confusing instructions to the Panamanian Defense Forces (PDF) on military radio frequencies. Muse was eventually turned in by the wife of a former co-conspirator and was jailed at Modelo, located a stone's throw from Noriega's command post/headquarters turned fortress called the *Comandancia*.

In the early morning hours of December 19, 1989, Muse was rescued by members of DELTA in a classic CT operation. Transported to the rooftop of the prison by an MH-6, the assault team, backed up by a man on the inside who disabled the facility's emergency generator, cleared the upper floors from the top down and fought their way to the cell holding area where Muse was imprisoned. White beams of light from the troopers' weapon–mounted pointers pierced the smoke–filled cell, after its door was blown, and Muse was whisked to the roof up a darkened stairwell as Specter gunships pummeled the *Comandancia* across the street.

Armed with MP5s of various configurations, the troopers took out the armed guards with lethal shock and firepower and used just enough explosives to open the door without harming Muse. The waiting MH-6 was piloted by a lone soldier from the 160th SOAR. Two troopers fought their way to Muse's cell, two more provided security on the stairwell, and four more were on the roof, exchanging fire with prison guards in the barracks beyond a small courtyard. The operation, so far, had unfolded with the clockwork precision of a Wally World exercise. As the security and rescue teams loaded into the helo and along its outside–mounted seats, the heavily laden Little Bird lifted into the night sky.

What Muse saw was as close to a living hell as Wagnerian opera. AC-130s were tearing great chunks out of the *Comandancia's* defenses, while tracers streamed upward at buzzing Black Hawk helicopters and, in the streets below, conventional mechanized infantry forces brought maximum pressure to bear on the PDF. In this deadly concert, the overloaded chopper, unlike a *Valkyrie* of lore, did not bear the men off to *Valhalla*, but was hit by ground fire and landed with an unceremonial thud on the street below. The iron–nerved aviator maneuvered it down the street like a taxi and pulled into a parking lot. Using several tall apartment buildings as a shield, the pilot again tried to make his getaway but the Little Bird was knocked down again, this time for good, and the men formed a defensive perimeter nearby. Seconds after one DELTA trooper held up an infrared strobe light, they were spotted by a Black Hawk, and the cavalry came to the rescue in the form of three 6th Infantry Regiment M-113 armored personnel carriers. Four DELTA troopers were hurt, one seriously, but unlike the events some nine years earlier in Iran, this plan was carried out and with the intended results.

(**Top**) The MH-6J Little Bird that lifted Kurt Muse to freedom is moved out of the street by US mechanized forces after they secured the area around General Manuel Noriega's headquarters. Note the three–man troop seats along each side and the large crane–like appendage for fast –rope operations. It folds forward against the side of the bird when not in use and inadvertently prevents troopers from easily exiting the interior from the right side. (**Right**) The battered *Comandancia*, located just across the street from Muse's prison cell. *Soldier of Fortune*

Air Support

Rotary– and Fixed–Wing Assets

The Holloway Report on Operation *Eagle Claw* laid bare the grevious deficiencies in special operations aviation that contributed to the disaster at *Desert I*; chief among them was the lack of interoperability between the armed services. The conglomeration of hardware fielded by special operations aviation was the most visible manifestation of this shortcoming.

Throughout the early 1980s, special operations aviation soldiered on with an unwieldy mix of helicopters. Depending on the mission (and what was available), a DELTA trooper might easily find himself working with CH-3 Jolly Green Giants, CH-53C Sea Stallions, UH1–1N Twin Hueys, CH-47D Chinooks, some newer (and extensively modified) UH-60A Black Hawks, HH-53B and C Pave Low IIIs, and substantially upgraded versions of the OH-6A Cayuse called AH and MH-6 "Little Birds." One highly capable helicopter that DELTA could *not* count on using, except, perhaps, in the most extreme emergency, was the RH-53Ds of *Eagle Claw*. The Navy's entire fleet of this counter–mine version of the Sea Stallion amounted to only twenty–four aircraft before a half–dozen were lost in the Dasht–e Kavir, severely degrading the fleet's mine–sweeping capability. They had been tapped for the mission because the stretched HH-53s, specifically designed for special ops, were literally too long to fit in the elevators of most aircraft carriers without time–consuming removal of their rotor blades, a problem that persists today, even though many of the vessels with smaller elevators have been retired.

Members of all armed services found themselves in general agreement with the Holloway Report's findings, and some organizational, equipment, and training improvements were made. But the most basic problem remained: the lack of "jointness" be-

A Pave Low jockey wearing AN/PVS-5A night vision goggles. Even relatively lightweight goggles require that a counterweight be attached to the back of a pilot's helmet, and after a year of night flying an airman's collar size often increases a size or two from the increased exercise of his neck muscles.

tween the Army, Navy, Marines, and Air Force. Under pressure from congress, the Department of Defense attempted, unsuccessfully, to put an end to the interservice rivalries by advocating that the Army become the sole operator of rotary–wing special operations assets, while the Air Force continued to develop its long–range, fixed–wing capability.

Although this particular proposal went nowhere fast because of both congressional backpedaling and continued resistance within the Air Force to anything that would cut into its turf, the future security of the nation was immeasurably enhanced by passage of the 1987 Defense Authorization Act, which established a unified command incorporating the special operations forces from all services. The new Special Operations Command (SOCOM) could train and deploy forces throughout the world and was given the authority to develop and acquire equipment, services, and supplies peculiar to special ops. Of particular interest to DELTA, was the funding and authorization to modify existing aircraft and develop new helicopter variants.

Under the act, the UH-60 Black Hawk would be reconfigured into three basic models to support all services. The Army's 160th Special Operations Aviation Regiment, Airborns (SOAR) would use the MH-60K Pave Hawk to replace its less–capable MH-60As* in the assault role; the HH-60H "Rescue

*The L variant Black Hawks, with their more–powerful engines, uprated transmissions, and HIRSS (Hover Infrared Supression Subsystem) would not enter service till the following year, 1988. All MH-60As and many UH-60As have since been retrofitted with the HIRSS.

(Above) The aftermath of an unscheduled Pave Low landing in Korea. No one was injured in the accident which occurred during a night training exercise. (Opposite) HC-130 Combat Shadow tankers and MH-53 Pave Low helicopters.

Hawk" would enhance the Navy's search and rescue as well as special warfare capability; and the Air Force MH-60G Pave Hawk would both replace its aging search and rescue aircraft as well as act as an armed escort for the new MH-53J Pave Low IIIs just entering service. All aircraft would be provided with tiedowns to allow shipboard operations.

The newest Pave Low III variant of the CH-53, called the MH-53J, was tasked to perform the heavy–lift, rotary–wing effort for the near future. A superb special ops aircraft, it is, unfortunately, rather short–legged, and even with the addition of a 600gal fuel bladder, it requires frequent air refuel-ing during long missions. Congressional sponsors of the 1987 legislation—as well as the Air Force hierarchy—envisioned that it would be phased out of special operations and into search and rescue as MH-47Es came on line.

The special operations variant of the venerable, heavy–lift CH-47D Chinook would complement the MH-60K's mission. Unlike the Pave Low IIIs, MH-47Es can easily fit into the elevators of all aircraft carriers and, thus, offers planners more de-ployment options. The MH-47E would also have an interoperable avionics system with its smaller cousin and could engage in full and open competi-tion with the CV-22A Osprey for the long–range strategic special ops mission. Unfortunately, the extremely versatile tilt–rotor Osprey, which in-corporated the lift, range and speed of a fixed–wing transport with the vertical–lift capability of a helicopter, was canceled by the Defense Department during the post–Cold War budget cuts.

Unlike other special ops helicopters, the AH and MH-6 Little Birds are not dealt with in the published versions of congressional defense appropriations. These descendants of the trusty old Cayuse were developd and fielded through the use of covert funds in much the same way as the F-117 stealth attack aircraft and, interestingly, started to edge out of the "black" at approximately the same time as the the F-117, primarily because of their high visibility during the 1987–1988 retaliatory attacks on Iranian targets in the Persian Gulf and the 1989 overthrow of Panamanian dictator Manuel Noriega.

The 160th SOAR, which carried out these operations, is known as the Night Stalkers, because of their effective use of darkness during missions, and many of its pilots have logged 2,000 or more flight hours wearing night vision goggles. The regiment, headquartered at Fort Campbell, Kentucky, is composed of four battalions: the 1st with eighteen AH-6s, eighteen MH-6s and thirty MH-60 (incorporating the forward–deployed 617th Special Operations Aviation Detachment (Airborne) in Panama); the 2d with twenty–four MH-47s; the 3d with ten MH-60s and eight MH-47s, based at Hunter Army Airfield, Savannah, Georgia, to support the 1st Ranger Battalion, as it did during the Grenada operation; and an Oklahoma National Guard battalion, the 1/245, based at Tulsa, Oklahoma, with more than three dozen aircraft including fifteen UH-60Ls which will eventually be replaced by MH-60s.

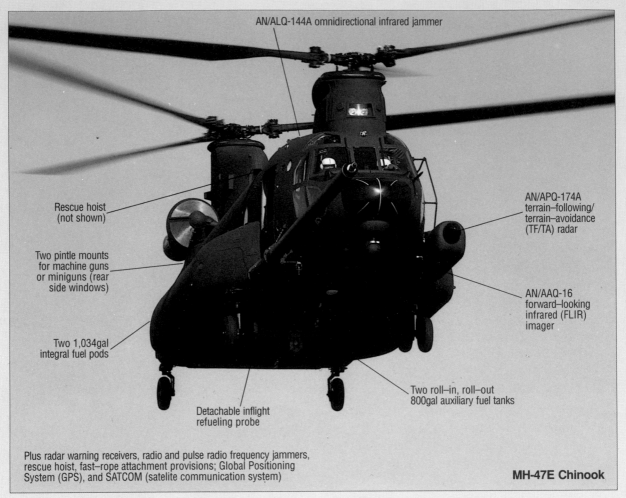

AN/ALQ-144A omnidirectional infrared jammer

Rescue hoist
(not shown)

Two pintle mounts
for machine guns
or miniguns (rear
side windows)

Two 1,034gal
integral fuel pods

AN/APQ-174A
terrain–following/
terrain–avoidance
(TF/TA) radar

AN/AAQ-16
forward–looking
infrared (FLIR)
imager

Two roll–in, roll–out
800gal auxiliary fuel tanks

Detachable inflight
refueling probe

Plus radar warning receivers, radio and pulse radio frequency jammers,
rescue hoist, fast–rope attachment provisions; Global Positioning
System (GPS), and SATCOM (satelite communication system)

MH-47E Chinook

MH-47E Chinook and
MH-60 Black Hawk Variants

(**Above**) The MH-47E's highly advanced, integrated avionics system and extended range allow it to complete clandestine, deep–penetration missions. The aircraft can easily use nap–of–the–earth tactics at night and in any weather conditions while placing a minimum workload on the pilot. Special operations enhanced UH-60 Black Hawks have performed spectacularly in long–range combat operations from Grenada to Iraq. (**Opposite top**) An MH-60 Enhanced Black Hawk (sometimes referred to as a Pave Hawk) of the Army's 160th SOAR named *Executioner*, upgraded from either an UH-60A or L. (**Opposite center**) A newly built MH-60G Pave Hawk undergoing flight testing. (**Opposite bottom**) An Air Force MH-60K Pave Hawk upgraded from a UH-60A. All of these helicopters wear infrared–suppressing paint.

MH-60 Enhanced Black Hawk

Two pintle mounts for machine guns or miniguns (forward side windows)

AN/ALQ-144 omnidirectional infrared jammer

Hover infrared suppression subsystem (HIRSS)

AN/AAQ-16 FLIR imager

Two 7.62mm miniguns

Two nineteen–round 70mm rockets launchers

M–130 flare/chaff dispenser tied to missile detector

Plus radar warning receiver, rescue hoist, fast–rope attachment provisions, GPS, and SATCOM

MH-60G Pave Hawk

Wire strike protection

Two pintle mounts for machine guns or miniguns (forward side windows)

AN/AAQ-16 FLIR imager

Inflight refueling probe

AN/APN-239 weather radar (with ground mapping modes)

M–130 flare/chaff dispenser tied to missile detector (will be replaced by ALE-40 dispensers)

Plus radar warning receiver, radio and pulse radio frequency jammers, rescue hoist, fast–rope rappelling system, GPS and SATCOM

MH-60K Pave Hawk

AN/ALQ-144A omnidirectional infrared jammer

Wire strike protection

HIRSS

M–130 flare/chaff dispensertied to missile detector

Two crash–worthy 230gal external auxiliary fuel tanks

AN/APQ-174A TF/TA radar

Inflight refueling probe

AN/AAQ-16 FLIR imager

Two pintle mounts for machine guns or miniguns

Mounts for air–to–air or air–to–ground rockets

Plus radar warning receivers, radio and pulse radio frequency jammers, rescue hoist, fast rope rappelling system, GPS, SATCOM, and laser detector

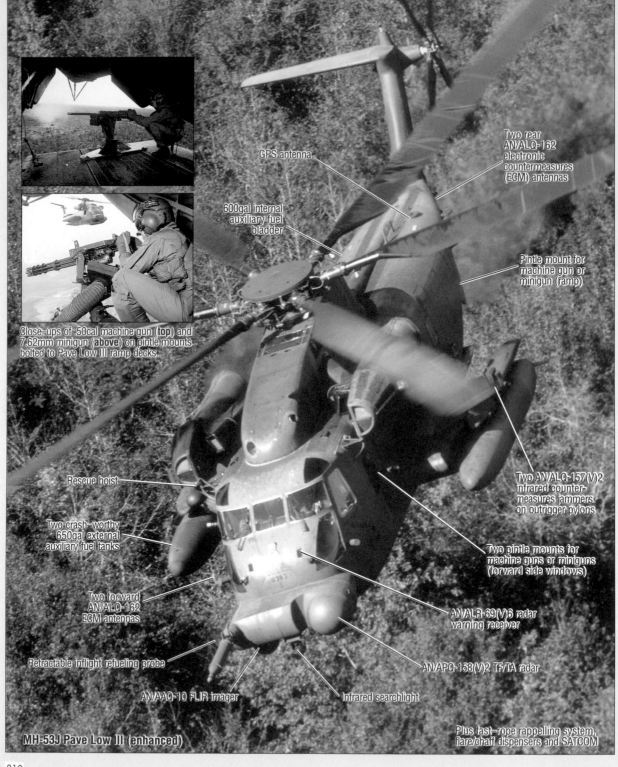

GPS antenna

Two rear AN/ALQ-162 electronic countermeasures (ECM) antennas

600gal internal auxiliary fuel bladder

Pintle mount for machine gun or minigun (ramp)

Close-ups of .50cal machine gun (**top**) and 7.62mm minigun (**above**) on pintle mounts bolted to Pave Low III ramp decks.

Rescue hoist

Two crash-worthy 650gal external auxiliary fuel tanks

Two forward AN/ALQ-162 ECM antennas

Retractable inflight refueling probe

AN/AAQ-10 FLIR imager

Infrared searchlight

Two AN/ALQ-157(V)2 infrared counter-measures jammers on outrigger pylons

Two pintle mounts for machine guns or miniguns (forward side windows)

AN/ALR-69(V)6 radar warning receiver

AN/APQ-158(V)2 TF/TA radar

MH-53J Pave Low III (enhanced)

Plus fast-rope rappelling system, flare/chaff dispensers and SATCOM

MH-53
Pave Low III

The MH-53H and J Pave Low IIIs are descended from a long line of Sikorsky helicopters that have performed rescue and special operations from the Korean War through Vietnam and the aborted 1980 raid to free American hostages in Iran. Of a family that is second only to the Soviet–built Mi-26 Halo in size and heavy–lift capability, the Pave Low III is capable of operating with pin–point accuracy in all weather conditions and at night. It also shares many components with other Air Force assets, such as the FLIR on the AC-130 Specter gunships and MC-130 Combat Talons transports. (**Top**) Special operations forces exit the rear of a Pave Low III via a flexable ladder and (**above**) by fast–rope. (**Opposite**) An MH-53J skimming the trees. One recent night training exercise included seven Pave Lows receiving four inflight refuelings each during a nearly eight–hour flight. The exercise concluded with the helicopters arriving within two seconds of their target time and unloading thirty men each in five seconds.

MD 530MG

Little Bird Variants

Based on an extremely popular airframe that can be found in extensive use by both civilian and government entities in every corner of the globe, the Little Bird offers great agility, adaptability, and its own version of visual stealth if such is warranted by a mission. The aircraft is manufactured by McDonnell Douglas and carries a basic civilian designation of either MD 500 or MD 530. The 500, 500C, and 500D aircraft were produced with a round, bubble–like nose through 1982 when all subsequent helicopters of these types were manufactured with the more pointed nose of the MD 500E, 500F, and 500MG, as well as the slightly larger and more powerful MD 520 and 530 series aircraft. The US Army's orders for these helicopters after 1982, however, have generally called for the retention of the bubble nose to maintain the option of installing a TOW antitank missile aiming sight and keep visual commonality with the large number of pre–1982, nonmilitary aircraft of this type.

The high civilian and foreign–military demand for a small, reliable, inexpensive helicopter was coupled with the manufacturer's effort to fill that demand by incorporating a large variety of powerplant, transmission, rotor, and other changes on what is essentially the same airframe. This proliferation of different aircraft types found its way into the 160th SOAR's inventory since there was never a specific production line opened for the US Army, all purchases being made in bits and pieces over a decade of off–the–shelf buying to supplement its original OH-6A Cayuse helicopters. This proliferation has led to a mind–boggling alphabet soup of aircraft types in the 160th's 1st Battalion, the unit that most directly supports DELTA. Jane's *All the World's Aircraft* states that the MH-6B and AH-6C are derived from the OH-6A; the AH-6F and MH-6E from MD 500MG; and the AH-6G, MH-6F and MH-6J from the MD 530MG. "A" designations are given to the heavily armed attack versions of the Little Bird, which can be armed with a variety of miniguns, machine guns, rockets, and missiles. Nearly all Little Birds are equipped with a swinging, crane–like arm for fast–rope rappeling and Stabo operations, and the AH-6G, MH-6E, MH-6F, and possibly the AH-6F, have multifunction displays and forward–looking infrared (FLIR) imagers to be used in association with night vision goggles.

(**Opposite**) MD 530MG unleashing a salvo of 70mm rockets during weapons testing at the US Army's Yuma Proving Grounds, Arizona and closeups of seven–tube 70mm rocket launcher and TOW antitank missile pod. (**Top to bottom**) 160th SOAR AH-6G Little Bird bereft of any identifying markings or "sterile"; an MD 530N equipped with NOTAR (no tail rotor) system, including close–up of steering louvres on underside of tail; and MD 530N configured for transportation with louver cone and tail fins folded upward and main rotor blades stowed along tail boom. Note that the MD 530 models in the lower photos have both the pointed nose, for streamlining, and the pre–1982 bubble nose of the MD 500 series aircraft still used on most military variants.

Of great benefit to DELTA in urban counterterrorist situations is the 160th SOAR's conversion to the NOTAR system on its Little Birds. The NOTAR uses a variable–pitch fan and direct jet thruster to push cool air through longitudinal steering louvres on a circulation control tailboom. Although early tests by the 160th showed "higher than desired pilot workload" due to a tendency for the nose to wander at low speeds, yaw–only stability augmentation corrected the problem. With the NOTAR system, AH/MH-6 aircraft display a greatly reduced acoustic signature, increased hover stability, and roughly double the lateral and rearward speeds of conventional helicopters. The absence of a tail rotor also eliminates the danger of tail strikes on ground crew and allows DELTA troopers more freedom of movement around the aircraft during operations.

AN/ALQ-144A omnidirectional infrared jammer

Two seven–tube 70mm rocket launchers

AN/AAQ-16 FLIR imager

AH-6G

MD 530N

MD 530N

AC-130 Specter Gunship

The AC-130 Specter gunship is a basic C-130 modified with side–mounted weapons and various sensors that make it highly adaptable to a variety of special missions. When fielded against targets with few antiaircraft defenses and a minimal air threat, the Specter is able to provide close air support much more efficiently than a large force of fighter aircraft and is a particularly effective platform for interdiction and armed reconnaissance missions. The Specter has the ability to aid in perimeter defense, escort, surveillance, search and rescue, infiltration/exfiltration, illumination, and landing zone support operations, as well as to conduct limited airborne command and control functions for other strike aircraft.

The AC-130H is armed with two 20mm Gatling–type guns, a rapid–firing 40mm cannon and 105mm howitzer supported by a laser rangefinder (which can also be used for marking targets for laser–guided bombs), an infrared sensor to identify heat sources such as people and vehicles, a beacon–tracking radar, a fire control computer, two–kilowatt searchlight and a low–light–level television capable of amplifying even faint traces of starlight to monitor both targets and friendly forces. The newer AC-130U models have retained the 40 and 105mm weapons but use a single 25mm Gatling–type gun fed by a two–canister, automated loading system instead of the H models' 20mm guns which required their linked ammunition to

be hand–loaded. Other new features have also been added such as the F-15's fire control radar, lightweight Kevlar armor, inflight refueling capability, and a highly efficient, soundproof battle management center.

Depending on the type of target, threat environment, weather, and desired level of destruction, weapons can be accurately employed at altitudes from 3,000 to 20,000 feet above ground level. The Specter fires from a constant angle of bank and, at a typical slant range of 10,000 feet, the remarkably stable gun platform can deliver ordnance within ten feet of its target even under conditions of low cloud ceilings or poor visibility. Unlike fighter aircraft, which must make separate runs on hostile forces, targets are continually visible throughout the gunship's entire orbit and can be fired on at will. But even though the run–in headings required by fighter aircraft are not needed, no–fire headings may be imposed from the ground or automatically computed by the aircrew if there is a risk of short rounds hitting friendly forces from a particular angle.

The Specter's two–kilowatt searchlight can be used to illuminate targets and landing zones, aid in search and rescue, and supply light for the television sensor if its illuminator is inoperative. In combat, the searchlight is normally used in a covert infrared mode, to provide illumination for night vision devices, since its overt white light mode would easily pinpoint the gunship's position for hostile forces. Its effectiveness is reduced with altitude and weather.

DELTA troopers in a tight spot can mark their ground position with a wide variety of items. First, Mk-6 and Mk-25 ground markers can be dropped by hand from the rear of the Specter, itself, and will burn for forty–five and thirty minutes, respectively. Next, transponders, including the handheld SST-101 miniponder, can be picked up by the aircraft's beacon tracking radar at up to ten nautical miles and the powerful AN/UPN-25 and SST-181x transponders can be received by the ship's navigation radar at up to sixty nautical miles. A standard survival vest strobe light with a removeable infrared filter can also be used either visually or with the filter installed. The infrared filter provides the same information to the aircrew as the unmasked strobe but prevents visible light from revealing the friendly ground position

to the enemy forces. Positive identification is provided by turning one or more strobes off and on in response to radio instructions for the aircrew. The old standby, lightweight three–by–five–foot cloth reflective panels, can clearly mark ground reference points when illuminated by the Specter, either overtly or covertly. Other methods of marking positions include flashlights, vehicle lights, pen gun flares, tracer rounds, fires, fire arrows, signal mirrors, and simply running a vehicle engine with the ignition unshielded.

(**Opposite**) An AC-130H Specter fires its 105mm gun during a night exercise; (**top**) airmen loading a Specter's 40mm gun; (**left**) twin 20mm Gatling–type guns aft of the cockpit; and (**right**) 40mm and 105mm guns forward of the aircraft's loading ramp.

MC-130 Combat Talon and HC-130 Combat Shadow

The mission of the MC-130E and H Combat Talons is to conduct day and night infiltration, exfiltration, resupply, psychological operations, and aerial reconnaissance into hostile or enemy controlled territory using air landings, air drops or surface–to–air recoveries. The use of FLIR imagers enables aircrews to visually identify targets and checkpoints at night while terrain–following/terrain–avoidance(TF/TA) radar and an inertial navigation system allow extreme accuracy while navigating to unmarked drop zones. Missions are normally flown at night using a high–low–high altitude profile. The high portion is flown prior to penetrating and after exiting the target area at an altitude that minimizes fuel consumption and enemy detection. The aircraft then descends to the lowest possible altitude consistent with flying safety and uses its TF/TA radar to penetrate and operate in hostile territory.

The Talon's range depends on several factors, including configuration, payload, en route winds and weather, and the length of time spent at fuel–guzzling, low–level flight. For planning purposes, its range (without refueling and factoring in two hours at low level) is 2,800 nautical miles. With inflight refueling, the Talon's range is limited only by the availability of tanker support and the effect

that crew fatigue may have on the mission. The Talon is not a rapid response aircraft. Operating deep in heavily defended enemy territory requires extensive preflight planning, and units normally receive notification at least forty–eight hours out with a final briefing on threats and positions of friendly forces before takeoff.

Aircrews are capable of successfully operating at unmarked drop zones (DZs) but usually have something they can hang their headphones on. When ground and air component commanders agree to use a specific DZ, reception committee personnel coordinate with the aircrew on the type of markings to be used, configuration of the DZ, method of authentication and release point determination. The most frequent cause for mission aborts is a lack of coordination or confusion over marking procedures; it is important to note that terrain–following is made difficult during moderate showers and even further degraded during heavy thunderstorms.

Depending on mission, an aircrew makes either a static–line, low–altitude air drop; a high–altitude, low–opening (HALO) air drop; a surface–to–air recovery (STAR) using a Fulton extraction system; or may simply land the aircraft. For static–line drops during combat operations, a Talon is flown as low as 750 feet while a HALO drop, which requires a free fall before parachute opening, is never conducted from lower than 1,500 feet. For static–line drops combining both men and equipment (such as rubber rafts), troops exit immediately after ejection of equipment. A STAR can be used for the extractions during either day or night but requires fairly good weather to accomplish the mission safely. Either two people or 500 pounds of equipment can be picked up over land or water per pass. During air landings, the minimum length necessary is the takeoff/landing roll plus 500 feet for a total of approximately 3,000 feet. The Talon's minimum required runway width is sixty feet and, while the capability exists to set down at a landing zone that has no lights or is lit with infrared lights, use of the Special Forces seven–light panel marking system (which includes a 250–foot/ten percent safety zone at each end out) is preferred.

The HC-130P Combat Shadow tankers have essentially the same extensive radar and navigational aids as the Combat Talon, as well as the ability to refuel two helicopters simultaneously in flight. After the tanker unreels its fuel line and slows to approximately 120mph, the Shadow's customer slowly edges its refuel probe closer to the drogue–tipped hose while making certain that it stays beneath or to the outside of the tankers turbulent slipstream. It generally takes an MH-53 less than ten minutes to top off and an MH-47, with its huge fuel blisters, can get its fill in about fifteen minutes.

(**Opposite**) The retracted nose prongs, which, when extended forward and out, snag the line of a target baloon during surface–to–air recoveries, can be clearly seen in this shot of a MC-130 receiving fuel from a KC-135 tanker. See page 120 for a complete recovery sequence. (**Top left**) A Vietnam–era MC-130 rigged for a pick–up with guard cables running from the top of its bulbous nose to its wingtips and (**top right**) a similarly configured MC-130E or H variant. Note the difference in radar bulge configuration on the newer aircraft, to accommodate its expanded TF/TA, FLIR, and other systems, as well as its lengthened prongs. (**Above left**) TF/TA radar screen, displaying an obstruction in the aircraft's path as a blob below the upwardly bowed line, and a portion of the FLIR display off to the left. These systems and all other internal controls can be made to glow in a subdued mode so that they do not interfere with the pilot's night vision goggles. (**Above right**) An MH-60 carefully maneuvering its refuel probe up to an HC-130's extended fuel line and drogue.

Chapter 5
Back to the Desert

The deep sleep of the early morning hours was interrupted by the familiar obnoxious sound of a pager going off. Reaching for his clothing, the young Sergeant kissed his wife's head and ambled down the hall to check on his son. Allowing the hall light to play over the boy's sandy hair, the trooper bent down to kiss him goodbye as he had so often in the past. Waiting until he had left the house, he sat on the front steps to pull on his well worn cowboy boots. He climbed into his pickup truck and drove to the post. In less than two hours, the young sergeant's troop was winging away from Pope Air Force Base near Fort Bragg. As the wheels of the lumbering C-141 Starlifter retracted into their wells, his troop commander was already scanning the initial intelligence reports from the agencies supporting the unit. Things were not so good in the land of oil and sand.

At 0400 on the morning of Thursday, August 2, 1990, mechanized elements of Saddam Hussein's elite Republican Guards stabbed across the desert frontier separating Iraq and Kuwait east of the disputed Rumalia oilfield. Iraqi forces had been massing steadily across the border for almost two weeks before the invasion, but both Western and Arabian governments believed this to be nothing more than a show of force to bolster Saddam's financial claims against the oil–rich kingdom. By midday, all meaningful resistance by Kuwait's tiny army had been crushed and its royal family had fled to a sumptuous exile in Saudi Arabia.

The Baathist government in Baghdad rejoiced

A thirsty trooper inhales bottled water in the shade of a C-141 StarLifter in Saudi Arabia.

over its quick victory and believed that it had been accomplished with such speed that the world was presented with a *fait accompli*. Saddam expected a toothless condemnation from the United Nations and perhaps even a half–hearted economic embargo that would soon fade away. But his analysis was fatally flawed. US and British leaders meeting in the United States immediately resolved that the rest of the Middle East's oil resources must be kept out of Saddam's bloodied hands, at all costs. Even before his generals gathered their forces for the next morning's move to the Saudi border, numerous elements of America's special operations forces were either already deployed or were going "wheels up" from bases in the United States and Europe.

From the first moment President George Bush was notified that Iraqi forces were plunging across

Kuwait's border, one of the prime challenges to face him as the National Command Authority was the possibility—indeed probability—that large numbers of Americans would become prisoners in a dangerous diplomatic game. The specter of a second major Middle East hostage crisis loomed over the Pentagon and the White House. Although public speculation was kept to a minimum, no one needed to be reminded that the Carter administration fell because of the prolonged hostage crisis in Iran. The extreme vulnerability of the US Embassy staff and numerous Americans associated with Kuwait's petroleum industry was evident. When coupled with the Baathist regime's close ties with terrorist groups, history of wanton aggression against its neighbors, and deadly abuse of its own people, the president had no choice but to act. Although special operations forces assets already in the Gulf were capable of performing the hasty option response, the National Command Authority launched the first DELTA assets into the Middle East.

Crisis action teams were dispatched to Saudi Arabia and other friendly nations to establish C^3 (command, control, and communications) sites for future operations and to provide a terminal for information to and from Washington. Launch sites for missions were identified and staging areas hastily opened. Meanwhile, back at Fort Bragg, the Joint Special Operations Command (JSOC) worked hard to avoid being caught flatfooted and began building a massive workup of target folders for the "long war" that was sure to come.

Other important assets moving into the area were elements of the Intelligence Support Activity (ISA). Like so many other parts of the special operations force, ISA was an offshoot of the *Desert I* after-action review. A critical failing during the hostage crisis in Iran was the lack of information from human intelligence sources or HUMINT. In Iran, DELTA did not have an "eyeball" on its target. In Iraq and

Kuwait, ISA would provide the needed eyes.

Various elements of the myriad special operations units in Europe and the United States continued to trickle in, and most of the burden of working with the resistance inside Kuwait was assumed by the Special Forces units that already had that mission in accordance with theater war plans. As predicted, US and other foreign nationals did indeed become "guests" at selected Iraqi strategic military and nuclear sites but were eventually allowed to leave as a "gesture of goodwill" when their continued captivity threatened to precipitate, not prevent, an assault on Iraq. DELTA remained.

Commencement of the coalition air campaign raised fears that hostages might be taken in retaliation at widely scattered locations around the globe, and additional target folders of possible hostage-holding centers began to take shape. While significant terrorist operations never emerged, the public display of Allied prisoners of war did cause concern at the highest levels, and plans were formulated to rescue those individuals. Small teams were also selected to carry out a number of sensitive, direct-action missions against targets in Iraq's command and control nets.

Initially, special operations units were faced with the same problem they have always had to deal with: How to get the conventional force commanders to use their capabilities properly or even at all. For example, the 75th Ranger Regiment's assessment team left the Gulf after finding out that there was very little they could do in the theater, and the elite light infantry of the 82d Airborne Division was severely handicapped on the billiard table–terrain without an immense amount of support.

Colonel Jessie Johnson, commander of Central Command's (CENTCOM's) Special Operations Command (SOC), drafted his campaign plans for the upcoming desert war from his headquarters at King Fahd International Airport near Dhahran. A

(**Right**) All–terrain Fast Attack Vehicles (FAVs) and motorcycles (**above**) saw extensive use by special operations forces, including DELTA, during operations in Iraq and Kuwait and operated from forward bases in Saudi Arabia or base camps established far behind Iraqi lines. Motorcycles with heavily muffled engines offered troopers individualized, high–speed movement coupled with the ability to approach a target from several axes simultaneously and, on some types of missions, would be used in combination with FAVs.

Capable of being armed with a wide assortment of goodies—machine guns, antitank weapons, grenade launchers and almost anything else one might think of—FAVs offered substantial hitting power and the ability to travel extended distances across the desert at speeds up to 80– plus mph. The vehicles pictured here both mount AT4 antitank missile launchers on the outsides of their frame roofs and M60E3 machine guns forward of the passenger seats. An additional gunner sits in the elevated, rear seat, which can swivel around for firing at targets behind the vehicle. In the top photo, this position mounts a .50cal machine gun while the vehicle above sports a 40mm grenade launcher. Note the dart board taped to the nose of the FAV at lower left, a not–so–subtle comment by its crew on their vulnerability. *Soldier of Fortune.*

veteran of *Desert I*, where he commanded the joint Ranger–DELTA road–watch teams, Johnson knew what difficulties awaited his forces. Luckily for him, his boss at CENTCOM, General H. Norman Schwarzkopf, had the utmost confidence in his special ops commander. Despite attempts by elements within the Joint Chiefs of Staff, to replace him with a two–star officer, Schwarzkopf kept his faith in Johnson, who in return, became the architect for several brilliantly executed operations.

Saddam's Vengence Weapon

As the war progressed, another in history's long line of terror weapons was unleashed in the Middle East: the Scud B medium–range ballistic missile, successor to Hitler's infamous V-1 and V-2 rockets

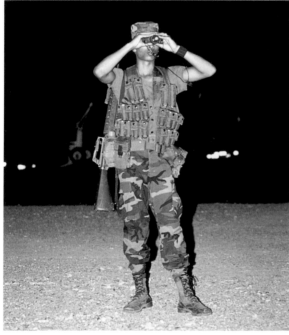

DELTA operated out of secure, remote bases dotting the desert wastes south of the Saudi–Iraqi border. (**Above**) A C-130, of unidentified type, sits baking under "big red" across from a special operations Black Hawk with external, add–on fuel tanks. (**Left**) Air base security armed for bear with a combination M16 assault rifle/M203 grenade launcher. His vest is packed with twenty 40mm grenades for the M203, and he is using night vision goggles, which turn even the blackest nights into a green day, to scan the perimeter.

of World War II. On those earlier weapons, The "V" designation was, itself, part of Hitler's psychological warfare campaign aimed at terrorizing the British people. Nazi English–language propaganda broadcasts gleefully warned Britons of the immense destruction that would be wreaked on their cities by the "vengeance" weapons. Since their target was an English–speaking public, the Nazis named their rockets the V-1 and V-2, instead of giving them an "R" designation for the equivalent German word, *rache*.

The Scud retained many of the V-2's basic characteristics, along with many deadly improvements. Highly mobile, it nevertheless required more than an hour to fuel and its involved targeting procedures took excruciatingly long to complete, even when performed by experienced crews at preplotted sites. To make matters even more interesting, homemade

(**Right**) A Scud B medium–range ballistic missile on its MAZ-543 transporter–erector–launcher and (**above**) a rare photograph of a Scud impact. Even before certain changes were made to the weapon that degraded its accuracy, it was not known for its ability to make pinpoint strikes. The weapon in the above photo was fired by Soviet forces at Afghan guerrillas who had surrounded Loyalist troops at an isolated garrison. It missed the guerrillas and instead landed within the government troops' defensive perimeter. Above: *Soldier of Fortune*.

versions of the missile, like the *al Hussein*, incorporated range enhancements that both reduced its warhead capacity and severely degraded its ability to strike near its target.

The Soviets designed the Scud to deliver small nuclear warheads, or as an area saturation system when fired in conventional battery salvos; the Iraqis instead used it as simply a fire–in–the–general–direction–of–your–adversary–and–then–wait–for–the–results weapon. Fixed launch sites containing both real and dummy missiles existed at airfields in western Iraq, targeting Israel, and in eastern Iraq, aimed at Iran and Saudi Arabia. These sites were well known to US and Israeli planners and could be easily removed from the picture. It was Saddam's surprisingly large number of wheeled launchers for the Scud and shorter–range Frog missiles that proved to be exceedingly difficult targets for air reconnaissance assets to locate. This difficulty in targeting the mobile launchers in the wide expanses of Iraq set the stage for one role the troopers of DELTA never dreamed of or trained for: Scud hunting.

The scenario thrust upon DELTA was a far cry from the world of takedowns and hostage rescues each man became immersed in the moment he entered Wally World. Many, if not all, the troops deployed to the Gulf had extensive training in their initial Special Forces specialties and were already experts in carrying out such standard missions as unconventional warfare, special reconnaissance, foreign internal defense, plus search and rescue operations, to name just a few, but it was the introduction of Saddam's terror weapons that forced the counterterrorists to revert to these basic war–fighting specialties and become what the press dubbed "super commandos." Curiously enough, though, since Scud missiles served no real military purpose —when used as they were by the Iraqis— DELTA troopers could still be said to be involved in a new, unanticipated form of counterterrorism.

The war was going poorly for the Iraqi warlord, and he knew that his best bet to overcome the military setbacks around was to drive a wedge between the Arab and Western elements in the coalition arrayed against him. If attacks on Jewish population centers could push Israel into a knee–jerk military response, Saddam believed that indignant Arab masses would finally heed his call for a *jihad*, or holy war, and either overthrow unfriendly governments like President Hosni Mubarak's in Egypt or, at the very least, force their governments to withdraw from the coalition. Western elements isolated at the end of a very long logistics line would be forced into an ignominious withdrawal.

Saddam's strategy was not difficult to anticipate,

and the White House made it crystal clear through strong public statements (coupled with a rapid, showy deployment of a Patriot surface–to–air missile battery to Tel Aviv) that the drawing of Israel into the war would be prevented at all costs. CENTCOM had no choice but to commit its Air Force component to a resource–consuming search for mobile launchers with little to show for its efforts.* This same mission was also handed to the Army's Special Forces, who, if necessary, would actually target individual vehicles for air strikes— an extremely risky business for the troops involved but a mission that was, in light of the strategic situation, of immense importance. CENTCOM quickly discovered, however, that a critical shortage of trained special recon teams existed in the Kuwaiti Theater of Operations (KTO).

Every available Green Beret was committed to serving as liaison with the Saudi Army, training Kuwaiti resistance forces, or conducting intelligence–gathering missions for General Schwarzkopf's headquarters. When it became necessary to scrape together additional assets to help locate Scuds, the only force in the KTO was the counterterrorists of DELTA, as well as some British SAS personnel. Reports by the European and American news media later referred to this use of DELTA as if the unit were some sort of key reserve, when, in reality, it was all Schwarzkopf had at the moment.

Special operations assets made available by the coalition forces, primarily DELTA and the desert–wise SAS, were formed into teams and prepared for the upcoming operations.* At first, though, Colonel

---

*The continued success of the Iraqis at hitting Israeli and Saudi population centers necessitated that a full squadron of F-15Es be essentially pulled from the air campaign and assigned the task of eliminating mobile Scuds. Other air assets were soon added as the equivalent of three squadrons became tied up by the effort, and the number of sorties by Scud–hunting intelligence, refueling and strike aircraft sometimes climbed to more than 300 per twenty–four hour period. Although a severe drain on US resources, this heavy and prolonged commitment was instrumental in convincing the Israelis to call off two planned raids into western Iraq that could have had a disastrous effect on the war effort.

Johnson's professionals from Smoke Bomb Hill and the Ranch were understandably missing from the almost–continuous Gulf news coverage, while other forces from Fort Bragg, the XVIIIth Airborne Corps, 1st Corps Support Command, and the renowned 82d Airborne Division received their share of the limelight. But it wasn't long before reporters were hearing strange tales of parachutes gliding silently through the Arabian night to deposit their human cargo on the desert floor. The stories are many, but all have the same theme and similar scenarios. The following is just one of them. Maybe it's just a good piece of propaganda; then again, maybe it's true.

Prepping the Battlefield

An in-depth mission analysis was conducted on the upcoming Scud hunt by the intelligence agencies supporting the theater's special operations forces. The intel experts looked at such subjects as the terrain and infiltration/exfiltration routes

US special operations forces did not truly "own the night" as the often–repeated slogan claimed, but did operate extremely effectively in that environment, due to a combination of superb training and equipment. (**Above** and **above right**) Troopers viewed through a NVG move out under cover of darkness and rappel from a Black Hawk.

through Iraqi antiaircraft belts and known locations of enemy units were plotted on the situation maps. As this information was analyzed, a clear picture emerged indicating that the majority of the target areas could be easily reached by Army MH-60 Pave Hawks of the 160th Special Operations Aviation Regiment (Airborne) or Air Force MH-53 Pave Low IIIs of the 1st Special Operations Wing.

Unfortunately, the extremely heavy demand for the specialized helicopters in the KTO, as well as various other considerations, meant that they could not be used in every situation. For tactical reasons, it was decided that the target area around which this story centers necessitated that DELTA conduct a HAHO infiltration. HAHO (pronounced *hey–ho*)

---

*The SAS not only retains a great deal of institutional knowledge on desert warfare but also makes frequent use of a training area in the Gulf state of Oman.

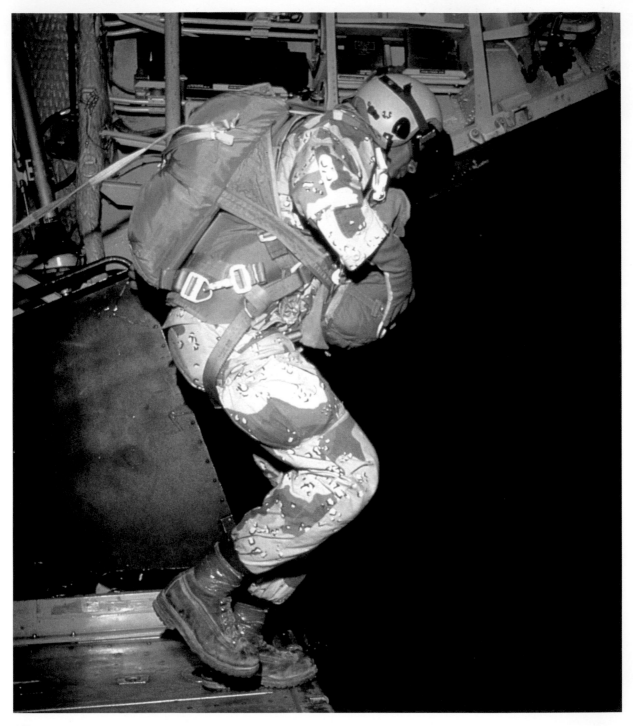

is the acronym for high–altitude, high–opening and essentially means that the drop is conducted at about 30,000 feet or higher, with the jumper opening his parachute almost immediately after clearing the plane. The trooper then glides his maneuverable, double–canopy parachute through the sky and lands with pinpoint accuracy at a predetermined site. The distance from the point that the jumper pulls his rip cord and where he lands can be as much as fifty miles.

The team participating in this unique Scud–hunting mission is required to prepare a "briefback" on how each trooper will carry out his duties. The briefback is standard operating procedure within the special operations community and covers the friendly versus enemy situation, the mission, its execution, support requirements, command structures, and a short, concise, yet detailed narrative of how the trooper will help accomplish the mission. The briefback is normally given to the leadership of the unit and not only demonstrates to the commander that his men are ready, but also assures the team that everyone is playing off the same sheet of music.

After a few carefully considered questions, the team is given the go–ahead and conducts final rehearsals, equipment checks, and other preparations. On this mission, they are more concerned with the "sneak and peek" than direct–action aspects of the operation. If they can find the missile's elusive transporter–erector–launchers (TELs), they will call

in an air strike and, if circumstances require it, use a portable laser to target the weapon for destruction by the fast–movers of the Air Force.

The basic plan is simple. The team will move undetected from their drop zone to a hidden observation point overlooking a likely area for Scud activity. When confirmed targets enter the area, SOC will be notified, and an E-2C Sentry's airborne warning and control system (AWACS) will vector strike aircraft into the target area. During their approach, the jets follow voice or signal beacon wavelengths to their prey. Air attacks will be conducted visually but any TELs obscured by darkness, camouflage, or poor weather will be lased, or "painted," by the recon team. Rolling in on their bomb runs, the fast–movers' sensors will lock on a laser guided bomb or rocket and release the "smart" munitions to glide along the laser's invisible path like a road map to the target. The jets will then maneuver away from the area, having only teased the outer perimeters of the lethal antiaircraft systems' kill zones, and the DELTA troopers, if necessary, will continue to lase targets for incoming aircraft from their concealed hideout. As many Iraqi units found out, the laser's invisible beam brought very visible destruction.

Reaching the austere departure airfield, the team is ushered into a secured hangar cordoned off from the rest of the facility. It is here that all of the specialized gear needed for the mission is stored. The departure airfield will also be the mission support site (MSS) for the operation, and a mobile communications van, mated to the main SOC communications bunker at King Khalid Military City,* has been moved into the hangar. The mobile van constitutes part of a duplex communications network

An Air Force Special Operations combat control team member exits from the open ramp of a MC-130 Combat Talon. Control teams are often inserted before the arrival of special operations or conventional forces to mark landing or drop zones that must be used at night by pilots using NVGs and arcraft fitted with infrared imagers. For example, a control team member had already arrived at and marked the *Desert I* refuel site in Iran before the arrival of the aircraft bearing DELTA. The lack of weapon and rucksack indicates that this was taken during a practice exercise.

*Designed and constructed by the US Army Corps of Engineers during the Iran–Iraq War, King Khalid Military City is one of three huge base complexes around which the outer defenses of the kingdom are formed. The "Emerald City" (as it was called by many US soldiers, who were surprised at the sight of it rising out of the desert wastes) is located roughly 110 miles southwest of Kuwait's westernmost point almost halfway to the major Saudi Arabian city of Buraydah.

(**Above**) The control and reporting center outside King Khalid Military City which linked US and Saudi mobile and airborne communications. (**Left**) An internal view.

that ensured reception of the team's vital intelligence even if one part of the network went down from either systems failure or enemy action. Except for the team's communications specialist, who is coordinating preselected frequencies and transmission times, the troopers take little notice of the signals experts moving to and from the van and stay focused on checking and rechecking their weapons and field gear. All weapons had been test–fired before leaving the isolation site, and at the hangar, a ritual of sorts takes place, which will wed the jumper to his air items and other essential

equipment. This union ends only when the mission is completed—or worse.

The six troopers wear sterile desert camouflage fatigues with the required face scarves and flop hats. Struggling mightily, they pull on cumbersome, insulated jumpsuits to help fight off the cold which sometimes exceeds –50 degrees at 35,000 feet, even in the Middle East. In addition to its insulation properties, the jumpsuits have radar–absorbing capabilities that will impede the enemy's ability to pick up the soldiers as they glide across the sky. Fortunately, the February night—cold even in the desert—engulfs the airfield, providing a small amount of relief as they don their main and reserve parachutes and oxygen masks. Before high–altitude drops like this one, both the jumpers and the crew of the unpressurized aircraft have to start breathing oxygen one hour before takeoff or "launch time." The team receives final jumpmaster inspections, and the troop commander arrives for that one last visit a leader makes. He is more of a fellow member than a commander, and everyone in the hangar knows the way the boss feels. He'd trade in his major's oak leaves to be going with them into Iraq.

Following the safety NCO out into the desert darkness, each man finds his own release to the inevitable tension. A flick of a "bird" finger to the top sergeant with a muffled, "Up yours, Top," or "See ya at the NCO club," mark the beginning of another mission. Their transportation, a huge C-141B, rests majestically next to the hangar, its gaping clamshell doors exposing the broad tail. The team struggles up the StarLifter's ramp into the cavernous cargo bay, while the crew chief and loadmaster guide the men around the small patches of hydraulic fluid habitually dotting its deck. An oxygen console rests securely in the center of the compartment, and each jumper

A C-141 prepares for a night takeoff from an airstrip in the Saudi desert.

plugs into it after disconnecting the oxygen mask from his individual bailout bottle.

As the StarLifter slowly pivots and then begins to taxi, the crew chief switches the internal lighting to the red lights required for the team to gain their night vision. The pilot reaches the main runway, and as he revs up the four powerful Pratt & Whitney turbofans for takeoff, each team member is caught in the thoughts of the moment: the myriad details that must be covered so that the mission succeeds, his wife, family, or the girl back home—the same thoughts soldiers have had to deal with since the second–oldest profession began.

The Jump

The C-141B flies on an easterly heading to its rendezvous point with two B-52s flying in from the tiny island base of Diego Garcia deep in the Indian Ocean. Snuggling into the number three slot, the formation portrays just another inbound bomber formation for any Iraqi radar still operating.

As the unlikely trio nears Iraqi airspace, the jumpmaster receives updates from the navigator. At prescribed checkpoints, he notifies the team of their exact coordinates so that all know where they are in the event that they are forced to bail out early. Thirty minutes from jump time, the team prepares for the "infil." The men assist each other in making sure that their rucksacks ride snugly against the bottom of the main parachute. Checking their padded–leather jump helmets, goggles, and oxygen masks one last time, they prepare to change over from the oxygen consoles to the bailout bottle strapped to their left sides. On command from the jumpmaster, the jumpers switch to their bailout bottles and waddle toward the open troop doors on each side of the fuselage.

Staff Sergeant Len Rodgers and the rest of the recon team work their way to positions along the walls of the StarLifter as their communications man, serving as jumpmaster, completes his visual checks and gives the hand signal for "Stand by." The cabin's eerie red lights, green jump light, and the howling winds whipping in the open troop doors could easily meet the needs of a good nightmare, and Staff Sergeant Rodgers is nearly deafened by the roaring wind and mournful banshee whine of the engines. He marvels that some people actually think this is fun! Moving closer to the door, he receives the "Go!" signal, as the jumpmaster disappears out the open troop door.

Pivoting on the ball of his right foot, Rodgers swings out behind him and falls into the position commonly referred to as the "frog." He's immediately followed in quick succession by the rest of the team. Plummeting through the moonless night, arms and legs extended, Rodgers begins to feel the penetrating cold. Behind him, each man monitors the altimeter securely strapped to his left wrist and assumes the glide position as they prepare to deploy their parachutes. At 30,000 feet, the aerial ballet continues as the team members pull their silver ripcords.

To the casual observer, this particular maneuver looks like a giant hand shaking each jumper loose from his very life. In reality, the men feel very little, and each checks the double–layer canopy above to see if his is fully inflated. Fortunately for this team, all now resemble airfoil–shaped wings, and the jumpers line up in a rough, follow–the-leader formation, taking the planned westerly heading as Staff Sergeant Rodgers navigates through the frozen night air. Settling into the parachute harness, he scans the panorama unfolding before him. Far to the north, flashes appear from the bombing mission the team's C-141 had joined. Craning his neck around to the southeast, he can barely make out green* tracers darting skyward in a futile search for the destroyers of a known Scud site's command and control bunker and wonders if it was done in by one of the F-117 stealth attack aircraft. He turns back and looks toward the unseen drop zone and toys with the idea that the display is for their benefit. He knows,

---

*Munitions manufactured by former Warsaw Pact countries such as the Soviet Union and Czechoslovakia give off green tracers, but the spectrum of hues sometimes runs to a yellow–green. US and many Western munitions give off a red trace.

however, that the distant explosions mean that real, flesh–and–blood men are dying.

As the team continues on its noiseless flight, each jumper lines up on the dull luminescent strip on the helmet below. Altimeter checks show that the gradual warming they feel is due to the descent. At 12,000 feet, they remove their individual masks and inhale the night air. With each passing minute, the team gets closer to the drop zone. This is when the paratroopers are most vulnerable. All are sure that the entire Iraqi Army is waiting to pounce on them, but the only living things awaiting the DELTA troopers are some stray goats from a Bedouin camp that run bleating into the night when they strike the earth. The men are relieved

Special Forces trooper on a practice jump, taking up the "frog" position. Note that the soldier wears an altimeter on his left wrist. Rucksacks are always strapped below the main parachutes and, in the second photo, a rucksack can be seen dangling fifteen feet below the jumper so that it will be out of his way when he lands.

that no reception committee is on hand to greet them, but there will be plenty of time for surprises. One of the greatest shocks of this desert war for the special operations soldiers was the fact that whenever you thought you were in the middle of nowhere, someone was always showing up—usually at the most inopportune time.

Chapter 6

The Scud Busters

The Lord said to Moses, "Send men to spy out the land of Canaan, . . . from each tribe of their fathers shall you send a man, everyone a leader among them."

Numbers 13

The team quickly assembles after landing. The troopers move to a nearby depression, and while half take up defensive positions, the others strip off their heavy jump suits and then roll them up with their 'chutes and jump helmets to make compact, easily buried bundles. The gear is quickly buried and the now–unencumbered troopers silently take their turn guarding the perimeter. Preparing to move out, each man goes through his mental checklist to ensure that every piece of equipment is in place. Faint vehicle noise drifts through the black night and the telltale signs of light are seen to the south.

Staff Sergeant Christopher Gleason, the point man for this operation, silently moves to his right, where the team leader is making last–minute com-

Troopers in the desert viewed through an image–intensification device.

pass checks and using his handheld satellite navigation system to pinpoint the team's exact location. Chief Warrant Officer Gary Van Hee intently studies the tiny screen's luminous, digital readout, which arrived as coded signals from a Global Positioning System (GPS) satellite drifting in orbit above the desert. Only one–third of the complete twenty–four–satelite constellation needed to blanket the earth had yet been sent aloft, so the lack of full–time, three–dimensional coverage sometimes made reception problematic. Tonight, though, Van Hee is having no trouble and he smiles broadly as the staff sergeant moves within whisper distance.

Gleason points out the rather obvious activity to the southwest, "The whole place is crawling with ragheads, Chief!" Van Hee's camouflaged face breaks into a devious grin and he retorts with his typical, "No shit, Sherlock." The team leader's time–honored response reassures the edgy point man, who steps gingerly back to his position and prepares to move out.

Each man's personal equipment is designed for specific tasks. Black balaclavas have been replaced with desert flop hats and face paint of pale yellow and brown. "No sweat" bandanas and camouflage scarves are wrapped tightly around necks and tucked into the now–familiar "chocolate chip"–patterned camouflage jackets. The men carry ammunition in pouches hung from their vests, and distributed about their bodies are canteens, first–aid equipment, a powerful miniature flashlight, and a Beretta pistol. Two of the six–man team also carry silencers so that their Barettas can be used to noiselessly kill an enemy guard or nosey point man. The unique silencers are so efficient that, using subsonic rounds, only the sound of the hammer striking the firing pin and the gun's action cycling can be heard—a small sound in this noisy environment.

The threat of "getting slimed" by Iraqi poison gas is far more than rhetorical in this war, so each trooper also carries a gas mask, securely strapped within easy reach on his left leg, and a complete protective suit in his rucksack. Rucks for this mission are configured with extra ammunition and smoke grenades. Additional water, medical supplies, a small quantity of food, and limited decontamination gear, complete the major items. Personal weapons are based on the defensive requirements of the mission, and the team carries either Colt M16A2 assault rifles or Heckler & Koch MP5 submachine guns.

While these final checks are being made, the communications expert, Sergeant First Class Michael Cranson, sends the team's initial entry report, a codeword transmission advising the MSS that they have arrived safely at the drop zone. For this signal, Cranson uses his radio's burst–transmission capability, and with the touch of a finger, the pre–

coded message is instantaneously sent. The split–second broadcast provides no time for hostile direction finders to get a fix on the team's position.

Armed with an integrally silenced MP5 SD3, Staff Sergeant Gleason slowly leads the way out of the depression and toward a large, rocky outcropping. The team members swing into their allotted positions behind him, forming a loose file. This and every action these soldiers will complete during the mission has been practiced over and over. Gleason and his fellow troopers use AN/PVS-7 night vision goggles to guide them through the rocky terrain. Popularly known as NODs, for night observation devices, the 1.5 pound goggles fit against a trooper's forehead and literally turn the desert darkness into a greenish, but very visible, day.

A Global Positioning System receiver.

By amplifying existing light, they enable man–sized targets to be recognized at almost 100 yards on all but the very darkest nights, with good moonlight extending their range by fifty percent or more. Operating under a last quarter moon, the men can see extremely well, but spotty cloud cover creates sudden, unexpected drops in visibility, in addition to the device's limited peripheral field of vision.

The point man's stubby, silenced MP5, his night vision goggles, and modified tactical vest give him an unearthly appearance. The bleak terrain, coupled with the patrol's appearance, could easily be mistaken for a Hollywood supernatural thriller. Walking behind the point man, the compass man, Staff Sergeant Rodgers, not only navigates for the patrol with his compass (for direction) and altimeter (for elevation), but also by watching his distance count (by how far he walks). The team leader occupies the number three position, and his communications, or "commo" man, Sergeant First Class Cranson, holds down number four. Positions five and six are rounded out by the team medic, Master Sergeant Frank Rodrigues, and the demolitions expert, another staff sergeant, who doubles as the patrol's tail gunner. His primary responsibility is to ensure that no one surprises the team from the rear and, like the point man, the tail gunner also resembles an alien stalking through a moonscape.

While approaching the low ridge where they will set up their observation post, it becomes painfully clear that they have, indeed, dropped into an area full of Iraqi units. Reaching their destination, the team immediately sets up security, sends out a two–man recon of the area, and digs in (one of the veterans later likened the experience to hacking into an asphalt parking lot). Flexible prefabricated covers are stretched over their holes to make the hide site complete, and the men will use disposable plastic bags to contain their bodily wastes so that no wild or stray animals will be attracted to their position—

a potentially disasterous occurrence that could attract curious Iraqi eyes and expose their position.

The troopers are prepared to lie low for days, watching for the elusive Scuds, but the arrival of dawn quickly reveals that part of Saddam's missile inventory is already operating in this area.

At first, only normal military, and civilian, traffic can be seen speeding along the east–west highway stretched out before them. It isn't long, though, before Van Hee recognizes some very familiar friends. Tailing along behind a westbound string of large civilian Mercedes tractor–trailers is a Ural-375 truck, mounting a mobile crane, and a pair of Type ZIL-157V tractors hauling elongated cargoes covered by tarps. The vehicles continue down the road for almost two miles and then pull off to the right about a hundred yards into the desert. Excitement is running high in the team and reaches a peak a half hour later when an eight–wheeled MAZ-543 transporter–erector–launcher (a TEL vehicle known to carry Scud missiles) and a ZIL-157V tanker towing a trailer appear to the east. They zoom by and continue on to the other waiting vehicles which, by now, include numerous supply trucks, C^3 vans, and a mix of towed quad 23mm and dual 30mm antiaircraft guns in the process of deploying on both sides of the highway. The top of the TEL is still well–covered by sand–colored tarps, but Van Hee is willing to bet his life and the lives of his men that it mounts a Scud missile.

The suspicious TEL remains with the other vehicles for only about ten minutes before all but the antiaircraft element suddenly begin to move off in column across the desert. After only a few hundred yards, the lead truck turns abruptly to the left into a deep wadi that arches back toward the road passing under it at a long, thin bridge a quarter mile past their original turnoff. As far as the team leader's concerned, this confirms it. There is no reason for an Iraqi unit this far afield of the main weight of coalition air attacks to go to this kind of trouble to hide itself unless it's a missile unit. At night, the TEL and select support vehicles will emerge back onto the flat, tabletop terrain to fire its terror weapon at Israel.

Sighting through his 7x40 Steiner binoculars, Van Hee begins to list what he sees as the vehicles disappear one by one down the now–apparent path bulldozed to the dry streambed. His time as an exchange member with one of West Germany's famed long–range reconnaissance companies is now paying off. As he reels off the NATO names, the team's radio operator writes them on his notepad. After one more sweep of the target area, Van Hee tells Cranson to inform headquarters that the "mother of all targets" is in front of them. He then slides back into the two–man foxhole, closes his eyes, and wearily tries to relax.

Opening his rucksack flap, Cranson closely examines the Satellite Communications System (SATCOM). From the ruck's outside pocket he pulls a miniature black satellite antenna folded in such a way that it looks like little more than a small, closed umbrella. Unfolding its legs and arms, Cranson places the device just beyond the lip of the hide hole and checks its frame to ensure that each prong is extended to its maximum position. With a diameter of only 17in, the antenna's profile will provide an observer with little clue as to what it is, even if the device could be seen from the highway. Cranson plugs the antenna's black, coaxial cable into the SATCOM and turns it on.

While the system hums and ticks through its self–checks and calibrations, the commo man listens through his headsets and consults the *Equatorial Satelite Antenna Pointing Guide* for the necessary elevation and azimuth angles required to orient the SATCOM's antenna for sending and receiving signals. Cranson moves the frame dish back and forth until he hears the unmistakable peep of the orbiting satel-

lite and then settles in to start his transmission. He speaks in slow, distinct tones into his microphone, sending the entire intelligence picture of what the recon team is viewing to a receiving station in the SOC communications bunker at King Khalid. Immediately, this vital information is passed through the US Air Force liaison officer to CENTCOM's air component tucked away in a basement corner of the Royal Saudi Air Force building in Riyadh.

Within minutes of the initial report being sent, coalition jets, pulled from the air campaign to hunt for Scuds, are vectored from their stations as others scramble from Saudi fields far to the southeast. Twenty–two minutes after the initial report, the first aircraft arrive over the highway. The jets briefly circle well out of range of the frustrated Iraqi anti-aircraft gunners while coordinating their attack, and then make straight for the well–camouflaged vehicles parked along the dry streambed.

Tipped off to the Iraqis' exact location, the ungainly looking A-10 Thunderbolt IIs (affectionately

A man–portable satelite communications system.

236

Mission accomplished. (**Left**) A missile and its mobile launching platform caught out in the open and destroyed. (**Above**) A missile rearm vehicle burned to the ground by Air Force jets.

called "Warthogs" or simply "Hogs") turn the wadi into a death trap. Resembling sharks during a feeding frenzy, the jets continuously roll in and pound the missile unit, and then begin to work on targets of opportunity up and down the highway. Their method of attack, however, seems strange to the hidden team members watching the show with intense interest. All had at one time or another seen live–fire exercises where the hog drivers swooped in and plastered targets from treetop heights, but now their hogs seemed to rarely venture below 8,000 or 10,000 feet because of the antiair assets.

Throughout the rest of the day, air strikes continue to hit what can only be described as "a target–rich environment." Periodic, huge explosions rend the wadi, and Cranson, who is monitoring the Warthogs' communications net, informs Van Hee that the hog drivers claim "two Scuds TANGO UNI-FORM" (Tits Up—slang for "destroyed"). Later strikes are conducted almost exclusively by F-16s, with some help from Tornado attack aircraft of unknown origin. The team hadn't been briefed that

Tornadoes would be in on the show, and although Cranson picks up their cryptic transmissions, he can only state that they are *not* speaking *American* English. He can't make out if they are piloted by Brits, Saudis, or Italians (all of whom field the multirole jet), and is the butt of several rude jokes from his friends until they, too, fail just as badly at deciphering the jet jockeys' nationalities.

These aircraft, and all others working the many targets, fly no lower than the Warthogs and, consequently, there are a lot of misses. But even through the smoke and dust kicked up by the strikes, Van Hee can clearly see that the cumulative weight of the air attacks has destroyed nearly every vehicle in the area by using a combination of rockets, iron bombs, and cluster munitions. The medium–altitude attacks have, moreover, rendered the defenders' antiaircraft guns nearly useless by striking from beyond their *effective* range. No one in the team sees any coalition aircraft go down.

As evening draws near, the team leader fears that their position is becoming increasingly vulnerable.

(**Opposite**) A night–stalking F-15 taking on fuel during *Desert Storm*. (**Above**) A disabled fuel truck in Iraq, and (**left**) an actual Scud TEL targeted by an F-15E. Target identification was often extremely difficult at night, even with the most sophisticated ground and airborne systems.

Although well–hidden on a barely perceptible ridge, they are, nevertheless, located on the highest terrain feature in the area. It might only be a matter of time before the increasingly active Iraqi patrols unearth them. As soon as it begins to turn dark, the team picks up their gear, quickly sanitizes the area, and heads south across the previously active road, now silent except for the crackling of a few vehicle fires still burning brightly. Moving carefully across undulating ground, the team settles into a steady, cautious march. Upon reaching a small depression dotted with low, thorny bushes, they form a perimeter and rest before continuing on to the exfiltration point that night.

But this is as far as they get. Gleason detects the hot thermal images of several trucks pulling off the highway barely 1,500 yards directly behind them. Both Gleason and Van Hee carry handheld AN/PAS-7 thermal viewers that pick up the heat of the vehicles several hundred yards beyond the system's stated range (the trucks can't be seen at all by the shorter–range NODs except for the occasional glint of reflected moonlight). Almost immediately, they are joined by a larger, semitrailer–sized vehicle.

Could it be another Scud TEL? Through their two thermal viewers, the team watches with nervous excitement—and no small amount of glee—as what appears to be more Scud launchers and support vehicles trickle in. Although the glowing, red, negative images provided by the viewers cannot produce an accurate picture at that distance, Van Hee and crew believe that their new neighbor is a full–blown battery preparing to launch a nasty surprise at the Jewish State.

Under normal circumstances, the lack of clear, sharp images would not prevent the team from determining if this is a Scud battery. With even the little elevation provided by a slight rise, they could look down on the spread of vehicles and make out the telltale signs unique to that type of unit's deployment pattern. Unfortunately, the recon team not only lacks altitude now, but is, in fact, slightly lower than the Iraqis. From their essentially eye–level view, all they can tell is that there are several dozen vehicles—some quite large—arrayed to the north.

Whoever they are, the darkness of night has given them a false sense of security and Van Hee can make out that they are neither properly dispersed nor making any effort at concealment. The team can easily call an air strike in on this unit, but even though the Iraqis are currently not well–dispersed, that could change in an instant. Moreover, if this is a Scud battery, even the fast–movers viewing the target area through their Maverick missiles' powerful infrared sensors will have great difficulty picking out the critical launch vehicles which, it turns out, are almost indistinguishable from fuel trucks and other lengthy vehicles at attack distances. Blanketing the area with cluster bombs will not guarantee the destruction of the mobile launchers either, although it would certainly "attrit" their crews and support personnel.

For obvious reasons, the Air Force was having a terrible time tracking down the nocturnal TELs and, true to the black humor that befriends men in war, the troopers nearly busted a gut a week earlier when they learned that a group of Jordanian tractor–trailer rigs had been rocketed and cluster–bombed when mistaken for one of Saddam's Scud units. It seems that their hapless drivers had pulled off the highway at one of its infrequent rest stops late at night and were inadvertently mistaken for a rearm and refuel site.* A Special Forces team on the ground soon confirmed that the blasted vehicles were civilian and, in any event, the Iraqis had immediately bussed foreign journalists to the scene to record "President Bush's most vile outrage." Word spread quickly from King Khalid "Emerald City" to the intelligence analysts, working out of prefab buildings on a Riyadh soccer field, and the shocked air unit that made the strike.

---

*If there was a plus side to the mistaken attack, it was the fact that fewer civilian drivers were now willing to brave the highway at night, thus making the job of target identification slightly less complicated.

Now, Van Hee finds the tables completely turned. Although the team leader is considerably closer than any fighter jockey releasing a Maverick missile and has all the time in the world to examine the glowing, shapes, there is no way he can confirm that they are what he believes them to be. Van Hee needs to know exactly what he is looking at before he calls in the fast–movers. Once committed to a strike here, on what is perhaps just some inconsequential heavy–lift unit, there might not be enough time or available air assets to immediately respond if a genuine Scud battery is detected.

Van Hee instructs Rodrigues and the tail gunner to move back toward the highway, to get a closer look, and hands over his thermal viewer. He wishes his team had gotten another of the precious thermal systems but is thankful that they

were able to get any at all. Many Special Forces long–range reconnaissance patrols didn't even have one of the scarce AN/PAS-7s, but the highly critical nature of DELTA's scud–hunting mission allowed Van Hee to get his mitts on two of the lightweight devices.

Gleason watches as their ghostly figures silently disappear into another depression, and settles into what is likely to be a long vigil on the perimeter. Everyone understands that the men may have to move in as close as 200 or 250 yards before their viewer will let them confirm the team's suspicions. If the approach to the Iraqi unit is difficult, the men might be gone for many hours. During their absence, the team checks and rehecks its equipment and notifies SOC of the situation.

The waiting is mercifully short. Helpful terrain features and a surprising lack of security have allowed the scouts to get their job done in barely three hours. Rodrigues reports that at least two of the mystery vehicles are "Spud" TELs, and Van Hee wastes no time setting back out with him to a spot where Rodrigues is confident that each of the confirmed launchers can be painted for incoming aircraft. When Gleason first spotted the gathering Iraqi vehicles at roughly 1,500 yards, they were beyond the effective range of Van Hee's AN/PAQ-3 MULE target designator, and the laser team has to travel almost one–third of the way back toward the road to ensure that their instrument can get a clear fix on the TELs. Newer, experimental handheld designators, that can accurately illuminate targets at roughly three times the distance had recently been sent to the Gulf, but Van Hee's team are not among the lucky few to receive one.

The route back is well known by this time, and the men are able to move with deliberate haste. The midnight hour Iraq often uses for launching its terror weapons is fast approaching, and through

A Scud missile erect on its launcher and ready to fire.

AN/AVS-6 Aviator's
night–vision imaging system

Comparative imagery from night vision
equipment used by US forces in *Desert
Storm*: (**top**) unaided, daylight photograph of an M606 Jeep and the same
vehicle shot from a slightly different
angle through (**center**) image intensification and (**bottom**) infrared devices.

AN/PVS-7A
Night vision goggles

AN/PAS-7 Thermal viewer

AN/PAQ-3 Modular universal laser
equipment (MULE) target designator

their thermal viewers, both the laser team and Gleason, at the hastily established patrol base, can see
the unmistakable pillar of a missile raised on one of
the erectors. A brief break in the clouds also allows
a faint, grainy image to be seen from the NODs.

At the base, Rodgers peers intently at the shad-
owy image of assembled Iraqi vehicles and nervously
fingers his M16. From his vantage point, he can see
only one other trooper, the tail gunner, about twenty
yards to his right, who has turned his way, as well,
and gives Rodgers a thumbs up. Rodgers knows that
he isn't the only man wondering if the fast–movers
will make it before the Iraqis launch. He doesn't feel

himself to be particularly expendable and hopes that
the Air Force will refrain from using cluster munitions against close–in, ground–lased targets as the
team had been briefed before the mission.

Activity suddenly picks up near the road. Several of the smaller Iraqi vehicles start hauling off in
all directions and a lone, dual 30mm antiaircraft
gun, positioned slightly east of the launch site, begins to pop green tracers into the air. The team
watches, mesmerized from their ringside seats as
other antiaircraft artillery, or "triple–A," quickly
comes to life, sending aloft crisscrossing streams
of fire. Cranson, meanwhile, listens in on the

approaching jets transmission: "Honey 1, sixty seconds, Maverick. . . . Honey 1, ten seconds. . . . Honey 1, laser on. . . . Spot. . . . Honey 1, lock–launch." *

The men have almost grown accustomed to the awe–inspiring spectacle of light and sound when a huge, double explosion bursts skyward. A Maverick air–to–ground missile has slammed into a TEL and ignited its fueled–up weapon.

Most of the triple–A falls silent for what seems like a long time, but one Iraqi gunner recovers from the shock of the explosion almost immediately and resumes shooting even before the fireball disappears into the air. Long strings of triple–A again arch into the sky as Rodgers and the others watch in fascination, knowing that Van Hee is already painting another Scud: "Honey 2, spot. . . . Lock–launch. . . . Honey 2, terminate." ** A second huge explosion lights the scene and more vehicles can be seen scurrying away from the carnage. As far as the Iraqi grunts are concerned, all Saddam's "little toys" do is attract death from above.

Secondary explosions begin to rock the target area as the laser team moves at a steady trot toward the patrol base. The Air Force is holding back from dropping its deadly packages of cluster bombs, to give them a jump at getting away from the target. Rodrigues and Van Hee's glowing green images can be seen quite clearly during their last 100–meter dash to the base, and some of the troopers can't refrain from greeting them with low–volume (very low–volume) whoops and hollers as they clear the perimeter. As if to join in the congratulations, the Air Force begins to hit the site again, and now the whole team moves out at a run. The troopers haven't covered a quarter mile when suddenly,

while cresting a wide ripple in the earth, they smack into an Iraqi squad barely thirty yards away. The Iraqis were apparently on patrol when the air strike erupted and are riding out the fireworks in this shallow depression.

The startled team comes under fire. Dropping to one knee, Gleason pumps two 9mm rounds into the nearest Iraqi's chest. Without pausing, he switches to the next target, who immediately crumples into a heap, his stomach perforated by two slugs from Gleason's H&K. Immediately sizing up the situation, Van Hee yells for the team to break contact. While moving through their leapfrog maneuver, a lucky round from an RPG-7 shoulder–fired rocket launcher lands between Rodgers and the tail gunner. Although most of the explosion is absorbed by the ground, shrapnel rips into Rodgers' right side and the tail gunner is killed instantly by a dime-sized piece of metal piercing his skull just above the right eye.

The four unhurt troopers immediately lay down an intense base of fire, which convinces the Iraqis to fall back to less dangerous surroundings. The firefight has lasted less than two minutes. One American is dead and another's life is leaking into the rocky earth. Hauling Rodgers and the fallen trooper along with them, the team hurriedly resumes their escape south while Air Force jets strike at Iraqi vehicles streaking pell–mell through the area. It is painfully obvious to all that they are in deep trouble, and, if action is not taken quickly, will either be killed or wind up being displayed on the evening news as prisoners of war.

Air–ground communications between the team and SOC is now being maintained by a "fast FAC," or forward air controller, who passes word to Cranson that immediate efforts are being initiated to get them out. They are instructed to keep moving south without delay, but each man knows that they are faced with a decision no soldier wants to make.

---

* "Sixty seconds to laser designator switch–on. . . . Ten seconds to switch–on. . . . Laser spot acquired. . . . Target locked–on and ordnance fired."
** "Laser spot acquired. . . . Target locked–on and ordnance fired. . . . Have visual contact; laser no longer needed."

The venerable A-10 Thunderbolt II "Warthog" and DELTA formed a deadly Scud hunter–killer team in Iraq. A-10s also proved themselves to be an effective search and rescue asset.

The young trooper's body hinders their movement to the extraction point, and they decide to bury him as quickly as possible. In a lonely defile, the team digs a grave for their comrade. It is not very much, as graves go, but it is made with love and respect, and the men dig as deeply as time will permit. Wrapping the staff sergeant up in his poncho liner, they gently lay his body into the desert soil. Van Hee carefully checks, then rechecks, the tight ten–digit grid coordinate he has plotted for the unmarked grave and silently swears to his fallen trooper that he'll be back for him. The team says a quick prayer over their friend, and then, carrying Rodgers, they strike out south again. Rodrigues, the team's medic, recognizes that the multiple shrapnel wounds are worse than previously thought. Rodgers is slipping in and out of consciousness and losing blood. Cranson radios the fast FAC that they have a man who will die if they don't get him out soon.

SOC knows that no special operations helicopters are currently available for a quick recovery, nor are there likely to be any until almost mid–morning.

Virtually everything is already committed to the far–flung operations in progress throughout what the Israelis call "Scudinavia" in western Iraq. SOC decides to use a MC-130 Combat Talon equipped with a Fulton Recovery System to conduct a sur-face–to–air recovery (STAR) of Rodgers. This is not generally a preferred method of extraction be-cause it takes so much time to set up the Fulton and is easily seen, but with helo assets unavailable, Rodgers' condition makes it necessary. Alerting the 1st Special Operations Wing, a hasty plan is worked out to recover the wounded DELTA trooper.

The Extractions

Arar Royal Military Airfield near Banadah is the launch site of some of *Desert Storm's* most inventive operations. It's not an unusual place to find one or two of the 1st Special Operations Wing's MC-130s, and when the call comes down, immediate prepa-rations are made for the STAR. First, a modified delivery canister resembling an old napalm bomb is loaded with all the items needed by the team to set

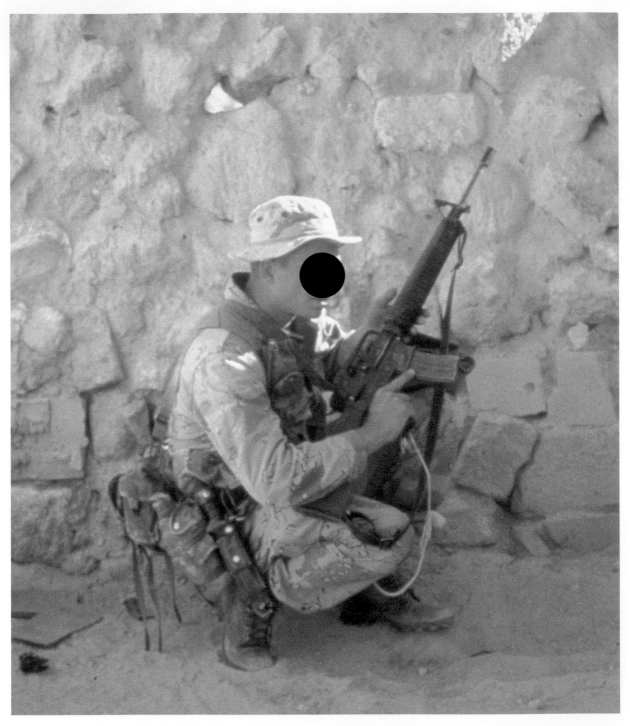

(**Opposite**) Intense concentration marks the face of a trooper keeping watch on the surrounding terrain from a desert ruin. (**Right**) An E-3A Sentry at Dhahran, Saudi Arabia.

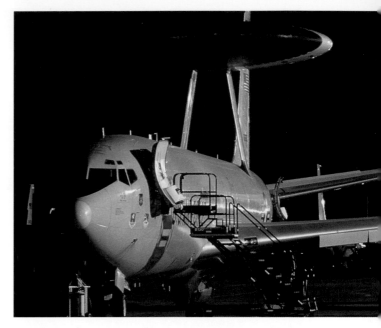

up the recovery. The canister is then affixed to a waiting A-10's weapons pylon, and the Warthog is immediately launched toward western Iraq. As the "Sandy"* Hog driver and his wingman speed north, the crew of the MC-130 receives their mission brief. Not uncharacteristically, the crew takes the briefing quite professionally; yet, underneath their calm exterior, there is a surge of adrenalin. They are going to execute a mission that they have trained hard for and has not been performed in combat for nearly twenty years. The airmen are confident that the improvements in technique and hardware introduced since the Vietnam War are sound.

Already deep in the desert, the recon team is now told to move beyond their original pickup point into an even more desolate area well away from any known military targets. After several hours, the exhausted team comes upon a group of ruined dwellings and sets up defensive positions as dawn begins to break. Rodrigues has just changed Rodgers' I-V and is connecting a new bag of saline solution when Cranson's radio crackles to life. The Sandy pilot is attempting to contact the team. Hopefully, it will appear to any nearby Iraqis that the hog driver and his wingman are out hunting for targets of opportunity and will avoid any curious overtures.

Van Hee is informed that he should mark their position for a "delivery." Using a mirror, Van Hee

---

*An A-10 pilot specially trained for rescue escort (RESCORT) missions. The rugged A-10's ability to loiter for extended periods of time makes it a perfect aircraft for conducting searches in a high-threat environment, and Sandy's are experts at locating survivors. By marking target locations and supressing enemy fire, they allow more vulnerable rescue aircraft to do their job. The term originated during the Vietnam war as a call sign used by A-1E Skyraider pilots providing gunfire suppression during rescue operations.

signals his location to the Sandys performing their lazy search pattern well away from the team. After receiving an acknowledgment from the pilot, Van Hee moves out about 175 yards from the perimeter, places a single orange panel in the gravel, and immediately moves back to the shelter of the ruins. The pair of Warthogs are continuing their indirect meander toward the ruins when they spot a group of Iraqi trucks moving parallel to the team approximately two miles out. Although they do not appear to be looking for the troopers, the Sandys take no chances and proceed to spoil the Iraqis' morning with fire from their 30mm Gatling nose cannons. As the hogs leave the burning vehicles, they approach the ruins indirectly by flying in a low, wide arc that, hopefully, will not draw attention to the hidden Americans. No extra passes are made over the site and the equipment canister is "pickled off" as the ugly jets roar overhead.

Thirty minutes behind the Sandys, the MC-130 Combat Talon penetrates into "Injun Country." While passing over the berm line, the special opera-

A surface–to–air recovery (STAR) of two troopers using a Fulton extraction system: (**Top row**) A canister containing the system is dropped by an Air Force fast–mover.' Helium bottles, balloon, line and attached suit in a recovered canister. The guard cables and whisker–like probes of an MC-130 yoke, opened to snare the Fulton's line. (**Center row**) Two volunteers with "Are we really going to do this?" looks on their faces. The line being snagged. Up, up, and away! (**Left**) The open rear ramp of the receiving aircraft as the soldiers are hauled aboard.

tions aircraft receives an ominous radio report from the E-3A Sentry orbiting in Saudi airspace behind them. Electronic warfare officers operating the AWACS's highly sophisticated sensors detect a number of hostile radar impulses. Despite the fact that the Air Force owns the sky, being painted over Iraqi territory always causes concern. Most of the Talon's crew had friends on the ill–fated AC-130 Specter gunship that failed to get out of Kuwaiti airspace when "locked on" by a surface–to–air missile. The result was charred debris floating in the Gulf and no survivors.

As the Talon closes on the team's location, Van Hee and Gleason open the canister. Extracting its contents, they find a balloon, nylon line, harness, and suit along with a bottle of helium. Rodrigues checks Rodgers' condition while Van Hee and Gleason prepare to inflate the balloon, and Cranson makes contact with the inbound Talon. Not only is the MC-130 approaching, but the pair of A-10s continue to ply the area in ostensibly random patterns, and a flight of F-16s has already assumed a guardian–angel role well to the east but within easy striking distance if trouble develops. The Warthogs again cruise past the ruins while Van Hee and Gleason affix the helium bottle to the balloon that will stretch Rodgers' lifeline in reach of the specially equipped rescue aircraft. As it inflates, the bulbous cream and silver balloon takes on the shape of a giant fish, its floppy fins growing firmer with each passing second.

While all this is going on, Rodrigues and Cranson gingerly ease Rodgers into the olive green recovery suit sewn firmly to the Fulton's harness. As its furlined hood is placed around Rodger's face, his glazed eyes open slightly to Rodrigues' familiar grin and thick, angular eyebrows. His medic friend has been in DELTA for a long time and has a well-earned reputation as a battlefield doctor. Patting Rodgers' thigh, he says with a chuckle, "You gonna go on a neat ride, my man. It's up, up, and away for you." Rodrigues does his best to put up a brave front for his buddy but fears that Rodgers may have lost too much blood. The furlined face is gray and expressionless, but it seems for a moment that he tries to acknowledge what the medic is saying.

Twenty minutes from the pickup, the balloon is allowed to creep slowly skyward. It reaches its full height and Rodgers sits securely attached to its tether while the team, minus the doc, stands guard in a circle resembling a herd of buffaloes shielding a wounded calf. Rodrigues continues his lively chatter to help keep his patient awake and gently pats and strokes his unhurt left arm. Although he doesn't know it, his determined "woofing" is paying off. Rodgers dimly comprehends that his buddies are doing everything they can for him and takes some comfort from the New Yorker's verbal blizzard.

At 525 feet in the air, the balloon attached to the tethered nylon rope is a beacon for all to see and is the reason that the team had to put so much distance between themselves and the highway. The incoming MC-130's unusual nose now resembles a snout with two large whiskers. These whiskers are actually probes swung outward to form the yoke. Their main function is to guide the line into place at the center of the nose as the plane makes the pickup.

Cautiously lining up on the balloon, the pilot throttles the fat, four–engine airplane down to 112, 105, then only 97 knots for the pickup and aims at the target area on the nylon rope marked by three orange streamers. Striking the target markers, the probes guide the line to the yoke and secure it as the plane flies over the DELTA team. With a minimum of fanfare, Rodgers is literally snatched from the gravity of earth and appears as a small dot hurtling behind the Talon. While the STAR is a nerve–wracking affair for the soldiers to watch, they know that Rodgers actually experiences less of a jolt during the pickup than he did when he opened his parachute.

In the gaping cargo bay, the loadmaster and crew chief now prepare to winch their human cargo on board. The nylon line is pressed firmly against the Talon's belly by the rush of air, and inside the bay, the crew chief and loadmaster move quickly to hook it, much as one snaps a fishing line. Reeling

A special operations helicopter streaking at low level across the night sky.

in the line and attaching it to the Talon's internal, hydraulic winch, the precious cargo is slowly drawn into the cargo bay. Soon, Rodgers is lying in the safety of the aircraft while Air Force Reserve trauma specialists work frantically to stabilize him. The only hitch during the pickup occurs when the balloon fails to release from the line. The Talon's navigator is forced to spear the playfully bouncing object with a harpoon–like device and cut it free with the help of the loadmaster.

As the MC-130 speeds toward friendly airspace, the remainder of the recon team moves out.

A well–timed air operation, centered mainly along the highway to the north, is initiated by the F-16s and a fresh pair of A-10s to mask their movement and the troopers head south by southwest toward a new pickup point several miles away. Although appropriate helo assets will be available in a few hours, SOC has decided to not make the extraction until after dark since Rodgers has been rescued and the recon team is in no immediate danger.

The team had flung their prefabricated hide site covers into their foxholes and buried them when they sanitized their original position, but the rough terrain the men are now moving into offers many opportunities for natural concealment and there is no worry that they no longer have the prefabs. They soon come upon a wadi that offers a reasonable amount of security and decide that it is as good a place as any to go to ground till nightfall. After the midnight firefight, Saddam's forces know that American commandos are in the area, but on-going airstrikes have given the Iraqis plenty of other things to worry about, and their movement has been heavily restricted for scores of miles in all directions.

The only enemy assaulting the men is a determined legion of sandfleas, which tirelessly press their attack as "big red" moved slowly across the sky. They do, however, also receive periodic visits from various Air Force jets. The pilots make it a point to fly close enough to the DELTA team to scout for hostile forces, yet their seemingly random passes are conducted at varied–enough intervals to give no clue to the whereabouts of the hidden soldiers.

Night comes quickly in this part of the world and the already–cool late January temperature drops like a stone even before the sun disappears from the horizon. As the four men make their final equipment checks before moving out, help is crossing the Saudi–Iraqi border 100 miles to the southeast. Boring through the gathering fog at sixty feet off the ground, a lone MH-60 Black Hawk is finally on its way to retrieve the soldiers.

Almost ten hours has passed since Rodgers was extracted, and Van Hee's team starts to move south again. The welcome night engulfs the dirty, un-shaven troopers and their night vision goggles allow them to move with the assurance of prowling nocturnal beasts unencumbered by darkness.

In spite of the sophisticated vision devices and their apparent isolation, the desert holds one more surprise. As they near the pickup point, a young goat herder casually emerges from a depression forty yards to their right. Upon seeing the ghost–like apparitions, he runs screaming through the darkness, scattering livestock in all directions. Fearing a return of Iraqi soldiers, the team moves through the area quickly and sets up a defensive perimeter 600 yards from their encounter. Speaking in hushed tones with the inbound chopper, Van Hee guides the bird in until the troopers can be seen on its infrared imager.

As the Black Hawk's wheels touch the hard–packed dirt, the remaining four troopers scramble aboard and slide across the metal floor plates to hold each other in the embrace only those who have faced the ultimate challenge know. "We made it!" Gleason yells above the pitch of the engines as the helicopter begins to rise above the desert floor.

After looking out of the waist gunner's hatch for any signs of Iraqi forces, Van Hee wearily leans back and says "Christ, I hope so."

Epilogue

Fort Bragg, North Carolina

Along Ardennes Road, framed by a stand of regal North Carolina pines, the John F. Kennedy Special Warfare Center Chapel occupies a place of dignity and serenity. Against the hustle and organized chaos that characterizes this sprawling Airborne post, it provides a safe haven of sanity and peace whether the visitor is a regular church–goer or just passing through.

Framed against the buildup of an incoming spring rain, a memorial service is taking place. It is a closed service designed to avoid the prying eyes of nosy newspaper reporters still trying to write a story connected to *Desert Storm*. Although the service was unannounced, the chapel is crowded. Word has passed quickly around the special operations community that one of their own is being remembered today. Conspicuous in their off–the–rack suits, cowboy boots, and nonregulation mustaches

A soldier is laid to rest.

and haircuts, the members of a DELTA troop have gathered once more. Along with their wives, they are here to help the young widow weather one more storm. It is a unique scene—one that rarely occurred in the past few years but has often been repeated since the operations "over there."

The widow's five–year–old son, sandy blond hair neatly combed and out of character, sits on the edge of his front–row seat. Gently poking an imagined spot on the chapel's maroon carpet with the toe of his Sunday best, he absently wonders, not quite knowing or understanding why he is here. He is aware that his mom's world is in disarray, and her sadness is something he has never seen before. All he knows is that the man whose picture occupies the table in front of the chapel room is not coming home. His father left home late one night "on business." That was not an unusual occurrence in his young life, but now a new twist has occurred. Mom said that his best friend has gone to live with God forever.

His father's friends, gathered around the family in a supportive ring, knew the story all too well. The smiling young soldier, pictured with the coveted green beret had been their friend, and in this close-knit group of professionals, that one word, "friend," was all that required their loyalty.

The emotion of these men was not a complicated show. Each behaved simply but with a degree of maturity in combat that comes only to a veteran. They accepted what was thrown their way in a businesslike manner, hiding their hatred, fear, confusion, and pride behind the mantle of a well-trained special operations soldier. To this group and the many others like them, the specter of death was always an additional member of the team. In this particular case, their friend was no longer able to avoid death's embrace. Thousands of miles away, hidden in an unmarked grave deep in Iraq's rugged western province, their trusted friend and the young boy's father had rested until a subsequent team, under Gary Van Hee, recovered his lifeless form.

As the chaplain exhorts the group not to grieve but to pray for the Great Jumpmaster's protection of their comrade's soul, the thoughts of many of the group drift to other places, other actions, and other services. The veterans of *Desert Storm* looks back over the madness of the past weeks which characterized the operations in the desert.

Hanging back a little from the rest of the mourners, a grizzled old warrior remembers similar services after such operations—code-named *Desert I, Urgent Fury,* or *Just Cause*—and drifts further back in time to days before he left Smoke Bomb Hill to join DELTA at the old stockade. His thoughts go back to the Green Beret Parachute Club, its cold beer, warm friendships and the old jukebox nestled in the corner next to the pool tables. He smiles to himself as he remembers that one song, a song from an unpopular war that saw so many of the special operations community answer the requirements of the ultimate test. Though not all of the DELTA troopers were initially Special Forces-qualified, most ended with that qualification, and an old war song expressed best the thoughts and feelings of this moment: "Her Green Beret has met his fate."

It's not all glory and gunsmoke in the realm of special operations—especially in covert operations. It can be boring for months at a time and then spiked with moments of sheer gut-wrenching, piss-in-your-pants horror. But that is what they signed up for. No yellow ribbons, no victory parades, or grand celebrations would greet these secret warriors. Just a gentle hug, a kind word, or a pat on the back that seemed to say, "Well done." That, plus "Clean up your gear and get ready for the next one!"

And there will certainly be a next one—somewhere, sometime. The odds are that the professionals from DELTA will be used not as they were during Iraq's stinging defeat, but in their traditional counterterrorist role.

For over a quarter of a century, the former Soviet Union and its surrogates in Eastern Europe, Latin America, and the Middle East gave safe haven to the world's most dangerous international terrorists. The collapse of Soviet communism, coupled with the shutting off of the terrorist's revenue by oil-rich Persian Gulf states angered over their backing of Iraq, have left terrorist organizations in disarray. Increasingly isolated politically and cut off from training and supplies from Europe and money from the Gulf, they bicker among themselves over how best to satisfy their grudge against the West and any Middle Eastern government unappreciative of their past deeds. They are, to put it bluntly, out of work and out of cash.

But the breather this has given the West is likely to be short–lived. As the world speeds toward the twenty–first century, it finds itself with more wild cards in its deck of nations. The familiar bipolar dominance of the United States and the former Soviet Union is gone for good, as the "evil empire" disintegrates into numerous successor states of questionable stability. These new countries are, themselves, not homogeneous entities and are likely to be rent by factional fighting in the decade to come. They are also the inheritors of at least 27,000 nuclear weapons. Despite pronouncements of their good intentions, their desperate need for hard currency and sporadic control of their own territory may result in some leakage of nuclear weapons ("loose nukes") or, more likely, nuclear materials and production expertise into the hands of terrorists.

This threat to peace and a new, ghastly form of warfare—environmental terrorism—may also cause elite counterterrorist units like DELTA to re-tool their operational methods. The sight of massive oil slicks released on the Persian Gulf and black clouds boiling up from oil fires to shut off the noonday sun will not be lost on the next generation of would–be terrorists. Moreover, their twisted logic will lead some terrorists to use the results of *Desert Storm* to add fuel to whatever cause is fashionable at the moment.

Literally dozens of captured Palestinian and Shiite terrorists have been dumped into this cauldron of change, let loose by the Iraqis when they invaded Kuwait or released by the Israelis as part of the package deal that freed a handful of Western hostages. Like the wandering free–lance warriors of feudal Japan who traded their violent skills for gold and fame, these modern–day *ronin* are available to any would–be despot or group fanning the flames of ethnic or religious unrest across Europe, Asia, and the Middle East. Key terrorist networks remain intact, and a number of groups and individuals dropped from sight when the vigilance of America's intelligence assets were directed to combat in the Gulf. Now that the flex of security operations has fallen to its normal lull, the specter of terrorists finding new work in the developing chaos is very real and Americans abroad are, as always, notoriously easy targets for any group desiring big headlines.

The pros of DELTA are ready.

13 12 79

U.S. SPECIAL FORCES

US NAVY SEALS

Hans Halberstadt

Acknowledgments

Many thanks to the friendly folks at USSO-COM public affairs at MacDill Air Force Base, Florida, particularly Col. Jake Dye.

This book wouldn't have been attempted without the reassurance of RADM Brent Baker, now retired, former Navy Chief of Information, who responded very graciously to some criticism of mine with an invitation to try working with the Navy again. The result is this book. Sir, I salute you.

Another salute to LCDR John Brindley and JO1 Mike Hayden, as hard a pair of public affairs officers as you'll find anywhere, with one of the most difficult missions in the fleet—smack dab in the middle between the media maniacs and the Naval Special Warfare community (whose motto is *No pictures!!! No names!!! No kidding!!!*). To two fine people doing what is usually a thankless job, let me say: Thanks! Well done!

I'd like to personally thank the many folks at BUD/S and SEAL Teams Three and Five who helped so graciously, and against tradi-tion, with this project. I'd like to, but I can't. National Security and all that. But the Desert Patrol Vehicle guys out at Niland, California, and the squad from Team Five went way out of their way to accommodate a bunch of media weenies and executed their op with a perfect blend of cooperation and consideration.

I *can* thank RADM Ray Smith—what a guy! He's largely responsible for a new, more open attitude toward public affairs within the Naval Special Warfare community, and it's about time. A salute to you, sir, as well.

CAPT Bob Gormly, USN (Ret.), and CDR Gary Stubblefield, USN (Ret.), both filled in the gaps in my Naval Special Warfare education, shared some wonderful war stories and lots of insights based on long careers in Naval Special Warfare. These are, despite the repu-tation of the SEALs, gentlemen—the kind of quiet professionals you seldom hear about in this community. It's too bad that more Americans can't know about the things these people and their teams have done for us all.

Chapter 1

Let Slip the Frogs of War

In the dark, damp hours before midnight, 19 December 1989, a small group of United States Navy SEALs put the finishing touches on their face paint, checked their weapons and equipment for the thousandth time, watched the clock, chatted nervously, and waited. There were twenty-one of them, all told, assembled and identified as Task Unit Whiskey.

As the time trickled away all of them knew that very soon blood would begin to flow. Whose and how much remained to be seen. At 0045 hours, according to the current plan, combined United States forces would initiate Operation Just Cause—combat operations against the Republic of Panama with the objective of seizing that nation's leader, Gen. Manuel Noriega. Tensions were high between the two nations, and there was no doubt that the operation would be costly.

The role of Task Unit Whiskey in all of this was small but potentially critical. Noriega had plenty of places to hide and lots of ways to escape. One of these was a Panama Defense Forces (PDF) patrol boat, the *Presidente Porras*, and the SEAL task force was detailed to immobilize it.

A scout/swimmer from Naval Special Warfare Group One. His fashionable attire is essentially the same as that worn by the dive pairs attacking the Panamanian patrol boat: wet suit with hood and a Draeger rebreathing system (not scuba).

The mission was launched from Rodman Naval Station in Balboa Harbor, one of many US Navy installations in the Canal Zone. At 2300 hours, not quite two hours before the scheduled kickoff, the men slid into their wet suits, donned their closed-circuit breathing apparatus, and clambered into their big, black rubber inflatable boats. When the Combat Rubber Raiding Craft (CRRC) were loaded, the engines were started and the boats pushed off from shore, moving into the soft, inky night at minimum speed to avoid notice.

In the first boat, CRRC number 1, rode two combat swimmers, LT Edward Coughlin and EN3 Tim Eppley (dive pair number 1); CDR Norm Carley (the on-scene mission commander); HMC George Riley (coxswain); and HT3 Chris Kinney (machine gunner). CRRC number 2 carried a second dive pair, ET1 Randy Beausoleil and PH2 Chris Dye; remaining in the boat would be IS3 Scott Neudecker (coxswain), OS2 Mark Dodd (communicator), and QM3 Pat Malone (automatic weapons man).

Ashore, within the Rodman facility but still within range of the objective, a fire-support team manned .50-caliber heavy machine guns, Mk 19 automatic grenade launchers, and 60mm mortars, all preregistered on likely targets and equipped with night sights. Afloat, in case of trouble, two PBRs (Patrol Boat, River) carried more SEALs ready to intervene if the vulnerable "rubber ducks" were engaged by the PDF.

As seems to so often be the case, there was tremendous tension in the boats. Special forces like the SEALs are in the business of high-risk, high-payoff operations. They are expensive, in every respect, and to be successful everything has to be planned, rehearsed, scheduled, and orchestrated in mind-numbing detail. Deviations from the plan traditionally mean mission failure and often death for the people out on the pointy end of the spear. So, at precisely one hour before midnight, an hour and forty-five minutes before the bullets will fly all over Panama, Task Unit Whiskey's operation was already turning into what SEALs call a "goatscrew."

All the planning and the schedules had been based on a 2330 hours insertion time to reach and attack the target at 0100 (H-hour), but then the COMJSOTF (Commander Joint Special Operations Task Force) changed the insertion time to 2300 hours, adding to the stress level. But late in the planning sequence,

just before the boats pushed off, Commander Carley was asked to push up his H-hour thirty minutes, to 0030. He refused; there wasn't enough time to get the swimmers to the target, arm the demolitions, and extract the swim teams with a thirty-minute advance in the schedule. The proposed change added another jolt of adrenaline to an already highly charged atmosphere.

Out in Balboa Harbor, the boats moved slowly and as silently as possible across the black water. There were bright lights ashore and boat traffic in the harbor, neither helping the SEALs with their stealthy approach to the point where the swimmers would slip over the gunwales and disappear on their mission. The outboards were not designed to run at such slow speeds; one began to run roughly and threatened to quit. But both boats made it to the shelter of a mangrove treeline on the north side of the harbor, across from Pier 18.

The SEALs waited and watched. Two

Hi ho, hi ho, it's off to work we go—with a Mk 138 satchel charge loaded with twenty pounds of water-resistant explosives, a dual priming system, and a pair of timers. The satchel charge is essentially iden- *tical to the old "mod zero" version of fifty years ago when the UDT swimmers cleared the beaches in Normandy and in the Pacific.*

boats moved across the harbor; was Noriega aboard? Were the Panamanians searching for US small boats or swimmers? The time for the boats to move out to the insertion point arrived. Boat number 1's engine fired up but boat number 2's refused to cooperate. Boat number 1 moved out alone while boat number 2, complete with frustrated boat crew and divers, stayed hidden in the mangroves.

In order to make up for the delays and still hit the required H-hour, the boat crew had to move a lot closer into the target than had been intended. At 2330 hours the first dive pair went over the side, into the water—on schedule. Commander Carley took boat number 1 back to the mangroves, took boat number 2 under tow, and got the second dive team out to the insertion point at 2335. Dive pair number 2 slipped over the side and disappeared.

After the swimmers departed, the SEALs were advised via radio that the H-hour for the whole show had been advanced fifteen minutes to 0045 local time, 20 December. This meant, of course, that the whole shooting match would kick off while the swimmers were at their objective and that their mission had suddenly become even more risky than anticipated. But there wasn't much to do except wait and watch and stay out of the way.

In the meantime, Commander Carley decided to take the boats back to Rodman and to change out the engine in CRRC number 2 with a spare. Boat number 2 was taken under tow again, and the little convoy slipped back across the water with practiced stealth. Two more Panamanian harbor craft transited Balboa Harbor; the SEALs evaded both and made it back to Rodman undetected and unscathed.

The dive pairs swam toward their objective about twenty feet below the surface. Instead of conventional scuba tanks, the swimmers wore Draeger rebreathing systems that recycle expelled air, clean it of carbon dioxide, then replenish it with oxygen. It is a closed system. No bubbles reached the surface to betray the swimmers' passage.

The swimmers had practiced for this mis-

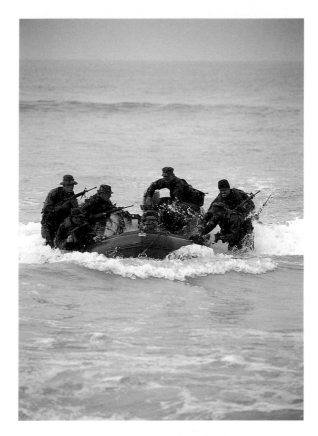

A "rubber duck" is launched into the Pacific for some play time. The design is another bit of World War II surplus—a lifeboat that has been used for covert operations for half a century. It is simple, stable, reliable, cheap, stealthy, low-tech—just the ticket for special operators in US Special Operations Command.

sion for all their careers. For most it was their first-ever combat mission. Instead of employing some exotic, high-tech navigation system to find their way through the water, they used a system older than they were—determining their direction with a simple, luminous compass and measuring their distance by counting the number of kicks they made. It is a primitive system, decades old, that still works. After about half an hour underwater, dive pair number 2 (Beausoleil and Eppley) surfaced

Here's another simple, stealthy, low-tech piece of gear used in Panama: the compass board. Once trained and experienced in its use, a diver can navi-gate with precision below the surface, using the compass to maintain course and measuring distance traveled by counting kicks.

under Pier 18. It was a noisy place to be; a firefight began just as they arrived, visible to the fire-support teams ashore and to the boat teams. Who was firing at whom was unclear to the SEALs, and the mission proceeded as planned, despite underwater explosions in the area, probably from PDF personnel throwing hand grenades in the water to discourage just this kind of mission.

 With the pier providing cover and concealment, Beausoleil and Eppley moved toward the target, still moored at its floating dock. They avoided swimming on the surface as they moved toward the patrol boat. At 0011 dive pair number 2 arrived at the *Presidente Porras,* positively identified it as the tar-get, and executed the attack on the vessel. The two SEALs swam down under the stern, found the port propeller shaft, and began attaching and arming the explosive charge—just as they heard the engines of the ship start up.

 The Mk 138 Mod 1 charge they'd carried through the dark water was a haversack loaded with twenty pounds of water-resistant explosive, complete with an MCS-1 clock, a Mk 39 safety and arming device, and a Mk 96 detonator, all designed to provide reliable delay and detonation of the main charge. In less than two minutes the charge was attached, armed, and ticking. Beausoleil and Eppley departed the target at 0013 hours, urged onward by explosions in the water nearby, and now made their way first to the shelter of nearby Pier 17, then to the extraction point where—they hoped—the boat would be waiting to pick them up.

A little late, dive pair number 1 arrived at 0014 and commenced their attack on the *Presidente Porras*. Despite the explosions and the firefight overhead, the SEALs moved along Pier 18 to the ship and installed their Mk 138 demolition system on the starboard propeller shaft. They tied a length of detonation cord from the haversack around the charge already in place on the port shaft, using a dual-priming technique to insure that both charges would detonate together for maximum effect.

At about 0017, after less than two minutes

at the target, Coughlin and Eppley removed the safeties and started the clock that would detonate the charges at 0100—if everything worked—and, as they say, got the hell out of Dodge. The PDF crews either knew or suspected what was going on and threw many grenades into the water, forcing the SEALs to the relative shelter of the pier pilings behind which they tried to avoid the effects of the nearby explosions. Finally they started to move away, but four more explosions sent shock waves through the water.

Because of the forty-five-minute delay on the charges and the enemy action in the vicinity of the target, both SEAL teams were trapped in the vicinity. They were still there

The first SEALs ashore are normally the scout/swimmer pair who precede the boat onto the beach, evaluate the threat level, then signal in the rubber duck with the rest of the crew. The wet suit is an important piece of gear, even for rough-tough SEALs—hypothermia is a problem for everybody.

A foundation for special operators from all services is the talent for popping up in the darndest places, unexpected and uninvited. This young lad looks a little waterlogged, as well he should because he and three teammates have been sitting on the bottom of San Diego Bay for an hour or so after navigating a few hundred meters below sailboats, water skiers, and the occasional recreational swimmer. He's been using a rebreather that recycles air, enriches it with oxygen, and emits no bubbles. The weapon is a Heckler & Koch MP4 9mm submachine gun, a favorite of special operators everywhere for urban and close combat.

at 0100 when the two Mk 138 demolition kits detonated as primed. While the swim pairs exited the target area, they noticed that all the PDF vessels in Balboa Harbor had started turning their propellers as an anti-swimmer defense.

The SEAL swimmers descended beneath the surface and swam out into the harbor on a course that brought them near the main shipping channel for vessels transiting the Panama Canal. In the grand tradition of military operations, yet another tactical problem presented itself now: a large, deep draft ship moving across the diver's intended course back to the extraction point. Although their Draegers were not designed for use at that depth, the swimmers descended to forty-five feet for ten minutes while the ship passed overhead, then ascended to the normal depth of twenty feet. At last they found the shelter of Pier 6 and from there proceeded to the pickup point at the end of the pier for extraction.

The two CRRCs were waiting. In fact, they'd been waiting for what had seemed an eternity, since about 0055. The dive pairs were extremely late for their planned extraction. The boat crews, the support teams, and the fire-support teams ashore had all seen the firefight in the vicinity of the target; they'd seen the charges go off on schedule. They'd endured a firefight of their own in the immediate vicinity of the extraction point, near Pier 6, where they'd held their fire while tracers zipped overhead, apparently at random. They'd monitored their radios, without word from the teams whose own waterproofed MX-300s had been unequal to the task of communicating with the support elements.

Commander Carley, worried that the dive pairs may have mistaken an adjacent pier for the extraction point, sent CRRC number 2 over to investigate, hoping that the swimmers were there; they weren't and the boat was recalled.

An hour later than planned, at 0200 hours, dive pair number 1 materialized from the gloom, much to the relief of the boat crews. About five minutes later the second group showed up, too, intact. The four SEALs were hauled back aboard the rubber boats, and the teams executed a tactical withdrawal. Using infrared strobes as a preplanned recognition device, the boats returned to the relative safety of Rodman at 0220 hours. An hour and a half later, Task Unit Whiskey was declared ready for retasking.

Mission Overview

Task Unit Whiskey's little adventure in Balboa Harbor is a kind of classic in the SEAL bag of tricks, revealing the hazards and virtues of naval special operations. Naval Special Warfare (NSW), as it is called, has been a very important and much abused subject for the last fifty years. For the US Navy it goes back to the Underwater Demolition Teams of World War II, who cleared beach obstacles and surveyed gradients for amphibious landings in the Pacific and against European shores, many dying in the attempt. It is an extremely dangerous set of missions that cannot be practically executed with other, less demanding means.

The organization and the people of the Naval Special Warfare is actually two communities, one being the men in the water, the Sea/Air/Land "commandos" (or SEALs), and the other being the men on the water, the Special Boat Squadrons (SBS). Both have a long and distinguished combat record, and both

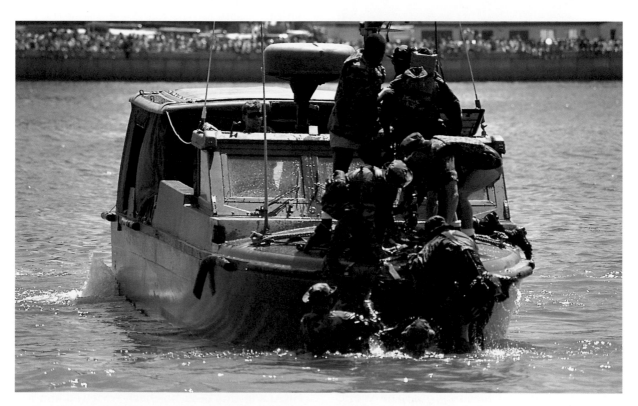

It can be a long, cold swim back to base, so when the bus stops to pick up the team there's always a scramble to get aboard. Here, a cargo net has been rigged off the bow to make recovery of the people in the water a bit more expeditious. The Naval Special Warfare community is well represented here, the guys in the water (SEALs) and the guys on the water (Special Boat Squadron members).

Membership in the SEALs is not for everyone. It requires tremendous toughness—some physical, most mental. While this healthy specimen looks as though he may have previously worked for a professional football team, most SEALs are of normal size and stature. These people are accepted into membership in a tiny community (about 1,200 men total) only after a long, rigorous process of testing, evaluation, and selection—more than actual training. Anyone can learn the technical skills required to do the things SEALs do, but few have the personal self-discipline to learn the internal, intangible skills needed to be a good operator.

communities have been linked together as Naval Special Warfare for about thirty years. While the SEALs get most of the attention and notoriety, the SBS have been doing a lot of the shooting and bleeding over the years. While most of the SBS crews are not graduates of the Basic Underwater Demolition /SEALS (BUD/S) training program the boat officers are SEALs, and SBS personnel are held

to the same high standard of performance as the more notorious part of the team. This story is about both.

The men in Naval Special Warfare are just one part of a big, broad spectrum of American combat power—in fact, a tiny slice of the pie. There are only about 1,500 of them in the US Navy, far fewer than the US Army's 7,000 or so Green Berets (active and reserve). SEALs, along with the Army's Ranger regiment and Special Forces groups, comprise the United States most elite surface combat operations resources. All are masters of basic infantry tactics; each has its own area of expertise. All train together at some points of their qualification. All, despite their parentage as components of the Navy or Army, are really on-call assets for the highest levels of the National Command Authority (NCA)—the president, the secretary of defense, and the Joint Chiefs of Staff. When they go to war, their mission will probably start at MacDill Air Force Base, Florida, where the United States Special Operations Command (USSOCOM) is headquartered. It is that kind of organization: powerful, dangerous, expensive, and above all, *special*. There is also something traditionally a bit odd about these special forces soldiers and sailors. They are isolated and aloof from the rest of the military and especially from the public, partly by design and partly by tradition. So how and why do a book like this one?

This book is the result of a policy of the US Department of Defense and the Navy to release as much information as possible about military institutions and activities while maintaining operational security. That can be a tough compromise sometimes, particularly with communities in special operations. In this case, it means that this book is the product of a close collaboration with the Navy, with the SEAL community, and with individual SEALs. All the photography of active-duty SEALs in this book has been reviewed and approved by both US Naval Special Warfare Command (SPECWARCOM) and SEAL Teams Three and Five, who assisted with its production.

The Big Picture: US Special Operations Command

Special Operations Command has become, in the years since the failed Iranian hostage rescue mission, one of the best funded, most secure, most competitive parts of the US force structure. All the services, including the Coast Guard, have been caught up to some extent in the reorientation away from what is called "high-intensity combat," with its need for nuclear weapons, long-range bombers, numerous tank divisions and aircraft carriers, to preparation for "low-intensity combat," the work of small teams of extremely adept people like SEALs and Green Berets.

USSOCOM is just one of eight "unified" commands within the US armed forces and has been a major player in the defenses of America since 1987. It integrates assets from all the services into one organization, with one commander, and with the same basic set of missions for everybody. That doesn't mean that everybody does the same thing; rather it means that the Navy, Army, and Air Force pool their talents and resources for planning, training, and executing missions.

Special operations forces have traditionally been the "bad boys" of all the services. Many senior officers have, over the years, been candid about their loathing of the "cowboys" within their large, conservative organizations. Special forces training and missions produce a kind of lunatic intensity that is accepted within these groups but that clashes badly with the larger Navy or Army community within which it is supposed to function. Special operators have a reputation (well earned by an earlier generation) of using their own, independent criteria for acceptable behavior. Green Berets used to say, when asked if they were in the Army, "No, I'm in Special Forces." Some still do.

Becoming a SEAL or a Green Beret has never, as a result, been considered the fast track to high rank. It was, and still is, a special place for special men (and, very rarely and not in the SEALs, a few incredible women) who consider these extremely demanding roles

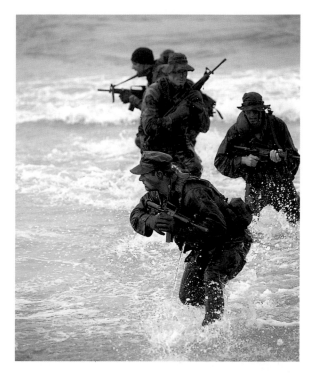

Naval Special Warfare is an interesting blend of high technology and the most basic, simple warrior skills. This fire team, coming ashore in a practiced ritual, functions much as small units have for thousands of years—with the same kinds of missions, the same concerns, discomforts, stresses. Norsemen invading England must, with minor changes in equipment and uniform, have looked like this.

a kind of calling. They aren't in the business to get rich or famous but to be measured by the highest standard of military performance and found acceptable. That is the real lure and the real reward of the special forces.

While the special operators may not always be personally popular within their services, the additional stress and funding for such missions has made for a very competitive budgetary environment. Both the Army and the Marine Corps compete with the Navy for the missions done by the SEALs. In fact, you could stand on a beach being infiltrated by combat swimmers and be very hard pressed to

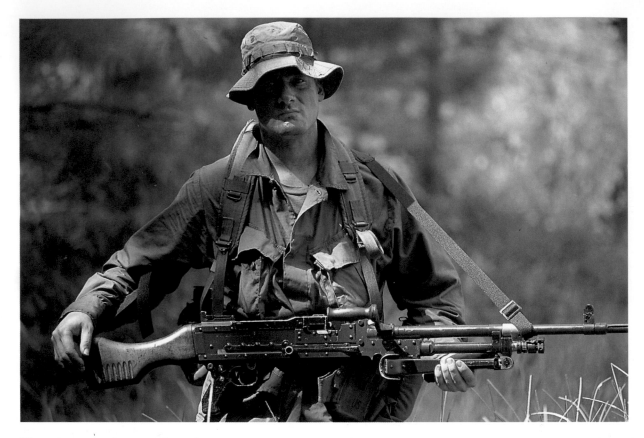

There is tremendous overlap of missions, training, aptitude, and command of all the organizations within US Special Operations Command. This Green Beret trains SEALs in the art and science of small arms like the German GPMG 7.62mm ma- *chine gun he's carrying. SEALs and Green Berets are essentially members of the same fraternity. They are likely to be on better terms with each other than with members of conventional units within their own branch of service.*

know who was about to kill you—American Army "Green Berets" or Rangers, Marine Corps Force Recon, or US Navy SEALs. All use precisely the same weapons, boats, dive gear, radios, and uniforms—and all train for what sometimes looks like the same exact mission. But it turns out that the missions are not quite exact, that there are distinctions, and that the overlap is not as great as it initially appears. Here, then, is a thumbnail description of how the confusing world of US Special Operations is split up and tied together.

JSOC

Joint Special Operations Command (JSOC) is a kind of planning and coordination cell, headquartered at Pope Air Force Base, North Carolina, (co-located with Fort Bragg). JSOC's primary mission is to study the techniques and requirements of all the Special Operation Forces (SOF) components, including Naval Special Warfare, to ensure that—as they say—everybody's playing off the same sheet of music.

USASOC

The Army contributes the "Green Berets" (properly but rarely called Special Forces), a

SEALs now have a hostage rescue/counterterrorist assignment to train for. These SEALs are training for it by being "proned-out" by some Marines during *a training exercise aboard the USNS Joshua Humphries in the Red Sea. This kind of joint training is a standard feature of life in the teams.*

regiment of Rangers, the Delta counterterrorist unit, a special operations aviation unit called Task Force 160 (TF-160), plus psychological, civil affairs, and signal units. Most of these units are headquartered at Fort Bragg, North Carolina, at the US Army Special Operations Command (USASOC).

AFSOC

The Air Force contribution to special warfare is the US Air Force Special Operations Command (AFSOC) with headquarters at Hurlburt Field, Florida. The Air Force provides special aircraft and crews to insert and extract Army and Navy combat elements and to support them from overhead. AFSOC owns and operates special versions of the C-130,

CH-53, and CH-60 within the 1st Special Operations Wing.

NAVSOC

The Navy's contribution to USSOCOM is called NAVSOC within the special operations community, but is in fact Naval Special Warfare Command—SEALs and Special Boat Squadrons.

SEAL Specialties

SEALs—by contrast with Air Force and Army special operators in the Ranger regiment and special forces groups—are generalists, although each will have a specialty (intelligence, submarine operations, weapons, engineering, communications), that he does in support of the organization in the planning process. But once the little squad of SEALs goes off to war, he has to be able to do the job of anybody else on the team. "If I'm the platoon commander on a mission and I take a hit," one SEAL officer says, "the assistant platoon commander can take over. It doesn't matter if he was the corpsman or the radioman—he can take over that operation and direct it to completion. I can pick up the radio, treat a wound, use any of the weapons. Green Berets say they can do that too, but I think we build *generalists* while they build *specialists*. That's probably because they operate in larger groups. We operate in groups anywhere from four to sixteen men, and any one of our guys can slip into the role of any other guy . . . within limitations."

SEAL Missions

Just about all the special operations forces have the same *basic* list of missions. Each of them adapts these missions to the unique talents of the force. For the NSW community the list looks like this:

1) Direct action (DA)—Short-term seize, destroy, damage, or capture operations. Attacks against facilities ashore or afloat; "prisoner snatch" operations; small offensive combat operations against hostile forces.

2) Special reconnaissance (SR)—Reconnaissance and surveillance operations. Covert beach surveys, listening posts, observation posts.

3) Unconventional warfare (UW)—training, leading, and equipping partisan and guer-

The Air Force contribution to Special Operations Command is two-fold: it offers a kind of bus service, like this SH-60 dropping a squad off in the Gulf, *complete with boat; and it provides a kind of body-guard service overhead, with Spectre gunships.*

rilla forces, behind enemy lines.

4) Foreign internal defense (FID)—Training, advising, and teaching the military, paramilitary, and law enforcement personnel of allied nations. Professional development, normally in a noncombat environment.

5) Counterterrorist operations (CT)—Operations conducted against terrorist units and individuals. May be as direct responses to terrorist operations or as indirect, preventive, deterrence measures.

All these missions have implications for their missionaries. To accomplish missions like these and survive, the people and the organizations they belong to need to be agile (individually and organizationally), trained to a far higher standard than conventional military personnel, and provided with far more resources, man for man, than conventional units. This assignment makes for organizations that are expensive and exclusive.

The "Wiring Diagram"

SPECWARCOM is an interesting community and a tremendous challenge to command. Although the SEAL teams are its most famous component, they are only one part of the whole business of Naval Special Warfare—a fairly small part, in fact.

RADM Ray Smith commands two major combat resources, Special Warfare Group One and Two. Each of these groups include three SEAL teams, a Special Boat Squadron, and a Swimmer Delivery Vehicle team.

Group One operates out of Coronado, California, and generally deploys forces to the Pacific and the Persian Gulf; SEAL teams One, Three, and Five are assigned to Group One. Group Two is headquartered at Little Creek, Virginia, with teams Two, Four, and Eight assigned, and a responsibility for operations in and around the Atlantic, including Europe and Latin America. These two headquarters are the administrative foundations for special warfare and, despite the sneers from the operators in the field about the "puzzle palace" (as such headquarters are often called) they are essential for the efficient coordination of as-

The fundamental component of the SEALs is the dive pair. A cardinal rule of life in the teams is you never abandon your swim buddy. It is too dangerous a business for solo operators.

sets and activities.

Coronado is not only home to Naval Special Warfare and Group One, but also to the notorious Naval Special Warfare Center where SEALs are trained. Basic Underwater Demolition/SEAL training is conducted at Coronado, the entry point for all new SEALs and SEAL Delivery Team members. The center also conducts advanced training and professional development programs for members of the SPECWARCOM community.

Little Creek, besides hosting Group Two, is responsible for the Special Warfare Development Group. This is the SEAL think tank

where new weapons, tactics, communication systems, and dive equipment is tested, evaluated, and written into doctrine. Little Creek is also responsible for the development of special operations tactics for air, ground, and maritime forces, in and out of Naval Special Warfare. SPECWARCOM includes detachments in Alaska and Hawaii, plus five Special Warfare Units.

What you don't see advertised are the semi-covert programs called Development Group and Red Cell. Development Group provides support for a variety of classified programs that—sorry—we aren't going to tell you about. Red Cell is an offshoot from the Naval Security Coordination Team and has the interesting mission of assisting navy commands around the world with their security problems. This help is not always welcomed because it is done in a sneaky way when the Red Cell members sneak or break into what are supposed to be secure facilities. They are supposed to act like terrorists or subversives—and that's the way a lot of people outside Naval Special Warfare think of them, too. Some commanders seem to think Red Cell creates more security problems than it solves. This program was at one time extremely notorious and the subject of a book by one of its former commanders (written while in prison) that scandalized Naval Special Warfare generally. It appears at this writing that the program will be transferred out of NSW into the more conventional Naval Investigative Service.

SEAL and Special Boat Squadron Basics

Although we usually refer to this community as SEALs, it is a bigger, more complicated business than the SEALs alone. The other

This fire team represents half a squad, a quarter of a platoon. Units this size are perfectly suited to most SEAL ops—ideal for ambushes, for example, and many strike missions. The fire team is small enough to be fast and agile and almost invisible; it is big enough to provide mutual support and to have enough diversity and cargo capacity to go inland for a raid or a recon.

SEALs get considerable latitude in the kind of gear and weapons they carry and use. This officer's non-standard combat vest is based on a design concept developed by the Israelis and adopted by the British, along with some US Special Operations Forces personnel. Rifle magazines are stowed in pouches designed for easy access—and to provide some protection against enemy small arms fire and grenade fragments.

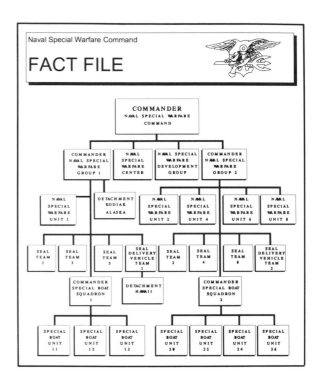

Naval Special Warfare Command

FACT FILE

COMMANDER
NAVAL SPECIAL WARFARE
COMMAND

COMMANDER NAVAL SPECIAL WARFARE GROUP 1 — NAVAL SPECIAL WARFARE CENTER — NAVAL SPECIAL WARFARE DEVELOPMENT GROUP — COMMANDER NAVAL SPECIAL WARFARE GROUP 2

NAVAL SPECIAL WARFARE UNIT 1 — DETACHMENT KODIAK ALASKA — NAVAL SPECIAL WARFARE UNIT 2 — NAVAL SPECIAL WARFARE UNIT 4 — NAVAL SPECIAL WARFARE UNIT 6 — NAVAL SPECIAL WARFARE UNIT 8

SEAL TEAM 1 — SEAL TEAM 3 — SEAL TEAM 5 — SEAL DELIVERY VEHICLE TEAM 1 — SEAL TEAM 2 — SEAL TEAM 4 — SEAL TEAM 8 — SEAL DELIVERY VEHICLE TEAM 2

COMMANDER SPECIAL BOAT SQUADRON 1 — DETACHMENT HAWAII — COMMANDER SPECIAL BOAT SQUADRON 3

SPECIAL BOAT UNIT 11 — SPECIAL BOAT UNIT 12 — SPECIAL BOAT UNIT 13 — SPECIAL BOAT UNIT 20 — SPECIAL BOAT UNIT 22 — SPECIAL BOAT UNIT 24 — SPECIAL BOAT UNIT 26

This is the "wiring diagram" for Naval Special Warfare—minus the "black" programs and units. Essentially it shows two major communities, Group One for the Pacific and Group Two for the Atlantic. The units are forward-deployment bases. Not shown are Red Cell and Development Group.

major part of SPECWARCOM is the guys on the surface who go through the same training at BUD/S, go off on the same missions, and bleed at least as much as the members of the SEAL teams—the Special Boat Squadrons and the members of the Special Warfare Units. They're all Naval Special Warfare members, although all the attention and glory seems to go to the SEALs alone. But, as the history of Naval Special Warfare in Vietnam and after shows, much of the combat and the killing has been done by the riverine warriors duking it out with the bad guys ashore with .50-caliber machine guns and Mk 19 grenade launchers, all while roaring around in their PBRs in an unstealthy way.

The idea behind the boat squadrons is to provide the SEAL teams with dedicated, "organic" mobility, as well as some kinds of special patrol and surface strike missions. These squadrons are commanded by SEALs but manned largely by sailors from the surface warfare community, what SEALs often call the "black shoe" navy. Although part of the Naval Special Warfare community, they are not quite SEALs but SEAL support units.

The home base for SEAL/SBS operations seems somehow out of place on the luxurious, tropical paradise of Coronado, California, just

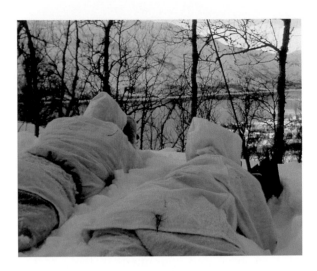

Far from the water but cold anyway, these two SEALs are participating in a training exercise in Norway. Special operators have to be extremely versatile and tolerant of extremes.

across the bay from San Diego. While tanned tourists frolic on the beach nearby, SEAL/SBS operations and training are planned and conducted at the Naval Special Warfare Command (SPECWARCOM), a component of US Special Warfare Command. The headquarters is just another rather modern concrete building, complete with the requisite lawn and landscaping, plus plenty of chain-link fence, guards, and razor wire.

The US Navy takes the prize for inventing and actually using the world's biggest and most awkward acronyms, one of which is SPECWARCOM. You might as well get used to words like this because everybody in the SEAL/SBS community uses them all the time; they are unavoidable. SPECWARCOM is the parent headquarters for all Navy special operations of which SEALs are only a part.

The commander of SPECWARCOM currently is a lean, bouncy, cheery, young-looking man with a star on his collar: he's Vice Admiral Ray Smith, fifty years old, who's been part of the community since 1970. Like all American commanders, he will have custody of SPECWARCOM for two or three years, then hand it over to a new boss. During those years he will be responsible for the health and wealth of the community, its training, its tactics, its fitness for combat. He, like his predecessors and successors, will try to guide SPECWARCOM through the hazards of annual budgets and Department of Defense policy changes.

SEAL Teams

On paper at least, a full-up SEAL team includes ten platoons of SEALs plus a small support staff from the black-shoe navy. This support staff are the yeomen for administrative support, radiomen, ordnance specialists, a navy diver to help with the dive locker—about twenty non-SEAL personnel. There is an additional command element including the commanding officer, executive officer, and operations officer, all of whom are fully SEAL-qualified.

While in theory there are ten platoons in each team, it doesn't usually work out that neatly. Each team has an intense training program that cuts into the number of people actually available to participate in a platoon. But each of the platoons will have sixteen SEALs assigned: two officers and fourteen enlisted members. These are grouped further into two squads of eight, each getting an officer and seven enlisted. The squads themselves are split into fire teams of four men, the fire teams each having two "swim pairs."

The squad has traditionally been the organization of choice for SEAL operations and has turned out to be a very efficient group for many missions.

A lot of SEAL equipment is designed around these groups. The Mk V patrol boat is designed to accommodate sixteen SEALs. Fire teams of four fully combat-loaded SEALs fit very nicely into a Combat Rubber Raiding Craft. The Patrol Craft, Mk 1 is designed to carry a squad of eight SEALs.

SEAL Mobile Training Teams

SEALs (and Green Berets, too) are deployed all over the world, all the time, on quiet little assignments that you never read about in the papers—even when dramatic things happen, and the proverbial poop hits that fabled propeller. These deployments have a couple of functions: one is to put the special forces people out near the scene of a possible crime, before it is committed, ready to respond; the other is to train in environments a lot more realistic than are available in the United States.

One of these quiet deployments ("dets" in the trade jargon) nobody ever hears about is in support of the anti-drug war in Central and South America. Although US law prohibits SEAL/SBSs and other American military personnel from active combat, US policy is to use special operations forces personnel to train the "trigger pullers" to a high standard. And executing that mission is the team of Naval Special Warfare Unit Eight (NSWU-8) and Special Boat Squadron Twenty-Six (SBS-26), forward based out of Rodman in Panama but

with people and boats busy in many Latin American nations.

These organizations, along with SEAL Team Four, are tasked with providing Mobile Training Teams (MTTs) to Bolivia, Argentina, Brazil, Colombia, Equador, and other nations where drugs are manufactured. All these countries have extensive river systems; there are more than 140,000 miles of navigable rivers in South America, with 20,000 in Bolivia alone. These become the highways for transportation of drugs. To control the drug flow requires efficient, effective patrol of the rivers, something the Special Boat Squadron folks do better than anybody.

The MTTs involve quite small numbers of US personnel and equipment to train rather large numbers of host-nation personnel. Sometimes the SBS/SEAL team doesn't even supply the boats. Once on scene the SBS team starts working with the boat operators from the host nation while the SEALs work with the police or military people who will do the patrolling ashore. In Bolivia this force is called the "Blue Devils"; it has been almost entirely trained by these MTTs. The SBS and SEAL dets have helped the Bolivians develop four bases for counterdrug operations deep in the jungle.

In Colombia the story is a little different. The US Marine Corps runs the show there,

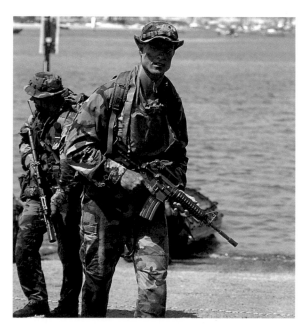

Although the basic uniform matches that of Army and some Navy units, the CAR-15 version of the M16 is pretty much unique to the special operators. The CAR-15 has a shorter barrel and a collapsible buttstock.

Special operators place a high premium on surprise, stealth, and speed. A lot of all three come from the SBS crews and their exotic little boats, like this 30-foot rigid inflatable boat (RIB) seen here zipping around with a fire team of SEALs embarked.

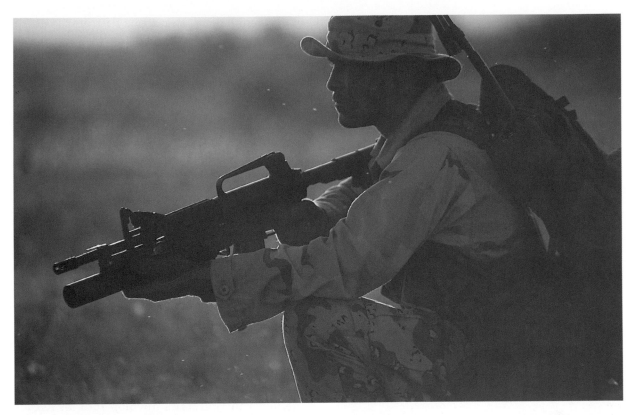

Deep recon and strike missions are usually the province of the Army's Rangers or Green Berets, but SEALs train hard to do the same thing. Who will get the call for one of these assignments will have a lot to do with who is closest to the scene of the crime, *rather than any particular special talent. All are good, but if the op happens to be a coastal target it may be a platoon or squad of SEALs who "take it down."*

where they've had a long and chummy relationship with the Colombian marines. The Colombian det includes one officer and four enlisted SBS/SEAL personnel, all with a special interest in riverine operations and with Spanish language skills. MTTs in Colombia, as elsewhere in the program, last six months.

Special Warfare Units and Forward Basing

Since there are so few SEALs to go around, and since the "real world" has a way of blowing up in your face unexpectedly, Naval Special Warfare has developed forward bases closer to the potential hot spots of the world than Coronado or Little Creek. These are the Naval Special Warfare Units (NSWUs), each with people, facilities, and equipment intended to speed up the process of planning and launching missions.

There are five NSWUs. When the "real world" starts acting up these are reorganized as Naval Special Warfare Task Groups and Units and start manning up with extra personnel from in and out of the NSW community. An emergency will probably find assets getting requisitioned from other NSWUs, particularly the exotic, complex Swimmer Delivery Vehicle (SDV), which may be flown in from the US.

279

Two SWUs serve the European Command area from bases in Spain and Scotland. The Naval Special Warfare Unit base in Spain (NSWU-6) uses Rigid Inflatable Boats (RIBs), Patrol Coastal boats (PCs), and Mk V patrol boats. The base in Scotland (NSWU-2) uses RIBs only. The Pacific Command is served by NSWU-1, recently repositioned from the Philippines to Guam; like NSWU-6, it uses RIBs, PCs, and Mk V patrol boats. NSWU-8 serves the extremely busy Southern Command out of Rodman Naval Station in Panama, supporting the busy counternarcotics operations with a mix of riverine and coastal patrol boats

This lieutenant commands a SEAL Team Three platoon conducting training in desert patrolling, small unit tactics, and live-fire exercises. Unlike many other units, particularly conventional ones, SEALs train their officers and enlisted people together at the same time. While it puts additional stresses on the officers, who must fulfill administrative duties as well as survive the program, it has the advantage of applying the same high standards to the commissioned officers, while their followers observe. The result is an extra measure of respect for a SEAL officer.

280

and the RIBs. Detachments in Hawaii and Alaska provide SEALs with a broad range of training options.

Besides these forward bases, two large Naval Special Warfare Groups on the east and west coasts of the US provide a continental United States (CONUS) foundation for operations "downrange."

For some Naval Special Warfare assets, forward basing is the only practical way to show up on time for the little "come as you are" wars that are the stock in trade of US Special Operations Forces. The PCs, for example, are far too big to go anywhere except under their own power. Although they are fast, it's a mighty big world. If they had to self-deploy from the US, it could take these ships almost three weeks to arrive at some possible operational areas.

Change of Mission

The "commander's intent" for American special operations has changed quite a bit since the idea was first used fifty years ago, at the outset of World War II. Back then the idea was to provide support for partisans and guerrillas in occupied France, Yugoslavia, China, and elsewhere. It involved very little—if any—direct combat. It was a training, leading, and supplying role for forces that tried their best to avoid direct contact with German or Japanese forces while collecting intelligence and sabotaging vehicles, railroads, and bridges and occasionally assassinating individual enemy.

Special Operations Forces today still train for that mission, and SEALs execute something like it every day, in nations all over the world. The trainees aren't guerrillas anymore, but soldiers, sailors, and law enforcement officers from nations such as Colombia, Bolivia, and Kuwait; and the "enemy" is now quite often the guerrilla-like forces who manufacture and distribute drugs or terrorists in Ireland, the Middle East, or Latin America.

The war against terrorist forces has, more than anything else, inspired much of the mission of today's SEALs and other SOF commu-

"Takedown" missions are complicated, dangerous raids that require tremendous skill to execute. When they go bad, they go real bad; the consequences aren't just death or embarrassment for the team, but possible dire international ramifications as well. Ever since the failed Iranian hostage rescue, this mission has been practiced over and over, in depth and detail.

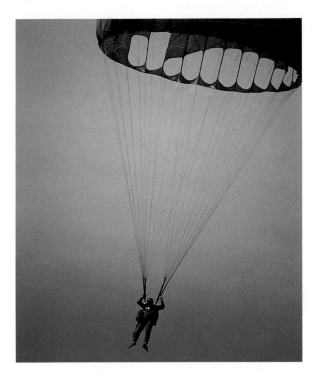

Although SEALs try to avoid airborne insertions like this (as one team commander says, "If you have to jump—find another way!"), the technique is still used occasionally and is practiced as just one way of getting from here to there.

nities. The tasking for Naval Special Warfare is now, essentially, to be prepared to *conduct short-notice small-unit operations at night, over the horizon, to infiltrate from sea, air or land, in adverse weather.* Instead of training others to fight large, conventional battles, SOF units, including the SEALs, are much more like global SWAT teams that can be sent to fight almost anybody, almost anywhere. Like a good SWAT team, these forces are task-organized and are based on stealth, shock, surprise, and precision. While some SEALs still study foreign languages and are charismatic instructors for people of extremely alien cultures, the heavy emphasis now is on preparing SEALs to be able to slither deep into hostile territory, up to easy pistol range of

very specific bad guys, put 9mm bullets between their eyes—and then get out without being obvious about it. The battlefield can be a hotel, an airliner, a civilian cargo ship, an oil platform, a factory, or an embassy. And the enemy may be one hostile man—or woman—surrounded by innocents.

This is a tall order. In fact, it is sometimes too tall; SEALs aren't, despite what you hear, supermen. They get tapped to do impossible missions sometimes because they are so skilled, so sneaky, so confident . . . and they die in the attempt, sometimes, as in Panama and Grenada, when they're pushed beyond their limits. There are only about 1,200 of them for a global set of responsibilities. It is a small community with a huge mission.

This motley crew is a squad of warrior SEALs from long ago and far away. Standing are Pierre Birtz, Bill Garnett, Charlie Bump, and Bob Gormly; kneeling are Jess Tollison and Fred McCarty; the photo was made in 1967. With Gormly (then a lieutenant) as squad leader, these men operated around the town of Binh Thuy, helping establish the reputation of the SEALs as among the most elite American *warriors. All made Naval Special Warfare a profession, and all are now retired except for Tollison, who was killed in an accident at the Niland, California, training facility in 1971. Gormly went on to command SEAL Teams Two and Six, UDT-12, and NSW Group Two before retiring in 1992 as a captain.* Bob Gormly collection

Chapter 2

A Short History Lesson

The keel for today's SEALs and Special Boat Squadrons was laid in May of 1942 with the formation of the Naval Combat Demolition Unit at Fort Pierce, Florida. The men who were selected for the program came from the Naval Construction Battalions and the Navy/Marine Corps Scout and Raider Volunteers. All had extensive swim experience; some were commercial divers; all were in superb physical condition. The training was not too different, fifty years ago, from today—lots of physical training (PT), lots of swimming, lots of demolitions. The stress level was high, by design. Training continued day and night, in the swamps with the alligators, on the beaches, and offshore.

The motivation for the program had come toward the end of the previous year. After less than a year of war, the United States was beginning to strike back at the entrenched Japanese, first at Guadalcanal, then, in November, at Tarawa . . . "terrible Tarawa," as it will always be known to the United States Marine Corps.

The US was badly unprepared for war, and even more unprepared for large-scale, long-range amphibious operations. One of the things that makes wars interesting is the ways in which individuals and nations respond to the surprises and stresses imposed on them by events. In the case of the US Navy and Marine Corps in 1942, this meant a re-quirement for not merely the attack of Japanese installations in the Pacific, but the seizure of critical bases.

Guadalcanal came first—and the invasion phase of the operation, at least, was a cakewalk. The Marines were able to step ashore, essentially unopposed, often with dry feet. Getting the force ashore was just about the least of the problems at Guadalcanal—most of which came soon thereafter. The Navy had been lucky with that phase of the operation. Tarawa was different. D-day for Tarawa was 20 November 1942. Information about the island, its defenses, and its approaches was limited. Hydrographic data was sketchy, tidal data almost nonexistent. The assault force commander took a risk, knowing the stakes, and lost.

The Marines were sent in aboard conventional landing craft. Five hundred yards offshore, within the range of Japanese machine guns, the boats ground to a halt against coral reefs. The Marines, in the grand tradition, jumped off the boat ramps for the long wade into the beach . . . and died in droves. Many stepped into depressions in the coral reef; heavily loaded, they sank and drowned. The rest had to endure the heavy, interlocking fields of fire from the Japanese defenders. It was a disaster.

Hundreds of Marines died before the battle for Tarawa really even began. In a way,

Many of the basic "frogman" techniques in use today were invented half a century ago in the pressure cooker of war. That includes this technique for de- *ploying a line of swimmers off an enemy-held beach from a high-speed boat.*

their lives were wasted, but in another way, by dying this way, they taught the Navy a lesson. The lesson was, and still is, that amphibious assaults are high-risk operations that require careful preparation. And that need for battlefield preparation was the idea for the development of the Navy Combat Demolition Unit.

Their mission was to scout possible invasion beaches and to clear, with explosives, obstacles that might prevent the invasion force from reaching the beach as had happened at

Tarawa. It was recognized that there were essentially four hazards to the force: enemy action from fortifications ashore, enemy-built obstacles such as concrete blocks placed in the water, natural obstacles such as the coral reef that stopped the Marines, and the time and range of the tides.

That was the program for the sturdy volunteers at Fort Pierce. The survivors of the challenging training were organized as small units, structured with six enlisted men and one officer per Combat Demolition Unit and shipped off to England with the rest of the American contingent building up for the invasion of France.

When finally, on 6 June 1944, Allied forces were ready to take Europe back from the Nazis, the first men ashore were the Navy Combat Demolition Teams (NCDTs). The NCDT members were tasked with the nasty chore of surveying and destroying the beach obstacles emplaced by the Germans along the Normandy coast of France. These obstacles were an ingenious and extensive array of concrete blocks, steel spikes, mines, and barbed wire that cluttered most of the beaches suitable for amphibious landings. Left in place, they certainly would deter any large force from putting men ashore. And in 1943 the Germans knew the Allies were going to come, sooner or later, and were working as fast as possible to make a beach passage as costly as possible.

When the Allies finally struck, the NCDT men were out in front of the first wave. With the most primitive equipment, utterly lacking effective protection from the chilly water, they swam in to the beach in the small hours before the invasion. Working from one massive obstacle to the next, hanging satchel charges linked with detonation cord, they prepared to clear the beaches for the assault elements.

Dawn that day found an incredible armada off the Normandy coast, thousands of ships and boats finally bringing hundreds of thousands of soldiers back to Europe—and the beaches still hadn't been completely cleared. The NCDT men had been given a tall order, and not all the obstacles had been blown by the time the infantry started in to the beach. As the cloudy sky brightened, German gunners could see, and engage, the men setting charges on the beach whose mission was obvious. While the NCDT men struggled frantically to avoid the fire, emplace the explosives, and blow the lanes for the landing craft, the first wave closed on the beaches.

Even without clear access to some of the beaches, the craft disgorged their cargoes of infantry when and where they could, often under intense artillery and heavy machine gun fire. The NCDT men worked as fast as they could, but even so they found infantry sheltering behind obstacles rigged and primed for demolition, despite warning devices. Some charges blew with infantry nearby, killing them, while other obstacles weren't blown because of the proximity of men from the first wave.

Even so, four lanes were cleared and the assault elements generally made it ashore—if not in good order, at least in one piece, one infantry division after another. The cost for the NCDT force was far higher than for the infantry—about thirty percent at Utah Beach, about sixty-five percent at Omaha, about forty percent casualties overall. But, from the point

February, 1969. A SEAL ties a block of C4 into a line of det cord before placing the charge in a Viet Cong (VC) tunnel complex. Vietnam honed the special warfare abilities of the little SEAL community to a sharp edge through an emphasis on small unit, independent operations that made individual platoons and squads responsible for "taking care of business."

of view of the planners, that was a small price to pay for getting a secure foothold on the heavily defended enemy shore.

Despite the losses and the problems the NCDT units encountered, their work was considered a success and adapted to the island-hopping campaign in the Pacific. They were rechristened Underwater Demolition Teams (UDT), each with 100 enlisted men and thirteen officers assigned, and retaining the seven-man unit foundation.

Out in the Pacific the UDT units developed a routine that became part of the standard operating procedure (SOP) for amphibious assaults, some of which survives to the present day. This routine started with a beach reconnaissance four days before the scheduled assault (D-minus-4) with the swimmers inserted just at first or last light. This recon would identify obstacles, natural and man-made, on the intended lanes for the landing craft and armored amphibious tractors (AAM-TRACs), recording each carefully and developing a chart of the offshore, nearshore, foreshore, backshore, and hinterland areas of the invasion beaches.

On D-minus-1 or on D-day itself the obstacles would be blown. The method developed fifty years ago is still taught today because it still works. Here's how they did it:

While naval gunfire and close air support aircraft light up the beach with guns, bombs, rockets, and cannon fire in this type of approach, a small, fast ship makes a high-speed run into the beach. During World War II, modified destroyer-escorts were used and designated APDs (Attack Personnel Destroyers). Several miles offshore the APD stopped and lowered four LCPR landing craft, each with a "rubber duck" lashed to the port side. These LCPRs then made a high-speed "splash run" parallel to the beach, about a thousand meters out, starboard side facing the shore. One after another the swimmers rolled out of the LCPR into the rubber duck and, on command, into the water, forming a line of swimmers. At a thousand meters the small portion of each man's head is essentially invisible, and while

the defenders might possibly have spotted one with powerful binoculars, the aerial bombardment and naval gunfire tended to make them worry about other issues.

The men swam ashore and executed their missions, either a reconnaissance or a beach clearance, then withdrew back to the thousand-meter line offshore for pickup, again forming a line of swimmers at intervals. The LCPR came zooming up the line again, with a rubber sling extended. By forming a crook with his right arm and kicking hard just before the boat came by, the swimmer could come up partially out of the water and snag the sling rigged from the inflatable boat, to then be smoothly plucked from the ocean slingshot fashion. One after another the line of swimmers could be quickly and (under the circumstances) safely recovered.

The actual demolition of the beach obstacles also became something of an art form, still practiced today. That technique sent swimmers in to assigned obstacles with satchel charges essentially identical to the ones used today. The flank swimmers at either end of the line carried long rolls of "det cord" instead of explosives; while the other swimmers were busy installing the satchel charges, the det cord was strung from one end of the beach to the other. The satchel charges were each tied into this det cord, and then most of the swimmers began to withdraw. Finally, the ends of the det cord were double-primed, once from each end, with a blasting cap and time fuse. Using waterproof fuse lighters, the fuse was lit, and the whole team formed up out at the thousand-meter line for pickup. When either of the fuses finally burned down to its blasting cap, the "powder train" was initiated; the det cord linked all the charges and caused all to go off within a small fraction of a second—hopefully while the swimmers were already well offshore and safe from the blast effect and chunks of concrete and steel that rained down after such a mission. After Normandy, UDT losses dropped to only about one percent from the approximately forty percent of the first large-scale operation, thanks large-

"Hey! You said the mud wasn't deep!" The op hasn't even started and this guy is already out of action— up to his knees in mud. The weapon is the infamous Stoner, a 5.56mm machine gun with a tendency to jam at embarrassing moments. When it worked, though, it could chew up whatever it was pointed at, and the idea behind it survives today in the light-weight version of the M60 still used by the squads.

ly to this technique. By the end of the war thirty-four teams, including about 3,500 officers and men, were in action in the Pacific.

Korea

In the grand American military tradition, much of the equipment and experience of the UDTs in World War II was discarded promptly after VJ-day—only to be reinvented a few years later. For UDT that came in September 1950 with the audacious amphibious landing at Inchon, Korea.

With United Nations (UN) forces trapped in a shrinking perimeter at the southern tip of Korea by a rampaging, nearly victorious North Korean army, Gen. Douglas MacArthur and his staff designed an "end run" operation on the enemy, with the port city of Inchon on the western coast of the peninsula, near the already fallen capital of Seoul, as the target.

The harbor at Inchon is a treacherous one, with an extreme range of tides that would make the timing and execution of any amphibious operation extremely critical. To minimize the danger, UDT was used to provide detailed information about channels, docks, tides, and defenses. They cleared channels of mines the hard way, by hand, swimming in line-abreast and attaching charges to the mines as they were encountered.

After the Inchon invasion totally changed the complexion of the war, with the North Koreans reeling back, the UDT units were used again, but not just for beach recons and clearance missions. Their skill and experience earned them assignments to blow bridges, railroads, tunnels, and similar targets well away from the beaches.

Korea was the first of a series of nasty little wars that didn't conform to the expectations of the strategic planners in Washington, but that didn't prevent soldiers, sailors, and Marines from having to fight them. Korea didn't really fit what the American public expected, either, and consequently support for the war and the men fighting it slowly ebbed a bit until the stalemate was formalized with a truce in 1953. But Korea expanded the mission of the organization that would soon be rechristened "SEALs" and included guerrilla operations behind the lines, parachute jumps, and other missions quite different from those envisioned ten years previously during the bigger conflict of World War II. And more was yet to come.

The Vietnam War

Although the ancestors of the units and the missions that would become the Navy's and Army's special operations forces existed during World War II, it was not until 1962 that they achieved real recognition and support. The support came from John F. Kennedy, a student of international conflict and unconventional warfare. Kennedy had read the works of Mao Tse Tung and Che Guevara, and he understood the changing nature of conflict away from nuclear confrontation to brush-fire wars. While the United States was reasonably well prepared for the former, he knew better than many of his generals and admirals how badly the US was prepared for unconventional warfare.

Kennedy was aware of the British success against guerrillas in Malaya in the late 1950s. The Brits learned to turn the guerrilla's tactics and strategies around on them, learned to live in the jungle—where they fought and won uncounted little battles. Kennedy perceived a warning and an opportunity. As a newly elected president, he was in a position to make things happen, and he did. He didn't invent the SEALs or the Green Berets—both organizations already existed but were allowed meager resources and roles.

The Army, in particular, loathed the fledgling special operations units that existed at the time. They refused to "play fair" in exercises and frequently disrupted the intended out-

The basic issue of gear is laid out for inspection in this Vietnam-era photograph: coral shoes, canteens, flippers, weight belt, wet suit, web gear, uniforms, and unshined boots. Gary Stubblefield

come. As a result, wearing the green beret was a court-martial offense at Fort Bragg—until Kennedy showed up. The Navy wasn't as parochial, but the UDTs were still hardly a barnacle on the chain of command.

Kennedy put the whole Department of Defense on notice that there was about to be a change of mission. The change was from a focus on a northern European, NATO versus Warsaw Pact conflict, to the kinds of wars Kennedy thought the US was likely to actually have to fight. He said, "This is another type of warfare, new in its intensity, ancient in its art—war by guerrillas, subversives, insurgents, assassins—war by ambush, instead of by combat—war by infiltration instead of aggression; seeking victory by eroding and exhausting the enemy instead of engaging him. And these are the kinds of challenges that will be before us in the next decade, if freedom is to be saved—a whole new kind of strategy, a wholly different kind of force, and therefore a new and wholly different kind of military training."

Kennedy insisted not only on new training, new organization, and new strategies, but on new weapons and equipment as well. He was responsible for the development and introduction of the AR-15/M16 rifle and the jungle boot, with its steel insert to protect against punji stakes. But it was the development of what became known as a *special warfare* capability within the US Department of Defense that was one of Kennedy's most inspired and enduring legacies.

The Army's Special Forces (known popularly but unofficially as the Green Berets) and the Navy's SEALs and SBSs share many things, including missions, heritage, and a strong sense of mutual respect. Both were developed, at Kennedy's insistence, in the early 1960s. At the outset, both were envisioned as extensions of the World War II Office of Strategic Services (OSS) teams that parachuted behind enemy lines to train, equip, lead, and inspire the native population, a catalyst that used a few men to put hundreds of soldiers in the field. It was called *unconventional warfare* and it was a good idea. It worked—in some times and in some places.

Birth of the SEALs and SBSs

The SEALs were officially born on 1 January 1962, with President Kennedy doing the honors, commissioning Team One and Two, assigned to the Pacific and Atlantic theaters. The original mission was to conduct Naval Special Warfare—which then meant unconventional warfare, counterguerrilla and clandestine operations in maritime and riverine environments. This meant, theoretically, the capability to: 1) destroy enemy shipping and harbor facilities; 2) infiltrate and extract friendly force agents, guerrillas, and escapees; 3) conduct reconnaissance and surveillance; 4) conduct counterinsurgency civic action; 5) organize, train, and lead paramilitary forces.

The new organization got its first taste of real world operations shortly thereafter, conducting operations in support of the Cuban Missile Crisis in 1962, and again in 1965, in the Dominican Republic. Neither lasted long or received much attention, but both put the teams under the kind of pressure that only happens during genuine hostilities. It was a useful rehearsal for the big war that was about to begin. SEALs in small numbers shipped out to Vietnam in 1962, working out of Da Nang and functioning in an advisory role to the Vietnamese Navy, much as the Green Berets were doing for the Army of Vietnam at the same time.

SEAL Team One trained up and deployed two platoons to Vietnam in 1965, assigned to operate in the Rung Sat Special Zone near the capital city, Saigon. These platoons started operating in areas never previously visited by American or Vietnamese forces, deep in the mazes of rivers, creeks, and channels where the VC (Viet Cong, communist South Vietnamese rebels) had been safe. The platoons set up listening posts to collect information on VC activity and ambushes to turn the VC activity off.

The poor VC would come cruising back from a night on the town, shooting up the nearest government outpost, collecting "taxes" from farmers going to market, or assassinating mayors or other officials who might be friendly to Saigon, putting along a deserted stretch of canal in their sampans on the way back to base all fat, dumb, and happy. Then, suddenly, the canal bank would erupt as machine guns and rifles opened up from an artfully prepared ambush. The VC were either killed or captured, their operational routine disrupted, and their influence over the local population severely reduced. The American SEALs were turning a VC tactic around and using it effectively. It just wasn't fair, somehow! It was stealthy, sneaky, and utterly unexpected—just what Americans were not supposed to be able to do, setting the tone for the conduct of Naval Special Warfare to the present day.

The results from this preliminary experiment were quite successful, and four additional platoons were soon sent, two assigned to Nha Be, one to Binh Thuy, and another to My Tho. With a headquarters element, Detachment Alpha, set up at Subic Bay in the Philippines, the SEALs were ready to "lock and load." Detachment Bravo went aboard an APD as a component of a beach recon group, Detachment Charlie went aboard two fleet submarines (the USS *Perch* and USS *Tunney*), and Detachment Delta was sent to Da Nang, Republic of Vietnam. Detachments Echo and Foxtrot went aboard the Amphibious Ready Group standing off the coast, with assignments to assist with demolitions and beach surveys. But it was "Dets" Golf and Hotel, the riverine patrols, that most frequently closed with the enemy and where much of the legend of the SEALs in that war was built.

SEALs were again deployed to Vietnam in 1966, first to the area around Saigon and later to the rich, heavily populated Mekong Delta. The platoons did their workup together, deployed together, and returned together after six-month tours. This made for a kind of intimacy and unit cohesion far stronger than the main force Army units in the country at the time, where soldiers rotated in and out of units individually for one-year tours.

In some important ways, the lessons of the SEAL platoons and teams during the war in Vietnam have been ignored and overlooked. Within the limited areas in which they operated, these little units became highly effective in a generally ineffective war. Their efforts were independent of a larger strategy and so failed to have a lasting impact on the bigger campaign, but they did show what could—and still can—be done by extremely small, stealthy units operating in a maritime environment.

The platoons were given tremendous freedom to conduct their operations as they saw fit. They developed their own intelligence, plans, and procedures, and executed their missions pretty much without interference or sup-

port from the Army or Air Force or from the local Vietnamese military commanders.

Although they avoided working with the local Army of the Republic of Vietnam (ARVN) as much as possible, the SEAL teams often included Vietnamese SEALs. Some of these men were very good. They provided excellent translation services and often exhibited a high degree of combat discipline.

The most common and appropriate use of the SEAL teams were in ambushes, recon missions, and prisoner snatches. The small size of the units, even when supported with gunboats and ground-support aircraft, normally kept the platoons from engaging anything bigger than an enemy platoon or, if it couldn't be avoided, a company or even a battalion. Their

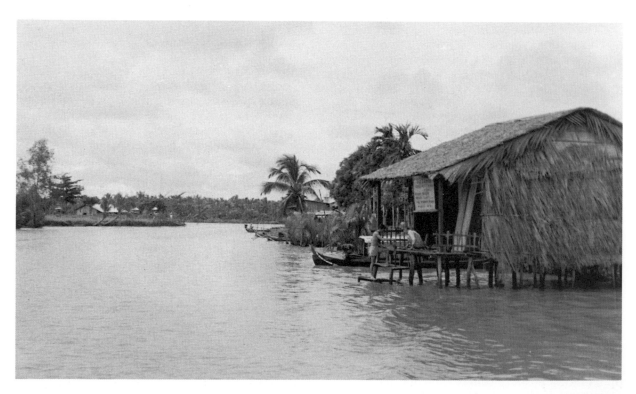

One of the most frustrating elements of combat operations in Vietnam was the way the VC and North Vietnamese Army (NVA) often used civilians for cover and concealment. Sorting out the good guys *from the bad guys was always a problem, particularly within the heavily populated Mekong delta where SEALs did most of their operations. Gary Stubblefield*

flexibility and experience, the effective and efficient support from the boat units, and the air and intelligence teams attached to the SEAL platoons all made for a successful fighting force and a style of operations that is extremely different than that used today.

In the Mekong Delta, particularly, SEAL operations ranged from simple ambushes to complex joint operations, staged from Navy ships located over the horizon, involving transit to the beach in small craft. SEALs used Army helicopter gunships, naval gunfire support, US Air Force "fast-movers," and Army helicopters again, this time the "slicks" for extraction from hot landing zones. SEALs also ran the Provincial Reconnaissance Units (PRUs) as part of the exotic Phoenix program.

Platoons at the time used fourteen men, but a typical mission usually called for no more than seven. Intelligence collection for an operation usually took several weeks and was developed concurrently with other operations. The platoon leader would design a mission around resources and objectives. Helicopters would be laid on for gunship fire support, the boats would be scheduled, an interpreter and a Vietnamese SEAL assigned. The helo crews were briefed, the squads received a warning order, and then, when the plan was fully refined, they got an operation order. Gary Stubblefield, a retired SEAL commander, says, "Briefings in those days took one hour, an hour and a half, max. We already knew our SOPs, we already knew our area. All we had to do was catch up with the changes required for the specific mission. The hard part was the 'actions at the objective' portion, where we got really detailed.

"Typically, we'd leave some time after dark, insert sometime before midnight, maintain an ambush until about daylight, break the ambush and get back in the boats to go back to the base."

A War Story

CAPT Bob Gormly has commanded SEAL Teams Two and Six, UDT-12, and NSW Group Two during a long career in Naval Special Warfare, just concluded. As a young lieu-tenant he went to Vietnam with SEAL Team Two's first deployment to the combat zone in 1967. SEAL Team Two was sent to the Mekong Delta, a hotbed of enemy activity, in the first use of the SEALs in that part of the country—though Team One had been working for some time up to the north, around Saigon.

"Our operations at first were kind of 'touch and feel,'" he says. "We were always searching for a strategy that we fitted into—and we never found it—but we had a lot of fun. Us young lieutenants had tremendous freedom about how we wanted to run an operation. We couldn't be told by anybody to run an operation that we didn't want to do."

Back then the entire delta was considered "Indian" country—hostile territory. The only real US presence was the Navy's River Patrol Force (CTF-116), which used PBRs to patrol the major rivers for about a year, getting shot at regularly. The VC had pretty much free run of the rest of the area.

The problem for the newly established SEALs from Team Two was first to find out what was going on. That required an intelligence information program, something that began immediately with requests for overflights, interrogations of prisoners, radio intercepts, and similar information-gathering techniques.

Gormly developed his own little plan for how he wanted to operate. First, the SEALs wouldn't go where other friendly forces could operate—because there probably wouldn't be anything there, and to make coordination with friendly forces more efficient.

After considering the available intelligence information—the "intel" as it's called—Gormly would call for a Navy Seawolf helicopter and go for a ride. He flew over the area he was interested in to get a sense of the lay of the land, looking for signs of enemy activity. Although there were no US forces in the area, other than CTF-116, there were a few trustworthy American officers in the delta who could help keep the chaos and confusion to a minimum.

"Then I'd land at the subsector headquarters to meet with the senior US advisor, usually a US Army captain or major, who would be working with the local Vietnamese provincial and subsector commanders. I'd walk in and tell him, 'Hi, I'm Bob Gormly. I've got a SEAL team, and we want to operate in your subsector—and I don't want anybody else to know about it but *you*.' To a man, they all agreed to that condition. Then I'd tell them, 'I'm going to be out there sometime in the next three or four days. I'm not going to tell you when. Just, please, don't put H & I [harassment and interdiction artillery fire] in there.'

"Then I'd go back to base, get the platoon together, start running whatever intel we had on the place, setting up to go. We usually went the next night.

"Just before we launched, within six hours, I sent a UNODIR [unless otherwise directed] message . . . a *flash* message that went to all higher headquarters that began 'Unless Otherwise Directed,' and indicated where we were going. Never once was I told not to go. Then we'd hop in the boat and head down river.

"We traveled very light, only small arms, plus an M60 machine gun and an M79 grenade launcher. The briefing was simple: I made sure everybody had the equipment they were assigned, then I told them where we were going, when, and what we were going to do. 'Any questions? No? Let's go!'

"We jumped in the boat, a twenty-two foot trimaran and took off. The boat was a 75mph boat that we made into a 25mph boat by adding a lot of weight in the form of ceramic armor, weapons, and a lot of people."

The SOP for ambushes involved cruising down one of the main rivers or canals into the general area of the objective, inserting several kilometers ("klicks," in the trade), and walking in to the ambush site along another canal. A typical mission involved a boat trip of fifty kilometers or so up the lazy river, as fast as possible for most of the trip, then as quietly and innocently as possible for the last few klicks. Navigation in the confused maze of canals was a tremendous problem, generally

one the skipper of the boat was responsible for. If he was good you arrived where you planned to go—if not, you could have a real problem.

The most dangerous and vulnerable concern was the problem of getting off the boat and into the local woodwork without being noticed. Nearly all insertions were done in the middle of the night. Rather than run the boat up into the weeds and debark the patrol in obvious fashion, the insertion was usually conducted in a more sneaky way. While the boat motored along in normal fashion, the team members merely stepped off the stern in patrol order, swam ashore, and slithered up on the bank. They all waited silently for ten minutes or so, listening for any movement that might indicate they'd been compromised and that enemy forces were moving in to investigate. If that happened, the boat could be recalled for an emergency extraction. Otherwise the mission proceeded according to SOP and to plan.

In the delta, the patrol would move out into the rice paddies, staying off the dikes and away from the treelines where enemy soldiers were most likely to be. Movement was extremely slow and careful, the SEALs moving quietly toward the intended ambush site, normally a canal bank, usually several klicks from the insertion point.

"Although we were in a free-fire zone where everything that moved at night was considered enemy," Gormly says, "we were more selective. Unless I actually saw weapons on the boats we would call the boat over to the bank and search it. If they were 'clean' I'd just take the sampan down the canal a ways and hold them there while we waited for somebody else to come along. One night we had to wait for four sampans before one came along that belonged to the bad guys."

SOP for that kind of contact was for the patrol leader to initiate the ambush, typically at quite short range where the M60, the M16s on full-auto, and the M79 grenade launcher's focused fire would shred the wooden vessel and its crew. The team would wait for the

From 1,000 feet overhead, the farms and rivers of the Mekong Delta look deceptively tranquil in this pre-op recon photo. Within the lush growth along the river are likely to be bunkers and fighting posi- *tions. Inland, among the fields and groves, may lurk more enemy facilities and stores—and the enemy himself.* Gary Stubblefield

leader to fire, sometimes with full-tracers, the signal to "hose down" the enemy vessel. "Seven guys carry a *lot* of firepower," Gormly recalls. "If it was a good hit and there were a lot of weapons aboard we might stick around to see what happened—maybe somebody would come over to investigate. Then we could ambush them too!"

After the patrol leader was satisfied with the evening's mayhem, the order to move would be given. The detained boats would be released, much to the relief of the fishermen aboard, and the SEALs would move off toward the extraction point. The pickup boat would already be somewhere in the vicinity for the scheduled recovery of the team, waiting for a radio call. The team would be recovered and would head back to base for debriefing and chow. In a couple of days it would be time for another briefing and another mission.

This pattern was used for the vast majority of SEAL missions of all types, including recons and prisoner snatches, with slight variations. Recons involved insertion around two or three in the morning, then patrolling into a predetermined overwatch location, setting up a "hide," and staying very still all day. Air or artillery fire could be called in on targets of opportunity. Finally, late at night, the SEALs would patrol back out to be extracted.

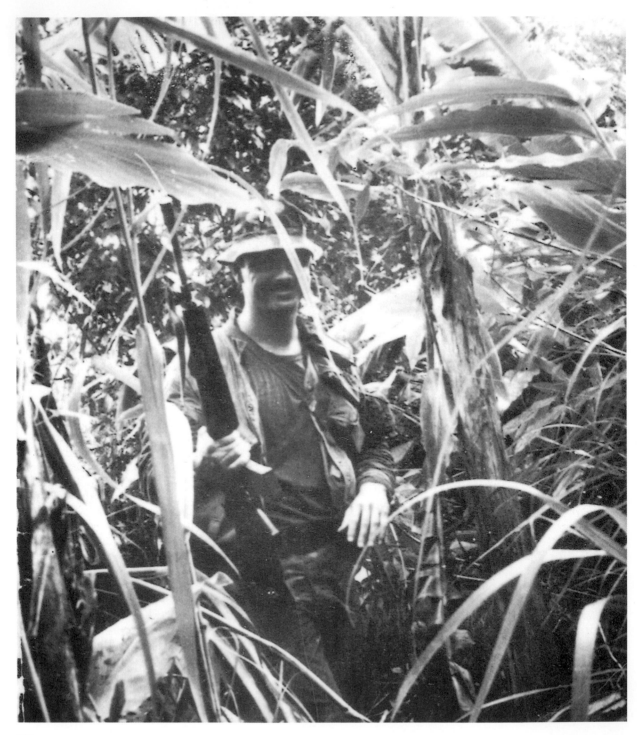

While this was a pretty efficient way of running operations, it was hardly without risk. Gormly was asked to send a team onto Cu Lao Tan Dinh, an island in the delta where enemy gunners routinely shot up passing patrol boats from fortified bunker complexes. With several patrol boats standing by for fire support, the team inserted at first light of 7 June 1967, loaded with hundreds of pounds of C4 explosive, blasting caps, detonation cord, and fuse.

Once ashore, Gormly's motley crew "sneaked and peeked" around for three or four hours, finding lots of bunkers in the process but not encountering any of the loyal opposing team. With the patrol boat supplying the demo materials, the team methodically blew up every bunker in sight. They did this for about four hours, moving steadily down the river from bunker site to bunker site. As they left what turned out to be the last bunker complex, Gormly noticed signs of human activity—bent grass where someone had stepped within the previous few minutes, leaving a trail away from the river. The patrol crawled thirty or forty meters forward, following the tracks, until Gormly (now on point) saw an enemy soldier, complete with helmet and weapon, in the weeds ahead. "I stood up and hosed him down. Then I got shot—and all hell broke loose! We had walked down the side of an L-shaped ambush—lucky us! We had a *big* firefight, then made our way back to the river where we directed fire on the VC until we could get a boat in to extract us. The helo gunships and the boats stayed there for about eight more hours, shooting it out with the VC. I got shot through the wrist. The guy that shot

Are we having fun yet? No, but we're about to . . . Lieutenant Gormly smiles for the camera just about the time that famous poop is about to hit the fabled propeller. It is August 1968, and the lieutenant and his tribe are on an excursion out near the Cambodian border, on Nui Coto mountain, looking for a cave and a large cache of weapons. They found the cave, and a dug-in force of NVA soldiers, too. After bumping heads, the SEALs elected to let the NVA keep their weapons and go home. Bob Gormly collection

me was no more than five feet behind me. We had a Vietnamese SEAL with us, and he hosed that guy down. I was *real* lucky—he shot me over my right shoulder. At first I didn't even know I was shot. I thought my rifle had jammed and blown up—then I noticed the gaping hole in my wrist and realized I'd been shot. That was kind of a stupid op but it was fun for a while!" It also turned out to be worth a Silver Star for Gormly after his SEALs wrote him up for the award.

Grenada

After Vietnam the armed forces of the United States suffered another postwar decline and was—as so often in the past—unprepared for the kinds of real world operations that always seem to materialize. But the failed Iranian hostage mission, among other factors, had begun to revitalize the conventional armed forces when, on 23 October 1983, the SEALs went off to war again, kicking off Operation Urgent Fury in Grenada.

Urgent Fury was, sad to say, pretty much a "goatscrew" for US Special Operations Forces generally, and for the SEALs in particular. The SOF community and the National Command Authority learned many lessons from the operation, but (as usual) it took the bloodshed of the former to educate the latter.

Point Salines Recon Air Insertion

On "point" for Operation Urgent Fury was one platoon of SEALs from Team Six tasked with a recon mission of Point Salines, a thin point of land at the extreme southwest end of the island on which the Grenadans had constructed a new airfield. The platoon's mission objective was a preinvasion recon of sites for amphibious and airborne landings. Their plan, which they developed themselves, involved an insertion by parachute of the sixteen men and their PBL (Patrol Boat, Light—a mil-spec Boston Whaler speed boat) near a Navy destroyer, the *Clifton Sprague*. Once in the water, the SEALs were to find the boat, assemble aboard it, rendezvous with the *Sprague*, take on more SEALs and three US Air Force combat controllers, and slip ashore for the recon. Planning such a complicated operation is one thing; making it happen in the real world is another.

Everything went wrong: instead of jumping at last light, as planned, the mission was late by six hours and the SEALs jumped into pitch black night, making link-up with the boats and the men extremely difficult. Then, overloaded with equipment, the SEALs were driven deep below the surface of the water on landing. Despite the use of flotation devices, three SEALs drowned at the very beginning of the insertion phase of the op. Others survived by jettisoning as much gear as possible from their 100-pound-plus loads. On the surface, one of the two PBLs couldn't be found. The five survivors simply floated on the surface, unable to execute the mission, awaiting rescue that would come at dawn with the arrival of the *Sprague*.

One of the SEALs in the other squad drowned on landing. That squad managed to recover its PBL, collect its survivors, and begin the execution phase of the mission. They found the *Sprague*, linked up with the other personnel, and headed in to the beach—only to encounter an enemy patrol boat and withdraw back to the destroyer.

They tried again the next night. This time another patrol boat came by; the crew killed the engine of their PBL and waited silently for the threat to pass. When the patrol boat was safely out of range, the SEALs tried to start the engine again—without success. They floated, dead in the water, for eleven hours before the *Sprague* came along. The airfield recon mission was, as they say, a "learning experience."

But elsewhere another SEAL recon mission was going off with more success. Using a more conventional (and less risky) fast boat insertion technique, elements from SEAL Team Four operated in direct support of the Marine Amphibious Unit preparing to conduct an assault on the Pearls airport, in the midsection of the little island. Bus service for SEAL Team Four was provided by Seafox crews from Special Boat Squadron Twenty. Late on the evening of 24 October the Seafox-

es, heavily armed with machine guns and grenade launchers, got the SEALs ashore.

One element moved off to scout the airfield while the other conducted a beach recon. The result was good news and bad news. The bad news was that the beach wouldn't work for an amphibious assault; the reef and surf made it too hazardous. There was more bad news, too: the airfield was well defended. But the good news was that the SEALs provided the information before the assault was launched, enabling the task force commander to execute Plan B, a heli-borne troop lift. (The Marines executed their part of the show with precision and grace—then got back on their ships and went off to their original mission in Lebanon).

Beausejour Radio Station Takedown

The SEALs had two other assignments: the first was a takedown of the radio station at Beausejour; the second was a rescue, with US Army Delta teams, of the imprisoned British Governor General, Sir Paul Scoon. Scoon was being held under house arrest by Cuban and Grenadan forces involved in the coup at Governor's House, on a hillside above St. Georges. Both went badly.

After difficulties with helicopter insertion at the radio station, the SEALs from Team Six successfully captured the facility and defended themselves, first from an enemy vehicle that blundered into their perimeter, and then from a counterattack force that included a potent, Russian-built BTR armored car. Although the BTR was killed, a lot of the infantry with it were not, and the SEALs had to beat a hasty withdrawal to the sea. After a successful escape and evasion, they made it to the water, swam out from the shore, and illuminated their infrared rescue strobes. The strobes, invisible to the naked eye but brilliant on thermal imaging systems used by the helos and ships, attracted attention quickly, and the team was quickly picked up. More lessons learned for all hands.

SEALs to the Rescue at Governor's House

Meanwhile, over at Governor's House, another learning experience was in progress.

A Patrol Boat, River (PBR) noses into the shoreline to de-bus a squad of SEALs. Swift, stealthy, surprising ops in the Mekong delta essentially turned guerrilla warfare around on the VC and NVA, keeping *them off balance and insecure. It was accomplished by a skillful combination of boat crews and SEAL teams, operating together in a way that still makes sense. US Navy*

First, the helicopter pilots couldn't even *find* the landing sites on the maps and photographs. Finally, after a lot of thrashing around, the sites were identified, but—oh joy—although they look usable in the aerial photographs, they turned out to be utterly unsuitable in reality. The defenders, alerted by all the activity overhead, had plenty of time to collect their weapons, ammunition, and a spot to work from. Then, instead of rolling over and playing dead as expected, they sat up and took

notice—and aim at the helicopters, which they then shot up.

A force of about two platoons of SEALs fast-roped to the ground and made a dash for the compound, quickly seized it from a light force of police, and collected the governor and his family and staff. They then took up defensive positions—just in time. Another reaction force, again using a BTR, arrived on scene, complete with about a platoon of infantry. With the BTR beating up Governor's House

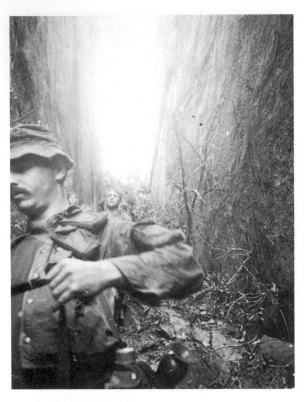

After calling for help, the squad runs off the mountain—right through this tiny pass. Overhead are the NVA, momentarily distracted by Cobra gunships firing up their positions. The squad, expecting a shower of enemy grenades at any moment, is on the run. Lieutenant Gormly leads the way, followed by Clay Grady and Ed Bowen, none of whom are too thrilled about the op. Bob Gormly collection

with its heavy machine gun and the infantry maneuvering on the place, the rescue operation was not going *quite* according to plan.

Among the many missing items from the SEALs bag of tricks was the radio they intended to use to call up support from the many gunships in the air. Instead, all that was available was a low-power, short-range squad radio designed essentially for coordination within the platoon. But at least it could talk to the Rangers and other units in the area and, by a series of relays, the SEALs were able to

get an Air Force AC-130 Spectre gunship overhead.

When a Spectre fires, it is essentially turning a firehose on the target, but with bullets instead of water pouring from its 20mm Vulcan rotary cannon. It is equipped with systems that permit incredible accuracy and precision target identification. And when the Spectre opened up on the reaction force, the party was over for most of them. According to one report, the crew of the aircraft reported to the SEALs after a firing run, "I see twenty 'flappers' and 'kickers' and seven 'runners.'"

Although the assault on Governor's House was held at bay, the enemy force was not driven off. The SEALs and the governor were to wait all night to be rescued by the Marines, over twenty-four hours after the operation began. It was, in the vernacular, a learning experience again.

While these operations were hardly textbook examples of the art, they were typical of the "first blood" encounters of inexperienced units throughout history. They revealed many inadequacies in doctrine, training, equipment, planning, and execution. Those lessons were studied and learned by all the armed forces, and major changes were then applied. The essence of these was to improve the integration of all the US Special Operations Forces into one force with different, mutually supporting talents: the US Special Operations Command assembled from Army, Navy, and Air Force units in 1986.

Panama

By the time Operation Just Cause kicked off in Panama in December of 1989, USSOCOM had come a long way in the process of integrating US special operators. In addition to better planning integration, all the forces had experienced better funding and received more attention as the NCA shifted the nation's military focus away from the Warsaw Pact threat toward the little brushfire wars and terrorist threats that now seemed more dangerous.

SEALs had two major assignments during Operation Just Cause: the *Presidente Porras* mission described earlier, and a mission with a similar objective, disabling Noriega's Neville Jet at Punta Paitilla airport. While the first mission went off pretty much according to the plan, the airport mission was a disaster.

The jet was identified as one of several likely ways Noriega might escape the noose prepared for him. While there were many options possible for taking it out of his game plan, the mission was assigned to the SEALs. The SEAL team, basing its plan on guidance from a higher headquarters, decided to send two platoons onto the airfield to seize the aircraft. When H-hour was pushed up fifteen minutes for the whole operation, the SEALs found themselves trying to play "beat the clock" and losing. The force of approximately forty men was discovered on the airfield and engaged in the open by some PDF who knew their stuff. The Panamanians fired low, skipping their bullets across the concrete. The SEALs took many hits—four dead, eight wounded. Although the Neville Jet was essentially destroyed, by accident, in the engagement, the mission was hardly a success. It even took an hour and a half to get the wounded out. Another learning experience, and a bitter lesson for all concerned.

But they did learn from it, directly and from the "after-action reviews" that followed, formally and informally. As the commander of the operation said to one critic, "You weren't there!" And he has a point—it is easy to be an armchair admiral (or lieutenant commander) and a different matter to do it under fire.

Persian Gulf, Round One

Special operations forces generally get tapped to fight the little wars and smaller skirmishes that tend to be forgotten rather quickly by the public and historians. One of these little operations, designated Ernest Will/Prime Chance, involved SEALs in the Persian Gulf long before that big "drive-by-shooting" called Desert Storm. These operations deployed US forces, in and out of USSO-COM, to the Persian Gulf during the war between Iran and Iraq. The purpose of the oper-

ations was to keep the sea lanes clear and secure for the passage of oil tankers, a rather tall order since the belligerents were indiscriminate about just who they were attacking and their use of mines, missiles, and the occasional small attack boat.

CDR Gary Stubblefield was one of the SEALs sent to the Gulf. His responsibility was to establish a kind of floating base to support a wide variety of "trigger pullers" from the Army, Marine Corps, and Navy—along with Air Force controllers—in a demonstration of what has come to be known as "jointness." The Army personnel operated AH-6 "Little Bird" attack helicopters and 20mm Vulcan cannons, the Marines provided defense for the platform, and all of them cooperated as a kind of guard force for the strategic waterway. For Stubblefield, the mission was twofold: support the guard force in the area with a secure, well-provisioned platform, and use the barge as a platform to stage offensive operations against hostile forces when required.

It was an interesting little operation. Several oil platforms were used by the Iranians as bases for offensive operations against shipping; the Marines took out some of these.

The SEALs *tried* to take down a couple of oil platforms, and probably would have done it well and perhaps with minimal loss of life. Instead, though, the "prep" cannon fire on the platforms that was intended to soften them up resulted in both platforms blowing up while the SEALs were about to land. As Stubblefield says, "We were *supposed* to capture the people on the platforms. But the wrong ammunition was used by the [navy gunners]; they were supposed to use armor piercing but used incendiary instead. While we were in the helicopters, on the way into the platforms, we got word that they blew up. There was no way we could land on them."

Persian Gulf, Round Two

Operation Desert Storm/Shield was the acid test for all the changes that had been incorporated in the US armed forces during the 1980s. SEALs and SBS crews played an active, early, and extremely successful role in

Urban combat skills have been a part of the SEALs' bag of tricks since the rise of terrorist groups and the necessity of hostage rescue operations began in the 1970s. This SEAL from Group Two is rehearsing his moves during a training op during Desert Storm. US Navy

the campaign.

One SEAL platoon, commanded by LT Tom Dietz, set up shop at a small naval base near the northern Saudi town of Ras al Mishab. After the air war kicked off in mid-January of 1991, the platoon started an aggressive reconnaissance program along the Kuwait coastline. Four special reconnaissance missions were executed, looking for any and all information about enemy defenses: Were there patrol boats operating in the area? Navigation aids still in place? Then, moving in closer to the beach, what kind of defenses were visible from offshore?

These recon missions had two or three phases. The first was supported by the SBS crews using their extremely fast, low, "cigarette" racing boats—designated HSBs (high-

speed boats)—for a fast tour of the area. Although not really designed for the recon mission, the HSBs are normally tasked with training the bigger ships in the fleet against anti-ship attacks from such small, fast vessels, and they don't have an official tactical mission. But that speed made them excellent for these recons. With a Zodiac CRRC lashed to the deck, the boats made nighttime forays along the coastline. Dietz says, "We didn't know if there was going to be an amphibious invasion or not. We were told to look for a beach where one could be conducted—or where a deception operation could be conducted."

The first two missions identified two possible invasion beaches from well offshore. The next two missions sent the SEALs ashore to scout the defenses. The plan for the recon missions used two Zodiac inflatables for the run into the beach each night. There were sixteen guys in each platoon, who all wanted to go in, but only room for five in each Zodiac; Dietz had to decide who would go in the Zodiacs and who would stay in the HSBs. "It wasn't an easy decision," he says. "I integrated everybody into the missions, and everybody got to go, but there were some guys that went in every night and some that got rotated."

Three SEALs surface swam in to each beach, without scuba or closed circuit breathing apparatus, which seemed unnecessary. Despite the wet suits they all wore and the training and experience they'd developed, all were chilled. As Dietz says, "The difficult thing about these missions was the cold. We were wet the whole time, from dusk until around dawn. That's why we go through BUD/S and why we go through Hell Week—so we can be wet and tired and still think!"

The Zodiacs were put in the water from about ten miles out, then sent in to about a thousand meters offshore where the swimmers slid over the side into the chilly, low 50-degree water. The SEALs surface swam into the beaches, but not out of the surf. They lay on the sand, using the water for cover and concealment, watching and waiting for about an hour. Then, on schedule, they slipped back into deeper water and back out to the Zodiacs.

After reviewing the results of the intelligence collection missions, one particularly suitable beach was selected, just north of a point called Mina Sa'Ud. The fourth mission went in to the selected beach to confirm the assumptions of the earlier recons. Dietz, as platoon commander, went ashore to have "eyes on" the target, still not knowing if the platoon was supporting an actual invasion or a deception operation. Finally, the decision was made: execute the deception plan.

The plan for the deception operation called for three Zodiacs, and all the men in the platoon would be committed to the mission. Six would swim ashore, a swim pair from each

boat; another three would stay behind to provide support. They were to install charges along the selected beach, primed with individual timers set for a two-hour delay. These charges were all supposed to detonate at about 0100 on the day the ground phase of Desert Storm kicked off, with coalition forces crossing their lines of departure at 0400. At about the same time the SBS crews and SEALs would close on the same beaches and fire them up with every suitable weapon they owned.

The charges and the gunfire didn't need to kill anybody or destroy anything to be effective. All they had to do was get the attention of the Iraqis and convince them that the Marines, who had been waiting offshore for just such an opportunity, were about to come across the beaches in a classic amphibious assault. If such an invasion actually happened and there was no one to meet it, the enemy commanders knew, the war would be over almost instantly.

But if there were no invasion and the enemy forces were still defending against one, that meant there were fewer enemy assets available to deal with the real assault, coming across the border to the west. So the SEAL platoon's sixteen men, plus the SBS crews in the HSBs, had the opportunity to take two whole divisions out of the war (about 20,000 enemy soldiers) with what amounted to a military version of a practical joke.

Execute The Deception Mission

"I've been asked how I picked the 'lucky' six who went in," Dietz says. "I basically chose the nine people who needed to stay back in the boats—my three best engine guys, three best machine gunners, three best radio operators—and the other six were left. But on the final operation I was able to take everybody. That's because we *needed* everybody."

Although the SEALs didn't see the need for Draeger scuba gear, they each took along a little "bail-out bottle" of air sufficient for about three minutes sub-surface swimming in case they made serious contact with any enemy defenders. The bottles were the kind of "field ex-

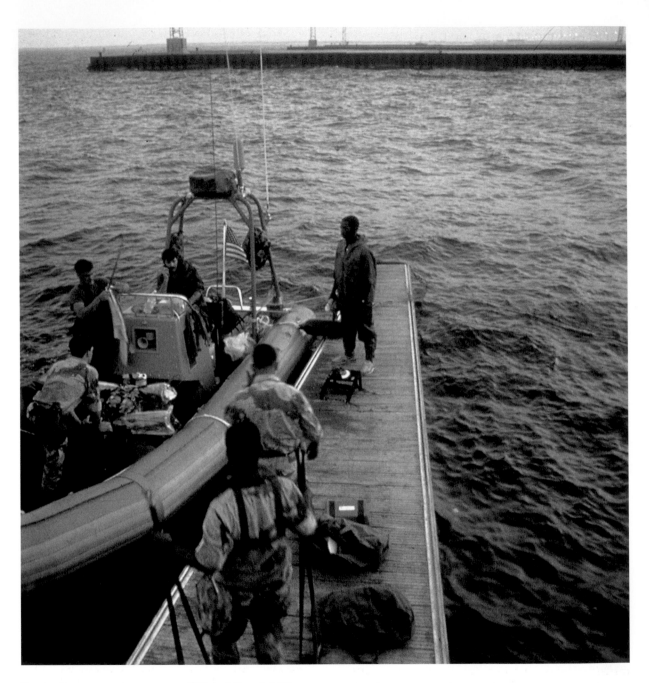

Desert Storm was a new test of Naval Special Warfare people, tactics, and equipment. This RIB is being prepared for a night operation in the Persian Gulf.

pedient" solution to a problem that seems to materialize during war—they'd been acquired from a helicopter unit and adapted to an entirely different use (and a prohibited one) than that for which they were designed.

Of the six SEALs who swam in, three carried CAR-15s, the compact version of the M16A2 with a shorter barrel and a stock assembly that could be retracted. The CARs all had M203 grenade launchers attached for serious, long-range, indirect fire. The other three carried the German Heckler & Koch MP5 submachine gun with suppressers (not silencers) attached. "The idea was that if a couple of sentries showed up on the beach, and we thought we were compromised, we could take them out with the suppressed weapons without giving away our positions," Dietz says. "But if something heavy opened up on us—a machine gun, for example—at longer range, we could lay some grenades on it."

Each of the six swimmers carried a Mk 138 satchel charge. Two timers were attached to each, set for two hours. This kind of "double priming" is SOP. In the bags were ten two-pound blocks of C4 explosive, dual primed, the charges all carefully prepared ashore before everybody climbed into the water.

The swimmers went in to the beach on line, about twenty feet apart. Once they could touch bottom with their flippers, they spread out, about fifty meters from each other across the 250-meter-wide beach. "You could just see the guy on either side of you," Dietz says, "and we didn't have to wait for any signals. Once we spread out, we swam into the beach and placed our charges in about one foot of water—since the tide was now receding—pulled the pins on the timers and swam back out to regroup." The Zodiacs, which had been standing by about 500 meters off the beach, were signaled in for the pickup. Once the swimmers were hauled aboard, the "rubber ducks" headed out into the Gulf, about seven miles off the beach, to the rendezvous point with the supporting SBS crews in the speedy HSB cigarette boats.

Four of the HSBs participated in the operation. Two HSBs collected the Zodiacs and the SEALs, counted noses, and secured the inflatables. In the meantime, the other two zipped in to about two miles. Now, at about 0030 hours, the active part of the deception plan began as the two HSBs closed to 500 meters of the shoreline and opened up with every weapon aboard: mini-guns, heavy machine guns, grenade launchers. "They ripped the beach apart," according to the platoon leader. The firing continued for about ten noisy minutes. For any Iraqis ashore, this would obviously not be bombing or naval gunfire, but a large scale, close in attack of the type preceding an amphibious assault. On their final pass up the beach, the HSBs chucked several additional explosive charges overboard—more C4, wrapped in plastic, primed to go off in the water at irregular intervals. These detonated as the boats made a break for the exit. About five minutes later, almost exactly at the scheduled hour of 0100, the satchel charges ashore started exploding. All went off within about thirty seconds of each other, with a series of tremendous *booms* that were audible far out to sea, where the HSBs beat a hasty strategic withdrawal.

All four linked up out at the seven-mile mark, then headed back to base. At 0230 they debriefed. "It was a very low-key, matter-of-fact debrief," Dietz says. "The operation went according to plan. We were happy but not really excited about it. What we were really excited about was that the ground war was now kicking off! It wasn't until later, after we'd gotten cleaned up and had something to eat, that we got a message from CAPT (now RADM) Smith, the Task Group commander, reporting that elements of two Iraqi divisions remained on the coastline even as the ground forces were going up behind them. They remained in position to defend against the amphibious invasion. That's what really pleased us—that the Iraqis paid attention to us, reacted to us, and hopefully we saved some lives."

Chapter 3

Earning Your Flippers at BUD/S

So you think you wanna be a SEAL? No problem—piece of cake. Anybody can do it! It only takes twenty-six weeks, and the training is mostly done on the beautiful, sandy beach at Coronado, California, right on the Pacific Ocean near warm, wonderful San Diego, and the program is run by a large, kindly, attentive, cheerful, and well-trained staff of SEALs. There are always plenty of beautiful women strolling by to admire the handsome sailors; the famous and luxurious Hotel Del Coronado, with its superb restaurants and bars, is right down the road. There is plenty of sailing, surfing, scuba diving, and other recreation available in the immediate vicinity. The beach is always available for a nice jog. And, best of all, every instructor at the Basic Underwater Demolition/SEAL program is committed to making sure that every day of those twenty-six weeks are just *loaded* with activities and experiences you will *never* forget. Sound like fun? Sign right here!

Well, Navy recruiters don't actually sell

One of the first and most terrifying tests of BUD/S is called "drown-proofing." This involves spending a half an hour or so in the water—with your hands tied behind your back, floating at the surface, coming up for a breath, and then relaxing for a bit underwater. These students are practicing the maneuver before the test. They'll also have to retrieve the masks without using their hands, which are tied behind them.

prospective recruits that rosy view of the program. But despite many cautions, SEAL candidates often show up at BUD/S without a realistic understanding of what is actually involved in the training required to earn the "Budweiser" trident emblem of a SEAL. The truth is that it is one of the most difficult, challenging, and actually brutal learning experiences anybody can have, and one of the things most people learn is that they don't really want to be a SEAL quite badly enough to finish the program.

Like the Army's Green Beret Qualification Course (or Q Course), BUD/S is a *selection* and training program that weeds out people who don't belong. That usually means most of them. They are weeded out the only way that anybody has ever found for reliably selecting people who can hack the problem—by cranking up the stress so high that only the strongest survive and the quitters quit—or break. It is not nice and it isn't pretty. There isn't any other way. And sometimes it results in nearly everyone of an entering class of SEAL candidates being eliminated. In one class *not one* single man graduated. It is a calculatedly brutal experience that is not pretty to watch and pushes its victims to their limits of physical and emotional endurance, and beyond. Injuries are routine and deaths in training occasionally occur.

But, in a way, it is true that anybody can

When BUD/S students take a swim test it is not always a heap of fun. This class is about to be tested on drown-proofing skills.

survive it—if they have the appropriate state of mind. It takes plenty of strength, but most of it isn't muscular; it's mental. Little scrawny guys that you'd never pick for a badminton team sometimes turn out to have more of the kind of internal toughness and physical strength that it takes to survive BUD/S and become a SEAL than the big weight lifters who seem to be naturals. If you've got the mental strength to work through the discomfort, the fatigue, and the humiliation, you can probably develop the physical strength, SEALs tell you. The head is the hard part. And no other test has, so far, been able to figure out how to find the men who won't quit from those who will without pushing them

both far beyond the normal limits of civilized routine.

The BUD/S training takes twenty-six weeks, but it is only one part of the process of becoming a fully qualified SEAL. Before even applying for training a prospective candidate must: pass the very strict physical examination for Navy divers; have eyesight at least 20/40 in one eye and 20/70 in the other, correctable to 20/20, without color blindness; score high on military written tests; be male, twenty-eight years of age or less; and pass the physical fitness test (extremely high scores are expected) that includes swim test (500 yards, breast or side stroke, in less than 12:30), rest for ten minutes, then at least forty-two

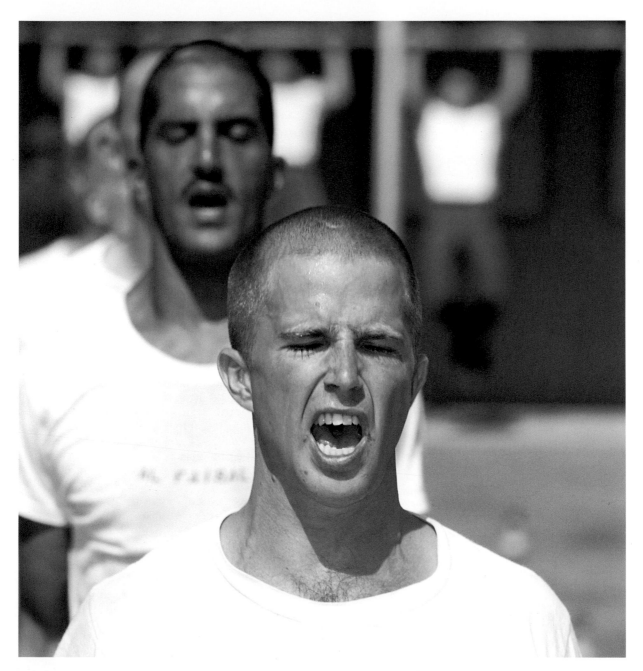

Out on the "grinder," BUD/S students get an hour or two of formal physical training (PT) everyday. They get another ten hours or so of informal PT, too, paddling the rubber ducks, running up and down the beach, and frolicking around the obstacle course. During all this they are all expected to show a high degree of enthusiasm, no matter how miserable they may feel.

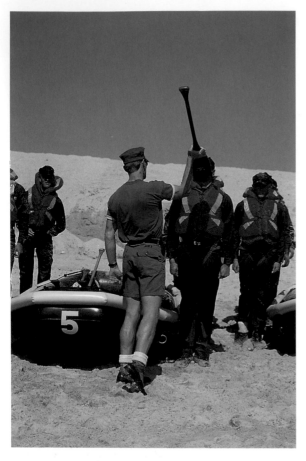

One of the kind and attentive staff of highly trained instructors helps a boat crew with their motivation. The technique is simple—a paddleful of sand, applied directly to the problem. Sand, it turns out, is a readily available, cheap, apparently effective material for helping people with their problems. It can be shoveled into boats and on hats, and the students can be rolled around in it, like a sugar cookie.

pushups in two minutes, at least fifty situps in two minutes, eight pullups, and run a mile and a half in boots and BDU pants in 11:30—all in less than an hour.

Applicants must come from certain Navy ratings, have the endorsement of their commanders, and have plenty of time remaining on their enlistment. If you fit all these require-

ments you can apply, and you might even be accepted and assigned a slot in a class. If that happens, don't wait to start your physical conditioning program. You don't go to BUD/S to get in shape; you *arrive* in shape, or you will fail almost instantly. "In order to even apply," RADM Ray Smith says, "you've got to be a top-notch sailor. We've got the pick of the guys coming out of the Naval Academy, more enlisted applicants than we can handle."

Although the published standards call for a cutoff age of twenty-eight, older men are sometimes accepted, and some are even recruited. Two thirty-six year olds have completed the program, and at least one man was thirty-two at the time. While the older bodies are a little less resilient sometimes, that can sometimes be offset by greater maturity and better self-discipline. One of these, a Polish refugee with extensive language skills, a former teacher and, at the time a competitive gymnast, was recruited for the program and made it through training on the first try.

New arrivals will indeed see the marvelous Hotel Del Coronado, the pretty sailboats, the girls sunbathing on the beach, and the glittering Pacific Ocean and will soon learn to loathe them all. They will soon learn that the Pacific is freezing, that the beach is for running on and rolling in, that the girls and the tourist attractions exist only as torture devices.

For seven long weeks the trainees endure a program of indoctrination and physical preconditioning, with long hours of classes, running, swimming, situps, pushups, calisthenics. They sweat and struggle . . . but they still haven't started BUD/S yet.

The Only Easy Day Was Yesterday

Phase One of BUD/S is the basic physical and mental conditioning portion of the program. It lasts nine weeks. It features a lot of running, swimming, and trips around the obstacle course. Every trainee is required to put his maximum effort into every test, every time. The minimum scores are raised each week. Each trainee is required to improve on his previous scores. Instructors watch and evaluate every hopeful trainee like hawks—or vultures—ready to pounce on any flaw or failure, real or imagined. It is an extremely abrasive, competitive process. The only way the instructors will leave you alone is if you've just beaten everybody else at an event; then you might be allowed a few minutes to gloat and relax while the rest of the class thrashes around in the surf zone.

This continues for five weeks. Each day the heat is turned up a little more. The instructors push harder and harder. The instructors never let up for a moment. As they say over and over, "The only easy day was *yesterday!*"

The students spend lots of time in the water, and the water is cold, even in summer. Hypothermia is a fact of life and occasional death. Wet suits are sometimes used, sometimes not; even with the suits, the cold Pacific Ocean seeps in, lowering body temperature. Students can be seen shivering violently sometimes after having come out of the cold ocean to stand in the cold wind. It is another stress, intentionally applied.

One by one people quit or are removed for injuries. Even quitting isn't easy, quick, or dignified; the trainee stands on the green painted frog footprints at one side of the "Grinder," the big blacktop space where calisthenics are performed, grasps the lanyard for the brass ship's bell attached to a column, rings the bell three times, and is gone. His green helmet liner remains in formation beside the bell with the others who've quit before him. While there is some disgrace to it, even these men get some credit (in private, away from the trainees) that it takes quite a man to get through any of BUD/S and that only a very select group even manage to get in the front door. While the quitters get credit for trying they are, just the same, an example to those who remain.

The O Course

One of the featured entertainments is the obstacle course—the "O course" in SEAL par-

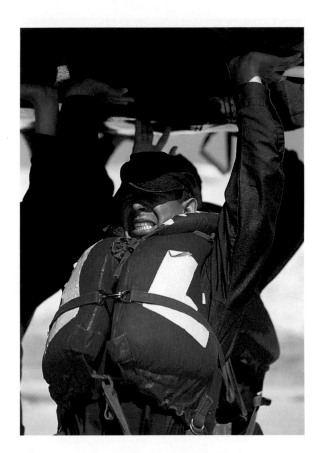

"Get it up! Get that boat up! Get it up! Get it up! You guys are the worst—get it up!" the instructor screams. After their first jaunt out into the Pacific in the rubber ducks, a crew has a few moments of quiet reflection on what they've seen and done—their new-found skills in small-boat handling and teamwork, with the help of the staff providing a running commentary and critique. After a few minutes supporting the 250-pound boat aloft, the crew tends to have an improved understanding of the lessons of BUD/S.

lance. It looks like a big sandbox with lots of play equipment: telephone poles assembled into a wide variety of structures. The BUD/S trainees are assembled here about once a week for an hour or two of play time. One after another, on command, the students dash off for a circuit of the course.

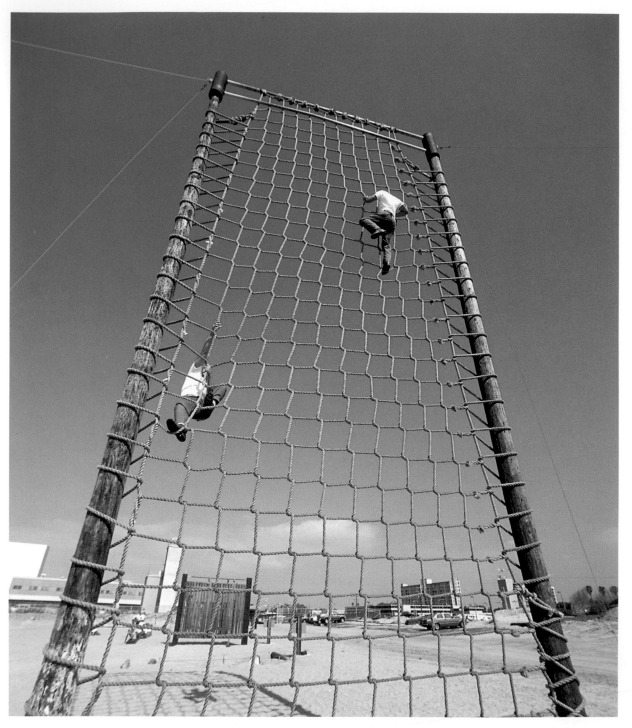

You start by running to the first event, a set of pole stumps set in the ground, their tops about two feet above the deck. You must run across them, jumping from one to the next without falling off. Then, from the last stump, leap to the top of a low wall, swing a foot over, drop to the other side, and start running. You'll go about fifty feet before you dive under a grid of barbed wire—crawl under the wire, then emerge and dash to the next structure, the net climb. A tall tower suspends a rope net that you climb to the top, swing over, and descend; the flexible net offers unstable footing and it is slow going. Once safely back on the ground, dash off to the next position, a pair of simple structures about four feet apart; you climb up on one and jump to the other, catching the crossbar across your chest; this is a favorite way to break a rib. They call this one "The Ugly Name." There are about ten more obstacles to negotiate, and your progress will be closely monitored by one of the attentive, helpful staff who are always ready with words of encouragement and advice. If you have trouble with part of the course the instructors will probably let you try the event all over again, just to make sure you get it right. Finally you return to your starting point and your time is recorded.

If you haven't done well you may get to cool off with a quick dip in the ocean, on the other side of a tall sand berm. Then, to dry off, you'll be expected to roll in the sand, then hustle back to rejoin the play group. As the trainees quickly learn, the O course is highly competitive, and people who don't do well are subject to extra, undesired, attention from the instructors.

You're expected to go all out every time you run the course, and you're expected to do better every week. Minimum times for the course are published, and they get shorter every week. It is just one of the stresses that

Look like fun? The obstacle course tests strength, agility, and speed—and mental toughness, too. All are expected to improve over the weeks, and a trainee's times must get progressively better.

are applied to the trainees to test their motivation and physical conditioning. But, as one of the staff says, "It isn't supposed to break you but to build up your confidence. It reveals a lot about the character of an individual. By the time you've gone through about three-fourths of it, every fiber of your muscles is burning, and you still have another quarter to go—and it's all through soft sand."

Hell Week

After five weeks of this comes the real

The circuit begins with a dash across the tops of these poles, a leap to the wall, over the wall to crawl under some barbed wire, then off to the net climb. It takes about eleven minutes to do them all, if you're in shape. The instructors provide helpful comments and critiques at most stations.

challenge that all have heard about and dreaded: Hell Week. It starts just before midnight on the Saturday before the sixth week with a gentle wakeup call from the instructors . . . using blank M60 machine gun fire and artillery simulators as an improvised alarm clock. The noise in the compound is deafening. Besides the firing, instructors scream incessantly. Chaos reigns supreme.

The trainees begin five and a half days of virtually constant activity. They will receive an average of about twenty minutes sleep per day, if they are lucky. They will go from one event to another, constantly: running on the beach, boat drills, PT, swims. They will crawl in slime, roll in the surf, and for a little extra torture, do "log PT."

Log PT requires boat teams to lift and maneuver sections of log weighing from 400 to 600 pounds. If your boat team hasn't been doing well (or if the instructors think you need a little extra help with your motivation), you'll get the 600-pound model. Then you can do situps with it on your chest, or try holding it over your head for a while. Needless to say the whole team has to work together to do anything with it at all.

The sun comes up on the first morning, and the day proceeds much like any other at BUD/S. The sun goes down, and the trainees know that somewhere people are returning to homes and wives, to quiet evenings and friendly conversations. In the tall apartment buildings overlooking the BUD/S compound the lights will start going out around nine or ten. The PT continues. By 1:00 a.m. they are nearly all out, but the activity on the beach continues. "The only easy day was *yesterday!*" scream the instructors.

When the sun comes up the next morning, the trainees will be a bit tired but will try not to think about it. All of them know what the routine is, that the really tough part is still days away. The competitions continue with boat races in the ocean and on the bay. Gradually, individuals will fail. When they do, their teams are subjected to more stress from the instructors and from the other teams.

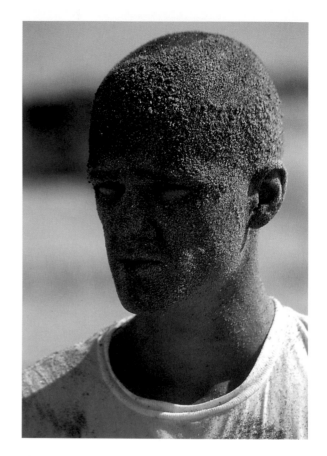

A recipient of the "sugar cookie" treatment—first get wet in the surf, then roll around in the sand. Then get back in line and try to do better. It's just one of the constant stresses and strains on trainees designed to separate those who will tolerate it from those who won't.

Although they don't get any real sleep, the trainees get plenty of food. They consume about 7,000 calories a day and still lose weight.

One day melts seamlessly into another without rest. There is no alternative but to tough it out, drive through the fatigue, and keep doing what they tell you to do. It is a test of mental toughness as much as the powers of physical endurance. After four days or so people start to hallucinate. And some people start

Log PT is another form of stress, this time applied to a whole boat crew all at the same time. US Navy

to quit. Hell Week is the most important part of the whole twenty-six week BUD/S experience, a physical and mental challenge that is intended to put the trainees under stress that is supposed to approach that of actual combat.

The hallucinations can be rather entertaining. While enduring a long night boat race out on the ocean, after a few days with no sleep and little rest, visions begin to appear. Sometimes it is mermaids, other times people picnicking on the beach, or a strange tunnel vision.

One of the rituals is the letter home. Toward the end of the week, when everybody is off in the ozone, they are all seated before tables and provided paper and pen. "Write me a letter explaining why you want to become a SEAL!" the instructor orders. This is not an easy thing to explain after going three or four days without sleep, wallowing in the mud, doing log PT, enduring endless boat drills, and slogging through competitive events like the "rubber duck" races on the ocean or the sixteen-mile runs on the beach. The students tend to stare at the paper for a while before attempting to write anything. The results tend to be gibberish. Later, after Hell Week is over, these essays are returned to their authors as an amusing reminder of the tremendous stress they were under and how it affected their performance of even this simple task.

As rough as Hell Week and the whole BUD/S program is, it has been toned down considerably from the past. Trainees no longer

Hell Week features rest breaks in the mud pit. Well, not really rest breaks but opportunities to work on your teamwork . . . and practice being miserable.

Not only do these guys get to stay awake for five and a half days straight, they get to do fun stuff like this day and night.

This is their first experience with a rubber duck in the ocean, dealing with the surf and having to function as a crew. Most will do rather badly and will overturn in the surf, lose paddles, and sometimes lose a man over the side. The instructors enjoy it all immensely—and pile on the punishment.

have to wallow in the mud of the Tijuana River, essentially an open sewer, after many came down with severe (and sometimes permanent) illnesses. That ended in 1983. A somewhat healthier goo is now available right in San Diego Bay. And after one trainee died on a five-mile winter swim around San Clemente Island, the staff started taking extra precautions to deal with extreme overexertion and hypothermia. An ambulance now trails along the beach behind the trainees on the long runs through the soft sand, trailing the "goon squad," as the slower runners are called; they can quit at any time, and many do.

BUD/S has been criticized, along with other extreme selection and training programs like the Army's Green Beret Q Course, for unnecessary extremes. The injuries, the high level of stress, the humiliation are all far more than anyone in civilian life or in normal military training ever must endure.

Why do it that way? As one SEAL officer explains, "One of the things I've noticed about many of the 'real world' combat operations I've been on is that you get a tremendous adrenaline rush—I call it *fear*. Once the operation begins that goes away, but on the way in you have a lot of time to sit and think. You *never* get that in a training situation! So one of the things I continually tell my troops while we are training is, 'Look, I can't give you the feeling of what it is really like to be in combat . . .

The famous bell is always waiting for anybody who's had enough. Then, you stand on the green frog footprints, grasp the lanyard, and strike the bell three times—and you can go back to the regular Navy, to conventional hours and conventional missions.

315

because I can't shoot at you and make you hurt. It's illegal, and I wouldn't want to do that anyway. What I *can* do is to make the conditions so tough, and try to make you so tired, put you under such stress, that you will get something of a feeling of what it is like."

When the trainees recover from Hell Week they begin a period of study intended to prepare them for "hydrographic reconnaissance," as beach surveys are called. This involves even more time spent wallowing around in the surf, cold and miserable, while the ever-attentive staff offers suggestions and encouragement from the beach. Once through Hell Week students are treated with a bit more respect and affection by the instructors. Finally, Phase One is over.

Swim fins, mask, and booties are all pretty much standard commercial gear, used in unconventional diving.

Phase Two

Survivors of the first part of training go on to Phase Two, where they will learn about diving operations. Each will learn just about all there is to know about scuba, closed-circuit rebreathing systems, and dive physiology. They will learn more than they ever wanted to know about the nasty things that happen to people who make mistakes underwater. They learn to deal with equipment failures, lost regulators, the hazards of nitrogen narcosis. They make long swims beneath the surface and learn to navigate in the cold, murky, dark waters in which SEALs operate. After seven busy weeks the BUD/S class will be missing a few more faces. The survivors will have the knowledge necessary to be basic combat divers, and the program is about to get really interesting.

Phase Three

By now the BUD/S class is beginning to see light at the end of the proverbial tunnel, and are pretty sure it is not from an oncoming train. They are far stronger physically and mentally than four months earlier. They've acquired a great deal of knowledge and confidence. Now they get to start putting the skills and the stamina together in practical exercises that simulate SEAL missions.

Phase Three is the Demolitions/Recon/Land Warfare part of the program. The BUD/S students learn land navigation, explosives, small unit tactics, rappelling, and patrolling skills and become expert in the employment of all the small arms and weapons used by SEALs in combat. After four weeks of classroom instruction and practical exercises, the trainees deploy to San Clemente Island for five weeks, where they put it all together.

One of the evolutions involves clearing beach obstacles like those that faced the amphibious operations of World War II—concrete blocks and steel rails dropped in shallow water to block the passage of landing craft. The students first make a careful hydrographic survey of the landing zone, noting the location of all obstacles, then plan a mission to demolish them with explosives. The quantity of

A "stick" of jumpers exits a Navy CH-46 helicopter. All SEALs are jump-qualified after they complete

BUD/S at the US Army's Basic Airborne Course at Fort Benning, Georgia.

explosive has to be carefully calculated, fuse measured. The students use their "rubber ducks" to get into the area, then dive to emplace the explosives. All the charges are linked with "det" cord to insure simultaneous explosion, and the divers are recovered to the boats. The last dive pair pulls the safety pins on the fuse-lighters, retracts the striker, and pops the igniter. Now it is time to get back to the boat. The instructors will time the delay, and it had better be within a few seconds of what was calculated. With a satisfying *whump* the surface of the water will boil, and the obstacles will (usually) be shattered.

BUD/S is probably the roughest, most demanding training and selection program in the US armed forces, at least outside the covert organizations. It has been loudly criticized as excessively brutal. Although it might not be quite as dangerous as at times in the past, it is a guaranteed way to get miserable fast and stay miserable for most of six months—or more, if you get injured. And the

injuries are common, almost with the intent of the staff. No other program tolerates such a high level of injuries. A lot of people outside Naval Special Warfare think the BUD/S program is sadistic and ought to be reformed. CDR Gary Stubblefield has an opposing view:

"It is the toughest military training in the world, and it's done that way on purpose. The Army's Special Forces don't have anything to compare to it. It's been this way since the days of the Scout and Raiders in World War II, a *very* difficult selection process. Most of the people who make it through the program are not premier athletes—they are *normal* people who have the ability to stick with something.

"There are injuries, some severe, in every class. But the business we are in is inherently dangerous, combat or not. If you take away the risk that goes with the training, you take away the mental stress that you put people under to know how they'll respond in the real world, in actual combat. Landing on rocks, long cold swims, surf passages—training where we have people break arms and legs—has to be part of the program. You *have* to be sure that they will stick with you when the going gets tough, and they have to know that, if you don't do things safely, there are consequences that include injury . . . or worse. Death in training is very, very rare, and it happens, I think, when the student doesn't follow the rules. The deaths are an anomaly but the injuries are not—those happen when someone does something they aren't supposed to."

Jump School

But even after surviving BUD/S, a trainee is still not a fully qualified SEAL and does not wear the trident insignia of Naval Special Warfare. First comes three weeks at the US Army's Fort Benning in Georgia, undergoing the Basic Airborne Course. Here each will have to confront a different fear, that of jumping from an airplane, to become a fully qualified military parachutist.

The first week involves physical condition-

The Naval Special Warfare trident insignia (the "Budweiser" in the SEAL vernacular) is awarded only after completion of BUD/S, airborne training, and a probationary period on a SEAL team that lasts from six months to more than a year.

ing, and since the Army school's standards are comparatively low, the BUD/S graduates manage this part of the program more or less with one hand tied behind their backs. The Army instructors will try to make the experience a little bit challenging for any SEALs, Rangers, Marines, or others they can identify, usually requiring extra PT to keep their attention, but BUD/S graduates generally consider this part of the program a kind of vacation.

Week two teaches the basic skills of military parachuting: donning the parachute, actions inside the aircraft, door position, jumpmaster commands, proper exit techniques, emergency procedures, and the Parachute Landing Fall (PLF). The students endlessly practice door position, exits, and PLFs from training aids: the suspended harness, the thirty-four-foot tower, the C-130 mock-up.

Finally, they start week three, Jump Week. Five jumps are required, three "Hollywood" daylight jumps without combat equipment plus one night jump and one jump with loaded rucksack and weapons container. The night jump is usually a sunrise or sunset jump rather than one in full darkness.

Jump school is actually a lot of fun for many of the people who attend, and the BUD/S graduates hardly work up a sweat. The jumps are often exciting, the instructors fairly civilized, the drop zone a soft, fluffy plowed field. The last jump is generally done on Friday morning, and students often invite friends and relatives to watch from nearby bleachers. Then the Army instructors break out the silver wings of a qualified military parachutist and pin them to the shirts of the students.

The "Budweiser"

Completion of the Basic Airborne Course is the final academic portion of the program required to join a SEAL or Swimmer Delivery Vehicle (SDV) team but the students are still not bona fide SEALs. First, each man is assigned to a team where he must complete a six-month probationary period. It is still possible to fail, and individuals occasionally are filtered out, even now, if they don't fit into the team or fail to meet spec somehow. But at the end of the six months, a year or more after starting the process, a few young men will pin on the big, gold symbol of Naval Special Warfare and finally be able to call themselves SEALs.

They enter a tiny, select community with a big reputation that sometimes gets in the way of business. Within the military SEALs are sometimes known as "cowboys" or "glass-eaters" who glory in their superman image. Instead they find a different kind of man on the teams: extremely confident without bravado, a man with tremendous talents and abilities, a person who knows his own limits. "We like to think of ourselves as quiet professionals," one says.

RADM Ray Smith says: "We are essentially a *people* business. We use a lot of exotic equipment—scuba, parachutes, radios—but all those things are peripheral to the essence of what we are. Our focus at BUD/S is on the human being, the nature of the person we want to have come on a SEAL team and do the things we have to do—always has been, always will. The finest equipment in the world (which we have) is not sufficient to accomplish our missions. You'll see guys in BUD/S who don't look very impressive physically—little guys, young guys—who'll surprise you and make it through. You can *never* successfully predict who will make it through! You can't measure what is inside the individual without subjecting him to BUD/S. In fact, this is a course in the development of human potential; all we are trying to do is to make the young man understand that the limits of the human being are practically unlimited."

Of the fifty or sixty students who begin BUD/S, the staff will tell you there will be five or six who *know* that they are going to complete the program, no matter what, and that there is no stopping them. There is another five or six who don't really want to be here, are not really ready for the challenge, and who will never be SEALs. In the middle are the eighty percent the instructors focus their efforts on. They probe for the fears that every

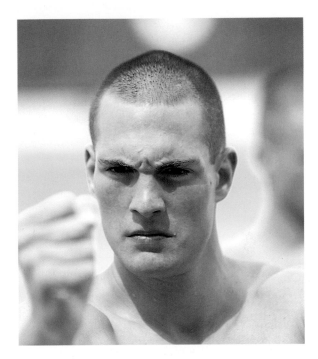

BUD/S is a selection process more than a training program, challenging people to use far more of their personal resources than most will ever need to do. It is a rather brutal program, by design, intended to help people survive and function in the far more brutal and stressful environment of combat.

man has—a fear of heights, of water, of jumping from high platforms—and each is confronted daily with his perceived limitations and pushed past them. "You can't call 'time out' in combat," one of the instructors says, "and that's what we try to teach them here."

Officers and enlisted personnel go through training together, unlike some other programs where officers sometimes get an easier ride. Both suffer and perform equally at BUD/S. It is a team-building system, developing trust up and down the chain of command. About thirty-five new officers and 250 enlisted personnel graduate from BUD/S annually and join the world of SPECWARCOM on the SEAL, Special Boat, and Swimmer Delivery Vehicle teams.

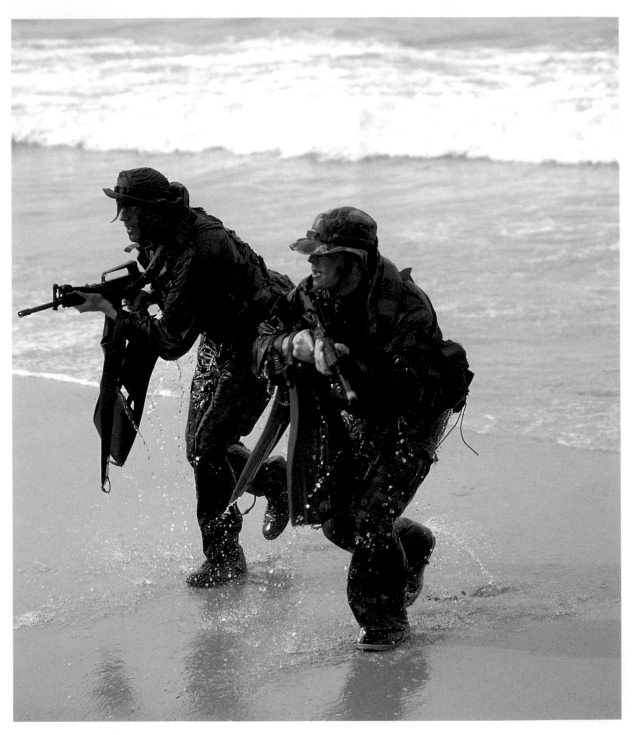

Chapter 4

Movement to Contact

Despite the way it is shown in the movies, the business of going into combat is a lot more complicated than picking up your weapon and following some resolute-looking lieutenant or sergeant who growls, "Okay, men, follow me!" The movies always manage to leave out all the paperwork, meetings, and related homework that comes first. In fact, it is just about impossible for American combat units to go off to battle without a great deal of this stuff. It can take weeks to prepare an operation of any kind, conventional or covert, but at the end of this long process will finally come two quite interesting "management/staff" meetings. The first of these is called a Warning Order; the other is called the Patrol Leader's Order.

The Warning Order

Before SEALs and SBS crews go anywhere or do anything, the mission has to be authorized, approved, and planned. A long time ago the units did most of this internally, but for the last decade or so, the missions have been conceived and tasked from outside NAVSPECWARCOM. Somewhere during the process somebody decides it is okay to actually

A swim pair secure the beach. Depending on the mission, SEALs wear wet suits or standard uniforms (which will be wet suits, too, in a way). The man on the left is one of the more unusual members of the special ops community—a "long hair" SEAL.

let the teams know that they can cancel those weekend plans. The way this is done is that the selected team is herded into a compartment or room, the area is secured, the doors are closed, and somebody, normally the unit commander, will issue a Warning Order.

In various forms, warning orders have been around since the Mongol hordes, since Attila, since Alexander the Great. In its short form it sounds something like, "We're going to break camp in the morning before sunrise and attack the infidels, sack their town, rape their women, and put the place to the torch. Bring your sword, spear, and all your armor. Questions?"

The modern version is more complicated, but the idea is identical. It gives the people involved an idea, usually incomplete, of what they are going to be doing and what they should do to prepare. The formal version (used by the Army and Marines as well) includes a brief description of the situation; the mission; general instructions, including organization, uniform, weapons, chain of command, schedule, including time for the more detailed patrol order, and for inspections and rehearsals; and specific instructions for subordinate leaders and individuals.

Everybody then scurries around, collecting weapons, demolition material, MREs, fresh batteries for the radios, and night vision goggles. *Nobody* gets to call home and say, "Guess what, Honey, I'm not gonna be home on time tonight 'cause we're off to defend freedom and democracy . . . "

Instead, they just don't come home in the evening. Sooner or later the families might get some extremely vague information, but that's one of the costs of admission to the special op-

Although they wear the same uniforms and carry the same weapons as other US forces, SEALs are unique in their combination of talents and tasking. SEALs train and fight in extremely small units with missions in or around the water. These missions may be to support either a Navy boss or a joint theater boss who could be an Army, Air Force, or Marine officer. They may be extremely covert, or extremely unconventional. Regardless, the basic weapon of Naval Special Warfare isn't the rifle but the man behind it, and the tiny team of which he is a part.

erations and rapid-deployment military communities. And not only do these call-ups happen for real world events, they are called for training, too, with irregular frequency.

The idea behind the Warning Order is that, once the order comes down to the unit, a fixed amount of time will be specified before the operation is supposed to be executed—perhaps twelve hours. The platoon or squad leader is expected to take a third of that time to make his own preliminary plan, and allocate two-thirds of the time to the subordinates to do their preparation and rehearsals. While it often doesn't work out that neatly, the idea is a sound one and is applied as much as circumstances permit.

SOPs

Each platoon has its own set of Standard Operating Procedures, its own identity, its unique reputation and subculture, all based somewhat on the characters on the team.

SOPs make planning and executing operations far faster and more efficient than otherwise. When a Patrol Leader's Order is issued only the unique details of the mission need to be discussed—radio frequencies, rendezvous points, routes in and out of the objective, commander's intent. All the other essentials—patrol order of march, actions on contact, reaction to ambush, individual responsibilities— all these things have been long since memorized as a kind of "company policy" that doesn't need repeating. Most of the members of the teams, like Bob Gormly's SEAL Team Two, had known each other for four or five years and could just about execute an operation without a word ever being spoken.

Patrol Leader's Order

The five-paragraph format used to formally brief the mission has been in use since World War I, its format memorized by millions of servicemen over the years. It forces the unit to plan logically to deal with an extremely stressful and dangerous experience. The elements of the order are the situation, the mission, the details of the execution, how the mis-

When SEALs jump, the rubber duck goes out first, followed promptly by the SEALs. The hard part is hustling out of the aircraft with those darn fins on.

sion will be supported and supplied, and command and communications. Depending on the complexity of the mission, the Orders Brief can last a few minutes or six hours; an hour or so is typical. SEALs may get some of the most difficult and dangerous missions, but they also get some of the very best and most expensive intelligence support, often custom-made for the specific mission. This will almost always include "overhead" imagery, photographs from all altitudes, from low level all the way up to the secret satellites like the KA-11. There may be radio and telephone intercepts, and reports from agents in the operations area. And (in extreme and rare cases) a prisoner may be snatched out of the target area, brought back to chat with the team, and held until the mis-

sion concludes and the team is safely extracted.

SEALs like to rehearse their missions, and if it is practical to do so, some kind of run-through will be done. This might be no more than a detailed brainstorming conference somewhere in the bowels of a submarine, or it might involve the construction of a mock-up of a target and a complete rehearsal of the entire mission ashore. Regardless, once the Patrol Leader's Order has been given, none of the players will be going anywhere or doing anything except preparing to launch into the op area.

When it is time to go to work, SEALs commute in dramatic and dangerous ways. Although trained for insertion to an operating

Water parachute landings are potentially treacherous, particularly at night. The MC-1 canopy used by this jumper is steerable and has a moderate forward speed. Now, about a hundred feet above the water, the jumper should be facing into the wind, chest band and reserve unfastened, reserve parachute shoved to the side. Assume a good prepare-to-land position: head up, eyes on the horizon, knees bent. US Navy photo

area by parachute, that's really not the SEALs' forte. Except in rare instances, the mission will begin with an insertion over or under the surface of the water.

At any time there are SEALs deployed aboard US submarines operating around the world, waiting for world events to call for their services. When the orders trickle down the chain of command, the SEALs plan their mission and use the most stealthy technique of all to drop in on the enemy—submarine insertion.

US subs have a small chamber, the "escape trunk," installed forward of the sail. This little chamber has two functions, the first allowing for trapped submariners to escape a boat sunken in shallow water, and the second (a secondary use) allowing for the deployment and recovery of combat swimmers.

Locking out of a sub is not for the faint of heart. The swimmers don their wet suits and their combat equipment, collect weapons, explosives, and related equipment, and prepare to enter the chamber; scuba or Draeger rigs are, believe it or not, optional. Then, one after another, they climb into the chamber, a spherical space about six feet across. Up to five combat swimmers can crowd into the chamber, but all will be extremely cramped and uncomfortable. Even among trained and experienced SEALs panic sometimes occurs as the water is slowly allowed in. There are mouthpieces and air lines installed in the chamber, and it is possible to use the sub's own air supply for breathing until the chamber is unlocked and it is time to leave. But SEALs normally use their own rigs—if they have any. It is quite possible to ascend to the surface without scuba or rebreather, and SEALs train for this "free ascent" or "blow and go" technique—as well as the reverse technique required to come back aboard.

The sub will slither in as close to shore as the skipper and the SEALs can agree on. Subs are not normally content to be in shallow water close to a hostile coast; SEALs are normally not pleased to swim in from over the horizon. So the typical mission will bring the SSN attack sub into a mile or two off the coast on a dark and hopefully stormy night. The sub

Here's another way to get to work—a Swimmer Delivery Vehicle being deployed by a submerged submarine. The SDV is kind of a submarine itself, although its passengers get cold and wet. US Navy photo

will come up to a depth of about forty feet, bring the periscope up for a quick peek at the neighborhood, then bring it back down. The 'scope makes a fair radar reflector, and if somebody is working a surface search radar tweaked for such targets, there could be a problem. So the sub crew gets extremely edgy about this kind of mission.

A typical insertion out of the chamber will have one man go out first, with scuba, and rig the Zodiac stored in the sail locker on deck. The boat will have to be taken to the surface while a tether is left attached to the submarine. This entire complex activity is done in darkness, almost entirely by touch, and takes about half an hour. When the diver has the boat properly infiltrated and on a tow, he signals the sub to send up the rest of the SEALs. Even this isn't quick or easy: he can flash a light signal at the periscope if the sub skipper is willing to raise it, he can swim down and rap on the hull, or he can even go back in the lockout chamber, repressurize and have a chat via microphone.

Usually, though, a simple rap on the hull will do it. Then the next batch of divers cram into the chamber, the water level rises, and finally somebody has to wriggle a hand over to the valves and latches that will open the hatch.

"You get into there, you've got all this weight on you, you close the bottom hatch, you stand there, doubled over—tanks on your back, equipment in your arms—three to five people jammed in there. Then somebody has to find a way to reach over to the valve so you can start to flood the chamber. There are some guys who are just more nervous about all this—everybody jammed in that small space, water coming up to your neck. I've seen guys panic in there."

It takes a long time, usually in cold, high seas, for the seven or eight men to rig the boats and exit the sub for a typical mission of

Locking out of a sub involves swimming out of a little chamber about the size of the hatch visible in this shot. US Navy photo

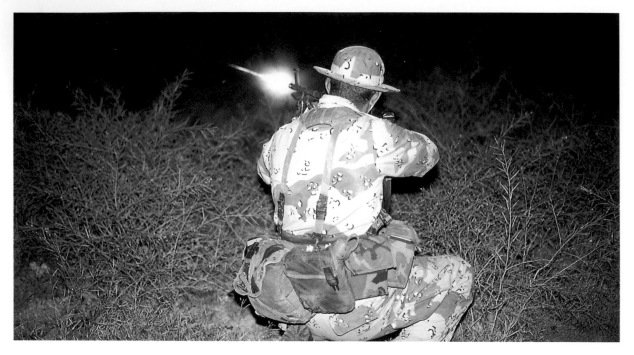

The M60 machine gun puts serious suppressive fire downrange. The M60 is an area weapon, used for delivering a heavy volume of fire at a distance.

this type. Hypothermia and seasickness will be a problem for those already in the boat up on the surface while the nervousness of the sub crew will be a problem for those still aboard. Even the rubber boats have a radar return signature, and if anybody is looking, the whole operation can suddenly become a target instead of a weapon. It is a very nervous time. But then, after perhaps a couple of hours, you're all set and its time to go ashore.

Dry Deck Shelter

There is an easier way, a bolt-on chamber that is called the Dry Deck Shelter (DDS). While it operates on the same principle as the lock-out chamber, it is far larger. The DDS is big enough to accommodate a whole platoon, with dive gear and rubber boats, radios and demolitions. It will also accommodate the Swimmer Deliver Vehicle, the SEAL-scooter

that is designed for zipping around underwater. Besides these handy features, it converts to a hyperbaric chamber for treating a diver who's been "bent" from staying under too long, too deep, and acquires the painful, potentially fatal condition called "decompression sickness."

While the general insertion technique for the DDS is the same as with the lock-out chamber, it is a lot faster and a lot less crowded. The whole evolution goes faster, much to the delight of the submarine crew.

To the Beach

Once everybody's safely in a Zodiak, it's time to break out the paddles or fire up the engine and head to the beach. Several hundred meters offshore, well outside the surf zone, a pair of divers—the scout swimmers—will slip over the gunwales of the Zodiac and, with weapons at the ready, move in to secure the section of beach where the landing is intended. After a quick check of the area, they signal the boats to come in. The "rubber ducks" run in through the surf, everybody alert for enemy contact, and the boats are promptly pulled up across the high water mark and either hidden or buried.

Once secure on the beach, the SEALs are ready to execute the mission. If it is a patrol or a "direct action" strike deep inland, the squad (or perhaps platoon if two boats have come ashore) assembles itself and prepares to move off into the hinterland without a word being spoken. Communication is done with hand and arm signals, visible and instantly recognizable even on dark, cloudy nights.

Out front, leading the patrol, is the point man who navigates the patrol to the objective. This is traditionally the most dangerous, difficult position in the patrol order, requiring superb land navigation skills and an extremely high level of alertness to the possibility of contact with enemy forces. A point man can walk you right into the kill zone of an ambush, or halt the patrol safely outside. Such choices can be (and often have been) the difference of life and death for an entire patrol. When contact with the enemy is made, the man on point is typically the first to fire or the first to die.

The point man's preferred weapon in wooded terrain is often not a rifle or machine gun but a military version of a standard twelve-gauge shotgun, loaded with five rounds of "double-ought" (size 00) buckshot. These are large, bullet-sized lead pellets that spread out in a lethal cone of destruction. One pellet will kill out to a range of about 100 meters, sometimes farther; at closer ranges, particularly within about ten meters, a well-placed load will punch a gaping hole through a torso, or rip off an arm or a head. It is the approximate equivalent of firing seven or so bullets at exactly the same instant in the same general direction.

An alternative load is the flachette round, with tiny steel darts in place of the buckshot. While these are not nearly as lethal or de-structive individually, there are many more of them, and they produce a denser cloud of projectiles, a handy way of providing a group of enemy soldiers at close range with something to think about besides the SEAL patrol. They are lethal out to several hundred meters.

There's yet another handy twelve-gauge round for the point man's shotgun, a single, heavy slug useful for opening locked doors and disabling machinery or electronics in one quick, brutal way. It is accurate out to a range of about five feet, maybe six. If it hits some-

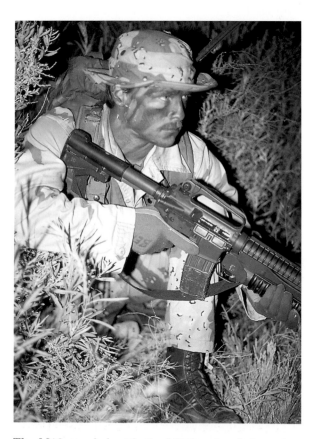

The M16 coupled with the M203 grenade launcher is a potent combination used to engage point targets out to about a quarter of a mile. The collapsible stock and short barrel make the weapon less awkward to get in and out of cramped places like lock-out chambers.

329

This sentry doesn't know it but he's got a little problem. That's an invisible infrared aim-point dot on his personal center-of-mass. Since the aiming device is attached to a rifle, that means the bullets from the weapon will strike within that dot, probably creating some discomfort for the target.

thing, the target stays hit. This is no precision munition, but it will punch a hole in the cast-iron block of an automobile engine, or the concrete wall of a house or bunker—or, if they cooperate, a whole row of enemy soldiers.

Riflemen

If the point man bumps into a bad guy at close range and gets the first shot off effectively, the patrol has the choice of either "going to ground" and duking it out with the opposing team or making a run for the beach. In either case the point man's shotgun will soon have limited utility—it will be out of range, out of ammunition, or both. That's why there are several riflemen on a normal patrol, each with an M16 rifle and five or six thirty-round magazines stashed in their load-carrying web gear.

M16A2 and Car-15

The M16A2 rifle is almost the same weapon that the father's of some of today's SEALs carried and fought with in Vietnam a generation ago. It's no longer the most exotic weapon on the battlefield, or on the teams, but it is still a good, light, accurate, effective weapon that has proven itself in countless battles. The latest version is more reliable than the first, which had a failure-to-feed problem for a while. The A2 also lacks the "full-auto" feature of the original, a modification based on the discovery that in the heat of combat the weapon was being used as a "bullet hose," ineffectively spraying rounds downrange. Instead, the rifle has a BURST position on the selector switch on the left side of the receiver, above the trigger; this permits three-round bursts that economize on ammunition while encouraging the rifleman to aim rather than point the weapon.

While the basic rifle issued to SEALs is essentially the same as the M16A2 issued to Army and Marine Corps infantry privates (and just about everybody else, too), the SEALs version tends to be an upgraded, customized weapon with specialized sights and a collapsible stock or a compact version of the

The little MP5 "room broom" is a super-compact little squirt gun that's a favorite of SEALs and other operators who have to deal face to face with terrorists at short range.

M16 that has been popular with special operators for the last twenty years, the CAR-15. This little squirt gun uses essentially the same receiver components as the bigger M16, but with an ingenious collapsible stock assembly and shorter barrel. It trades bulk for a little fragility and a slightly greater inclination to jam. The decision to carry the CAR-15 or M16 is—as with similar decisions on a team—partly a matter of personal choice. SEALs, along with other special operators, are permitted to exercise a lot more latitude in the choice of accessories than are troopers in more conventional units.

Depending on the particular mission, the sights installed may be a night-vision scope or a laser aim-point system. The first of these, the night-vision scope, amplifies existing light and presents the shooter with a magnified, green and black picture of the target through a somewhat conventional rifle scope. The other device mounts a small laser pointer under the barrel; once activated it puts a bright red dot where the bullet will strike. You

don't need to peep through a scope or iron sights—just put the red dot on your intended victim and squeeze. It is not a long-range, sniping system; but for night combat in confined spaces it is often the system of choice.

The M16 fires a small, 5.56mm (.223-caliber) bullet at high velocity. This makes for a very flat trajectory and a lot of retained energy at practical ranges. The Vietnam-era version of the M16 was supposed to be good out to about 300 meters; today's weapon/cartridge combination is rated to 460 meters—about a quarter of a mile. That means that a trained rifleman can hit a man-sized target at that range with about fifty percent of his carefully aimed shots. The bullet, of course, is lethal out to a couple of miles, but hitting things with it at extreme ranges has more to do with luck than gun control.

MP4 and MP5

The M16 and CAR-15 are not the only choices for a SEAL rifleman to take on a mission. His weapon can be almost anything that he and the patrol leader think is appropriate.

One favorite alternative is the Heckler & Koch (H&K) MP5 "room broom" submachine gun. It fires the diminutive 9mm Parabellum pistol round and is well matched to the laser aimpoint sight system for urban combat situations. It is extremely compact—you can wear it under a jacket for those formal events. Like the shotgun, it is accurate and effective only out to fifty meters or so, and its projectiles aren't guaranteed to have the desired effect. But you can carry (and shoot) a lot of those little 9mm rounds; if you squirt a burst of them into a bunker the folks inside will probably wish you hadn't.

The bigger brother of the MP5 is a beefy submachine gun called the MP4 , brought to you by those fine folks at H&K, builders of fine military weapons used around the world. Both of these German weapons possess a qual-ity that, in many ways, is more important than accuracy, hitting power, weight or rate of fire: when you pull the trigger the gun goes *bang*. This reputation for reliability has sold a lot of H&K weapons to a lot of operators, and it is the reason you'll so often see them, dripping sea water and covered with sand, coming across a beach in the hands of SEALs.

Silencers

On the muzzles of all these rifles and submachine guns you'll sometimes see tubular devices about eight inches long and an inch and a half in diameter. These are sound suppressers, or silencers as they are sometimes called. For weapons such as the 9mm H&Ks, with subsonic ammunition, they can convert the loud report to a subtle pop by slowing the propellant gasses as they rush out the muzzle behind the bullet. This can be a very handy

The MP4 is very popular with the teams, and rightfully so. It is compact, reliable, and tolerant of saltwater immersion. Its little 9mm round isn't the *hardest hitting bullet on the block, but it works well enough at close range.*

feature in those sneaky, close-in fights that SEALs sometimes encounter.

Suppressers work on the M16, too, but not nearly as well. The standard ammunition for the weapon is designed to produce very high velocities, far faster than the speed of sound. Much of the noise from the firing of an M16 comes from the sonic boom produced by the bullet's flight through air. Even so, some of the noise can be reduced, and suppressers are often attached even to M16s, particularly in urban combat situations. As with the aimpoint and night sights and so many other tools of the trade, suppressers have their specialized role in the SEALs' bag of tricks.

M203 Grenade Launcher

One of the most interesting and useful weapons you'll find carried on a SEAL mission is the M203 grenade launcher, a fairly simple weapon with a complex variety of ammunition and uses. It isn't much more than a short length of aluminum tube with a breech block and trigger assembly. It bolts to an M16 rifle, under the barrel; the magazine provides the hand grip. The 203 fires a 40mm cartridge with one of several warheads. It is a bit like a mortar, although it is called a grenade launcher. Its lobbing trajectory allows you to toss projectiles over berms and other forms of cover that your opponent may use to hide from direct fire weapons. Within about two or three hundred meters you should, with training, be able to put one of the rounds through a doorway or bunker aperture (although it might take a few tries).

Projectiles come in several flavors. There is a high explosive model (HE) that is one of the most popular. It will reach out about 500

The M203 grenade launcher throws a 40mm projectile out several hundred yards with precision. It's not much more than a simple aluminum tube with a breech and trigger. The hand grip is the rifle's magazine. With it, you can pump a few anti-personnel rounds through the aperture of a bunker, or an illumination round up in the air, or an anti-armor round into the side of an armored personnel carrier, normally with the desired results.

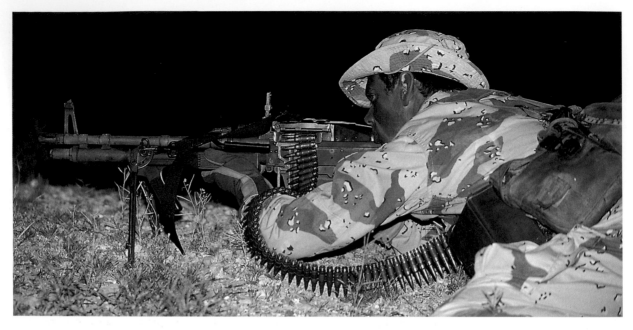

In conventional units the automatic weapons man gets an assistant to feed the ammunition. SEALs manage this chore themselves. The orange bullet tip indicates a tracer round; the others are ball.

Another view of the M203. It's not much more than a simple aluminum tube with a breech and trigger. The hand grip is the rifle's magazine.

Combat Time

Although Naval Special Warfare represents some of the best trained, most experienced warriors in the US Department of Defense, there is still something just a little naive about the vast majority of the people in this community. While they train to the highest standards and with the most realistic training aids, there is still something missing from the resumes of nearly all the 1,200 SEALs and SBS crews today: combat time.

About twenty years have now passed since the end of America's last prolonged conflict. With those years have gradually gone the SEALs who planned and executed the missions in the Mekong during the long, difficult years the teams fought in Vietnam. The result of that is that, in some ways, the teams are becoming *less* qualified rather than more so as time goes by. The lessons learned from prolonged combat operations in what military folks call the "real world" cannot be duplicated in peacetime. Now, when SEALs go to war, it is typically the first real combat operation of a career, and perhaps the only combat experience a man will ever have. Of the 200-plus men on one of today's teams, there is probably not one left with Vietnam experience, and very, very few with actual trigger-pulling experience in any operation since.

Real combat makes people do things they don't do in training. The big, heroic guys sometimes go numb and ineffective on you while the wimpy little guys who always screw up during training execute the mission with calm and grace and not a trace of fear.

In training you shoot at a cardboard or plastic target that pops up for a few mechanically timed seconds, usually in a predictable place, then disappears. If you hit it, the target folds down, mechanically, and a computer records your hit. In combat your target will appear anywhere, often unpredictably, often for a fraction of a second. The target may be a woman or a child, may be trying to shoot you, or may not know you exist. You can see its eyes, sometimes; you can identify it as a person, somewhat like you. The target probably has a family, a mission of his own, and maybe a target of his own—you. It is a bit like hunting; you must expect the unexpected, be alert without fixation, all

in a complicated, emotional, supremely frightening situation. When your target appears, it will probably be for a fleeting glimpse. If you are completely prepared, you may be able to get a shot off. If you do, you will certainly invite the same treatment on yourself.

Things they don't show you on television:

No matter how well you've maintained your weapon, no matter how full the magazine is or how carefully it has been loaded, there will be times when you pull the trigger on somebody and it will go *click* instead of *bang.* This can be quite embarrassing. It happens a lot more often than you can possibly imagine.

Gunfights on TV and in the movies are fought with weapons that have magical, bottomless magazines, that never run out of ammunition. Real world gunfights use weapons with magazines that are good for about three seconds full-auto, less if they jam (which they often will). And magazines that you can easily change in training, at night and with gloves on, you will find yourself utterly incapable of fitting into the well of the weapon. You will run out of ammunition far faster than you could imagine possible.

In a real world gunfight you can spot a target, align the sights, cut loose with a long burst from your trusty M60, and watch the tracers dance downrange at the man you intend to kill, when, just like in the movies, the dust kicks up around him, the bullets hammer his surroundings—and he runs off, untouched.

But if you somehow achieve that Zen-like state of mind that some men do, all things are possible. An enemy soldier can materialize out of the weeds, with your personal weapon jammed or broken, and now it is *his* turn to forget in nervous haste to move the safety on his AK-74 from "safe" to "fire." Then, perhaps, you will remember why you carry that Sig-Sauer 9mm handgun on your hip. If you get to the Sig quick enough, get it up, focus on the front sight, align with center-of-mass, and squeeze—if you are blessed this day—your bullet will strike your man in the lower sternum. He'll go down, and you can stay up; you'll live through another mission. If you're lucky and good, together.

None of these things will ever happen to you on an exercise or in training, but they will all happen to you if you go to war with a combat unit and stay there awhile. Trust me on this.

meters and will kill or injure anybody within about five meters of impact, a useful device when enemy infantry are closing in on your position. The 203 will also fire illumination rounds, like the mortar, that will light up the battlefield at night; and tear gas, white phosphorus, and flachette rounds for other times and places.

M60 Machine Gun

A SEAL squad with an inland patrol mission will carry plenty of "organic" firepower in the form of two stripped down M60 machine guns. The M60 is another old design that has been improved since the years when the dad of today's SEAL carried one back in the "big war." It fires the bigger 7.62mm (.308-caliber) NATO cartridge, delivering accurate, high-volume fire on area targets at ranges well beyond what the M16 can effectively engage.

It is a heavy weapon, with heavy ammunition, often cursed on those long walks in the woods and swamps—until, that is, the opposing team materializes out of the woodwork, spoiling for a fight. Then the M60 is worth its weight in gold or blood.

If this seems like a lot of choices, it is. A team commander explains his personal attitude toward weapons used by SEALs:

"I think we really do need a variety of weapons on the teams. Certain operations call for specific capabilities. I also don't think every guy should have a different weapon, just because he has his own personal preference. I should be able to switch magazines with the guy next to me if I run out and he hasn't. But, for the rifleman, the choice can be between the M14, the MP5, or the M16. The MP5 is for use in brush or urban combat situations. The M16 is a good, general, all-around weapon, and you can put the M203 under it. The M14 has extra power for penetration and range.

"Riflemen are for engaging *point* targets and they should be shooting single shots; personally, I don't even believe in three-round bursts. I don't even believe in 'double-tap' [firing two quick shots at a target instead of one], although the idea is currently quite popular. If you put the first shot where you're supposed

The M60 as used by the SEALs is a stripped-down, lightweight version that is a lot more tolerant of sand than the early versions were. After firing a hundred rounds or so the barrel will begin to glow.

to, you don't *need* another one! If you need another one, pull the trigger again. Why waste ammunition? You should be calm enough under fire to know what you are doing rather than just opening up 'full-auto' and spraying the riverbank.

"The automatic weapon man is not to take out point targets; he's supposed to keep the enemy's head down and to give you covering fire while the riflemen take care of the point targets."

RTO

The patrol can be far from a friendly face but still be in contact with the civilized world, thanks to the battery-powered high technology that the RTO (an old expression, short for radio telephone operator) carries. There are any number of systems he can carry, and with some of them you can chat with the big bosses

The RTO is the squad communicator. His duties include carrying the radio and batteries and managing the communications plan. The antenna will identify him as a prime target to any enemy snipers within rifle range.

in Washington and in the Pentagon—although that's not usually something the team will think is a good idea.

That's because you're on the ground, with eyes on the target, and the admirals and the assistant secretary of defense sitting next to him are both in a comfortable room in a safe place. When the sun goes down, they will go off for cocktails somewhere, have a nice dinner, and watch TV. You will crawl through the mud and perhaps have people shoot at you, all while attempting to do the bidding of these "experts" with the clean fingernails, thanks to that little "satcom" transceiver carried by the RTO.

Satellite radios are now extremely compact and can easily be taken along on operations with a very moderate weight penalty. They allow the team leader to communicate with almost anybody, almost anywhere (if he can get a channel on the satellite). That, believe it or not, can be a real problem. Although

you can call for help from almost anywhere on the globe with these little systems, if some politician in the "puzzle palace" comes up with a wild hair idea, they can call *you* and task you with this death-defying scheme, all from the comfort and safety of Washington, DC.

The RTO is, in some ways, a pack mule for the patrol leader; he carries the radio and operates it, but under the control of the patrol leader, whom the RTO shadows. The RTO is, along with the officer, a natural target for any sensible sniper on the opposing team who manages to identify and engage the patrol. The radio is the patrol's link to the close air support gunships overhead, the naval gunfire support offshore, and the "slicks" (unarmed helicopters) ready to swoop in to rescue the patrol in an emergency. By eliminating the RTO and his equipment, the enemy can isolate the squad and chop it to small pieces. That's why RTOs fold the aerials of their radios down and do their best to look as innocent as possible.

A funny thing about these radios, though, is that—despite their usually excellent reliability and reception—at moments like these they may suddenly stop working. As one officer explains:

"We have better communications now than we used to, but that works both ways. If I need to get ahold of somebody I probably can. It also means that guy can get ahold of me—and give me directions that I might not want. I can remember two times, during 1965 operations in Vietnam, when somebody tried to tell me what to do while I was on the ground. I didn't like it—and in one case I turned off the radio. Now, if the National Command Authority wants to talk to me while I'm on a hot operation, they very well may. This is not necessarily a good thing. To me, the guy on the scene calls the shots. He should receive *nothing* from those guys except support, when he calls up and asks for it. We make a plan and should stick to the plan, unless the guy on the ground wants to do differently. Now, if somebody has some information that can help you, if they see a platoon of enemy, for example, coming down the road toward you, they ought to be able to let you know. But don't tell me to go left or right in reaction to that platoon—let *me* make that decision!

"We have a tendency, because we have such good communications, to let responsibility slip upwards where sometimes it doesn't belong. Look what happened at Desert One [the failed Iranian hostage rescue mission]. Jimmy Carter was in the position where he could call up Colonel Beckwith [the on-scene commander] and tell him what to do. I don't like that! Most people in the SEALs don't like that. Some people submit to that. And some people automatically get their hackles up—don't submit to it; put the radio down and say 'Dang, something just went wrong with the radio!' The problem with letting decisions be made someplace, with letting somebody else be re-

PRC-112 squad radio is another example in the revolution in miniaturization that has transformed the command and control problem for managing SEALs during combat operations.

sponsible, is that I'm still responsible for the people who are with me. I want to make the decision for what happens once we launch the mission. Tell me what to do *before* I leave, and then if I buy off on it, fine. Just don't tell me what to do once I'm out there. While we have the advantage of better communications, we get with that the disadvantage of potential micro-management by people not on the scene."

Patrol Leader

The patrol leader on a SEAL operation is going to be one of the platoon's two commissioned officers, the platoon leader (normally a lieutenant) or executive officer (lieutenant junior grade or possibly ensign). The role of a combat leader is an odd kind of combination of duties that sometimes conflict. A combat leader has two heavy responsibilities: to complete the mission, and to preserve the force. That means that the leader takes himself and his followers to complete a mission that, in war, will probably involve great hazard. How much hazard is sometimes influenced by the officer; it may depend on how much risk he's willing to take in a given time and place. Just how important the mission is he has to judge. He has to judge how much it is worth, in time, effort, ammunition, and the blood of his men. So the patrol leader is stuck in the middle, with a responsibility upward, to his commanders who've tasked him with a mission, and downward, to his followers who trust his judgment.

The officer is part of the platoon, and he is aloof from it. He guards his men, is responsible for their welfare as a parent is for a child—and may send them knowingly to their deaths or dismemberment. He is trained, at Annapolis or OCS (Officer Candidate School), to be careful to avoid playing favorites and developing the natural kind of friendships that are common among civilians—fraternization, it is called.

The officer discovers, early in his career, that while the troops will automatically salute and call him *sir*, the respect may not be sincere. An officer learns that respect is earned in two phases: first through the commissioning process that awards gold bars and officer rank, then all over again in the units where real competence and leadership are demonstrated. For SEALs there is another part, BUD/S, where officers must perform alongside the enlisted sailors, suffer all the same insults and indignities, the same stresses and fatigue. It is an important part of the bonding between the leaders and the followers in the SEALs.

As officer candidates quickly learn at Annapolis, NROTC, or OCS, it's a complicated business to lead men in combat. It is a bit like leading an orchestra; you don't need to be the best player of every instrument, but you have to know perfectly what each can do—then to be able to make sure its resources are integrated into the big score. But the terrible,

This is one of the little compact SATCOM radios that have transformed the business of communicating in the field. This is the LST-5C transceiver; it weighs about ten pounds.

wonderful thing about military operations is that they are, always and invariably, partially improvisations. There is an old military saying: No plan survives contact with the enemy. That means that, no matter how well you think you've prepared, something is going to go wrong. And when it does, one person needs to be responsible for selecting an alternative course of action. That's what officers are for.

The platoon leader will normally have been personally given the mission and then designed the plan, with help from above and below. He takes the plan to the field and makes it happen with the help of his SEALs. When the shooting starts he is expected to direct, manage, and control the firing. When the ambush is triggered, he initiates it with a squeeze of the trigger or the "clacker" for the Claymore. His M16 magazines may be full of nothing but tracers, which he uses to indicate targets for the rest of the squad to fire on.

On the march, the patrol leader will typically be toward the front of the line of march. He may take the point sometimes, but usually will be the number two man, where he can provide direction for the man on point and still control the squad in case of contact. The RTO will be right behind the patrol leader, however, wherever he is.

Tail Gunner

The two most vulnerable areas for the patrol are its front and its back; it will either bump into trouble, or trouble will come sneaking up on it. That's why both the man on point and the last man in line, the tail gunner, have to be especially sharp. The tail gunner will probably have one of the squad's cut-down M60 machine guns—and eyes in the back of his head.

In actual combat, on deep penetration missions, he'll probably carry a variety of goodies to help break contact if the patrol finds itself compromised and on the run. Then he'll pull out the tear gas grenades, the devastating WP (white phosphorous) grenades, and perhaps a Claymore to rig as a booby trap against the pursuers.

339

Chapter 5

Actions at the Objective

As mentioned before, SEALs have five different general types of missions to perform: direct action, recon, foreign internal defense, unconventional warfare, and counterterrorist. This is a broad spectrum of responsibilities for a small organization, no matter how well trained or funded. Some of these are primary SEAL missions; others are secondary.

Counterterrorist operations, for example, are really the stock-in-trade for Delta, the Army's superb, extremely exclusive counterterrorist unit. The men (and—promise not to tell where you heard this—women) in Delta are going to get the call for such operations except under extreme circumstances. SEALs are trained and prepared to execute the operation, and there are a few "long hair" team members available for extremely covert ops, but it is hardly a prime talent for aquatic warriors.

Likewise, foreign internal defense (FID) and unconventional warfare (UW) are prime Army missions that are backed up by SEALs. Both require the language skills and charm of a diplomat, the charisma of an evangelist, and the patience of a saint. The FID mission turns

When you're a SEAL you don't have to worry too much about what the sign says, particularly when you've got a riot shotgun and an MP4. Close combat in confined spaces is a new skill required of SEALs. US Navy photo by PH2 Milton Savage

out to be one that a few SEALs excel at, about five guys of the 200 or so on a team, according to one team commander. This mission occupies a few SEALs in Latin America now, and it kept a lot busy during the workup to Desert Storm in training Saudi and other Arab naval personnel in the Gulf. As one of the team commanders says:

"I think we're quite good at the traditional Green Beret mission of foreign internal defense; we have a very high degree of success when we include foreign military personnel in our operations. For some reason we've thrown that back to the Army. We were very good in the Gulf when we took two or three SEALs and used them with ten or twelve host-nation personnel. We 'force-multiplied.' We had all the advantages of the host-nation expertise, plus our skills and experience in executing that type of operation. It was a Cracker Jack setup!"

But it is not one most SEALs find very appealing. It takes many months of study at DLI, the Defense Language Institute at Monterey, California, to acquire the skill to speak Arabic, for example, or Estonian, and that means time away from the teams. Unconventional warfare is the behind-the-lines version of FID, and hasn't really been used much since World War II—although it is still sitting there as a tasking for the Special Operations Forces.

So the principal missions, the ones that get the attention, the time, the rehearsals, are recon and strike. The first is stealthy and the second isn't.

Recons, Deep and Shallow

Despite all the wonderful, expensive technology that has gone into intelligence gathering, with billions of dollars spent on camera systems for aircraft and satellites, there is still no substitute for having someone go ashore for a "hands on, eyes on" study of a potential target. One of the lessons learned from Urgent

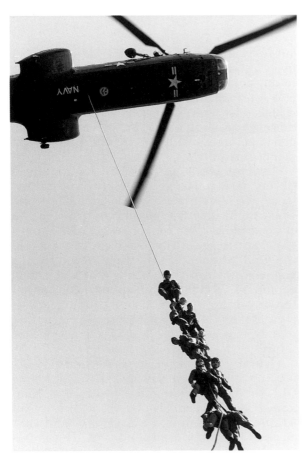

The SPIE (Special Purpose Insertion and Extraction) rig is one way to extract and insert SEALs in a hurry. It is a breezy and hazardous technique, but one that a lot of people actually enjoy. US Navy photo by PH2 Milton Savage

Fury was that overhead intel only begins to provide essential planning information and that things like landing zones can look completely different to a helicopter pilot than to a high-flying aircraft—with potentially catastrophic results.

Although not as glamorous as the strike missions, recon ops are just as important now as ever. As the recons in the Panama Just Cause op and the beach survey during Desert Storm both demonstrate, SEALs still get tasked with these jobs, and it is their particular art form.

The recon mission can be just about anything, anywhere. The classic one, of course, is the beach recon preceding an amphibious operation. While the Marines think their own recon guys can do this better than anybody, SEALs politely disagree. While it doesn't get much attention, it is still a tremendously important mission when you consider how much investment the US has in putting Marines across the beach anywhere in the world. The memory of Tarawa half a century ago haunts the Marines—and the Navy, too. Beach recons, consequently, are a big part of the course of instruction at BUD/S, where they're called "hydrographic surveys." They can be as simple or as detailed as you and your commanders want—and as circumstances permit.

There are many different types of hydrographic surveys and beach recons, from simple to complex. The amphibious task force commander who is planning an across-the-beach op will want to know gradient and composition of the beach, littoral current across the beach, surf size and type, beach exits, defenses, and obstacles underwater.

It takes a lot of people—or a lot of time—to develop this information. Without getting into the technical details, here's how they do it:

Swim pairs are dropped in the water off the beach at intervals of about twenty-five meters, on line, by a high-speed boat—just like they did fifty years ago out in the Pacific. Under command of the officer in charge (OIC), the swimmers move in toward the beach, mak-

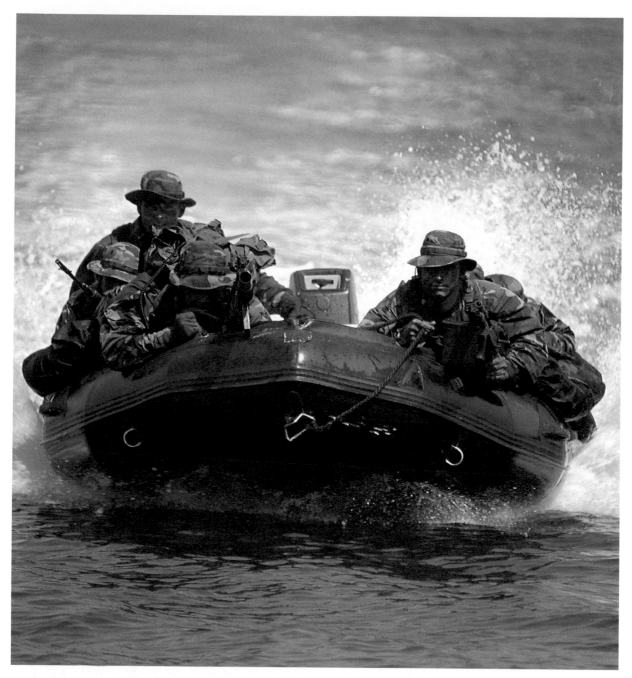

A fire team (half a squad) fits neatly into a rubber duck for a semi-stealthy insertion. Although the little inflatable is rated for over-the-horizon ranges, you don't want to ride around like this for long out on the open ocean.

First ashore during a combat insertion are the scout swimmers, who secure the beach before the rest of the unit comes ashore. They operate in pairs, for mutual security.

ing soundings with a lead-line (a lead sinker on a line marked in one-foot increments). While one man measures the depth, the other records the data on a slate. Since all the swimmers make these soundings at the same time, a set of coordinated data is assembled across a wide frontage of possible landing zone.

The line of swimmers moves in to the beach together, with the OIC controlling the intervals between soundings. Both depth and composition are recorded on each swim-pair's

slate. The Marine task force commander's staff will want to know what they have to contend with. Coral reef? Mud? Jagged rocks? Man-made obstacles with antitank mines attached? Is the foreshore (the surf zone) too shallow for LSTs, or is it steep and suitable for ramped vessels? Is the surf high and violent or short and mild? Is the current across the beach strong and likely to force the AAM-TRACs away from their intended beaches? Then, what's beyond the beach—will tanks and armored vehicles be "channeled" by sea walls, cliffs, embankments? Are there enemy-prepared fighting positions dominating the beach? Are they manned? Is there a beach patrol? Are there mines?

The survey party moves all the way into the beach and perhaps beyond, then withdraws back to the water. Under the direction of the OIC, they reform a line offshore for pickup. Then, perhaps aboard the flagship for the amphibious task force or wherever the SEAL unit has set up shop, the data from each swim pair is assembled as a detailed chart and presented to the plans-and-operations guys who are trying to figure out what to do. They (through their recommendation to the task force commander) make the call on the amphibious operation, not the SEALs, using the data provided.

There is another kind of recon for which the Army and Navy SOF communities compete, called *deep recon* or *strategic recon*, and this one might not involve even getting wet. Deep recon involves the study of a target or area of interest that typically requires covert travel overland or covert insertion inland. SOF teams did this during Desert Shield/Desert Storm in Kuwait and Iraq, watching for enemy SCUD launchers, for example, and reporting their location for attack by other "theater assets" like US Air Force F-15E Strike Eagle aircraft. A SEAL recon team was on the Saudi/Kuwait border when the Iraqis attacked the town of Kafji and participated in the coordinated engagement of the enemy armored column by air and coalition ground units.

HAHO and HALO Insertion

These recon teams can be delivered in some quite exotic ways. One of the sneakiest is by parachute, but SOF teams don't consider the standard 500- or 1,200-foot drop altitude used for mass tactical airborne operations to be very covert; having a C-130 fly low over the neighborhood is one sure way to get noticed. Instead, the drop aircraft goes way up to 30,000 feet or so—where the commercial airliners fly. The jumpers, rigged with special equipment to cope with the incredible cold and the lack of oxygen at that altitude, jump and free fall before deploying their canopies.

The HAHO technique (High-Altitude exit/High-altitude Opening) allows a jumper to glide for many miles under his canopy, through the dark, virtually without fear of detection, to a predetermined landing zone.

The HALO technique (High-Altitude exit/Low-altitude Opening) is a similar way to have the jumper move away from the ground track of the aircraft, making it difficult to find him. This time, though, the jumper uses free-fall parachuting techniques to "fly" through the air, opening his canopy only when very close to the ground.

Once down, the mission proceeds as planned. When it is over, one way or another, it is time to go home. While, again, there are many ways to do this, the quickest will again be by aircraft. Unfortunately, though, pickup aircraft are a lot less subtle.

Once the scouts determine the beach to be suitable for a visit, the rest of the squad comes ashore, but they are hardly complacent about it. This is a vulnerable moment for the SEALs, and they are extremely cautious at this phase of insertion.

STABO Extraction

An extremely unsubtle extraction technique, STABO (Stabilized Tactical Airborne Body Operations), involves having a helicopter arrive over the team on the ground with a special harness deployed, coming to a hover, and then plucking the SEALs out of harm's way. The SEALs all wear harnesses similar to those used for parachuting and attach the harnesses to the sling dangling from the helicopter. When all are secured, it's up, up, and away . . . for a very breezy ride.

Strike

The mission against the Panamanian patrol boat was a classic strike or direct action mission, a carefully planned, precision attack against a point target under difficult circumstances. Using any special ops unit for such an attack is a lot more expensive, in every respect, than using conventional resources to do the same kind of thing, so there is usually a good reason for sending SEALs to blow the propellers off a boat instead of (for example)

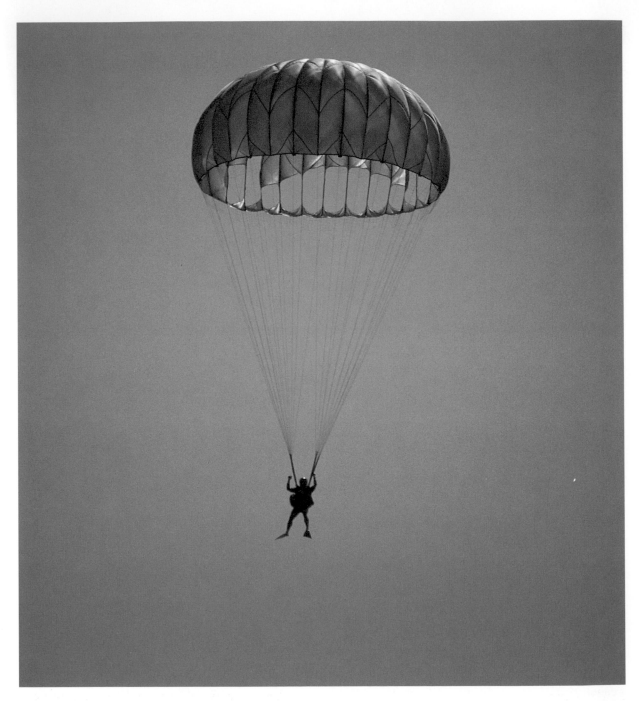

Airborne insertions are also typically done at night,
but that makes for dull photographs.

One way to make a quick getaway is to call the helo back for a pickup. The crew will toss a ladder over the ramp, and then it's up to the swimmer to climb back aboard.

having an F/A-18 drop a bomb or smart missile on the target. Collateral damage and loss of life has been one of the driving concerns lately; in Panama, certainly, and in Grenada, too, this caution has created risks of its own.

But ambushes and attacks on point targets are still a major talent of SEALs, another area where they compete with the Army's Rangers and Special Forces. These can be conducted in many imaginative ways, most of which are of the high-risk, high-payoff variety (although SEALs sometimes think some of these are high-risk, low-payoff missions).

Ambushes

The ambush is a kind of classic special op mission. SEALs conducted probably thousands of them in Vietnam—and were on the receiving end of quite a few, too. The "plain vanilla" version of the operation works like this: first, find a place where your enemy regularly travels—a road or trail—and find a nice sharp bend in the route. The "kill zone" will be determined by the patrol leader, normally the long axis of what is an L-shaped portion of the road. The leader will position himself at the corner and will control the whole thing, usually with his own fire and with the triggering of a Claymore mine or two.

Ambushes are marvelously effective when everything works properly—the carnage is *incredible*. But if you screw one up, the carnage can be on your end. And ambushes are easy to screw up; the key is fire discipline and timing.

The little $50,000 dune buggy called the Desert Patrol Vehicle is a fast, potent machine for rescuing downed pilots, scouting large sections of potential battlefield, or inserting snipers into an operational area. It will do at least 70mph, fly through space, and—with the machine guns and AT-4 rocket launchers—duke it out with carefully selected enemy forces.

SEALs practice executing raids on oil platforms and other semi-urban spaces. These guys have just landed on a ship and, like buccaneers of old, are swarming aboard to take control. US Navy photo by PH2 Milton Savage

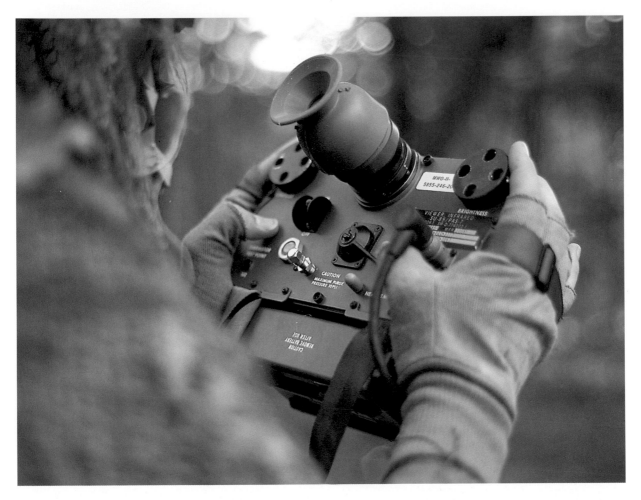

The PAS-7 infrared viewing system. SEALs use a variety of sensor systems to inspect terrain at night; thermal imaging systems such as this make objects *like people and vehicles instantly visible out of the gloom.*

Ambushes don't take a lot of people or a lot of resources (depending on the target, of course), but they do take planning and teamwork.

If available, Claymores are installed along the kill zone with overlapping fields of fire and with careful attention to protecting the team from the substantial back-blast. If the ambush is along a road, detonation cord can be placed in the ditches that survivors will naturally use

for cover after the Claymores fire, and they can be taken out with another squeeze on another "clacker," firing the electric blasting cap that will fire the det cord.

When all the preparations are made, the responsibilities and fields of fire assigned, you and the rest of the crew slither into the woodwork without a trace and wait . . . and wait . . . and wait some more. At last, in the distance, somebody is moving toward you; it can be chil-

349

dren on their way to school, innocent civilians going to market. You have to sit, silently, waiting for them to pass. What if one of the kids sees the Claymore? What if somebody notices your face peeping out of the brush? Anything that can go wrong, will go wrong to somebody, sooner or later—usually sooner—so it pays to set these things up with exquisite attention to detail.

The way these things are *supposed* to work, an enemy unit will come rolling down the road. With luck (for you, anyway) they will fit the ambush resources; don't pop a Claymore against a platoon of main battle tanks, for example. But if any enemy squad comes bopping down the bunny trail (laughing, playing radios the way they sometimes do), everybody in the ambush waits for the signal to fire. That signal is usually the patrol leader's detonation of the Claymores, hurling their pellets in wide, deadly arcs. If the timing is right and the patrol is within the kill zone, they will all go down—maybe. Some guys are just luckier than others, and fit into a hole in the pattern of the spray of ball bearings. Others may be outside the kill zone. Regardless, this is the time to use all those marksmanship skills they taught you at BUD/S and since. You engage the closest guy with a gun in your field of fire (got a round in the chamber? safety off?), and you keep engaging until there is no more resistance or the patrol leader calls, "Cease fire!" There will be a terrible mess where the patrol was, and this will be a good time to start moving toward the exits.

Ambushes go wrong in lots of ways. Often, the enemy doesn't cooperate. They either won't show up, or they send the wrong victims (like tanks), or they decide not to use the road today, but move along in the woods—where you're hiding. Or they notice you before they get to the kill zone, and then it's *turnabout is fair play*. Then it's your turn to be the vic-

Conflict resolution and power projection in the special operations community generally means something like this—either threatening or actually using deadly force against people to make them behave.

351

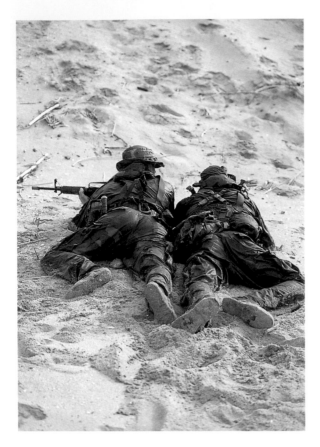

There is something extremely primitive about much of the work of a SEAL team; while drivers of stealth bombers and F-15 Strike Eagles operate multimillion dollar weapons systems in relative comfort, SEALs use skills as old as war. This swim pair crawls up out of the surf, just as their forefathers did in World War II, for a peek inland, hoping and praying that there won't be an enemy sentry on top of the sand dune.

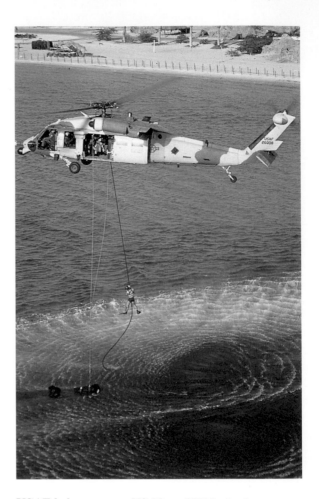

USAF helos support US Navy SEALs in the new co-operative relationship called "joint operations." This kind of integration has had profound effects on things like radios, weapons, training, and doctrine, ensuring that different services can all "play off the same sheet of music," as the operators like to say.

tim—and practice those escape-and-evasion skills they taught you in BUD/S. Just remember what they told you at BUD/S: The only easy day was yesterday.

Raids

The diversion operation at Mina Sa'Ud that helped kick off Desert Storm was one kind of raid, as was the attack on the Noriega

Neville Jet, the rescue of Sir Paul Scoon, and hundreds of similar missions executed by SEALs since World War II. Raids are quick-in, quick-out strikes against high-value targets that can't be attacked efficiently or effectively otherwise. This is another area where SEALs compete with the Army, whose Rangers are masters of the art of the raid. Rangers, however, are specialists in the "blunt instrument"

This role-playing sentry might have a bit of a problem—and a headache not even Anacin could help. Much of the training, equipment, and doctrine used by SEALs today is oriented toward dealing with unconventional forces like terrorists.

style of raid, with lots of people (very large, muscular ones) and lots of firepower landing on top of an enemy target, typically by parachute, and ripping it to shreds.

The SEAL raid is more surgical and subtle. It still might arrive by parachute, but—unlike with our beloved Ranger Regiment—the enemy target of a SEAL op might never know what hit them. That's because a SEAL strike mission might only involve two men, a sniper and his spotter/security man. With their big .50-caliber sniper rifle and woodcraft skills, these two can move across terrain unseen and disappear into the woodwork.

(Rangers attempting this would leave a trail of scorched earth and destruction visible at a mile). Then the sniper team can sit and wait until the SCUDs come home—and then drill holes in their rocket motors from a mile and a half, without anybody knowing where the bullets came from or how it happened. That same sniper team can, if desired, kill a senior enemy staff officer or commander riding in his Mercedes, pick off a tank commander standing in his hatch, or disable an aircraft taxiing for take-off. In fact, people who weren't part of the Neville Jet take-down op during Operation Just Cause wonder why forty SEALs were

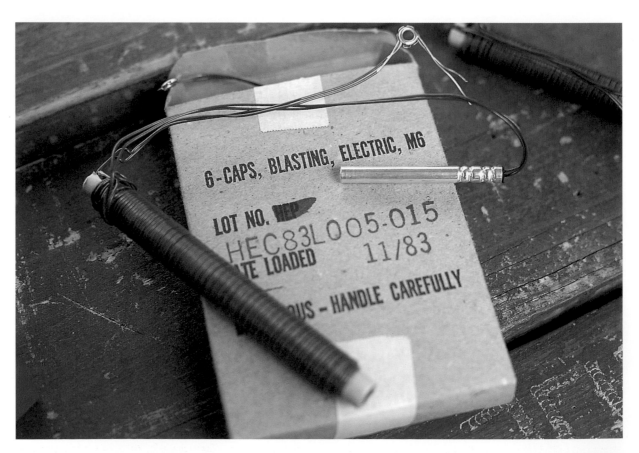

An electrical blasting cap, fresh from the box, ready to prime any military explosive. It contains three stages of material, each setting off the next. The last, a material called PETN, will reliably set off just about anything.*

sent across the airfield to attack the jet when a sniper team ought to have been able to do it from the safety of the far side of the runways.

Among the most challenging kind of raid SEALs train for is the counterterrorist hostage rescue mission. This is the kind of op that you only get one shot at; it has to be done perfectly or the wrong folks get killed. Consequently SEALs practice all the ancient arts of rapid insertion, extraction, close-quarters target identification, and precision shooting. According to people who've been there, you've got seven seconds in a room with the bad guys to conduct business—sort out the good from the bad, kill the bad guys, protect the good guys— or the operation goes to hell. When you consider that this must often be done at night, in unfamiliar territory, with alert and fanatic enemies, this becomes a tall order. But it can be done, and has, successfully.

Killing People and Destroying Things

A sad but unavoidable consequence of all military missions involves taking perfectly good buildings, airplanes, vehicles, bridges, boats, and people, then taking them apart and converting them into smaller, less useful junk. This process is generally thought to help ac-

A mixed bag of things that go bump in the night— TNT, dynamite, and det cord, with a partial box of blasting caps (time fuse variety). These explosives are quite stable and difficult to detonate without a blasting cap. For example, to prime the dynamite you have to poke a hole in it with a pointed tool, then insert the blasting cap-fuse assembly.

Kids—don't try this at home! Somebody's used a lot of explosive to do a bit of body and fender work on this old car.

complish national policy objectives. While this behavior isn't always considered very nice, it usually works. This is conflict resolution, US Navy SEALs style.

There are many ways SEALs use to accomplish their mission, but basically there are only two fundamental techniques used by the teams. One of these uses individual weapons—rifles, machine guns, mortars—to engage other hostile forces. The other involves using explosives in one form or another to blow things up. "Hostile forces" is a military expression for the loyal soldiers or sailors opposing the SEAL mission, and "engage" is a military expression for the business of shooting up these folks in an organized way. If this seems like kindergarten, it is only because we generally talk around the seamier side of the business of war.

SEAL missions often involve the destruction of some enemy facility—a radio transmitter, a bridge, a bunker complex, a headquarters, or (as in the attack on the *Presidente Porras* in the beginning of this book) a naval vessel. This usually involves the use of high explosives in one of many forms, and one thing most SEALs quickly discover in BUD/S is that

explosives are *fun*. As one blaster says with a smirk, "There are very few of life's troubles that can't be cured with high explosives."

A Short Course in Demolitions and High Explosives

Despite what you hear, high explosives are quite safe to handle and are actually difficult to detonate. Most of the military varieties can be pounded with a hammer (old, runny dynamite excepted) without going off. One of the best materials for blasting passages through coral reefs is a simple mixture of fertilizer and diesel fuel. You can break off a chunk of TNT from a quarter-pound block and set fire to it; so it's not only a great explosive, it's also a great heat source for warming up your lunch. C4, the famous "plastic explosive," looks, feels, and acts like putty—a white material that you can easily form and shape with your fingers, in complete safety. The same is true of virtually all other military explosives, with the possible exception of dynamite, a combination of nitroglycerine and gun-cotton, that can become quite unstable if stored improperly. Most of these materials can sit on the shelf for decades without any significant decay, and it isn't unusual to be issued cratering charges, for example, that were made during World War II.

For these and other reasons, explosives are very interesting and useful materials, available in many forms. There is Primacord or "det cord," a material that looks like fuse, a flexible plastic-like quarter-inch cord that contains a very high explosive, PETN, and is used to connect main charges. The PETN cord is set off with a blasting cap or other charge—then it explodes at a linear rate of about four miles per second with enough force to detonate any US military explosive the cord is tied to. It is very handy stuff for making a lot of little charges all go off at the same time—and other, sneakier applications discussed later.

In every case, including that of dynamite, you must work hard and carefully to actually get the stuff to go off. And that's accomplished with a little device that is quite dangerous and that will go off if you fail to handle it with care, caution, and respect—the blasting cap. These come in two flavors: electric and fused. Both are tubes of aluminum or copper, a quarter of an inch in diameter, partially filled with a three-stage mixture of specialized explosives, an ignition charge, a priming charge, and a base charge. Although things happen quickly, these charges go off in sequence, and the last one, the base charge, is the one that *should* set off the main charge.

As an example, let's set off a one-pound block of TNT. The main charge comes in a cardboard tube with a threaded receptacle on the ends to hold the blasting cap. We'll use common fuse instead of an electrical cap for this charge; it's more traditional. Also less safe.

First we take the fuse, cut six inches off the end and discard it. This should remove any contaminated and unreliable material. Then we cut a section six feet long, light one end, and time the delay. After about four minutes, a little flash of fire will come from the end. Note the time, divide by six, and you know what the delay of the fuse is in seconds per foot; normally it is about forty seconds per foot. Now, using your combination tool designed for demolitions work, cut a good, healthy length of fuse sufficient for five minutes' delay. The ends should be clean, square cuts.

Remove a blasting cap from the storage box where they are kept for safety and inspect the fuse well for foreign matter. *Gently* slip the fuse into the open end—about an inch—and into contact with the ignition charge. Crimp the fuse to the cap with the crimper part of the tool, about a quarter inch from the end of the cap. Now gently insert the cap into the priming well of the TNT block, place it on the ground, and extend the fuse so that it doesn't coil over on itself. We could use a fuse-lighter to get things started, but you might as well learn the traditional way first: split the fuse end about half an inch, insert a match head in the core, and strike it. The match will ignite the black powder inside, a bit of flame will sputter, a little smoke will be emitted,

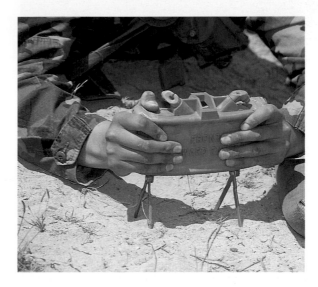

Emplacing an M18 Claymore. The device is not much more than a slab of C4 explosives and a lot of ball bearings, electrically primed. It sprays a cloud of steel pellets that will kill or maim anyone within about fifty meters to the front.

and it is time to vacate the premises. It is considered good manners to shout, "Fire in the hole!" at this point unless there are bad guys in the vicinity. You walk, not run, well away, take cover, note the time, and await developments.

When the fuse burns down inside a non-electric blasting cap, a little squirt of flame shoots out, into the cap. If everything works as planned, the ignition charge goes off, then the priming charge, which detonates the base charge of the cap, and that little blast will usually set off the TNT. There will be a loud *Boom!*, and dust and rocks will scatter for a hundred meters in all directions. But don't expect any gaping crater—even a pound of TNT won't do much unless it is artfully placed and prepared. Instead, we have a patch of ground that is lightly depressed and not much more.

Explosives are used to do very specific things and are used with mathematical precision. You can cut a twelve-inch diameter tree with a half-pound block and have it fall across

The M67 hand grenade is thrown like a baseball. With practice you can put it into a machine-gun pit, a bunker, or a room. Without practice it tends to *bounce back, fall short, or otherwise embarrass its thrower.*

a roadway, blocking traffic. You can make a ribbon out of C4 plastic explosive, stick it to a steel girder, and cut a bridge support. You can shape it into a flat diamond and wrap it around an eighteen-inch diameter ship's propeller shaft, prime both points with blasting caps, and cut off the shaft neatly when the charge goes off. Put two identical charges on both sides of a concrete wall or abutment and prime electrically so both go off at the same instant, and a small amount of explosive (a pound and a half per foot of thickness) will crumble the concrete.

The most common application of explosives for SEALs has been clearing beach obstacles prior to amphibious landings, a technique developed to a minor art form by the UDT swimmers during World War II and Korea. Besides that use, vast quantities of C4

went up in smoke in Vietnam and, more recently, in the Gulf, blowing up bunkers and creating diversions. You can make a foxhole in a hurry with it, crater a road, cut a railroad line or a thick telephone cable. In the form of a Bangalore torpedo (a long section of steel pipe filled with explosive) you can blast a gap through a barbed wire obstacle or a minefield. It is mighty handy stuff.

Det cord, all by itself, has an interesting application for those occasional ambushes where you have plenty of time to set up shop. It can be electrically primed and hidden in roadside ditches alongside the "kill zone." When the ambush is initiated, you can be reasonably certain that the survivors of the first blast of small arms fire will dive for the presumed protection of the handy ditch. If the SEAL with the "hell box" (as the blasting machine is called) remembers to twist the handle about now, the det cord will explode in the ditch, adding to the consternation and woe of the enemy force.

Claymore Mines

The Claymore mine was developed in Vietnam to deal with those nasty situations when a couple of hundred little fellers in black pajamas were swarming across the barbed wire defenses of a compound with intentions of committing mayhem on the residents. The Claymore is a simple little package of C4 explosive and a few hundred steel ball bearings, fired with an electric blasting cap and a "clacker" (a one-handed electric generator that, when squeezed, will fire the cap). When the explosive detonates, the ball bearings

If this sniper team wasn't posing for the camera you wouldn't know they were there at all. The rifle is a bolt-action .50-caliber model designed specifically for special operations use. The bolt has to be removed to load each round. Its effective range is about two kilometers—more than a mile and a half.

Haskins .50-caliber sniper rifle. Despite the rumor, there is no prohibition against using the .50-caliber against individual enemy targets. This weapon is designed, among other things, to kill a man with the first shot at ranges over a half mile. The tremendous recoil is partly absorbed by twin hydraulic shock absorbers in the stock—and partially by the shoulder of the firer.

A sniper team in "ghillie" suits. These camouflage suits are handmade by the men as part of their training at the Special Operations Target Interdic- *tion Course. In them they blend into the terrain, virtually disappearing—although they do have a tendency to stand out a bit on the street.*

spray a wide area with deadly effect, usually helping to convince the enemy force that there may be other, better, things to do than to attack this particular place.

Claymores have since become favorites for temporary defensive fighting positions and for ambushes, where they excel. Like virtually all other weapons, they are not perfect or foolproof. One sneaky trick the VC learned was to find them and turn them around.

The guy with the "clacker" in an ambush setup has to be a very cool dude, sufficiently self-disciplined to wait until the enemy is properly within the kill zone before firing the weapon. Lots of perfectly good ambushes have been ruined by the premature detonation of the Claymore, removing the element of surprise quickly and completely.

SEALs carry a Claymore or two along on some of their excursions, the whole kit of mine, clacker, wire, and blasting cap all stored neatly in a little bundle complete with carrying strap.

.50-Caliber Sniper Rifle

One fine, somewhat neglected military art is that of the sniper. SEALs and Green Berets study this skill at the Target Interdiction Course, part of the Special Operations Command Center and School at the Army's Fort Bragg, North Carolina. Here, out among the weeds and chiggers, apprentice SEAL snipers learn how to move invisibly across any terrain, to build a hide so natural that an enemy can stand on top of it and not know that two Navy SEALs are in residence below, and to shoot so well that enemy soldiers over a half mile away die with the first shot, tank commanders standing in the turrets of their tanks lose their heads (literally), and antennas and vision ports on armored vehicles become useless.

The key to all this is a relatively simple, relatively ancient weapon—the rifle. The one favored by special operators like the SEALs these days is the big .50-caliber single-shot, bolt-action model that weighs about twenty pounds with scope and bipod. For a variety of reasons the big half-inch bullet will fly very accurately, very far. It will reliably strike a man-sized target so far away that the noise from its firing is practically inaudible, out to ranges of two kilometers, more than a mile and a half. But to achieve such accuracy requires far more than just an accurate weapon and sights. A SEAL sniper team out in the bush must deal with wind, moving targets, slant angles, and heat distortion.

Snipers work as two-man teams: the shooter and the spotter. They are inserted near their objective by boat or parachute, or swim ashore from a submarine, or come by Volkswagen bus—whatever works for the tactical situation. They will travel the last kilometer or so to their hide by crawling. It can take a day or more. Their weapons and equipment are contained in a "drag bag," pulled along behind each. Under cover of darkness, they carefully, methodically carve a hole in the ground, then re-cover it so artfully that it seems perfectly undisturbed. In this hole the pair will live for a day or two, observing, recording, and possibly reporting by radio. Normally the sniper's mission will not include actually firing on an enemy force but calling in artillery or aviation to do the job.

Determining range to the target and wind effect are the two principal problems confronting the sniper team, and the pair will expend considerable effort preparing to fire the first shot. A big .50-caliber round is inserted into the breech, the bolt brought forward, locked, and the sights carefully aligned on a computed aim point.

The spotter uses a compact telescope to look downrange. Instead of watching the target, the spotter watches for the *bullet* as it streaks toward the victim. With proper training and the right weather conditions, you can actually see a bullet and the vapor trail produced as it flies through the atmosphere. The spotter reports the point of impact to the shooter for any corrections.

Another version of the .50-caliber sniper rifle, used in Desert Storm.

Chapter 6

Special Boat Squadrons—
The Brown Water Navy

As mentioned earlier, the Special Boat Squadrons have typically been somewhat neglected in favor of the higher profile SEAL teams in the development of Naval Special Warfare. That's too bad because the boats have as rich a combat history as the teams, and both have worked closely together for nearly three decades. In fact, one of the big selling points for Naval Special Warfare in the competitive business of special operations is the unique resource SPECWARCOM has in its fleet of boats designed to take the fight close to the beach and up all those lazy rivers.

The Special Boat Squadrons are teamed with the SEALs to provide a kind of mutual support. And, just as the SEALs have a variety of weapons to choose from for their missions, the SBS crews have a menu of boats as well. There are little IBS inflatables, RIBs, PBRs, and fast-attack patrol boats. Most are stunningly fast, with thirty-knot-plus speeds . . . although you only get speeds like that from an IBS (a little seven-man rubber duck) when all the BUD/S are screaming and the students are paddling like crazy.

Mission mobility for Naval Special Warfare provides an extremely diverse set of problems for the "Coronado Yacht Club." Here is a breakdown of the three basic areas of respon-

Thirty-foot rigid hull inflatable boat (RIB) with fire team of SEALs embarked. The crew are from the Special Boat Squadrons.

sibility for the SBS part of NSW. But don't think that there's a sharp line between any of these assignments—the real world has a way of mixing and matching them. The boat that is primarily intended for coastal patrol may find itself occasionally on a riverine mission, or executing some exotic special operations support assignment.

Coastal Patrol and Interdiction

The first of these, requiring the biggest vessels, is the coastal patrol mission. The offshore patrol and interdiction mission is very different than, say, the clandestine insertion of a couple of combat swimmers for a demolition raid. It takes a good-sized vessel to provide the kind of platform needed to stay offshore for very long, to provide reasonable comfort for the crew, and to have the speed and firepower to accomplish anything useful. These missions are currently assigned to the Patrol Boat Coastal (PBC), Mk III Swift Patrol Boat, and the Mk IV Patrol Boat.

Neither the PBR or PBL provide much speed or comfort out past the surf zone; they're flat water boats with a specific set of missions. For the offshore jobs, where the Sea State goes up to five or so and the waves swell up to twelve feet, even froggy SEALs want something sturdy and stable. That pretty well eliminates the light little flat-bottomed boats in favor of something longer and beamier,

The Naval Special Warfare community finally gets a real ship in the form of the new Patrol Boat, Coastal (PBC) vessel. While it isn't all that fast, light, or stealthy, it at least provides organic support for long missions offshore, with facilities for SEALs or other small teams of operators.

The Mk III patrol boat was intended to be a fast, inshore weapons platform that can mount mortars, heavy machine guns, and a big 40mm canon. With a length of 65 feet and three high-power, light-weight diesel engines and an extensive rack of radars and radios, the Mk III is a fast, potent little vessel. Its missions include coastal and river patrol, gunfire support, and insertion and extraction of a complete SEAL squad.

with a nice, sharp V-hull to slide through the waves instead of pound along on top of them.

Patrol Boat, Coastal (PBC)

The PBC is something of a major change for the Naval Special Warfare community—the introduction of an entirely new class of ship to support NAVSPECWARCOM missions. In the past such support has been improvised, based on whatever happens to be around. The PC-1 class formalizes the support.

Ships of this class, starting with the *Cyclone* (PC-1), are designed for serious patrol work, their primary mission. Naval Special Warfare support is secondary, but a dedicated assignment. With an overall length of 170 feet, the PBCs are big enough for serious offshore work, reasonably comfortable, and commodi-ous enough for a rather large number of embarked SEALs and Naval Special Warfare players.

The ships are the biggest platform the Special Boat Squadrons have ever had. They're funded by Special Operations Command and are assigned to the NSW Groups at Coronado and Little River, but are likely to be forward based. There will be a total of thirteen of the PBCs when the program is complete.

Obviously, it is hard to be very covert with 170 feet of warship. Rather than sneaking and peeking like the little boats, the PCs will be used to "show the flag" while maintaining a US presence in regions where the National Command Authority wants a show of force. The ships will be tasked with monitoring and detection missions, escort operations, noncom-

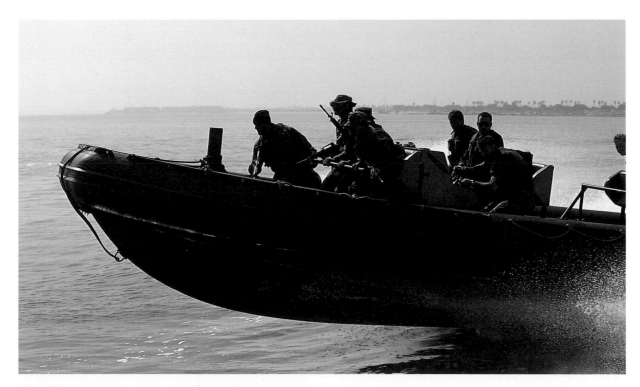

The RIB is quite capable of getting airborne, and throwing its passengers overboard, too, if they aren't careful.

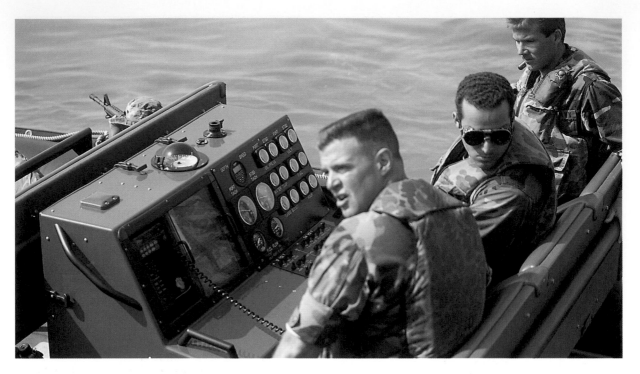

The coxswain's control console is pretty fancy for a rubber boat, but appropriate for such an expensive, high-performance craft.

batant evacuation, and foreign internal defense—all pretty much the plain-vanilla patrol mission assigned to any of the Navy's or Coast Guard's smaller ships.

The more interesting missions, and the ones the Naval Special Warfare community is involved in, are for long-range insertion and extraction of SEAL teams, tactical-swimmer operations, intelligence collection, operational deception, and coastal or riverine support.

The PBC's steel hull with aluminum superstructure has a beam of twenty-five feet and a draft of about eight feet; it displaces about 330 tons (full load). Propulsion comes from twin diesels that can drive the ship at thirty-five knots. A tank of fuel (about 13,000 gallons) will give a range of about 2,000 nautical miles at a moderate cruise speed of twelve knots. The ship will tolerate Sea State 5 conditions—rough seas with waves of 8–12 feet. There is a platform on the stern for launching and recovering combat swimmers, and the ships each have two CRRCs available for SEAL operations.

Normal complement is four officers and twenty-four enlisted personnel. Unlike previous SBS vessels, the commander of the PBC ships is not likely to be a SEAL but a surface warfare officer. While there is some apprehension about this, there is also the realization that this is an entirely new asset for the community, with a somewhat different mission—and how it all works out remains to be seen. There will probably be at least a few SEALs assigned. Besides the crew, there is berthing for a nine-man SOF or law-enforcement detachment aboard.

Appropriate to its size and missions, the

PCs will be the most heavily armed of Naval Special Warfare craft. A Mk 38 25mm rapid-fire gun is installed, along with a station for the Stinger antiaircraft missile system. Four mounts for heavy automatic weapons are available for the Mk 19 40mm grenade launcher, M2 .50-caliber machine gun, and the M60 7.62mm machine gun. For antiship missile defense, a Mk 52 chaff/decoy system is installed.

Mk III Swift Patrol Boat

The Mk III is a big, 65-foot boat designed back in the 1960s with a coastal mission in mind. These boats have been used extensively in combat over the years, particularly to patrol the waters off the coast of Vietnam and, more recently, the Latin American coastal waters used by drug traffickers and the Persian Gulf waters in support of Desert Storm. The basic mission is to serve as a high-speed weapons platform for Naval Special Warfare units. The deck is reinforced to tolerate recoil stresses from the many weapons that can be mounted on the Mk III—any mix of 20mm cannon, 81mm or 60mm mortar, Mk 19 40mm grenade launcher, .50-caliber machine gun, and the faithful old M60 7.62mm machine gun.

The boat is rated at thirty-plus knots, needs a crew of eleven, and can stay out up to five days. It is powered by three big diesel engines installed in an all-aluminum hull with a low-profile radar and acoustic signature (for this kind of boat, anyway) that makes it comparatively easy to accomplish some kinds of covert missions. The Navy will tell you officially that it is "reasonably" stable in "moderately" heavy seas, but most experienced offshore operators will tell you that a 65-foot hull fits neatly in the troughs of most any sea and will wallow like a pig in mud given half an opportunity.

But Naval Special Warfare boats aren't intended to be pleasure craft. The Mk III is tasked with patrol and interdiction missions, with fire-support missions against targets ashore or afloat, and the insertion of SEAL team elements. One of their users, an SBS unit commander, says of them, "They've lasted

SEALs support a US Marine Corps beach landing operation during Operation Desert Storm. US Navy photo

through everything we've sent them to, from Vietnam to the Persian Gulf—and in fact the Persian Gulf is where they've gotten their heaviest workout." The Mk III is an old boat now, nearing retirement. An improved model, the Mk IV, is in service, but a completely new version, to be called the Mk V, is in the long design and acquisition process.

Mk IV Patrol Boat

The Sea Spectre 68-foot patrol boat is an improved version of the Mk III, an evolution of a proven design with some substantial upgrades. The missions, specifications, and weapons remain about the same, but the boat is designed to be more easily adaptable to the wide variety of missions that such boats are tasked for. Like its older brother, it is not a heavy weather offshore boat (that doesn't mean you don't have to operate in those conditions, just that you'll be uncomfortable when you do).

Special Operations Support Mission

Support for special operations doesn't have the same kind of requirements for station time that patrol does, and the boats used for inserting and supporting SEALs and other

A Swimmer Delivery Vehicle (SDV) being deployed from a Dry Deck Shelter (DDS) of a submarine. US Navy photo

Locking out of a sub. Rigging the SDV is the business of the members of the SDV support unit, who are tasked with maintaining a complicated system plus maintaining their SEAL skills. US Navy photo

SOC operators are designed with things other than comfort in mind: speed, range, capacity, and a low radar signature are far more important than stability or fuel economy.

And the SBS crews and boats aren't always supporting strictly SEALs or Naval Special Warfare personnel; part of the idea of the Joint Special Operations Forces when it was established was to coordinate and integrate all the operators going downrange. So these SBS and NSW assets give rides to Green Berets and Rangers as well as to SEALs, and even to the occasional Force Recon Marine.

Rigid Inflatable Boats (RIB)

RIBs are the boat of the hour. Everybody's making and using them. Pretty soon you'll probably be able to take a Caribbean cruise on one. They're simple, cheap, fairly economical, and faster than a speeding bullet. They are used by the Navy, the Coast Guard, and many

foreign nations. They combine some of the best features of rigid hull and inflatable designs in one fast, stable, buoyant platform.

There are three variants of the big rubber duck used by the SEALs: 24-foot, 30-foot, and 10-meter RIBs. All use fiberglass hulls with a V-shaped cross section, offering stability, a rigid motor mount, and firm footing, along with an inflatable gunwale section. The inflatable part of the boat is fabricated from an extremely tough material, a combination of hypalon neoprene and nylon reinforced fabric. It won't shed bullets, but it will take a lot of lesser abuse, including the pounding you get from jamming around offshore, punching through the waves. The hammering a boat takes in normal service can be pretty severe, cracking fiberglass and aluminum hulls with the constant flexing. That is not a problem with an inflatable.

The RIBs are extremely tolerant, for a small boat, of heavy seas. With light loads the boats have operated offshore in extreme conditions—Sea State 6 and winds of forty-five knots. That means waves up to twenty feet high, when even SEALs would rather be ashore, even at BUD/S. While the boats can operate in such conditions, they normally don't go out when things get that bad; the SOP calls for a Sea State 5/thirty-four-knot wind limit on use. All the boats are normally crewed by three SBS sailors.

The 24-foot RIB weighs in at about 10,000 pounds fully loaded. It is powered by a single Volvo inboard engine/outboard drive powerplant and has a rated maximum speed of twenty-eight knots. Range is 175 nautical miles at twenty-five-knot speeds. Even this little boat mounts a radar—and an M60 7.62mm machine gun. Its principal mission is to deliver a single SEAL fire team (half a squad, four men) to an insertion point. It isn't the stealthiest way to insert a SEAL element on a covert mission, but not all missions require invisibility.

The 30-foot RIB is quite similar to the 24-foot version, but with two engines driving water jet drives and a higher rated maximum speed of thirty-two knots. The 30-footer is, as a result, half again heavier, weighing in at a combat weight of about 15,000 pounds. Range is slightly less, at 150 nautical miles, and the payload is a bit bigger.

The biggest of the breed is the 10-meter (33-foot) inflatable. This one will accommodate a whole squad. This means that an entire eight-man SEAL combat element can be cold, wet, and miserable while they huddle behind the dubious armor of two thin sheets of high-tech rubber and about two feet of compressed air on the run in to that hostile shore. The boat can be pumped up to forty knots, just in case the coxswain decides to race an aircraft carrier or perhaps outflank the fleet. And when he gets in range, this inflatable warship carries two weapons mounts accommodating either M60s or Mk 19 grenade launchers. There's enough fuel aboard for about an eight-hour mission, providing a range of around 250 nautical miles.

Combat Rubber Raiding Craft (CRRC)

One of the most used and useful boats in the inventory is a kind of war-surplus model left over from World War II, the CRRC—the legendary little rubber duck. Originally designed as a life raft, the boat has been adopted and adapted to all sorts of offensive missions. Marines use it, the Army Rangers and Green Berets use it, and of course the SEALs use it, for clandestine surface insertions and extractions. The CRRC weighs only 265 pounds. It gets tossed out of C-130 airplanes or from cargo helicopters, along with the SEALs, into the ocean. It is also launched from submarines, either from the surface or submerged, or gets chucked over the side of larger surface craft.

It's only about fifteen feet long, with a six-foot beam, but it will do about twenty knots. That, of course, requires an outboard engine, a single fifty-five horsepower powerplant with an eighteen-gallon fuel bladder providing a range of about sixty-five miles. That offers

The DDS is a temporary, hangar-like arrangement that bolts to the hull of the sub. It can accommodate a whole SEAL squad in relative comfort, or the squad and the SDV, in which case the squad is less comfortable. US Navy photo

over-the-horizon capability, but—trust me on this—you don't want to ride one in to the beach from over the horizon except on the *nicest* of days.

It is an extremely versatile piece of gear. While civilians spend hundreds or thousands of dollars on health clubs and Nordic Track exercise machines, the Navy uses the CRRC at BUD/S to build better bodies eight ways. In fact, the BUD/S instructors have discovered that you don't need fancy machines or chrome-plated weights, just a CRRC; if you have the students hold one overhead for a few minutes it *really* works those upper-body muscles. And, for a little extra help for those who need it, the CRRC can easily hold plenty of wet sand, bringing its weight up to something more challenging.

These inflatables have another virtue lacking in most other Navy property: they are, at times, considered disposable. Rather than go through the time and trouble to bring one back aboard a submerged sub, you may, during real world combat operations, stick your dive knife into one when you're done with your mission and let it sink to the bottom, engine and all. Just make sure that the submarine is standing by for you first!

SEALs are hauled back aboard a Patrol Boat, River (PBR)

Swimmer Delivery Vehicle (SDV) Mk VIII

Perhaps the most interesting, least publicized, most covert boat the Naval Special Warfare community operates is the wet submersible called the SDV Mk VIII. It's an odd little submarine SEALs use for fast, covert sub-surface insertions. The SDV is like a little speed boat, with rechargeable batteries and an electric motor for propulsion. Like other submarines, the SDV is visually blind and relies on sensors and instrumentation to navigate without bumping into things.

The embarked SEALs climb into a fully enclosed cabin. Although they wear scuba or closed-circuit breathing systems for backup and for work outside the vehicle, the SDV has its own supply of breathing air.

SDVs are launched from surface craft sometimes, but the dry deck shelter (DDS) attached to a submarine is a more typical point of departure. The DDS is like a small hanger, big enough for the SDV and with enough room for the swimmers to enter from the sub and climb into the SDV. The DDS is gradually flooded, the hatch opened, and out goes the SDV in search of adventure. The divers are now essentially in an expensive tin can full of water. It can be a cold ride. As one of its users says:

"It's a strange ride. You can't see out. You fly on instruments the entire time. You are a diver the entire time you're in it. The SDV provides more speed and range than swimming. Quite honestly, the boat will go farther than the man will. Exposure to the cold and to the ambient sea pressure put tremendous strains on the human body that become a limiting factor for missions with the SDV. I don't think it's used enough, perhaps because its reliability hasn't always been too great. It is a complicated thing to support and deliver. But if you plan its use properly, if you get it within its range, it is an extremely effective tool because it is almost nondetectable. The ability to deliver either SEALs or ordnance is just phenomenal!"

The vehicle has its own support unit, the SDV team, within SPECWARCOM. These teams maintain and operate the SDV, SEALs who actually man the boats on missions. An operator and a navigator are always assigned; both are fully qualified SEALs who have what amounts to a kind of bus driver job in addition to the usual combat assignments in the objective area.

The SDV is rated to carry six swimmers and their equipment, including the crew of two. A sonar sensor (for object avoidance) and an inertial navigation system allow the operator to cruise around underwater. A third sensor system is sometimes installed as part of a developmental program, but that remains "buggy," a side-scanning sonar for target identification of objects like mines as well as to record bottom contour. Not too surprisingly, a lot of specific performance information about these exotic little boats is classified. While the specifics are secret, we are authorized to hint a lot: The vehicle is about twice as fast as a submerged swimmer; vehicle endurance is probably a lot longer than crew endurance; and the SDV will tolerate up to 500 feet of water pressure without failing, and that's a lot farther than the crew will go before their subsystems start to fail! We could tell you more, but then we'd have to kill you.

Actually, though, the whole vehicle was extremely classified for a very long time. It couldn't be moved without being covered, and of course no photographs could be released showing it. But a few years ago, the then commander of SPECWARCOM decided the SDV would be a nice addition to the unit's annual float in the Coronado 4th of July parade and ordered it displayed on the flatbed trailer, along with the usual "cammied" Naval SPECWARCOM warriors. That's the way it is sometimes around Naval Special Warfare—things that are super-secret on one day and in one place are proudly displayed to the world the next.

Riverine Patrol and Interdiction

SEAL experience in Vietnam strongly demonstrated the need for good shallow-draft boats with plenty of speed, stealth, space for

Boat coxswain. Although the SBS coxswains don't go through BUD/S and aren't SEALs, they play an essential role in Naval Special Warfare.

combat-equipped SEALs, and provisions for both defending and attacking when in contact with enemy forces. That mission still exists today, in Latin America, where the US is involved in a quiet war in the backwaters of the Amazon basin and elsewhere. The boats from that previous war, along with some new ones, are helping to fight this one. Sometimes SEALs are embarked, sometimes not. In some cases the operators are foreign military or law enforcement people who are equipped and trained by the US, often by SEALs in the Foreign Internal Defense mission.

Patrol Boat, River (PBR)

The PBR has been around since quite

The SBS crews are the unsung heroes of Naval Special Warfare—or so they say, anyway. But at least they aren't shy when the media shows up.

early in the Vietnam war. It is still serving long after most of its crews have retired, a design with an interesting history.

When SEAL Team One packed its bags and shipped out to the combat zone in 1966 it was pretty much without a really good boat to support its new missions. Existing Navy LCPL (Landing Craft, Personnel, Launch) fleet craft had been modified for the purpose but just didn't seem suitable for the riverine mission of fast, long-range, shallow-draft patrol. That's why, in September 1965, the Navy's Bureau of Ships published a request for bids on a twenty-five to thirty-knot boat with a "dead-in-the-water" draft of eighteen inches and a draft at speed of only nine inches. A slightly modified commercial design from the Hattaras Yacht Company was selected, a 28-foot boat with "Jacuzzi" type propulsion.

The prototype was delivered only two weeks later. After testing, the design was modified, lengthened a bit to thirty-one feet,

and christened the PBR Mk I. The boats were being delivered to the Navy only a year after the program began. Not much later they were zooming around the Mekong Delta, trading shots with the VC and providing a kind of taxi service for SEALs off on nocturnal excursions.

The PBR was designed for high-speed patrol and insertion operations in rivers and bays. It is a heavily armed and armored boat, designed for combat at close quarters, with special ceramic armor similar to that used on tanks applied to the vessels' crew compartment. The hull is made of thick, reinforced fiberglass and is designed to accept the stresses of recoiling heavy machine guns and grenade launchers. The current PBR in service is 32-feet long, with a beam of about 12-feet. It weighs about 18,000 pounds—light enough to be transported on C-5 Galaxy aircraft.

While fairly ancient as military systems go, it is still an amazing boat. The two big

This High-Speed Boat (HSB) has just shot up a golf course with that big .50-caliber machine gun, terrorizing much of the tourist trade of Coronado, California, without so much as an apology. The HSB was originally intended to catch the small and medium-sized vessels that had been tormenting merchant and military shipping in odd corners of the world during the last decade or two. Very few of the costly, complex boats were purchased, and they've mainly been used as "adversaries" to train the Navy to deal with the fast, hit-and-run attacks of the sort mounted by Iraq and Iran. Even so, the HSBs were used during the deception campaign against Iraqi forces near Kuwait City, zooming along just off the beach, firing machine guns and tossing explosive charges over the side.

One of the 24-foot RIBs at speed. These extremely popular boats are used for many purposes by SEALs and other hard-charging units. They tolerate a lot of abuse (not including bullets), are fast, stable, and relatively easy to maintain and transport.

The Patrol Boat, Light (PBL) is a Boston Whaler with an attitude problem. The attitude comes from all those machine guns and the knowledge that, no matter how many holes the enemy puts in the hull, the fragments of the boat are unsinkable. US Navy photo

General Electric diesel engines will tootle along quietly or crank up 215hp each when required. Those engines each drive a 14-inch Jacuzzi pump; the water squirts out of 5.75-inch nozzles, making the boat go faster than thirty knots—in excess of thirty-five miles an hour to you landlubbers. Of course, that's with the water jets clean, and they do clog up. It has a range of 200 miles on 160 gallons of fuel. Normal crew complement is four.

A lot of bullets have dinged off the hulls and armor of PBRs, and a lot of crewmen have died aboard them. The boats have done a lot of shooting of their own. Standard equipment includes a tub-mounted twin M2 .50-caliber machine gun system in the bow; that's industrial-strength firepower guaranteed to "clean the clock" of almost any point target within two kilometers. There is also a pedestal mount for another M2 .50-caliber and a mount for the marvelous Mk 19 grenade launcher, a type of machine gun that fires 40mm, baseball-sized projectiles to better than two kilometers. As options you can sometimes get a 60mm mortar installed, with or without M60 machine-guns, and additional .50-caliber and 40mm machine

guns mounted amidship. Of the more than 500 PBRs built since 1966 only twenty-four or so remain in service. A new design is in the works.

Patrol Boat, Light (PBL)

The PBL is another modified off-the-shelf civilian design from that distant era; still in use is the 25-foot military version of the Boston Whaler, an unsinkable little boat powered by a pair of big engines and mounting two heavy weapons, the M2 .50-caliber machine gun and/or the Mk 19 grenade launcher. The PBL is a light, fast, air-portable, quiet, somewhat vulnerable boat that has evolved a bit over the years, but continues to support the riverine mission after almost three decades in the inventory.

Like the PBR, it uses water-jet propulsion to achieve better than thirty-knot speeds on flat water. It will turn on a proverbial dime—in fact, the boat will turn a lot faster than the coxswain and crew will probably find comfortable, a 180-degree about-face in less than 30-feet while doing thirty knots. While the G-load of such a maneuver could easily toss most everybody right out of the boat, it is a handy capability for those times you come blasting around a bend and find a horde of bad guys waiting for your arrival.

Two pedestal-mounted "Ma Duce" heavy machine guns are mounted just forward of the coxswain's position. This provides all-aspect firepower for breaking contact when the crew of three thinks it is necessary. There is also a third mount farther forward, and any combination of .50-caliber and 7.62mm machine guns can be installed.

Although the PBL draws about a foot and a half of water when stopped, at speed it will just about operate in a mud puddle, skimming along on the surface of the water rather than through it. The two engines will run at full throttle for eight hours on a tank of fuel, driving the boat across about 160 nautical miles of river or canal at more than twenty-five knots. It uses standard twin engines, with dual steerage, ignition, and controls for back-up redundancy.

It is an extremely mobile little boat, in and out of the water. The PBL can travel on a conventional trailer, be rigged as a sling load for a helicopter, or be loaded aboard a C-130. A lot of PBLs have traveled to Latin American military forces, where they are justifiably popular with the counter-narcotics forces patrolling the Amazon delta and other riverine battlefields.

Mini-Armored Troop Carrier (MATC)

The MATC is a kind of small landing craft similar to the ones Marines have been using to come ashore for decades, only smaller. It has a flat, ramp-type bow that drops forward to eject a whole platoon of sixteen combat-equipped SEALs onto a beach. It is a riverine craft with shallow draft and all the sea-keeping qualities of a cork. Like the PBR and most other riverine craft, the MATC has a water-jet propulsion system that "vacuums" the boat through the water, Jacuzzi fashion. A crew of three operates the boat.

Its hull is thirty-six feet long, made of aluminum, and is designed for high-speed patrol, interdiction, and combat assault missions on the relatively flat waters of bays, rivers, canals, and protected coastal areas. It is serious about all this—there are seven weapons stations for heavy machine guns or grenade launchers and a 60mm mortar can be installed. It comes with a high-resolution radar and a rack of radios for every taste and purpose. The boat weighs about 25,000 pounds, is good for about thirty knots and a range of 230 nautical miles from 430 gallons of fuel.

In the grand SEAL tradition, the boat is fast and sneaky. It has a low six-foot profile that's hard to see or pick up on radar (well, for a slab-sided metal-hulled boat). The engines are extremely quiet. What this all means is that you can pile a bunch of weapons and troops aboard, run up the river to a likely spot, slide into the weeds and woodwork along the bank, and wait, engine at idle. With good "comms" you can talk to surveillance aircraft overhead, other teams ashore and afloat in the area, and wait for your victim to come chugging down the creek. When the perpetrators of the crime arrive on scene, the MATC has the troops and the firepower to negotiate with just about anybody and win through intimidation.

Chapter 7

Leader's Recon

Before a combat operation, particularly ashore, a commander will, time permitting, travel to the objective area for "eyes on" the target, as LT Tom Dietz did before the diversionary raid on the Iraqi coastal defenses in Kuwait. This personal study by a combat commander of an area where conflict will occur is called "leader's recon." There is no good substitute for this kind of personal, direct contact by the combat leader with the battlefield. For people within military communities there are all kinds of battlefields besides the kind we usually think of. Some are institutional, within the unit, while others are the political, doctrinal, policy arenas. For the past fifty years, SEALS have had to adapt to changes in the world, in the US armed forces, in the Navy, and within Naval Special Warfare itself. These internal battles shape the nature of the institution that will fight the wars of the future. These institutional, peacetime conflicts are tremendously dangerous—not for the present, but for the time when push comes to shove, as it always seem to do.

Among the most dangerous things SEALS need to worry about is complacency on their own part, about bad tactical habits, about inexperience and overconfidence. Despite several combat operations over the last couple of decades, the SEAL community today is almost completely inexperienced in war—and this is a dangerous thing. War is different than training, no matter how tough that training may be.

Combat experience is slipping away from the Navy. The last Navy Medal of Honor winner retired in 1992, and nearly all the Vietnam combat veterans have left the formal military service. One of these men with a great deal of combat time is CDR Gary Stubblefield, recently retired but still actively working with Naval Special Warfare as a consultant and contractor. With retirement comes a greater freedom to discuss Naval Special Warfare issues. The following are a kind of "leader's recon" offered by Commander Stubblefield, a selection of opinions and insights about the life and times of SEALs today and in the future. His observations are a rare insight into the challenges of the present and future for Naval Special Warfare.

Deployment & Tasking

"Since the time I started in this business twenty-five years ago, I've seen a lot of changes. One is that now our people expect to receive their missions while sitting here in the States or in some forward-deployed base overseas—receipt of mission from higher authority, rather than developing our own missions from within the area where we will operate. In Vietnam we set up our own bases, designed our own missions, and, unless somebody thought we were doing something really stupid, we were left alone. Now we are directed by higher authority. When Ray Smith was operating in the Gulf, he was getting messages from the CINC saying, 'Conduct SEAL operations here, here, and here.'"

Planning and Accountability

"We've become very good at developing 'overhead' intelligence-collecting from aircraft and satellites. We've lost the ability to develop good 'human intelligence,' the ability to develop information from people, face-to-face. We were *great* at that, and it was so much better than what we even get now from the overhead systems. But you only get human intelligence by living there, by being part of the community, by building rapport with the host nation—it's the only way that will work. Now we do our planning in an insular way.

"Now I receive my intel, develop a concept or a series of options for an operation, and then I have to send it back to my boss and say, 'Here's what I intend to do; what do you think?' He may have to run the idea up the chain of command even further! Then he'll come back and say, 'This is the one I choose for you.' Then I have to develop that option—and send it up to my boss for approval again! It comes back with his changes . . . and only then can you brief your people. All this time the platoon is milling around, trying to get organized for something—but they aren't at all sure just what it will be.

"This kind of micro-management is the sort of thing we were getting into down in Panama. We were getting into operations where we required outside people, who weren't on the ground with us, telling us how we were going to do things, based on our written plan—asking for permission, which is asking for trouble.

"We tend to do more of our planning now for somebody else, rather than for the teams, to demonstrate that we know how to do something when we're evaluated by our higher authority, or in an exercise where we're demonstrating to an umpire that we're doing things according to doctrine. If you were to take that same platoon and turn them out into an op area for six months where they eat, breathe, and live in the area, like we did on the barges in the Persian Gulf during the Iran-Iraq War, pretty soon you fall into the old habits. You know your operations area, you know your platoon—you go back to basics. You plan your operation on the basis of the lowest common denominator and use the KISS principle [keep it simple, stupid!]. That way you have fewer things go wrong, you have a simpler operation to run, you rely on your knowledge of your platoon to deal with contingencies. That's called *flexibility*."

SEAL Virtues & Vices

"We're quite good at maritime direct action missions—where we ourselves are out there, in the water, delivering the munitions, collecting reconnaissance. Second, we are capable of doing long-range, long-duration missions—but we haven't typically been very good at it. The reason is that when you do these long missions, with all their logistics support requirements, you lose the ability to be fast, light, mobile. The minute you start putting on hundred-pound packs you lose that ability to do what we've traditionally done best."

The Training Environment Vs. the Real World

"I see a lot of guys who just don't get serious about our business. People have a tendency in training, in noncombat exercises, to take shortcuts. We can't afford to do that in this business. The way that you train is the way that you fight. If you get used to taking shortcuts because it's not dangerous, you'll get killed by that shortcut out in the real world. The business that we do is inherently dangerous anyway—parachuting, diving with closed-circuit rigs, locking out of submarines, working with explosives, shooting close to each other—those things are dangerous, but there is a difference even between doing them in training and in combat.

"I cannot explain to somebody until they see it for themselves what it is like to have somebody fall down beside them with a bullet in them, blood coming out of them—to lose a friend—to explain to them that they are vulnerable. You feel like you are almost invincible until you see something like that—and you never get that same feeling in any exercise, no matter how tough we make it. It takes something like that to make you really get serious about this business.

"Because there aren't real bullets going by overhead, people today don't realize you don't go very far very fast in combat. We have a tendency today to say we can travel twelve nautical miles an hour—a figure that is only realistic in a noncombat environment. It was not unusual in Vietnam to take an hour to go 100 meters back then; you had noise control, mud to contend with, water up to your chest. A hundred meters in an hour was rather fast. But we typically expect much faster movement from our SEALs today.

"Another thing we need to learn is to stop carrying all this extra gear; lighter, faster, smaller is better! I see guys going out with 200 rounds—you don't need all that. You need to stay mobile, you need to stay light, you don't want to sink too deep in the mud. You need to go back to basics again . . . when you get in the real world.

"But when I left SEAL Team Three we had only five guys out of 205 people who ever had any combat time—and I'll bet that, out of those five guys, not all of them had ever seen anybody get hurt! So you've got five guys who are serious and about 200 who say, 'I like this job, it's neat, it's fun . . . ' Years ago, when we had teams come back with ten of the fourteen guys on a platoon having been wounded, we had a lot of guys who said ' . . . Uh, look, I don't want to do this anymore, I think I'll get out.' We don't have that now because we don't have all those casualties."

Technology—A Blessing and a Curse

"Our weapons system, operating gear, and radios are all better now than ever before. Technology has helped us in many ways—but now, we tend to load up on this stuff, because

we have it. I've actually stopped people getting ready for an operation and had them weigh their packs—which turned out to weigh 110 pounds—for a three-day operation, and I say, 'What's wrong with this picture?' You don't need to do that! You need a couple of LRRPs [similar to MREs], enough water to get you by for that period, your weapon and ammunition—and *that's it*. Let's go! Batteries, maybe an extra radio, no more than that.

"We have a tendency today to do more 'whizbang' stuff—night vision sight systems, laser aim-point systems—it's smaller/lighter/faster today. If I had to go back over there today, I think we'd operate pretty much the same kind of ops. The radios are better now, the waterproofing is better.

"We don't have a tendency to move into an area and get to know it before an operation now, although the Persian Gulf was something of an exception. I think that's very important—you have to move into your area and become familiar with your territory. And we have a tendency to really overdo the briefings—I see briefings lasting five and six hours! It's ludicrous! A human being can't remember all that. When we're going out for a two-day operation, why do you need to brief for five or six hours? If you're working well together on the team, patrolling and training together, you're familiar with your op area and you know your guys, and you don't need to brief that long. Instead of briefing for the benefit of the senior commander present, I think we need to remember that you're briefing your *platoon.*"

Joint Operations and the Multi-service Environment

"In Vietnam, our boat support units lived with us in the same hut. I could go over to the next bunk and say, 'We're going on an op tomorrow night—can you have this boat ready to go?' *Nowadays* assets like boats are coordinated by multi-services. If I need a boat now, even though it's internal, I have to make sure everybody knows about it because somebody else may be planning to use the same boat—so

I have to go to higher authority, tell them I need this boat, get my ticket punched, *then* I can go over to the guy on the next bunk and talk to him about it. If it's a helicopter that could belong to the Air Force or the Army, I might have to go all the way up the chain of command, find out if it's okay, involve them in my planning process, make them part of the mission planning. Since I'm not living in my op area, I have to rely on higher headquarters to 'de-conflict' my mission, to make sure that they aren't sending an Army Green Beret A team into the same area, where we might end up shooting at each other.

"We used to be well-segregated from other friendly units in Vietnam. We all had our assigned AO [Area of Operations], and you didn't cross over without checking with the other team. The same thing applied to the boat units—I could go to the riverine boat comman-der and say, 'You guys working in here? No? Well, we are, and I don't want you going in there with your boats now.' Nowadays you can't do it that simple."

Parachute Operations for Seals

"The rule for parachute operations is: If you *have* to jump, go find another way; if you still can't find another way, make sure you observe the restrictions on wind speed, weights, all that. We have a tendency to make things more complicated than they need to be—we should always go to the lowest common denominator. We have a tendency to send more people than we need when instead we ought to take the minimum. That makes for much better command and control. We get into trouble, as in Grenada and Panama, when we make things too complex."

One Foot in the Water

Special ops is a kind of military art form, a team sport that takes special talents and years to learn. Despite overlap of missions and training, each American special forces unit has a limited set of talents. For the SEALs, that means missions that are somehow linked to the sea. As one SEAL team commander explains, "The US military has Green Berets that dive, US Army Rangers that do across-the-beach operations with the same kind of Combat Rubber Raiding Craft that SEALs use—there are lots of similar examples in the Army and Marine Corps. We in the SEALs are the United States military's *small unit maritime special operations force*. We don't operate in larger than sixteen-man units. We don't belong in anything that involves multi-platoon operations—we've never been successful at it, we've never trained in it, and any time we've tried it we have failed. We keep our units small and separate from large force operations.

We have a niche there to be very good, in units most often less than eight men. That makes us harder to detect, easier to command and control, better at the small, unique operations that we train for. The Green Berets may conduct dive operations to get to their objective; we can conduct operations entirely underwater. US Army Rangers conduct large unit across-the-beach operations, and it isn't unusual to see them use twelve or more CRRCs. You probably will never see more than two in our business.

"We keep one foot in the water. That means that *if* we must do inland operations it is because they are attached to some maritime reason—that was the only available insertion technique, or it happens to be a coastal target. *Keeping one foot in the water* means that we don't get into areas that properly belong to other operators."

Index

INDEX

INDEX